A SHEARWATER BOOK

the wilderness *from* chamberlain farm

the wilderness from chamberlain farm

A Story of Hope for the American Wild

DEAN B. BENNETT

FOREWORD BY
STEWART L. UDALL

Island Press / SHEARWATER BOOKS
Washington • Covelo • London

All rights reserved under International and Pan-American Copyright Conventions. No part of this book may be reproduced in any form or by any means without permission in writing from the publisher: Island Press, 1718 Connecticut Avenue, N.W., Suite 300, Washington, DC 20009.

ISLAND PRESS is a trademark of The Center for Resource Economics.

The author gratefully acknowledges permission to publish papers and writings of William O. Douglas. Published with permission of the William O. Douglas Estate

Library of Congress Cataloging-in-Publication Data

Bennett, Dean B.
The wilderness from Chamberlain Farm : a story of hope for the American wild / Dean B. Bennett ; foreword by Steward L. Udall.
p. cm.
Includes bibliographical references (p.   ).
ISBN 1-55963-729-3 (cloth : alk. paper) —
ISBN 1-55963-730-7 (pbk. : alk. paper)
1. Wilderness areas—Maine—Chamberlain Farm—History.
2. Human ecology—Maine—Chamberlain Farm—History.
3. Nature—Effect of human beings on—Maine—Chamberlain Farm—History.
4. Chamberlain Farm (Me.)—History. I. Title.
QH76.5.M2 B46 2001
333.78'2'0974125—dc21
2001003844

Printed on recycled, acid-free paper
British Cataloguing-in-Publication Data available

Manufactured in the United States of America
10 9 8 7 6 5 4 3 2 1

To Sheila,
who makes it all possible

Contents

Foreword

By Stewart L. Udall

This is an important book. It is important because it concerns the historic Allagash River, the premiere canoe river in the eastern United States. It is important, too, because the author traces the never-ending vigilance needed in this country to preserve the quality and the essence of natural treasures we are prone to assume we have "saved."

A highlight of my first year as secretary of the interior was a trip into the wild Allagash country of northern Maine in 1961, with Senator Edmund Muskie as my guide. This was an immensely valuable learning experience for me. I had never been to Maine, and the trip offered me an opportunity both to study the resources of that state and to form a friendship with a new senator who would become one of the giants of the nascent environmental movement.

Our float-plane safari was the outgrowth of a meeting we had with President John F. Kennedy in the Oval Office, where the senator outlined what he hoped might be accomplished in his state during the Kennedy administration. Ed told the president he wanted support to preserve the legendary Allagash as a free-flowing tributary stream by moving a planned federal hydroelectric dam on the St. John River upstream. He also wanted my engineers to study the feasibility of reviving the famous Passamaquoddy Tidal Power Project on the coast of eastern Maine, which had been proposed by President Franklin Roosevelt in the 1930s. JFK was amenable, and our low-flying inspection trip got under way on a weekend in late June.

As one familiar with the West's wild country, I viewed the remote woods, lakes, and mountains of northern Maine with surprise and a bit of wonder. I had read Henry David Thoreau's memorable account of his canoe trip on the Allagash in 1857 but had assumed that the region, in heavily developed New England, had lost the pristine qualities he described.

From our conversations, I realized that Ed Muskie loved this spacious, unspoiled part of his home state. Moreover, the fact that an up-and-coming eastern senator not only had just voted for the wilderness bill but also was ready to champion the concept of leaving some rivers undammed and natural made me wonder whether a time was coming when members of Congress would support legislation to create a national system of wild rivers.

Ed Muskie was a tough, tenacious person, and a provocative thinker in the bargain. In the course of our conversation about the merits and demerits of the high dam on the St. John River, we discussed rivers in general and agreed that since most of the country's rivers were already "harnessed" with huge flood control and hydroelectric dams, it would be a good idea to begin deciding which streams and tributaries should be left in their natural condition. Muskie's great crusade against river pollution lay in the future, but as we flew across his home state, I sensed his dismay as he pointed out its polluted rivers and outdated mill dams that had eliminated the migration of Atlantic salmon.

Senator Muskie took pride in having our pilot fly alongside the magnificent roof of Mt. Katahdin, Maine's highest mountain. En route, the senator told me how a former governor, Percival P. Baxter, had failed to persuade the legislature to appropriate sufficient funds to preserve the spectacular Katahdin landscape as a state park. Undaunted, Baxter had made it a personal project and, over a twenty-year period, purchased 200,000 acres and presented them to his beloved state with this admonition:

Man is born to die. His works are short lived.
Buildings crumble, monuments decay, wealth van-
ishes but Katahdin in all its glory forever shall
remain the mountain of the people of Maine.

My adventure on the Allagash with Ed Muskie—and a similar
outing I had a few months later in the Ozark Mountains of Missouri—evoked a land stewardship concept that I floated as a trial
balloon in my book *The Quiet Crisis* in 1963. I wrote:

Generations to follow will judge us by our success
in preserving in their natural state certain rivers
having superior outdoor recreation values. The
Allagash of Maine, the Suwannee of Georgia and
Florida, the Rogue of Oregon, the Salmon of
Idaho, the Buffalo of Arkansas, and the Ozark
Mountain rivers in the State of Missouri are some
of the waterways that should be kept as clean, wild
rivers—a part of a rich outdoor heritage.

The seeds of this concept sprouted in 1968 as a new national
policy embodied in a law known as the Wild and Scenic Rivers Act.
Missouri conservationists had nurtured the idea that lands surrounding the Current River and its tributaries should be acquired by
the federal government and designated as a "national river" administered by the National Park Service. When this concept was over-
whelmingly endorsed by Congress in 1964, it sent a signal that
emboldened President Lyndon Johnson to propose comprehensive
wild rivers legislation in his State of the Union message in 1965.

Dean Bennett describes in a clear and detailed manner the values related to wilderness areas and wild rivers everywhere. He shows
how the fascinating story of the Allagash reveals these values and
how they influenced the river's watershed during its long, rich his-

tory, culminating in preservation of the Allagash Wilderness Waterway. We see in the following pages the political obstacles that must be overcome to preserve wild places in a society in which freedom allows many values to compete.

A wonderful quotation in this book is Wallace Stegner's imperishable phrase in which he suggests that leaving special landscapes alone provides a "geography of hope." Stegner, like me, was acquainted with the vast spaces and rivers of the Rocky Mountains and the West, but here in the East, Senator Muskie reminded me that wild rivers remained that must be preserved.

Dean Bennett also tells us how Senator Muskie amended the Wild and Scenic Rivers Act so that states could nominate their own rivers to be part of the National Wild and Scenic Rivers System. This vital amendment encouraged states such as Oklahoma and Oregon to pass comparable laws setting up state systems of wild rivers. Muskie's vision was brought to fulfillment in 1970 by Maine's governor Kenneth Curtis with his successful application for designation of the Allagash Wilderness Waterway as a wild river area in the National Wild and Scenic Rivers System.

The story of the Allagash, however, does not stop with the laws that preserved it. Dean Bennett emphasizes the crucial lesson that conservation legislation must be accompanied by everyday vigilance. There are people who will push and push to undermine the protections we have given our rivers and who will succeed in gradually whittling away gains thought to be permanent and lasting. We must remember that the battle, whether to protect a park, a seashore, or a river, is never won. Those who esteem what they have saved must continually stand guard.

Wild rivers are things to be prized, and the Allagash is something special. This fine book illustrates the role of wild rivers in our nation's history and the changing values regarding nature and wilderness that lie at the heart of this conservation concept.

Preface

This is a story of hope for the American wild. It is a true story about a place deep in the wildlands of northern Maine, a remote piece of land with a small point sheltering a shallow cove along the shore of an expansive lake. Once part of a vast wilderness, it served as a camping place for early indigenous peoples who, for thousands of years, traveled by the point on a well-known canoe route. In the mid-1800s, the site caught the eye of lumbermen, who cleared and developed it for a lumbering depot and named it Chamberlain Farm. For nearly a century, the farm served as a supply center for loggers. Following a period of disuse, it attracted those who catered to hunting and fishing enthusiasts. As changes came to the region, some of its visitors registered concern over threats to the historic and wilderness character of the farm's environs. A long political struggle ensued, and though it resulted in the preservation and return of a touch of the wildness once present along the waterway in which the remnants of the farm now reside, the years following have taught a lesson on the need for watchfulness over what was saved.

In the five years during which I worked to uncover and document this story, I looked beneath the events surrounding the dynamic history of the farm and its setting for clues to their causes and discovered a quiet change under way in our society's perspective on the rest of nature. The change was apparent when I looked into the thoughts and actions expressed by those individuals who were drawn to Chamberlain Farm and its vicinity. Their reasons for coming and their effect on this wildland area reflected society's evolving beliefs and attitudes regarding nature and wilderness, including a shifting perception of ethical conduct toward the natural world. These changes stemmed from a variety of factors, including developments in science and technology, governmental and political influences, economic conditions, and population factors. For example, in my own lifetime our world's population has gone from 2 billion to 6 billion individuals, and if I live another twenty years, it may reach 8 billion.

It is difficult to separate the causes of values from their effects, to sort out the interaction between cultural values on the one hand and changes in society's sociological, institutional, and technological development and environment on the other. It is even more difficult to draw conclusions about society's influence on a particular individual's perspective. I am therefore cautious in drawing definitive conclusions about the views of nature held by the principal subjects in the following story, and especially cautious about judging their behavior. I believe that humans are too complex to be identified with a single value. Competing values may come into play to influence behavior when one is faced with a decision. People also change, and a values decision made at one time in a person's life under a given set of circumstances may not be made the same way another time.

For the foregoing reasons, I focus on describing and explaining in a general way major perspectives, or viewpoints, on nature revealed by those attracted at different times to the farm and its environment. Thus, the story of Chamberlain Farm is presented in four parts, each part presenting the evolution of a different perspective. Because these viewpoints overlapped in their appearance at the farm and their influence on the surrounding wildlands, as they did throughout the United States, each part in the story's narrative has its own chronology and principal characters, who by their words and actions suggest the defining elements of our society's changing perspectives on nature and wilderness. The hope that I found in this story lies in the kind of change I saw in these perspectives. From that hope springs the will and energy to care for the earth that sustains us and the other forms of life in our natural community.

Our civilization evolved from the wild, and after thousands of years we are still unable to exist without it, both physically and psychologically. I believe that deep within us resides an ancient memory of our vital link with a wild nature—an instinctive need for this connection. Awakening this intuitive sense, perhaps even a longing, is the purpose of this book. As the following story shows, there is reason to believe that such an awareness is already developing.

Acknowledgments

This book required the assistance of a great many individuals and institutions, spanning the United States from the Atlantic to Pacific Oceans and from the country's northern border with Canada to its southernmost states. When I set out to write about a place that nature had begun to erase, and a remote and obscure one at that, I had no idea that its past was woven from threads of history that extended so far and wide. I did have a feeling that Chamberlain Farm and the lakeshore where it began its life more than a century and a half ago had a story behind it that could illustrate some fundamental ideas about our relationship with nature and wildlands, but I did not know how rich it would be as a source of insight. Not until I had begun to trace the lives and thoughts and feelings of those who were attracted to this place and its wildness did I discover this. By the time I had completed my investigation, more than 150 people, nearly 60 of whom represented public and private institutions, had answered my questions and helped me complete the story.

First and foremost, I thank my wife and best friend, Sheila, without whom this book would not have been possible. For more than a quarter of a century we have skied and paddled the Allagash Wilderness Waterway together. Her constant companionship in this North Woods region is a source of great happiness, and her unwavering and enthusiastic support of this project and keen insight and advice have been a wellspring of encouragement. I also appreciate the interest and support of my daughter, Cheryl Martin, and her husband, Chuck Martin, who accompanied Sheila and me on a canoe trip to retrace part of Henry David Thoreau's 1857 trip down the West Branch of the Penobscot River and across Mud Pond Carry into Chamberlain Lake. And I thank my son, Rick Bennett, for being a great booster of my writing projects and for a wonderful day we spent together during my search into the life of E. S. Coe.

I am grateful for the support I have received from my many colleagues and friends at my professional home, the University of Maine at Farmington, located in the foothills of the mountains in western Maine. The administration and faculty liberally granted me leaves and research funds, and the students in my honors course, Perspectives on Nature, contributed much to my thinking and inspired me throughout this undertaking. So many staff and faculty members helped in so many ways that it would not be possible to list them all here, but I do wish to single out a few who were especially helpful: Janine Bonk, Dorothy Chouinard, Fred H. Dearnley, Rod Farmer, Alan Hart, Stacey Hodges, Sylvia Hodgkins, Shirley Martin, and Ellen Robillard.

I thank the following individuals who contributed information, ideas, photographs, and, in some cases, their own writing, to this project: Tony Altiere, David Backes, Priscilla Bartlett, Camille Beaulieu, Avis Harkness Black, Mrs. John Boeger, Tom Carboni, Herbert Cochrane, Warren Cochrane, Howard Collins, Curtis Cooper, Brad Crafts, Betty Donovan, Jack Donovan, Joel Eastman, Durward J. Ferland Jr., Dick Folsom, Steve Foster, Paul J. Fournier, Gil Gilpatrick, Lawrence Hadley, Faye Hafford, Bradford Hall, Nathan Hamilton, Charles M. Hamlin Jr., Earl Hamm, Jeanne Hamm, Terrance Harper, Barbara Herrick, Clarence R. Herrick, Horace A. Hildreth Jr., the late Lee Hoar, Dabney Y. Hofammann, Robin Holyoke, Anne Howe, Gary Hoyle, Etta M. Hubbard, J. Parker Huber, David Hubley, George L. Jacobson Jr., Phyllis Jalbert, John M. Kauffmann, Michael Kellert, Dorothy Boone Kidney, George King, Linda Koski, the late Gene L. Letourneau, Matt Libby, Lynn G. Llewellyn, Barry Lord, Robert Manning, Joseph J.

Moldenhauer, Pauline Nelson, Donald E. Nicoll, Larry L. Niska-
nen, Lidia Nugent, Miles Nugent, Robert K. Olson, Sigurd T.
Olson, W. Kent Olson, John Penfold, Mike Penfold, Trudy Price,
David C. Priest Sr., Lillian Priest, Randall Probert, David E. Put-
nam, John Richardson, Neil Rolde, William Rossi, Jym St. Pierre,
Harry A. Sanders III, Geraldine Tidd Scott, Dana R. Shaw, Richard
Shaw, John G. Sinclair, David C. Smith, James Smith, Liz Soares,
Betty D. Steele, Lawrence Stuart, Theodor R. Swem, Anthony
Tomah, Stewart L. Udall, Henry Van de Bogert, Earl Vickery, Ray-
mond F. Vigue, Elinor Walker, Regina Webster, Alice Wellman,
Edward C. Werler, Martha Werler, Harold Whiteneck, Eric Wight,
Norman Wight, and Austin H. Wilkins.

I am also grateful to a number of public and private institutions
and their staff members who provided information and materials.
These include the following: Abbe Museum—Rebecca Cole-Will
and Diane Kopec; Allagash Alliance Group—David Hubley;
Amherst College Archives and Special Collections—Daria
D'Arienzo and Carol Trabulsi; *Bangor Daily News*—Richard Shaw;
Bangor Historical Society—Norma J. Towne and Jeem Trowbridge;
Bangor Hydro-Electric Company—Alan Spear; Bangor Public
Library—Molly Larson and Cindy Todd; Bates College, Edmund
S. Muskie Archives—Christopher M. Beam and Ralph Perkins;
Bowater Great Northern Paper, Inc.—Kenneth M. Laustsen; Bow-
doin College, Hawthorne-Longfellow Library, Special Collections
and Archives; Brewer Historical Society—Brian Higgins; Brown
University, Special Collections Library—Martha L. Mitchell; Colby
College, Miller Library, Special Collections—Nancy Reinhardt;
Concord Free Public Library, Special Collections—Leslie Perrin
Wilson; The Connecticut Historical Society—Stephen Rice; Dart-
mouth College Library, Special Collections—Philip N. Cronen-
wett; Denver Public Library, Conservation Collection; Earlham
College—Charles W. Martin; *Echoes: The Northern Maine Journal*—

Kathryn J. Olmstead; Forest History Society—Cheryl Oakes; James W. Sewall Company—Scott Bergquist, Peralie M. Hallett, and Lynn Smith; L. C. Bates Museum—Deborah Staber; Library of Congress—John E. Haynes; Maine Bureau of Forestry—James Blanck and Tom Parent; Maine Bureau of Parks and Lands—Thomas Cieslinski, Richard S. Coffin, and Herbert Hartman; Maine Department of Inland Fisheries and Wildlife—Fred Hurley, Mark Latti, Thomas A. Santaguida, and Parker Tripp; Maine Historical Society—William Barry; Maine Historic Preservation Commission—Earle G. Shettleworth Jr.; Maine State Archives; Maine State Law and Legislative Reference Library; Maine State Library—Patty Bouchard, Ben Keating, Gary Nichols, and staff; Millinocket Memorial Library—Lori Fitzgerald; Minnesota Historical Society—Steve Nielsen; Moosehead Historical Society—Everett L. Parker; *Moosehead Messenger;* National Archives and Records Administration—Mike McGinn; New Brunswick Museum—Regina C. Mantin; Ohio Historical Society—Thomas J. Rieder; Outdoor Writers Association of America; Patten Lumbermen's Museum—Carol M. Baldwin; Phillips Academy, Robert S. Peabody Museum of Archaeology—Sara W. Germain; The Pierpont-Morgan Library; Piscataquis County Historical Society; The Portland Newspapers—Julia McCue; Seven Islands Land Company—Sara Medina; Thoreau Institute—Bradley P. Dean; The Thoreau Society—Thomas S. Harris; University of California, Santa Barbara, The Writings of Henry D. Thoreau Library—Elizabeth Witherell; University of Maine at Augusta, Bennett D. Katz Library—Gabriella Howard; University of Maine, Maine Folklife Center—Steve Green; University of Maine, Raymond H. Fogler Library, Special Collections Department—Bill Cook, Betsy Paradis, and Muriel A. Sanford; University of Maine at Presque Isle, Northeast Archives; University of Michigan, Bentley Historical Library—Nancy Bartlett, Karen L. Jamia, Kim Mager, and Kathleen Marquis;

University of Southern Maine, Osher Map Library—Yolanda I. Theunissen; The Wilderness Society—Bennett Beach; William O. Douglas Estate—Cathleen Douglas Stone; and Yakima Valley Museum—Martin M. Humphrey.

I especially thank Robert Kimber, who read the entire manuscript and gave me many invaluable suggestions for improving the writing. He was especially generous, as is his nature, taking time from his own writing to meet with me for extended periods of time.

I also thank the following individuals for their careful reading of portions of the manuscript about which they had special knowledge: Irvin C. Caverly Jr., Tim Caverly, Warren Cochrane, Bradley P. Dean, Richard W. Judd, William B. Krohn, Pauleena MacDougall, Robert Patterson Jr., David C. Priest Sr., Lilian Priest, David E. Putnam, John Richardson, Cathleen Douglas Stone, and Regina Webster.

One of my great pleasures was making the acquaintance of Stewart L. Udall, and I deeply appreciate his interest in this book. I thank him, too, for the inspiration and leadership he continues to give to those who work to preserve and protect our natural treasures.

I thank my agent, Mark Melnicove, for his faith in me and his help in the publishing of this book. And finally, I am indebted to the staff and editors of Island Press, especially Barbara Dean, for her enthusiasm, sensitivity, careful editing, and many helpful suggestions as I worked my way through the intricacies of telling the story of Chamberlain Farm, and Barbara Youngblood, for her pleasant and attentive guidance on manuscript preparation and submission.

Prologue
THE SAFE

IMAGES RACING ACROSS MY TELEVISION screen ploughed up lost memories and took me back nearly forty years, to June 25, 1962. I pressed the "pause" button on the videocassette recorder and stared hard at the opening on the far shore that I now knew so intimately. A mile or so in the distance the old fields still showed clearly, swathed in the bright green of early summer. The view was as eye-catching as I remembered it—an unexpected opening in a shoreline of dark spruce and fir. I fast-forwarded the tape and paused again. The scene jumped in size with a change to a telephoto lens. There were buildings over there, I guessed, but they were terribly blurred. Frustrating! I wanted so much to get a clearer view. But what could one expect from images produced by a handheld eight-millimeter movie camera and made even less distinct by conversion to video-tape? The memories became clearer as I watched the scene. "That's Chamberlain Farm," I heard someone say. "The last caribou in Maine was shot over there," another voice added.

We had stopped for lunch halfway up Chamberlain Lake on the first day of a ten-day canoe trip through northern Maine's Allagash country—a party of twenty-eight in fourteen canoes. Ostensibly on an Explorer Scout trip, the group comprised sixteen adult "advisors" to twelve boys. This ratio had nothing to do with the boys' needs; it reflected instead the adults' desire to experience a wild part of Maine that by then had become almost mythical in its reputation as a des-tination for wilderness canoe trips.

Soon we relaunched our canoes and left the farm behind,

Chamberlain Farm from across Chamberlain Lake, 1962
The author first saw this view of Chamberlain Lake and
Chamberlain Farm in June 1962. In this photograph, taken two
months later by Robert W. Patterson Sr., the farm appears on
the right as a clearing on the lake's dark, wooded shore.
Photograph courtesy of Robert W. Patterson Jr.

unaware of the lessons its story could teach us about the future of
wildlands and about ourselves. Nine days and 120 miles later, I came
off the trip feeling somehow changed. I could not define what I felt
at the time, but I remember being excited and energized. As I look
back, I realize that feeling probably contributed to a career change
that led to almost forty years of environmental education and advocacy. Throughout that time, trips to the Allagash have provided a
source of renewal and energy. On one of those excursions, only a few
years ago as I write this, something unexpected happened, setting
me on a course of exploration that eventually led to this book and to
insights about our relationship with nature—insights from Chamberlain Farm.

Author's First Visit to Chamberlain Farm, 1975
Nine years after Chamberlain Farm became part of the Allagash
Wilderness Waterway, the author and his wife, Sheila, skied to the
farm from Nugent's Chamberlain Lake Camps, a distance of less than three
and a half miles. The Katahdin range of mountains provides a spectacular
backdrop for the farm site. Photograph by Dean B. Bennett.

I had come up to the farm in a boat with John Richardson from
Nugent's Chamberlain Lake Camps, located on the shore about
three and a quarter miles down the lake. John runs the camps with
Regina Webster under a lease from the state of Maine; they maintain a housekeeping cabin at the farm, the only building remaining
of the old complex. Perhaps it was originally a boathouse or storehouse—whatever; remodeling over the years has obliterated its original use. While John worked around the camp, I took advantage of
the beach, revealed by the low water of late summer, and strolled
toward Hog Point, which forms a protective cove in front of the
farm. I passed the rusting remains of an old steam-powered paddle
wheeler, the *H. W. Marsh*, once used to tow booms of logs down

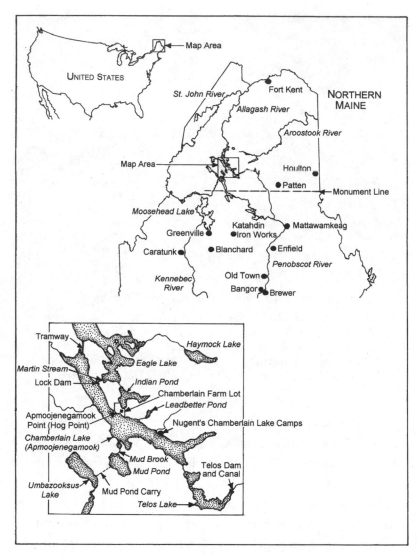

Chamberlain Farm Location

Chamberlain and into Telos Lake, nine miles away. From there, the lumbermen sluiced the logs into Webster Brook and drove them down the Penobscot River to the mills.

Out on the end of the point, I could see down the lake to a range of mountains, including Mt. Katahdin, which, at about a mile in elevation, distinguishes itself as Maine's highest mountain. Although they were thirty miles away, the mountains looked closer, their silhouettes etched sharply against the sky. Turning around, I could see the low, distant profile of Allagash Mountain, some thirteen miles to the west, and, looking hard, I thought I could even make out the old, abandoned fire lookout tower on its summit. I sat in a dreamlike state for some time, watching the light slowly change the color of the scene as the sun dropped lower. How many others, I wondered, had sat in this same spot, mesmerized by this panoramic view?

After a while, I decided to explore a part of the old farm site still unfamiliar to me and perhaps discover a little more of its history. I knew, for example, that Henry David Thoreau had camped on this very point in 1857, and as I walked, I wondered where he had pitched his tent. I made my way through a tangle of shrubs, around a swale of sedges, and through a grove of aspens. Soon I broke out into one of the old fields, now sprouted with small trees. The land sloped upward. I passed a collapsed, decaying barn, timbers piled helter-skelter, and parts of rusting farm machinery scattered about. Higher up, I circled behind the farm's cabin. A clump of aspens and firs attracted me, and as I groped my way through them, I nearly stepped into a large cellar hole. Although large trees in the cellar obscured its true size, I could see sections of rocked-up foundation walls, still in place despite years of exposure and disuse. But one thing attracted my eye: a safe.

It lay there in the shadows on its side, open, disemboweled, its contents gone. In its useful life, people had put their faith in the safe. Now, however, it was a hulk of unwanted metal rusting between crumbling stone walls in a darkened, tree-choked cellar hole—all that remained, I would learn later, of a farmhouse ravaged

Moosehead–Chamberlain Lakes Region

by fire some seventy years ago. The safe intrigued me. This was remote, wooded country. No road led to this old cellar and its safe, the nearest being miles away. Yet I was looking down on a product

*Opened Safe in Cellar
Hole of Farmhouse at
Chamberlain Farm, 1996*
This old safe, lying empty and
rusting, symbolizes values different from those that existed when
this setting was a wilderness—
values different, too, from those
that today guide this place
toward a return to wilderness
character. Photograph by
Dean B. Bennett.

associated with the making of money, with bustling businesses on busy streets.

The differing values juxtaposed in that scene reminded me a little of the way I had felt on encountering two giant railroad locomotives abandoned in the woods a few miles to the north. The advancing forest surrounding this old cellar hole would soon obliterate most of this bygone lumbering depot, for in this fading opening, nature was returning by intent: In 1966, the citizens of Maine had created a wilderness waterway here, setting aside 23,000 acres of publicly owned land in a thin ribbon a few hundred feet wide enfolding nearly 100 miles of the Northeast's premier wild and scenic waterway. The cellar hole lay within this narrow area now protected for its natural qualities—a place where human activity was restricted so the land might realize its promise of wildness, of solitude, of quiet communion with nature, of undisturbed beauty.

The safe, on the other hand, symbolized the promotion of human activity for private gain through use of the land for production of goods and material wealth, certainly not for benefits to be derived from keeping it wild. Its contents once held the promise of human comfort and security, probably in the form of wages, monies from sales, promissory notes, and other records derived from the conversion of capital, labor, and the surrounding forest into products for the market. And its presence here prompted a nagging question: What caused such a change in the use of this land?

One might conclude that this place represented a struggle between two extreme views of nature: one in which humans dominate and control nature for materialistic, utilitarian ends and another in which humans live in nature as part of it, appreciating and caring for its integrity. But a danger in seeing our relationship with nature from such dipolar perspectives is that we might exclude the possibility of a continuum of intervening beliefs, attitudes, and values. Stephanie Kaza commented in *The Future of the Northern Forest,* a book about this region, that "there is no one way to view the Northern Forest. Each person, town, corporate landholder, tree, moose, and salamander has a different perspective of and experience with the Northern Forest."[1] Not recognizing this diversity of views or values, I believe, works against our finding consensus or compromise on issues or, more specifically, resolving conflicts among values, including the values of a tree, moose, and salamander, all of which contribute to a measure of wildness.

With these thoughts running around in my mind, I left the dark hole, stepped through the surrounding clump of trees, and began making my way past the camp and down to the lakeshore. As I ripped past raspberry bushes and fended off dogwoods and alders, I became more aware of the change in values taking place here, with the forest closing around the opened safe, the foundations falling, and the rusting farm implements disappearing beneath layers of vegetation.

These signs of a shift in controlling values, from "unwilding" the land to preserving wilderness, would not be so easily discerned in the Katahdin mountain range, which again drew my eye when I stepped onto the beach. Unless one was familiar with the history of that complex of highlands overlooking Chamberlain and the other Allagash lakes, one would not know that more than 200,000 acres surrounding Katahdin had been wrested by one man from a future heavily directed by goals of material consumption and given over to a future controlled by a love for wild nature. The irony is that materialism, with its businesses, profits, banks, and, yes, its safes, had provided the economic power to save this outstanding piece of land, now Baxter State Park. The real power behind its acquisition and philosophy, however, was the vision and will of a former governor of Maine, Percival P. Baxter. For more than thirty years, he patiently assembled the park, purchasing it with his own money. He gave it to the people of Maine, directing that most of it be kept "forever wild." Today, it remains New England's largest wilderness area.

What, we may ask, is so important about these two areas that provide a measure of wildness on the landscape? Most will agree that it is prudent, in a time of growing population and widespread land development, to set aside some areas before they are lost, especially those that are good examples of different types of ecological systems. Many believe that such areas should be free from human influences that would hinder the continuation of natural evolutionary processes. They see that unaltered ecosystems allow us to make comparisons with ecosystems we have changed—harvested forests, for example—so we can better judge our effects on them. Others support keeping some areas wild because they believe it is ethical to respect the rest of nature in its own right. Then, too, there are those who believe that economic value exists in wild areas because people value them enough to pay for the benefits they derive from visiting them. Such benefits may be physical, such as the opportunity to develop skills in wilderness survival, or they may be psychological, such as the pleasure and peace of mind one receives from solitude, quiet, and undisturbed beauty.

We can derive other, more subtle psychological benefits from wild areas, and the wilder the area, the stronger the benefits. When we enter a wild area, we are given the opportunity to reflect on the developed, or altered, world we left behind and compare it with the pristine environment we have entered.[2] Such a sharp contrast allows us to see more clearly our effects on the natural world and encourages us to search for those values that guide our conduct toward the rest of nature. In this sense, wilderness can help us discover, clarify, and develop values regarding nature that lead to an ethical relationship. A firsthand experience, we know, can be a powerful educational tool.

Wilderness areas also allow us to experience the wildlands our ancestors faced when they carved out a civilization. Wild areas are living museums of the past. Additionally, there are those who gain pleasure by simply knowing that such areas exist. And still others receive pleasure in knowing that their generation can pass them on to future generations.

In the decades since the Allagash and Katahdin areas were set aside, the preservation of such places for their wilderness values has faced increasing obstacles. Why should this be? Does our society no longer believe that wilderness is relevant to our lives? That the protection of wild areas is no longer meaningful in this day or for a future day? And if such areas are relevant and meaningful, is there still hope for their preservation and restoration? I pondered these questions as I stood on the shore in the late afternoon sun, feeling a slight breeze on my face and listening to the light wash of waves on the beach—the only sound.

I looked up toward the farm and realized: There *is* hope for wild nature and the values it stands for. It is in the closing of the clearing here. It is in the unbroken shoreline, the distant mountains. It is even in the deteriorating safe: No longer does one set of values predominate here, as it did when the farm appeared on this shore. This place has seen a range of perspectives toward nature, each of which has experienced shifts of relative influence over the years. It occurred to me that if I could open the door to the history of this place, I might see the causes of these changes clearly enough to articulate them to others. I would need to find out who came here, why they came, the values they held, and what influence they had on this wildland region, and the region on them. I believed that if I could answer these questions, I would find in the history of Chamberlain Farm the true meaning of Wallace Stegner's view of wilderness; he called it a "geography of hope."[3]

It has been several years since that old cellar hole and its safe spawned my questions. The questions were valid, for they led me deeper and deeper into the cultural elements that influence our minds and behavior, eventually revealing those beliefs, attitudes, and values that form our perspectives on nature. Inevitably, my search led me to contemplate the naturalness of humanity. If we are as much of nature as anything else, is what we produce natural—our pollution, for example, or our burgeoning population? If so, does that somehow relieve us of our responsibility? The answer, I believe, relates to environmental ethics. Given the power of our technology and our political and economic systems, it is possible for even one individual today to have a tremendous influence on the natural world, even to the extent of affecting our future as a species, as well as that of all others. It thus becomes imperative for us to know as much as we can about the values that enable us to form ethical relationships with the rest of nature so we can be guided, individually and collectively, in our choices. This is what I looked for in the past of Chamberlain Farm.

Although my search raised more questions than it answered, the fascinating story of the farm and the people who worked there, visited, or passed by revealed more than I imagined, renewing my hope for the future of our relationship with nature and for the preservation of wildness everywhere. It contains lessons for all those who wish to protect wilderness areas, especially wild rivers, for the story of Chamberlain Farm is not an isolated example. There are other places throughout our world where this story has unfolded, albeit on different stages and with different actors, but the plot has been essentially the same: People encounter a wild place, seeing its value from a certain viewpoint, and engage in behavior that over time changes the natural character of the place and diminishes its wildness. New perspectives emerge to influence the way people behave toward the area, leading, in some cases, to its protection, restoration, and return to a semblance of its original wild state. Thus, in this scenario one can see a kind of cycle of values. This I saw at Chamberlain Farm, and when I looked for it in our society, I discerned something of a curve, reflecting a part of the cycle and suggesting similar changes in our cultural perspectives toward nature. It is this trend, manifested in places such as Chamberlain Farm and its surrounding Allagash country, that underlies this story of hope for the American wild. And it begins with a people who, one day long ago, named the lake in front of Chamberlain Farm Apmoojenegamook.

PART I

Apmoojenegamook

Kinship with Nature

I FIRST SAW THE NAME *Apmoojenegamook* on an old map, a copy of the map Henry David Thoreau used during his trip into Allagash country in 1857. The map had been more than twenty years old at the time of Thoreau's trip, and I viewed it with interest. The point of land I associated with Chamberlain Farm showed clearly, but a large island I had never seen, today obliterated by an artificial water level, stood between the point and the opposite shore. It brought me closer to a time when the lake was unchanged by humans, when it was known by a different people, who knew it as I longed to know it.

Who were those people who called this lake Apmoojeneg-amook? The name became a common utterance in their language—a language of spoken words that had little written expression but evoked images and ideas to a depth of feeling and understanding most of us living today will never experience. In their time, Apmoo-jenegamook resided near the eastern edge of a large continent with forests humans will rarely, if ever, see again—a true wilderness where nature worked and changed with little conscious human disturbance. Theirs was a time when a vast primeval land extended back from its shores hundreds of miles in some directions, thousands in others. For millennia, the land had experienced little more than the work of climate and natural disturbances on its rocks, soils, and waters and on its vegetation and wildlife—all interacting and responding to random rhythms of nature.

They were a people who arrived more than a hundred centuries ago, when a cold, barren country surrounded Apmoojenegamook—a people who through evolving cultural traditions would come to be collectively called Wabanaki, or People of the Dawn. For ten thousand years, these indigenous people lived off this land touched by the first rays of the morning sun. Here, in reverential adaptation, they conjoined with the natural world. The land and waters; the rocks, earth, plants, and animals; the sun, stars, and moon; the wind and rain—these and all the other natural elements of this place were their kin. They were one with nature. This was their home.

Because they shared this home, this wilderness, with others of their kind, they gave names to its places. One was Apmoojeneg-amook, meaning Lake That Is Crossed or Cross Lake, for one must cross its expanse, at times with great difficulty and risk from strong winds and high waves, to follow the ancient canoe route that passed through this wild region of the Dawnland and by a point of land where there would one day be a farm.[1] Perhaps here they camped or sat, wind-bound, waiting to cross. If so, were there still signs of their presence?

Chapter 1

The Dawnland

"YOU HAVE PEOPLE CAMPED THERE," David Putnam says, waving his hand toward the point we have just waded around. His voice quickens, displaying a tinge of excitement, as he explains the findings to me and the other three in our group: Anthony Tomah, a Maliseet Indian from Houlton, Maine; my wife, Sheila, a biologist; and John Richardson, who has a deep and caring interest in this waterway in which he lives. David is a professional archaeologist with training in the natural sciences as well as in anthropology and archaeology; he researches prehistoric archaeological sites across the northern portions of North America, especially in Alaska. Recently, he has begun to focus seriously on the lakes of the Allagash region. When he learned of my interest in exploring for signs of early indigenous people in the area around Chamberlain Farm, he volunteered to lead a trip, and because he strongly believes in working closely with people of indigenous cultures, he invited Tony to join us.

And so, on a hot, sunny June day in 1999, I find myself on the point of land in front of the farm, listening intently to David's enthusiastic explanation of evidence he has just discovered that suggests an encampment here thousands of years ago. We are looking at fire-cracked rocks and learning that there are two kinds: those that were arranged to form a hearth and those that were heated by a campfire and then dropped into a bark or skin cooking vessel to heat water or make soup. In both cases, the heat of the fire caused the rock's outer layer to redden, and this is what catches David's eye when he is in the field. The cooking rocks tend to be fractured, he explains, because they exploded from the center outward when they were superheated and then immersed in cold liquid. The rock fragments lay at the bottom of the vessel during cooking and were dumped out in a telltale pile after the people finished their meal.

Searching for Signs of an Ancient People at Chamberlain Farm, 1999
Archaeologist David E. Putnam, at right, describes to Anthony Tomah of the Houlton Band of Maliseet Indians the artifacts he hopes to find in front of Chamberlain Farm. The farm's one remaining building is near the shore of the cove behind them. Before the day is over, Putnam will discover an ancient camping site used by indigenous people who passed by this point of land thousands of years ago. Photograph by Dean B. Bennett.

David discovers another kind of artifact in the water off the point: flaked rock that was worked by hand. He demonstrates how it might have been held and struck to produce the desired shape for a tool. He points out its flaked conchoidal shape. This rock, however, is not what he hopes to show us; he is looking for red Munsungun chert and greenish Kineo rhyolite, both of which were highly valued by early toolmakers. David asks for a name to designate this archaeological site; I suggest Apmoojenegamook Point.

Later, we leave the point, elated by our discovery that ancient people camped here. Most such sites, David tells us, probably lie far offshore, covered by several feet of water. Not only have dams raised Chamberlain Lake, but also, scientists believe, sometime after 10,000 years ago a very dry period occurred here in the north, lowering the lake levels significantly. Even if no dams existed today, water would probably cover some early sites.

John boats us two miles almost directly south across the lake to the mouth of Mud Brook, the way to a major carry trail into the adjacent watershed of the Penobscot River. We inspect the shore, and here David finds what he is looking for—a chunk of dark Kineo rhyolite and many flakes of red Munsungun chert, unusable pieces of worked stone that were discarded along this historic canoe route. The high water level this spring limits our search, but we feel successful and realize just how much indigenous people used this way of passage.

In the afternoon we investigate another carry at Lock Dam, a few miles northwest of the farm, where some of Chamberlain Lake's water goes north into Eagle Lake. The carry trail runs between the two lakes for about half a mile along Martin Stream. On the way, we pass a park campsite. Here, David takes the opportunity to compare this modern version with campsites thousands of years old he has recently studied. There are some similarities, he notes, such as the size of the site, which measures about fifteen feet in diameter, and the effect of heat on the fireplace rocks. When we arrive at the Eagle Lake side, the water is too high for us to survey the shore, as David expected it would be. Three years earlier, during replacement of the dam, David had led an archaeological study on the shores of this lake and the next, Churchill Lake. We discuss the desirability of the new dam; David says he supported its development because the raised water level would better protect the archaeological sites from looting, a major problem where artifacts exist. Perhaps in the distant future, when another drawdown occurs, we will have even better methods of archaeological study and learn even more from these sites.

We stand on the shore, looking north. I remember David saying as he picked up a flake of chert at Mud Brook Cove that he was probably the first person to hold it since it was held by a toolmaker thousands of years before. For a moment, I could see that his mind had connected to an ancient time and place, to a people who saw a much different land from what we see today.

About 11,000 years ago, some twenty miles north of the point of land we searched on that June day in 1999, a group of people sets up camp on the shore of a large lake. The ice-cold breath of the last glacier sweeps over their encampment and the surrounding land, a vast, treeless expanse of tundra and silty lakes of glacial meltwater. Immediately to the south, a wasting mass of ice, perhaps twenty miles wide and thirty miles long, overlies the basin of a lake that will one day be named Apmoojenegamook. To the north lies another remnant of what was once a powerful continental ice sheet, now reduced to isolated, stagnating mounds of melting ice and rubble. Sedges, grasses, ferns, mosses, and woody dwarf willows and birches compose the tundra and attract a range of grazing animals, from beetles to caribou and perhaps musk oxen, and giant mastodons and mammoths. The large animals are visible for great distances on the treeless landscape. The trees will come later, after the climate warms enough to melt the permafrost, which prevents penetration of roots and anchoring of trees.[1]

Such was the image David helped fix in my mind on that June day when he related to us the discoveries of the archaeological team he had led there two years previously. His party had found an assemblage of stone tools attributable to the period of around 11,000 years before the present (B.P.).[2] But archaeologists know comparatively little about these Paleo-Indians, who came here during the Late Pleistocene epoch, except what they can infer from the few artifacts that have been discovered: stone tools and implements, charcoal and fire-cracked hearth rocks, and calcined bones—bones that were probably discarded into campfires and changed by the heat to become greatly resistant to deterioration by soil acidity and bacterial decay. The people must have been hardy souls to withstand the harsh conditions. There can be little doubt that they accepted enormous risks in order to survive here, and one might infer that they calculated the safety of their decisions on the basis of an intimate knowledge of the land. The land offered them opportunities to hunt large game animals, particularly caribou. It also provided stone suitable for tools—stone more easily discovered than now, for it was a glacially stripped, barely revegetated, rocky landscape the Paleo-Indians saw.[3]

A truly amazing story lies beneath the tundra-covered land chosen for that encampment and in the rocky outcrops from which the Paleo-Indians obtained the stone for their implements (see the table). The story deals with time and events staggering in their

Geologic Time Scale

Era	Period	Epoch	Years B.P. (Millions)	Geologic Events, Allagash Region
Cenozoic	Quaternary	Holocene	0.01	0.011: Ice sheet retreats from Maine.
		Pleistocene	ca. 2.6	0.025: Laurentide ice sheet advances. Last Ice Age begins.
	Tertiary		65	
Mesozoic	Cretaceous		146	Erosional processes remove bedrock to a depth measured in miles.
	Jurassic		208	
	Triassic		245	
	Permian		286	
	Carboniferous		360	Erosional processes are under way.
	Devonian		410	Volcanic activity produces materials that form Kineo rhyolite. Avalon Terrane collides with the continent (Acadian Orogeny).
Paleozoic	Silurian		440	Avalon Terrane approaches. Long period of erosion—sediments form Seboomook Formation of rocks.
	Ordovician		505	Sediments of silica and volcanic rock accumulate that subsequently form the Munsungun chert beds. Gander–Boundary Mountain Terrane drifts in and docks on the edge of Old North America (Taconic Orogeny)—underlies the Allagash region.
	Cambrian		544	Allagash region lies below the equator as part of the continent of Old North America.

dimensions and taxing to the imagination. A little more than 500 million years ago, late in a geologic time period called the Cambrian, this part of the continent of Old North America lay below the equator, its shores washed by tropical seas. For the next 150 million years, give or take a few million, two drifting landmasses called terranes closed in and docked on the edge of the old continent, creating what is now the state of Maine. The first of these, the Gander–Boundary Mountain Terrane, drifted in between 500 million and 440 million years ago, during a period called the Ordovician. Today, it underlies the region in which Apmoojenegamook resides. The collision of the continent with this landmass and an accompanying mountain-building event known as the Taconic Orogeny produced a period of volcanic activity. Sometime during this period, in a sea at the edge of an arc of volcanoes, tiny skeletons of marine plankton called radiolarians accumulated on the seafloor, along with minute spicules, or spikes, of sponges, both containing silica. Subsequently, the silica-laden sediments, which also contained small amounts of clayey and volcanic materials, underwent compaction, cementation, and other changes. The result was beds of chert, a tough, dense rock that produces smooth, curved surfaces, or conchoidal fractures, when broken. Outcroppings of this rock lie near a lake eighteen miles northeast of Apmoojenegamook, a place that would be discovered by Paleo-Indian toolmakers and today carries the name *Munsungun,* or Quarry Lake, given to it by Penobscot Indians.

Following the Taconic mountain-building event, a long period of weathering and erosion ensued through a span of time called the Silurian period, which began 440 million years ago, and extended into the Devonian, a period that began about 410 million years ago. During this time a second terrane, the Avalon Terrane, neared this edge of the continent. Through erosion, it, too, shed enormous quantities of sediment, fine sand, silt, and clay, which settled into a narrowing sea between the continent's edge and the approaching terrane. These materials accumulated to depths of two to three miles, at times entombing marine organisms that lived on the ocean floor. Many of these life-forms were fossilized. The enormous pressure generated by the weight of the sedimentary material solidified it into the Seboomook Formation of rocks, which now makes up a large part of the bedrock basin of Apmoojenegamook.

The approach and eventual docking of the Avalon Terrane on the continent's edge triggered a second major mountain-building event called the Acadian Orogeny. It deformed and tilted the Seboomook rocks, changing them through heat and pressure into metamorphic rocks such as slate. Many of the rocks, however, experienced only weak metamorphism, and the fossilized remains of the ancient animals that roamed the seafloor remained intact, their patterns to be revealed one day to curious eyes.

The Acadian Orogeny spawned a period of volcanic activity. Forty miles southwest of Apmoojenegamook, at a place the native people named Kineo, volcanoes erupted violently. Molten materials spewed out, forming a dense, hard rock called rhyolite. This rock, like flint, will flake off when struck sharply, leaving thin, sharp edges. Its color varies by locale, ranging from dark gray with flecks of lighter minerals to bluish, greenish, reddish, and yellowish hues.

From that ancient time to the present, erosional processes wore away the bedrock to a depth measured in miles, removing hundreds of millions of years of geologic record around Apmoojenegamook. Today, one sees here a variety of rock groups and formations: both sedimentary and igneous rocks that have undergone metamorphosis and some that were organically derived, such as fossiliferous limestone and old reef material. And during these events, the region of Apmoojenegamook moved from below the equator in the Southern Hemisphere to a latitude of 46 degrees above the equator in the Northern Hemisphere.[4]

About 2.6 million years ago, at the beginning of the Quaternary period, began the last ice age, in which a number of glacial episodes occurred. The last great ice sheets began to grow about 90,000 years ago; the largest of these in North America, the Laurentide Ice Sheet, expanded from central Canada. Between 25,000 and 18,000 years ago, it reached its maximum extent, burying what is now Maine under ice a mile or more thick. It moved across the area on a southeastern course, subjecting the surface to tremendous weight and massive removal by abrasion. Softer materials disappeared beneath the ice mass; more resistant bedrock underwent contouring, scratching, and grooving. The orientation and shape of Apmoo-jenegamook's basin were undoubtedly determined during this time.[5]

The glacier began melting about 18,000 years ago, and by 11,000 years ago all that remained was a few wasting blocks of ice, several square miles in dimension, surrounded by a landscape of glacial debris that included deposits of gravel and sand. The retreat of the ice sheet, its effects on the Gulf Stream off the coast of Maine, and the shift in the drainage of the Great Lakes from the Mississippi River to the St. Lawrence River created a warmer and wetter climate with increased snowfall. Revegetation started immediately with lichens, mosses, sedges, and grasses, but for possibly two or three hundred years, unstable conditions prevailed until the plants covered a good portion of the ground. Large quantities of rock flour from glacial grinding clouded the meltwater in the region's many lakes and streams. Animal life in this changing environment followed the plants, and it was into this wilderness the Paleo-Indian came.[6]

Throughout its habitation by indigenous peoples, from deglaciation to European contact, the region experienced pronounced environmental change. The rivers settled into their channels and lake levels stabilized. Currents and waves ground and sorted the glacial materials. Soil slowly accumulated from weathering of the bedrock and glacial debris and from buildup of organic matter. The basin and shores of Apmoojenegamook continued to change until in time there appeared, halfway down the lake on its northeastern shore, a small projection of bedrock, Apmoojenegamook Point, jutting into the lake and backed by a slight slope rising to a low ridge. The point protected a small cove on its eastern side from the prevailing westerly winds. Two miles directly south across the lake, a brook flowed from a small, muddy pond the indigenous people named Pockwockamus, or Mud Pond. Just south of the pond, at the top of a low rise of land, the drainage changed and flowed into the Penobscot River, away from Apmoojenegamook and the river beginning at its outlet, named Allagash. The name was perhaps a contraction of *Allagaskwigamook,* or Bark Lake, the native people's name for the lake at the river's source, now called Allagash Lake.[7]

North of Apmoojenegamook, receiving its outflow, lay two large lakes that came to be called Pongokwahem or Pongokwahemook, also called Heron Lake (now Eagle Lake), and Wallahgosquegamook (now Churchill Lake). On their shores, archaeologists have found evidence of the presence of early peoples during all the major periods of Maine's archaeological history. Most discoveries were made at times when the dam at the head of the Allagash River was not functioning and low water levels revealed the beaches, sandbars, and riverbanks the people favored for encampments. These sites occurred along a major canoe route winding through a complex of waterways connecting the St. Lawrence River and areas north of it to the St. John River and watercourses to the south.[8]

Warren K. Moorehead, the first archaeologist to explore the region, traveled through it by canoe in May 1912. The North Woods had barely emerged from winter when he and his Penobscot guide, Frank Capino, came into Chamberlain Lake from Mud Pond Carry and paddled past the point of land on the opposite shore. This trip was the first of many conducted in Maine from 1912 to 1920 by

Moorehead, who was director of the Department of Anthropology at Phillips Academy in Andover, Massachusetts. Lured by the suggestion that "felsite from Mt. Kineo, which the Indians had worked extensively, . . . might have been taken from Moosehead down the Allagash" and by the knowledge that "Indian sites had been reported on Chamberlain, Chesuncook, and other lakes," Moorehead saw the exploration as a preliminary survey. Later, he reported that "many sportsmen and pleasure seekers have taken the Allegash trip, but no one seems to have looked at the banks of these rivers and lakes with a view of recording aboriginal sites. The water being unusually high,

Archaeologist Warren K. Moorehead and
Crew at Camp along Maine's Penobscot River, 1912

Warren K. Moorehead, at far left, was the first archaeologist to survey the Allagash region for artifacts left by indigenous peoples. However, his reconnaissance trip, which took him past Chamberlain Farm, yielded little evidence. Photograph by Charles A. Perkins, © Robert S. Peabody Museum of Archaeology, Phillips Academy, Andover, Massachusetts. All rights reserved. Reprinted by permission.

many places at which guides reported that arrow heads and chips of the Kineo flint had been found, were unaccessible." In a footnote, Moorehead complained of "the obliteration of archaeological sites in Maine by the erection of modern dams," noting that "it will probably never be possible to carry out archaeological researches on Lake Chesuncook or Lake Chamberlain."[9]

It should be said that Moorehead's eagerness to explore new locations and sites, according to one biographer, caused him to leave for others the task of answering questions raised by his searches.[10] And his work in excavating sites, such as the so-called Red Paint cemeteries, which contain bright red ochre (powdered hematite), has been called "far more aggressive and much less careful" than that of other archaeologists.[11] However, this pioneering archaeologist, known as a kindly and gracious gentleman, made many discoveries and contributions to the field and worked tirelessly to improve the welfare of indigenous people in the United States. And one day he would raise his voice for preservation of this wilderness surrounding Apmoojenegamook.

In the late 1940s, Milton and Minna Hall acquired a sporting camp on Munsungun Lake and soon afterward discovered that their area contained much evidence of early peoples. When they extended their search into the nearby Allagash lakes in the early 1950s, the Halls discovered many camp locations and hundreds of artifacts. They were systematic in their searches, making maps, saving all the material they found, and photographing and cataloging their findings. Beginning in 1953 and continuing into the early 1960s, under supervision by archaeologist Wendell S. Hadlock and in cooperation with John B. Hudson and others, the Halls excavated sites and discovered artifacts dating from about 10,000 B.P. to modern times.[12]

When David Putnam arrived on the scene, bringing with him an acute understanding of the relationship between culture and environment, his work led him to observe that as the vegetation had changed in the years following glaciation, "the people's lifeway changed from one adapted to open country to one dependent upon the waterways in a forested environment, a pattern that existed to historic times."[13] And, added archaeologist Bruce J. Bourque of the Maine State Museum, their cultures evolved from interaction not only with a changing environment but also with external forces, "human contacts outside the region through trade, technological exchange, population pressure, and war."[14] The waterways traveled by the early peoples played an important role in these human interactions, and along their Allagash routes, archaeologists have detected several cultural changes that took place during the wide span of postglacial time.

Between 10,000 and 5,000 B.P., during a period archaeologists call the Archaic, climatic warming promoted forest closure of the open tundra region around Apmoojenegamook hunted by the Paleo-Indians (see the table). At first, sometime between 11,000 and 10,000 B.P., isolated individual trees or groves of trees such as poplar, spruce, and paper birch began to appear on the tundra, ending with a closed forest dominated by spruces, firs, paper birches, and alders. By 9,000 B.P., white pines, oaks, and other temperate species had partly replaced the boreal, or northern, tree species, and around 8,000 to 7,000 B.P., white pines occupied as much as 20 percent of the forest, which was at that time probably warmer and drier. By 5,000 B.P., hemlocks, beeches, and yellow birches had invaded the forest.[15] The change to a forested environment required adaptations in the way its human inhabitants carried out their lives; it is worth noting that the artifacts Putnam discovered from this period include axes, adzes, and gouges.[16]

Through the Late Archaic and Ceramic periods, a time spanning 6,000 to 500 B.P., the forests around Apmoojenegamook continued to change as a result of climate, disease, and disturbances such as fires and windstorms. Studies of pollen grains show a dra-

Maine Archaeological Periods

Years b.p.	Period	Culture Tradition
Present		
	Contact	
ca. 500		
	Late Ceramic	
1,000		
	Middle Ceramic	
2,000		
	Early Ceramic	
ca. 3,000		
		Susquehanna (ca. 3,800–3,500 b.p.)
4,000		Red Paint People or Moorehead
	Late Archaic	Phase (ca. 4,500–3,800 b.p.)
5,000		Maritime Archaic
		Laurentian (ca. 6,000–5,000 b.p.)
ca. 6,000		
	Middle Archaic	
ca. 7,500		
	Early Archaic	
ca. 10,000		
	Paleo-Indian	
ca. 11,000		

matic decrease in hemlocks around 5,000 b.p., probably because of a pathogen, with recovery by 4,000 b.p. Beech and yellow birch forests also declined. From 1,500 to 1,000 b.p., a boreal forest of spruce and fir began to increase in the region, most likely in response to cooling in north-temperate latitudes. Over the past 4,000 years, white pines decreased in abundance with the cooling of the climate and undoubtedly with the decreasing frequency of fire, which produces the exposed soil conditions necessary for reseeding. Over the past

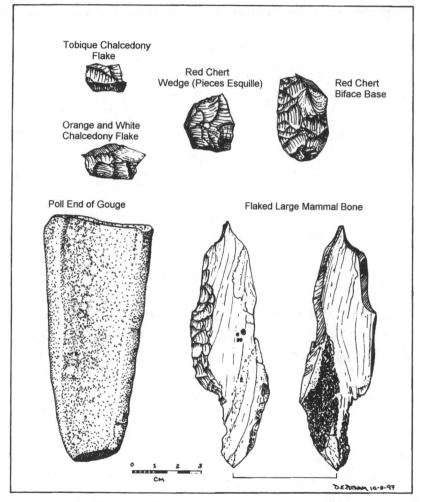

Artifacts Left by Indigenous Peoples along the Allagash Lakes
These drawings by archaeologist David E. Putnam show the diversity of artifacts he and his team discovered at the headwaters of the Allagash River. Courtesy of David E. Putnam.

1,000 years, spruces and firs came to dominate the forest around Apmoojenegamook.[17]

During these changes in the forests of northern Maine, some-time from the Late Archaic period to or before the Ceramic period, though the time span is difficult to determine accurately, the birch-bark canoe replaced the dugout. Bourque noted that "a phenomenon which may mark the arrival of the bark canoe in Maine is the decline in abundance of large woodworking tools during the Ceramic period" and, interestingly, the "almost simultaneous appearance of other forms of smaller tools made of raw materials originating from the interior sections of Maine."[18] With its light-ness and portability, this innovation provided a much easier means of travel throughout the interior of Maine, most likely expanding the use of small streams and portages and increasing the number of traveled routes. Although it is not known, one might assume that human traffic through Apmoojenegamook increased during this time.

Thirteen miles north of Apmoojenegamook Point, Putnam and his crew in 1996 discovered a Kineo rhyolite projectile point and a large, thin tool of red chert, evidence of Late Archaic peoples dur-ing the period of 6,000 to 3,000 B.P. A few miles closer, they found a large number of stone flakes, charcoal pieces, calcined mammal bones, and projectile points of green Kineo rhyolite and red and green chert of the Late Ceramic period, a time when people adopted the use of pottery.[19] Evidence of quarrying at Mt. Kineo and Mun-sungun Lake during these periods indicates that they were likely sources for the rhyolite and chert.[20]

The archaeological record of early use of the Allagash waterway shows a progressive change in the way early indigenous peoples lived.[21] It is a record of change that continues through the time of European contact and into the colonial period.[22] But with the arrival of Europeans on New England's shores in the early 1600s and the spread of their settlements, a cultural change began that drastically and irreversibly altered the cultural traditions of these people. In the words of Maine anthropologist David Sanger: "In a profound sense, that contact effectively altered a culture and way of life which could never again be reproduced or restored. As archaeologists, our job is to recover and interpret those native peoples' long history."[23]

For archaeologists such as Putnam who try to interpret this history, the Allagash sites represent more than potential for scientific study. Viewing them, he believes, "evokes an emotional sense of wonder about a past we can only imagine." He can "stand quietly by a series of fire hearths and hear the bark of dogs, mothers scolding their children, the notes of a flute as a young man courts the love of his life, and smell the cooking moose, fish, or goose mingling with the woodsmoke, wafting across the millennia."[24] Such a graphic image probes beneath the scientific observation of artifacts left by those early peoples who visited Apmoojenegamook to imagine individuals full of life, carrying on their day-to-day living. Deeper still lie their beliefs and feelings about this primeval land and how they should live on it.

Clues to indigenous peoples' perspectives on their natural environment come from many sources. Some hints of their attitudes and values may be revealed by their campsites, stone quarries, cemeteries, rock art, and other artifacts—the stuff of archaeology. The brittle, yellowing pages of journals, reports, letters, maps, and sketches left by European explorers, settlers, traders, and visitors involved in early encounters with the native people are another source. A wellspring of clues about native views of nature are found in the tales, legends, and songs handed down from generation to generation through storytelling and ceremonial traditions. "Myth and folklore," in the view of Kenneth M. Morrison, a professor of religious studies, "document the vital mentality and adaptive imagination used by

Indigenous People Canoeing, 1791
Sketch by Patrick Campbell of New Brunswick, from original in the
collection of the Champlain Society, New Brunswick Museum. Reprinted by
permission of New Brunswick Museum, St. John, New Brunswick, Canada.

the northeastern Algonquians."[25] Scientific descriptions of the individual cultural groups that are considered Wabanaki—Micmac, Maliseet, Passamaquoddy, Penobscot, and others—also help reconstruct possible emotional connections to the natural world of those peoples who came to Apmoojenegamook.

Despite the various avenues that can be explored to reveal the indigenous peoples' view of nature before European contact, the task is not an easy one. Environmental philosopher J. Baird Callicott puts it thus: "Reconstructing the traditional Indian attitude toward nature is . . . to some extent a speculative matter. On the other hand, we must not abandon the inquiry as utterly hopeless."[26] Like other scholars, he is aware that firsthand accounts and personal recollections are filtered through the cultural biases, perspectives, and memories of the observers and that cultural traditions conveyed by living members of indigenous communities have suffered the effects of

European influence and cultural change. Yet despite the difficulties, the way those indigenous people viewed their natural world as they passed by Apmoojenegamook Point is far from a complete mystery.

The folklore, legends, and myths of Wabanaki people shed light on how they viewed their place, or position, in the natural world and its creation. They believed they were children of a giant man or spiritual man they called Gluskap. He came from their world of origin, a world they believed to be an island earth called Ketakamigwa (the Big Land on the Seacoast). Their legends of Gluskap show a connection to this world through him. He possessed the ability to transform or shape the earth so it would be suitable for humans and a place where they would be happy.[27]

One idea is seen repeatedly by those who study indigenous cultures, an idea that perhaps best describes these early peoples' place in nature. It is kinship with the other living and nonliving entities in their environment. Anthropologist Harald E. L. Prins noted, for example, that some Wabanaki people and their southern neighbors wore tattoos and otherwise decorated themselves with images of animals, which "probably represented their animal guardian spirits or family totems," and thus "endowed them with special spirit power."[28] Morrison also wrote of their idea of solidarity between humans and animals.[29] Callicott, too, on the basis of his review of studies that included Algonkian Indians, a broad group that included the Wabanaki people, generalized that "the typical traditional American Indian attitude was to regard all features of the environment as enspirited. These entities possessed a consciousness, reason, and volition no less intense and complete than a human being's. . . . The world around . . . [was] bound together through bonds of kinship, mutuality, and reciprocity."[30] Calvin Martin, author of *Keepers of the Game: Indian–American Relationships and the Fur Trade*, found that many, if not all, indigenous peoples' ideologies seemed to share "a genuine respect for the welfare of other life forms."[31] And researchers of human–land relations Annie Booth and Harvey Jacobs, in their broad review of Native American thought, found that "the idea which appears over and over is 'kinship' with other living beings. . . . Not only do Native Americans see themselves as part of the land, they consider the land to be part of them."[32]

The indigenous peoples' consciousness of the land also shows up in their place-names. As several Abenaki living in the northeastern part of the North Woods region pointed out in the 1990s, "behind each name are traditions linking us to the ancient life of this land."[33] More than a century earlier, North Woods writer and adventurer Lucius L. Hubbard analyzed 139 Penobscot Indian place-names and found that the people had an intimate geographic understanding of the wildlands they inhabited. Their names described locations of features in relation to others on the landscape (as in Abahtacook, indicating a stream that runs parallel with a big river); described the details of places, often in terms relative to efficient and safe travel (Aboljackarmegas, meaning no trees, all smooth, and Kawapskitchwak, denoting sharp, rough rips); provided specific directions (Ahsedakwasic, place on a stream where a stick or rod points to some branch stream); gave historical information (Mahnekebahntic, place where people used to get cedar bark for packs); and indicated the location of wildlife resources (Macwahoc, beaver place) and plant resources (Musquacook, birch-bark place).[34] Among these places, the Penobscots lived as fully integrated members of a natural community, on equal standing with all other living and nonliving things. Such was their place in nature.

The people's place-names not only suggest they valued nature to provide for their material needs; they also show an aesthetic appreciation—for example, Woolastook or Wulustook, their name for the St. John, translates as Beautiful River.[35] Geologist Stephen Pollock and his colleagues noted in their report on the geology and archaeology of Munsungun chert that the early people's "choice of materials, and the specific manner in which they were used to produce the artifact, suggests to us that aesthetics played a role in the lives of these individuals." The chert and exotic stone became economically valuable in a far-reaching exchange network that ranged from western Pennsylvania to Labrador.[36] It is also well known that the Wabanaki people decorated their pottery, birch-bark containers, and other products; ornamented themselves with bird feathers, paint, and wampum; and beautified their clothing.

Yet the role in nature of Maine's indigenous peoples—their behavior toward their natural environment—appears to have been driven by much more than material and aesthetic needs. Martin saw their land-use relations as reflecting "spiritual-social obligations and understandings."[37] Tales of their culture hero Gluskap show him teaching them to have concern for others, human and nonhuman; advising them to face their troubles positively and constructively; and warning them never to abuse the spirits of animals, although they were permitted to kill animals in order to eat their flesh.[38] In their stories, Gluskap transforms the world for human well-being and practices a kind of ethical code by punishing people for greediness, selfishness, excessiveness, hoarding, abuse of power, disrespect, and cruelty. Gluskap, however, was not above making his own mistakes and learning from them, as in a story in which he wishes for a game-bag of hair so he might more easily capture the creatures of the land. His grandmother Woodchuck makes him one from the hairs of her belly. He thanks her and then goes into the woods and calls all the animals, telling them the world is coming to an end and promising them that if they get into the bag, they will not perish. On returning to the wigwam, he shows his grandmother what he has caught. "You have not done well, Grandson," she scolds. "Our descendants will in the future die of starvation. I have great hopes in you for our descendants. Do not do what you have done." Gluskap then goes out and opens the bag, releasing all the animals.[39]

To what extent did these indigenous peoples' views of right and wrong reflect what today is called a land ethic? From a social viewpoint, Callicott noted that their philosophy of living as coequals with other life-forms and natural features, which they saw as socially organized, personal beings, required of them a certain correctness in behavior: "They are courteous, cautious, mutual, reciprocal, deferential, diplomatic—forms of conduct which must be maintained to sustain the interspecies social structure and, so to speak, the international balance of power. From a sociobiological point of view, this is the sum and substance of an ethic—an American Indian land or environmental ethic." Still, Callicott struggled with the question of how all of nature's elements could be viewed as living personal and social beings yet at the same time seen as impersonal natural resources to be carefully used and conserved. He was, however, persuaded that at least among some groups, these views come together to "inhibit thoughtless destruction and overexploitation of nature."[40]

Politics also seems to have played a role in leading some groups in the direction of preventing overexploitation of natural resources. Early observations of Wabanaki people indicated that their sagamores, or chiefs, made formal agreements with their allies to divide up the country into territories. In this way, regional bands could adjust their hunting, fishing, and other food-gathering activities to their own needs and to seasonal cycles without competition and conflict.[41]

Putnam, however, stated that for indigenous peoples whose way of life was based on hunting, fishing, and gathering, such as those who frequented the Apmoojenegamook region, the "real issue [was] economic," and he questioned "the applicability of the concept of an 'ethic.'" He pointed to the fact that "highly mobile societies cannot afford to transport large volumes of possessions." Further, the indigenous peoples had a cultural "emphasis . . . on relationships, both with people and other living and non-living elements of their environment, rather than a social hierarchy based on material goods." These factors, when combined with "small numbers of people, an ephemeral presence, and a lifeway based on expediency, reflect a light 'footprint' on the land. . . . In contrast [to hunter-gatherer groups], Native American agriculturalists were more sedentary, more concerned with material goods, more warlike, more organized socially, had stratified societies, and had significantly greater impact on the environment."[42]

Martin questioned the idea that the relationship between Indians and the land involved ethical ties, preferring to think of it as a compact in which people and nature (which was a community of animal species regarded as people) were joined on the basis of protecting each other's interests and fulfilling common needs.[43] Some critics point to accounts of mass slaughter of buffalo on the western plains and overtrapping of furbearing animals, such as beavers in the eastern forests, as evidence that an ethic did not exist. But others counter that even though we may discover such events in the history of native peoples, they were not the norm in pre-European groups and should not be seen as reflecting the moral standards of the whole culture, any more than violations of ethical norms today should be seen as reflections of modern society.[44]

Although opinions clearly differ among those who study and interpret the environmental role and influence of American indigenous cultures, there appears to be ample reason to believe that those who camped on or passed by that point of land on the northern shore of Apmoojenegamook viewed themselves as one with the natural world, their home, and in kinship with everything that composed and lived in that home. They lived by the natural changes, rhythms, and cycles. Booth and Jacobs wrote that although the indigenous peoples were responsible for changes in their environment, in some instances negatively so, "the great majority of natural communities remained ecologically functional while supporting both Native American cultures and a great diversity of different plant and animal species."[45]

But 500 years ago, the Dawnland at Apmoojenegamook faced a change unlike any that it, or North America as a whole, had ever before experienced—a change that would be devastating to indigenous peoples' way of life, health, and numbers. People of a different culture would soon arrive, bringing a different set of perspectives and values concerning humans' relationship with their natural environment. Newcomers looking out at their surroundings from the point on that lakeshore would see the world differently, and they would begin by renaming the lake—not for any relationship to its natural character or for their interaction with it, but for the name of one of their own. They would call it Chamberlain.

PART II

T7 R12 and the Farm

Control of Nature

THE PAINTED AXE MARKS of the blazed town line led north from the shore near the arm of Chamberlain Lake. I encountered them one bright, crisp March day while cross-country skiing on a ridge behind Nugent's Chamberlain Lake Camps, and I saw them again when I photographed a patch of old-growth forest five miles directly north of Chamberlain Farm. Another time, while climbing Bear Mountain, overlooking Pillsbury Island on Eagle Lake, Thoreau's northernmost point of penetration into Allagash country, I discovered a town corner post at the place where the first one was planted between 1835 and 1840.

Initially, those who followed the European settlers came slowly into the headwater lakes of Allagash country, like the beginning trickle of the annual snowmelt. They called it trackless, dark, and gloomy—a wilderness. Among the first were surveyors who marked lines on the ground and put them in people's minds, set off towns and lots, and left maps and reports. They came with their compasses and measuring chains in service of those who had visions of public and private ownership and wealth, whose ambitions required that they control the land, who hoped to harvest an abundance of untapped resources—timber, minerals, and furbearing animals—and to remake the land into productive settlements and farms.

Almost everyone who had dreams for this wildland's future saw the need to change it. Some went so far as to say it would be evil to let it remain wild. Scientist Charles T. Jackson, on seeing the unbroken shores of Moosehead Lake in 1838, remarked that "the scenery is picturesque, but an amateur of fine views would find it yet too wild, and not relieved by the habitations of man; an evil which time will remedy."[1]

And so they were compelled to transform this land, the Dawnland, the home of the Wabanaki people. In the headwaters of the Allagash River, they bounded a point of land in a lake named

Chamberlain, placed it in a town they called T7 R12, and built a farm—a lumbering depot—where many would come who sought to control the errant ways of nature.

C h a p t e r   2

Wealth in a Bounded Land

*L*IKE THE FIRST tentative beams of morning sunlight striking the eastern edge of the continent, the tiny, crowded European vessels sailed in, touching the ragged coastline quietly, gently, their bright sails shining against the ocean's waters. The Dawnlanders saw them, but the straggling arrival of the newcomers in the early years of the 1600s and the unassuming size and appearance of their ships belied the mind-set, conviction, and resolve that accompanied them. There was little hint of their orientation toward the nature of the new world they encountered, that it would brew up into small squalls of change to the land and then become a tempest that would alter the face of the North American landscape.

When those early settlers of New England arrived, they found an incredible natural abundance of plants and animals, made more unbelievable by their memories of the impoverished land they had left behind. "The commodiousnesse of the country . . . and . . . The foure Elements, Earth, Water, Aire, and Fire . . . and convenient use of these, consisteth the only well-being both of Man and Beast in a more comfortable measure," exclaimed the Reverend Francis Higginson in 1630.[1] Unlike the bounded, domesticated pastoral land they had left, this vast wilderness promised unlimited wealth for the taking. But it was by no means a paradise to them.

In contrast to the indigenous peoples, who saw the land as their home and were familiar with its nooks and cubbies, many of these new arrivals saw it as mysterious and threatening. They called it *wild*, a *wilderness*—terms that described a conceptual chasm between their view and that of its native inhabitants. When the first settlers of the Plymouth Colony arrived in 1620, "the whole countrey, full of woods and thickets, represented a wild and savage hue," wrote William Bradford.[2] Some years later, when a visitor named John Josselyn went into the mountains of interior western Maine, he saw that "the Country beyond these Hills Northward is daunting and terrible."[3] And to many, it seemed entirely consistent that such a place would be inhabited by savage, animal-like heathens who needed to be tamed of their barbarous ways, just as the wilderness needed to be subdued.

In an atmosphere permeated by these beliefs, the settlements spread northward and westward from the southern New England coast, in a pattern reminiscent of the revegetation that had occurred thousands of years before when plant life recolonized the land as it followed the retreating glacier. By 1760, cabins, farms, and villages covered most of southern New England, breaking the silence with sounds of the forge, axe, and saw. A hundred years later, only northwestern Maine remained unsettled—a vast forested area known as the wildlands, in which lay a lake carrying the dual name Apmoojenegamook and Chamberlain. Although the origin of the name *Chamberlain* is uncertain, a noted Maine folklorist suggested that it originated with a hunter rather than a logger because lumbering had not begun in the vicinity of the lake when the name first appeared. In fact, the 1790 census of Maine, at that time a district of the Commonwealth of Massachusetts, showed a hunter, Moses Chamberlain, living at Caratunk, then the northernmost settlement on the Kennebec River, about eighty miles south of the lake.[4]

The conquest of New England was, in principle, fairly simple and direct: claim the land, exert control over it, and take its wealth—in a word, dominate it. At first, all of New England was claimed by England.[5] But in 1697, under the Treaty of Ryswick, France laid claim to a large land area including the Allagash region—a claim that lasted until 1763.[6] Following the Revolutionary War, the United States and Great Britain concluded a treaty designating a northern boundary between the British possessions and Massachusetts' District of Maine "along the said Highlands which divide those rivers that empty themselves into the river St. Lawrence from those which fall into the Atlantic Ocean, to the northwesternmost head of Connecticut River."[7] The United States interpreted this to mean the highlands that separated the St. John River's watershed from that of the St. Lawrence River, including the Allagash River and Apmoojenegamook. However, as we shall see, the British did not agree.

The war for independence set in motion other events that would profoundly affect the future of the wilderness surrounding Apmoojenegamook but would also provide one of its first descriptions. Bankruptcy threatened Massachusetts, the war having left its treasury empty and its paper currency worth scarcely 10 percent of its value. Facing huge war debts and unable to burden the people with increased taxes, the commonwealth turned to the sale of its wildlands, opening a land office in 1783 to survey the lands and place them on the market.[8]

In 1793, a wealthy land speculator, William Bingham, began acquiring millions of acres in Maine; his acquisitions included a contract for a million-acre tract in the northern part of the district, just east of Apmoojenegamook and extending to the highlands dividing the St. John River from the St. Lawrence. Unable to close the bargain until the land could be surveyed, the Massachusetts Land Committee sought a surveyor. This, however, proved difficult because the territory was unexplored, with no connecting water routes or portages, uncertain distances, and little information available from the local indigenous people. Finally, the committee persuaded Park Holland to survey the tract along with his friend and fellow officer in the Revolutionary War, Jonathan Maynard.[9]

Born in 1752, Park Holland grew up on a farm in Petersham, Massachusetts, where he also received the benefits of a good education. Following service in the war, he settled on a farm, but in 1784 he began surveying for the commonwealth in the District of Maine while periodically serving as a representative in the General Court. He was described as honest, industrious, and benevolent, a man who had the confidence of all—a confidence that would be tested in the wildlands of northern Maine.[10]

Surveying of the Bingham purchase began in August 1794, with a great deal of uncertainty and potential danger. Holland did not realize that the line he and his men were expected to run had been underestimated by 175 miles. But even had he known, it would not have been in his nature to quit or shirk the responsibilities of a job. And so, with "much reluctance and no anticipation of anything but hardship," he and Maynard set off with their crew.[11]

Starting around August 12 at a point in eastern Maine, loaded with as much provision as they could carry on their backs, Holland and five men headed north. They planned to leave the line in a month and travel west to meet Maynard at Grand Lake Matagamon, at the head of the East Branch of the Penobscot River, for reprovisioning. For the first fifty miles, they worked their way through the thick, wet tangle of a "continued cedar swamp."[12] The surveyors' methods and instruments were by today's standards crude and imprecise.[13] Using compasses, axes, record books, and a sixty-six-foot iron measuring chain made up of a hundred links, the party spotted trees along the line, with Holland keeping records as they went. "It was generally very hard traveling," Holland recorded in his diary.[14]

They emerged from the swamp to find "high hard-wood land" and easier going. After about ten more miles, the party left the line and struck off westward to meet Maynard. They were out of provisions except for one partridge to divide among them, and to make matters worse, they were unknowingly not on the stream where they wished to be. But luck was still with the surveyors because, as Holland later wrote, "to our great joy we saw an Indian coming down the river towards us." Holland hired the man, who helped the party obtain food and guided them to Maynard, who, it turned out, was thirty miles away.[15]

Holland and Maynard sent a man downriver for supplies and new clothing. However, he failed to return, and on September 13, with the season getting late, the two made the difficult decision to leave. They packed up all their provisions, which consisted of thirty-five pounds of pork and twenty of bread, and in their tattered clothing set off with three men to continue the line. Although they saw "fine prospects," traversed "good hard-wood land," and struck a "beautiful river," they ran out of food, survived a dangerous lake crossing on a raft in gale-force winds, and passed "a wretched night for want of water" before arriving at the St. John River on September 29.[16]

Reprovisioned at the village of Madawaska and helped by a hunter who gave them a small yellow dog for company, they were back on the line in four days. On a hardwood hill between the St. John and St. Lawrence Rivers, 152 miles from their starting point, they marked a nearby tree with the letters *J. M. P. H. W. B. N. E. B.*, representing Jonathan Maynard and Park Holland's surveyors' mark and William Bingham's northeastern bounds. A short distance away, they laid up a pile of stones to mark the true corner.

For the next several days, the party ran the northern boundary westward, not realizing what lay ahead of them. All too soon they dipped into a "horrible" valley, and on October 9, the weather turned cold and rainy. With their linen jackets and trousers worn and torn and their provisions nearly spent, they decided to turn toward the southwest. On October 10, after rafting a river with great difficulty against a hard wind, they arrived at what they considered the northwestern corner. Turning south the next day, they experienced worsening conditions. On October 13, they once again encountered the St. John River, which they waded, emerging cold, wet, and worried about their soaked tinder. Holland, however, was able to get a fire going, and in its warmth they shared a meager supper of chocolate-root (water avens) and one biscuit divided among them. On October 14, they marked a white birch tree and decided not to chain any farther because it was impossible for them to use their field books with everything so wet. They wrapped their books in birch bark, put them away, and crossed the Allagash River. The next day, with their clothes and moccasins about gone and only a few biscuits left, they woke up to several inches of snow. Following their compass, they went as fast as their "weakened limbs" would take them, trying to outdistance the now real threat of starvation and growing fatigue. On October 17, while discussing the prospect of eating their dog, good luck befell them and the dog when it discovered a hedgehog. The dog held the hedgehog at bay until the men had a chance to dispatch it, whereupon it was immediately cooked.[17]

On October 19, with more than 250 miles behind them, the party reached a point twenty miles east of Apmoojenegamook, with only two biscuits and tea made of juniper bark and chocolate root to share. They had started early, stopping along the way to examine the works of beavers. At noon, they came to a stream in the headwaters of the Aroostook River and found an old camp and a line Maynard had run earlier. By good luck, they were able to kill another hedgehog their dog had chased into a hollow log. Holland recorded in his diary, "Here we concluded to remain the rest of the day, and a pleasant one it was to us, for we now felt that we should live to get out of this wilderness, supposing that the hedgehog and two biscuits would help us from starving until we reached our batteau, which if we had good luck, would not take us longer than four days." On October 22, "very faint, weak, and hungry" and with only berries to sustain them, they reached their bateau on the East Branch of the Penobscot, where they had cached some food.[18] It was early November when Holland landed in Boston.

During the time of Holland's survey and into the early part of the next century, while the fires of statehood for the District of Maine were being fanned, Massachusetts continued to sell and grant its northern wildlands. The commonwealth traded wilderness for war pensions, educational endowments, roads, mills, and even ministerial services to spread the gospel, establishing a custom of money-raising that Maine citizens would later continue with sales of their own public lands. Generally, however, the public knew little about those great tracts of wildland. Then, in 1816, Moses Greenleaf, an entrepreneur and developer with a strong interest in describing and mapping the interior of Maine, published his *Statistical View of the District of Maine*. Without a doubt, this publication directed the attention of public leaders and entrepreneurs toward the development possibilities of the wildlands.

Greenleaf devoted a long chapter to an examination of the extensive, unsettled wilderness of Maine and "its importance . . . as a source of revenue to be obtained from future sales; and more especially as affording a foundation, on which, by proper measures, may be established a vast access of wealth and strength to the State." He estimated that the territory under consideration contained 16,031,000 acres, most of which was continuous forest, the largest section being the country watered by the St. John River. Discussing opportunities for inland navigation, he noted that "the St. John is passable for boats ascending and descending, from the Grand falls, near the eastern boundary, to its source in the lake Ahpmoojeenegamook." Expounding on this theme, he predicted that "if a line of communication, by means of canals, could be opened through the District at a comparatively trifling expense, it will be readily conceived, that the real value of the land must be much enhanced, and the population and improvement of the country highly promoted."[19]

Noting that nearly half of that country lay in St. John waters, which provided the cheapest means of conveying lumber and produce but were under the jurisdiction or control of a foreign power, Greenleaf proposed that three major routes, each with canals, be built to deliver goods to Maine seaports. One of these would follow an old canoe route of indigenous peoples up the Kennebec River from coastal Maine to Moosehead Lake and thence continue by a canal of a mile and one-half to the West Branch of the Penobscot River. He explained the route from this point as follows:

> The passage of the river is safe and easy to Chesun
> cook lake. From thence, up the Umbazukscus is
> smooth water 10 or 12 miles, and with the excep
> tion of one short portage, it is passable for boats to
> a small pond at its head. From this pond it is low
> land about 1 1/2 mile to another, issuing and afford
> ing a good passage for boats to Ahpmoojeeng
> amook lake. This lake, with two smaller ones below
> it, affords good navigation for about 40 miles far
> ther, to their outlet in the river St. John; which is
> passable for boats, for more than 100 miles to the
> Grand falls, with the exception of one portage of
> about 20 rods. . . . The benefits, which might result

to the State from the opening of such an extensive
inland navigation, would probably be found, in a
great increase in the intrinsic value of its land;
encouraging the settlement of the country, and preserving to itself its surplus population, with its con-
sequent wealth and strength; anticipating the revenue to be derived, from the sales of land; opening
new fields, for the employment of the industry and
enterprise of its citizens.[20]

On March 15, 1820, a jubilant Maine became an independent
state in the Union. At this time, timberland covered 90 percent of
the state. Maine and Massachusetts divided the public lands, with
Massachusetts' ownership consisting of more than 8 million acres.[21]
The new state created a land office, and following its failure to rat-
ify an agreement to purchase Massachusetts' public lands, the two
states worked jointly in granting and selling them.[22] However, an
international boundary dispute loomed over a large area of wildlands in northern Maine that included Lake Apmoojenegamook—
an ownership dispute between Great Britain and the United States
that would last until 1842.

By 1820, a number of developments had occurred in and outside
the new state that would portend changes in the vicinity of Apmoojenegamook Point. The steam engine and its application in steamboats and locomotives had already been developed. The first efficient mechanized papermaking plant in America had been in
production for three years.[23] Log driving had been instituted as a
means of transport to mills for at least a decade.[24] The first important road north of Bangor had been extended to Howland, seventy
miles south of the lake.[25] In another event significant to the future
of Apmoojenegamook, swampers cleared a tote road from Patten to
the East Branch of the Penobscot River, sixteen miles away.[26] Five

years later, a stage line offered public transportation between Portland and Bangor.[27]

With these developments promoting greater interest in northern Maine's resources and in the sale of public land for income, surveying became a necessity. Between 1825 and 1833, surveyors ran an east–west baseline, called the Monument Line, for laying out public townships. The line began at a cedar post at the head of the St. Croix River in eastern Maine. From there, it ran westward for ninety miles. Mapmakers and surveyors began laying out townships north and south of the line in squares six miles on a side, or thirty-six square miles per town. Each town received two numbers: a town number for the row of towns in which it was located, all towns in the same row receiving the same number, and a range number for the column of towns it was in. The numbering of towns began three rows below the Monument Line and progressed northward. Range numbers began at the eastern boundary line of the state. A town, for example, might be given the designation T6 R10 W.E.L.S., meaning a town in the sixth row and the tenth range column west of the eastern line of the state.

Gradually, the surveyors and mapmakers turned Maine into a grid of townships. Yet as late as 1829, a map by Daniel Rose of towns surveyed westward from the eastern line of the state stopped short of Lake Apmoojenegamook. A map published by George W. Coffin in 1835 showed township lines, but they were incorrectly drawn and labeled.[28] However, sometime before 1840 the surveyors arrived, and Apmoojenegamook Point lay in a town mapped as T7 R12 W.E.L.S., a designation it holds to this day.

In the 1830s, interest in the wildlands continued to grow. Some seventy miles directly east of Chamberlain Lake and near the state's boundary, builders completed Aroostook Road from Lincoln to Houlton, and Military Road opened from Mattawamkeag to Houlton, improving access to the northeastern areas of Maine. In the

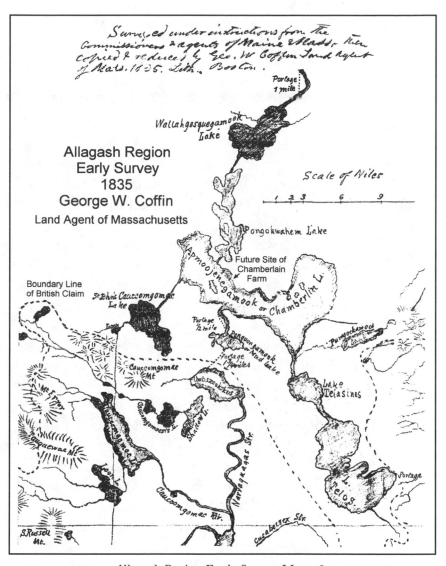

Allagash Region Early Survey Map, 1835

George W. Coffin's map of the Chamberlain Lake region depicted
incorrectly its features and township boundaries. Modified from
A Plan of the Public Lands in the State of Maine, 1835, cage box 2,
Oscar Fellows Papers, Special Collections Department,
Raymond H. Fogler Library, University of Maine, Orono.

mid-1830s a railroad came to Maine, operating a few miles between Bangor and Old Town. Steamboats also ran at this time on Moosehead Lake and on the Penobscot River between Old Town and Mattawamkeag.[29] All these developments presaged change in the Allagash region, and lands passed rapidly among owners as speculation and fortunes mounted.

With the increasing promise of more settlers and a growing speculative interest in land sales came the need to know the nature and value of the internationally disputed wildlands. The Massachusetts legislature passed a resolution on March 21, 1836, to conduct a two-year geologic survey of the public lands in the state of Maine to ascertain their worth. Maine also authorized a three-year geologic survey of the state. The two states appointed Charles T. Jackson, a graduate of Harvard Medical School and a member of the country's scientific elite, to conduct the surveys. In his first report to the governor of Massachusetts, he noted that "all the essential particulars respecting the nature, extent, and value of the mineral treasures of the useful rocks, soils, and many facts concerning the physical topography of the country, and the nature of the agricultural and manufacturing opportunities which are afforded will become the objects of my study while engaged in the survey."[30]

On July 22, 1837, three men struggled to portage their bateau and utensils over a dark, muddy trail through a swamp overhung by spruces, firs, and cedars amid "the greatest abundance of pine." Rays of sunlight spattered a mossy forest floor, and newly hatched mosquitoes hunted for exposed flesh. James Hodge, a twenty-one-year-old geologist and recent Harvard graduate, led the trio as an assistant in Charles Jackson's survey of the wildlands of Maine. That evening, as the sun settled behind the forested shoreline of a small pond, Hodge made notes in his journal that would later become the basis for his report to Jackson about this area:

We spent the night of the 21st on this portage; the next day passed over it, and across Mud lake, and the portage of 80 rods at its foot, the outlet being too shallow to float the batteau. Mud lake, as its name indicates, is low and muddy. Its level has been found to be fourteen feet above that of the Umbazookskus. A canal might be cut, with little expense to the state, across to some part of Umbazookskus pond or stream, which would increase that branch of the Penobscot, and furnish a means of getting down some of the timber, which lies between Mud lake and lake Pelos, and around the upper Allagash lakes, which region comprises the best timber land in the state. This is the only way by which this timber can be brought to market, for the Allagash lakes are too long and dead to allow of its being carried to Madawaska. But this has already been proposed by others.[31]

The next day, Hodge and his party completed their portage into Chamberlain Lake, coming out directly across from Apmoojeneg-amook Point, unnoticeable from their side of the lake. His report provides the first written description of the lake:

The outlet of Mud pond, down which we passed on the 23rd, is very small and shallow for the first mile; almost filled with rounded boulders of siliceous and argillaceous slates. Its banks abound with juniper and hackmetack, and rise to the height of small hills. For the last mile above Chamberlain lake, the stream is deeper and easily navigated. This lake, called also Baamchenungamook and Appmoo-

> jeenegamook, or Great Cross lake, is the largest of
> the Allagash lakes. . . . The shores are low, covered
> with gravel and small boulders of slate and quartz
> rock, and the country around is level, with some
> good scattering pines. The outlet is three or four
> miles from the inlet, across a part of the lake. . . .
> This is wide and quick, but shallow. At the island
> there is a good opportunity for building a dam
> across the stream, and erecting a saw mill.[32]

The reports of Hodge and Jackson contained another dimension of value that Jackson discussed at length and with great concern—the value of the reports in helping the United States' case against Great Britain's claim over the wildlands. "We should know accurately the nature and value of the district in dispute," he advised.[33] "The claim set up by Great Britain to more than *ten thousand square miles* of the territory of Maine, on the plea that the . . . chain of highlands designated in the treaty of 1783, is the range which divides the Penobscot and Kennebec waters from the Allagash and Walloostook [St. John River], is certainly too absurd for serious refutation, and shows only an earnest and grasping desire of that country to extend its territory into lands belonging justly to this country."[34]

The British, however, were not to stand idly by. Two years after Hodge's exploration of Chamberlain Lake and the Allagash country, on a chilly October 1, a party of eleven men coming from the north reached the swift but shallow stream flowing out of Chamberlain Lake. The aspens and red maples on the surrounding shores glowed in the sun's final rays as the tantalizing smell of frying moose meat wafted through their streamside campsite.

George Featherstonhaugh, a fifty-nine-year-old expatriate Englishman and experienced geologist, led the group. Appointed jointly with another Englishman and surveyor, Lieutenant Colonel

Richard Mudge, Featherstonhaugh served as part of a diplomatic offensive by the British to secure this disputed area from the United States in the boundary controversy. The two men had been out since September 11 with instructions to report on, among other things, the extent of the country that could be designated as the highlands. On the morning of October 1, Mudge and other members of the expedition had gone down the Allagash River to the St. John, some sixty miles north, where Mudge would travel with a party up that river and meet Featherstonhaugh at Baker Lake in the St. John's headwaters before going on to Quebec, Canada.

Featherstonhaugh, a London-born intellectual, had received a classical education and acquired proficiency in music, languages, and writing. At the age of twenty-eight he had moved to New York, where his accomplishments included stock breeding, co-founding of the Mohawk and Hudson Railroad, and publishing. In 1834, he received an appointment as the first United States geologist. Aristocratic in his ways, he revealed in his journal entries a rather scornful intolerance of many of the settlers and woodsmen he encountered, calling them ferocious, ill-mannered, low, poor ruffians and vagabonds. He had little patience with Mudge and others in his party who did not hold to his standards in personal neatness, planning, and work.

On Wednesday, October 2, Featherstonhaugh and his men paddled down Chamberlain Lake and passed Apmoojenegamook Point before turning into Mud Brook toward the carry. Featherstonhaugh's journal gives us our second view of this area while it was still an unaltered wilderness. And even though his mission was to gain control of the land and its resources, he took pleasure from its wildness:

> This Lake Umgenaygamuc [Chamberlain Lake] is
> an extensive sheet of water about 15 miles long . . .
> with a great bay extending from near the foot of the

lake to the N.E. In crossing the lake we had a perfect view of Mount Katahdin, saw its shape: there is
a fine set of mountains between us and it. . . . We
arrived at a portage of 1 3/4 miles leading to Lake
Obscuskus [Umbazooksus] or Reed Lake. This
portage for the first third part is a deep black mire
which it would be almost impossible to get through
but for the old logs blown down, and other small
ones which have occasionally been thrown in, upon
which there is some footing to be had. It is a very
old portage, wide enough to carry a bateau. . . .
Generally speaking, the land is very good in this
part of the country, capable of maintaining a
numerous agricultural population. In beauty nothing can exceed parts of it: extensive lakes and
mountains of a lofty kind in the foreground, as on
Lake Umgenaygamuc, whilst the hills bordering
upon the lake frequently slope down in a very
graceful manner. Take the country altogether, it is
the most elegant solitude imaginable.[35]

While Great Britain and the United States jousted over the
northeastern boundary, surveying of the wildlands proceeded. On a
day in 1840, one year after Featherstonhaugh's expedition, two surveyors, William P. Parrott and Zebulon Bradley, landed on the
windy shore of Chamberlain Lake near Apmoojenegamook Point.
One of them, Captain Parrott, had been appointed two years before
by Maine's governor, Edward Kent, to a state commission charged
with surveying the northeastern boundary. In 1839, Parrott had
served as deputy land agent in charge of the Aroostook Boom and
the building of two blockhouses at Fort Fairfield.

That day in 1840 found Parrott and Bradley in the process of surveying the boundary lines of six townships surrounding Chamberlain Lake, among them T7 R12. Their survey provides the first detailed description of the true undisturbed character of this plot of land. From their general remarks, we learn the following:

General description of township 7 in the 12th Range.

Watered by Apmogenegamook or Heron Lakes, and Ponds and streams tributary thereto.

The surface is uneven, lying in high hills and ridges.

The soil is mostly of the 2° & 3° quality, and yet there are some ridges from 50 to 300 acres in a body, of good soil and hard wood, spruce & hem

There is much fine timber in the SE & NW quarters, and is standing less compact on the residue. Perhaps one half or more is small sapling, under twenty inches in diameter, much which if suffered to remain growing, will be sought after and taken off within twenty years, but is worth nothing to manufacture at present.

Much spruce, and some larch and cedar may be found in various parts of the township.

We estimate the pine timber suitable to be taken off immediately for board logs, at eight or ten millions feet, board measure, two thirds of which may go into Apmoogenegamook Lake.

Contains 24,240.03 acres.

Bangor, September 1st
AD 1840
Zebulon Bradley
Wm. P. Parrott[36]

From the field notes these two surveyors made as they proceeded around the boundary lines of T7 R12, further details come to light regarding the land and water surrounding Apmoojenegamook Point. Their survey began on the western line, at the southwestern corner across the lake from Apmoojenegamook Point, and proceeded northward. They crossed Chamberlain Lake (139 chains and 75 links); lined through some good large pines to the Allagash River (130 links wide), running rapidly eastward (now known as Martin Stream between Chamberlain and Eagle Lakes); continued through an area of large pines, many of which appeared to be sound; and finally encountered a ledge and climbed a small hill known today as Bear Mountain. Here, they reached the northwestern corner and marked a cedar post, noting its location 44 links east of a tree marked by someone who had located the corners of the township the previous spring.

Along the northern line, running west, the surveyors noted land that had been burned about twenty-three years earlier; hardwood and spruce trees extending to the summit of a hill; and some very good pines—perhaps those found today in the Eagle Lake Old-growth White Pine Stand, one of Maine's largest stands of old-growth pine, which has been aged to before the Revolutionary War. Running north from the southeastern corner, the surveyors recorded ridges; ledges; cedar and juniper swamps and much spruce and fir, as well as beeches, maples, and yellow birches; a small pond; a beaver pond; streams; a brown ash swale; and burnt land.[37]

Thus, Parrott and Bradley gave us a tour of T7 R12 at a time when it was a primeval wilderness. From their descriptions and those of Park Holland, James Hodge, and George Featherston-haugh, we know it was a pathless virgin woods cluttered with blow-down trees and occasionally broken by openings blackened and charred by natural burns, where one could climb a tree or hill and see a vast, untouched forest extending for great distances. One could literally walk hundreds of miles and never encounter a road, a house, a settlement, or another person. Clear rivers and lakes flowed freely and contained abundant populations of fish and other life. Native plants and animals dominated. Only natural sights, sounds, and smells stimulated the senses, and beyond them a feeling of the unknown, of mystery, hung over the land. The surveyors knew that their survival depended on a knowledge of the land, an ability to endure physical hardship, and, under some conditions, a strong will to live.

It is against this description of the wilderness around Apmoo-jenegamook that the changes the region experienced after 1840 unfold, and their effects on the natural character of these wildlands can be seen with greater clarity. Just as the history of this place reflects a continuum of changing values, so does it illustrate a continuousness of change from a wilderness to a region more altered and controlled by humans. The extent to which it remained a wilderness in the minds of those who encountered it depended on their point of reference—for example, whether they were from the country or the city. Thus, the degree to which the region remained a wilderness became a subjective judgment and a point of increasing debate through the years. A possible means of resolving the argument would be advanced in the last half of the twentieth century by two thinkers, Roderick Nash and Michael Frome. They proposed consideration of a range of conditions, from pure wilderness to pure civilization, and recognition that along such a continuum, wildness has different meanings for different people (see the table).[38]

In 1840, the purely wild landscape of T7 R12 that Parrott and Bradley surveyed was about to move in the direction of more human control, for that was the reason for the two men's presence. Some of the change for the area around Apmoojenegamook would also be related to settlement of the northeastern boundary dispute. On June 27, 1840, the same year Parrott and Bradley published their survey,

A Wilderness Continuum

Purely Civilized (City)	Rural, Pastoral, Managed (Working Forest)	Purely Wild (Wilderness)

Perception of naturalness, remoteness, quietness, aloneness, ancientness

1	2	3	4	5

Note: See appendix B for further explanation.

President Martin Van Buren received the report and maps made by Featherstonhaugh and Mudge. Expecting that the British would use this information to their advantage, President Van Buren and the United States Congress authorized the exploration and survey of the boundary line between the states of Maine and New Hampshire and the British provinces. Three commissioners were subsequently appointed: James Renwick, James D. Graham, and Captain Andrew Talcott. Renwick, a professor of natural experimental philosophy and chemistry at Columbia College, was an experienced topographical engineer and proficient in the sciences, scholarly writing, languages, and watercolor painting. Graham, a graduate of the United States Military Academy at West Point, had served as a major in the Corps of Topographical Engineers and was skilled in astronomy. Talcott, also a West Point graduate and skilled in mathematics and astronomy, had served in the U.S. Army Corps of Engineers before resigning his commission in 1836 to work as a civil engineer.

In the course of three surveying seasons in 1840, 1841, and 1842, two parties surveyed Chamberlain Lake and its vicinity. This area interested the commissioners because the line claimed by the British ran just south of the lake, placing it within the territory the United States hoped to acquire. A party under the direction of Captain Talcott made the first survey of the area during the summer and

U.S. Boundary Commission Surveyors on Chamberlain Lake, 1841

This camera lucida image, signed by P. Harry, is titled "Katahdin,
bearing about South 30° East . . . as seen from the Eastern Shore of
Lake Chamberlain." The scene was captured a few miles east of where
Chamberlain Farm would be built five years later. Talcott print #1, "Maps
and Sketches from Surveys Led by Talcott" (P.I 170, Entry 104), Records
of Boundary and Claims Commissions and Arbitrations, Record Group 76,
National Archives and Record Administration, College Park, Md.

autumn of 1841. The assistant engineer, P. Harry, provided not only
a fairly detailed description of the Chamberlain Lake country but
also the earliest known drawing of Chamberlain Lake. By means of
a prism in an instrument called a camera lucida, an image of the lake
was projected on a sheet of paper and traced. Later, the artist added
details and color to the picture, which is almost photographic in its
exactness.[39]

According to P. Harry's account, the party progressed westward
from the headwaters of the Aroostook River, following the British
line that separated Allagash waters from those of the Penobscot.
The description of the land provided yet another firsthand view of a

relatively untouched wilderness in the vicinity of Apmoojenegamook Point, except for one important change:

> The line of "division of waters" retains a general
> southerly direction until we arrive at the point
> where the waters of Lake Telos (St. John water) and
> those of Webster Pond (Penobscot water) were for-
> merly divided by a very slight obstacle,—which has
> been removed by the Lumbermen who have cut a
> channel [later named Telos Cut or Telos Canal], by
> which the waters of Lake Telos and Lake Cham-
> berlain (dammed up at the outlet of the latter) now
> flow into Webster Pond, and consequently into the
> Penobscot.[40]

As we shall learn, this "very slight obstacle" caused a very large
change in the Allagash watershed and created a significant issue in
the region's logging history.

The report of the commissioners came the next year, during delicate negotiations between the United States and Great Britain, and
failed to be introduced into the deliberations. On August 9, 1842,
the Webster-Ashburton Treaty was ratified, and Chamberlain Lake
and T7 R12 became an undisputed part of the United States. It
would be only a matter of time before Charles Jackson's predictions
came true. Four years earlier, he had foreseen that "the moment the
boundary line is adjusted, agreeably to our claim . . . many active
enterprising individuals . . . will turn their labor towards the Eastern
forests, soils and minerals . . . and the need to "finish the great
roads."[41] Although good all-season roads to Chamberlain Lake
would take another century to arrive, lumbering appeared imminent. In the words of historian Richard Judd, "the successful negotiation of this international agreement paved the way for logging
operations in the Allagash."[42]

The control of nature, however, had already begun by those who had an eye on the timber in this region. Unlike the indigenous peoples, who had dealt with this place on its terms, the newcomers intended to adapt it to their needs. This new approach would have a profound effect on the wilderness around Apmoojenegamook Point.

The surveyors' blaze marks had hardly begun to weather before the land around Chamberlain Lake and Apmoojenegamook Point attracted the attention of practical, entrepreneurial, and politically inclined individuals—shrewd businessmen who would play a high-stakes game on the newly surveyed checkerboard of Maine townships. They would bring jobs to many—jobs that would result in physical hardship and little money for some and comfort and prosperity for others. In some instances, they cared for the interests of people; in others, they put their fortune-seeking ahead of other considerations. This is not to say that they did not enjoy watching a sunset, seeing the beauty of a forest, listening to the sounds of loons, or being surrounded by the peacefulness and tranquility of a quiet lakeshore, or that they showed little concern about social welfare, justice, harmony, and stability or setting standards of honesty. Many, probably most, did, but as a group they demonstrated values that directed their lives toward control over resources and people for such reasons as achieving personal success, independence, pleasure, social status and prestige, authority, wealth, creative proficiency, triumph over challenges, and excitement in life. Most of them expressed drives that reflected the social standards of American culture at the time. This is the way it was with most of those entrepreneurs who came with an eye on the land and water surrounding Apmoojenegamook Point in the mid-1800s. But within two decades, other val-

ues would flicker in the minds of some who sat in the light of campfires and lamps there.

Until 1840, pine ranked as the principal tree species used in
commercial manufacture, and by then one-third of the original pine
forest in Maine had been cut, though most of the state's forest
remained in primeval condition.[43] With few roads in the state, the
Penobscot River provided access to a huge portion of Maine's interior country and its pines, as well as a means of getting the logs out.
As early as 1836, a survey of the headwaters of the river's East and
West Branches reported many signs of lumbermen in the region.
Throughout the years, both branches would experience major devel-
opment, including the diversion of Chamberlain Lake and other
Allagash waters into the East Branch.[44]

The Penobscot River flowed past Bangor, a port at head tide that
accommodated large vessels and a mill town, which in 1840 found
itself on the way to becoming the lumber capital of the world. The
market for wood products appeared bright. In that year, Maine's
population had reached 0.5 million, and the U.S. population numbered 17 million. The practical and potential value of scientific
endeavors had caught the public's attention, and those in the lumber business looked with more than a casual interest at a growing
number of technological advancements, including steam-powered
mills and, perhaps, the prospect of the rotary saw, which would
arrive a decade later. Loggers had begun using the crosscut saw to
fell and cut up trees. Haulers continued to favor the use of oxen,
although horses shared some of the work.[45] The building of tote
roads to supply logging camps and lumbering operations, primarily
in winter, expanded into new areas of virgin forest.

In the years just before 1840, lumbermen on the Penobscot
River, practicing a "cut and move on policy," began casting their eyes
in the direction of Allagash pines.[46] The upper reaches of both the
East and West Branches of the Penobscot River came close to the

Log Hauling, 1850s

Oxen were commonly used in the nineteenth century to haul logs
to the water's edge, where they would then be driven to the mills.
Reprinted from John S. Springer, *Forest Life and Forest Trees*
(New York: Harper and Brothers, 1851), 83.

headwaters of the Allagash River: the West Branch at Mud Pond
Carry, between Umbazooksus and Chamberlain Lakes, and the East
Branch at a short carry trail along a rocky ravine between Webster
and Telos Lakes. As we have seen, for years both of these places had
been considered as possible canal routes. Having enough water for
log driving represented an economic risk factor that occupied lumbermen's minds, but major river improvements were prohibitively
expensive for any one logger to deal with. To overcome this draw-
back, the state of Maine provided a legal means for loggers to collectively improve rivers by delegating control over publicly navigable
rivers and streams to private interests.[47] Furthermore, the public's
mood at this time all over the country supported canal building.
Between 1821 and 1855, Maine authorized thirty toll canals to
facilitate the transportation of logs.[48]

All this serves to explain why in the year 1839 Shepard Boody, a lumberman, passed by Apmoojenegamook Point on a mission. His task: to determine the feasibility of diverting the waters of Chamberlain Lake, Telos Lake, and their feeder lakes and streams into Webster Lake and the East Branch of the Penobscot. In Boody's words: "We found we could raise over eleven feet by Chamberlin's dam. The water would run over [Telos Lake] into the pond [Webster Lake]. . . . From the point at sixty rods from Telos, there was a valley—a little run. No other place to make a cut."[49]

Two years later, he returned to help build two dams. He later described the operation as follows:

> In March 1841, Major Strickland employed me to go up and assist him, and show him where to build a dam at Chamberlin outlet, to turn the water this way; and to work for him there. I went up; went to Chamberlin lake. He sent for us to come back to Telos; concluded to build a dam at Telos. . . . The object in building this dam was to regulate the water—to keep the water that might come from Chamberlin. Strickland wanted the water to help drive logs from Webster pond, which they were cutting that year. . . . They built the Chamberlin and Telos dams. . . . When Telos rose high enough, the water run over the height into Webster pond. The Stricklands got their logs out. . . . In the winter of 1842, Gen. Strickland put some men on to work below the Telos dam, removing obstructions, etc.[50]

And so, with the completion of the Telos Canal, or Cut, Allagash water flowed southward past Apmoojenegamook Point, and for all purposes Chamberlain Lake resided in the Penobscot water-

Telos Dam from Telos Canal, 1879

Telos Dam, along with a dam at the outlet of Chamberlain Lake,
controlled the flow of Allagash waters into a canal, or cut, grubbed out by
lumbermen so they could drive logs down the East Branch of the Penobscot
River to the mills in Bangor. In essence, this engineering operation changed
the watershed of the Allagash River. Reprinted from Thomas Sedgwick
Steele, *Canoe and Camera: A Two Hundred Mile Tour through the
Maine Forests* (Boston, Mass.: Estes & Lauriat, 1880), 80.

shed. Control of the waters had been achieved. To someone standing on that point of land at that time, the change would have been
apparent: flooded shores with trees standing in water, soon to die
and bleach in the sun before toppling over and littering the shore
with a barrier of broken and twisted trunks and limbs. In the spring,
booms of logs would be laboriously winched down the lake toward
Chamberlain Thoroughfare into Telos.

That same year, 1841, a wealthy shipping merchant from Salem,
Massachusetts, named David Pingree made his first purchase of
Maine timberlands. Pingree has been portrayed as a man of busi-
ness, a merchant of integrity, a deep thinker with broad views, and

Log Boom, 1879
Floating logs were collected and confined in booms to be transported across
lakes and then sorted at the mills. Reprinted from Thomas Sedgwick Steele,
Canoe and Camera: A Two Hundred Mile Tour through the Maine Forests
(Boston, Mass.: Estes & Lauriat, 1880), 109.

a person of untiring industry. Some said that recollections of his
boyhood in Maine led him to give some attention to the state's
lands.[51]

The next year, 1842, an event occurred in Pingree's life that led
to his increasing investment in Maine's forestlands. Ebenezer Coe,
a business acquaintance who owned land in Stetson, Maine, introduced Pingree to his twenty-eight-year-old son, Eben Smith Coe,
an engineer of experience and training. Eben Coe, or E. S. Coe, as
he preferred to be known, was born in Northwood, New Hampshire, of a well-to-do family and had the privilege of a private education. Although he was not fond of study and preferred outdoor
work, he nevertheless completed a program at a private engineering

E. S. Coe

Eben Smith (E. S.) Coe built
Chamberlain Farm in 1846 and
supervised its management for
more than half a century. Coe
became an influential landowner
and lumberman in Maine.
Reprinted by permission of the
Bangor Historical Society.

school in Hartford, Connecticut, to become a civil engineer. For the
next few years, he found irregular employment surveying for new
railroads during the early phase of the industry. But an economic
depression and opposition to the railroads presented difficulties for
the promoters for whom he worked, limiting their ability to pay
their employees. Discouraged, Coe returned home to Northwood to
rest and seek advice from his father, who arranged his meeting with
Pingree.

The meeting went well, and Pingree hired Coe as an agent to
explore and develop his land purchase in Maine. While there, Coe
explored the Allagash wildlands around Chamberlain Lake, and
after he had seen the virgin pine forests of T7 R12 and the other
surrounding townships, he returned to report to Pingree on his esti-
mates of the timber. It was a turning point in both men's lives.

E. S. Coe had discovered his life's work and an environment he
enjoyed—the Maine woods. Here he found direction and opportunity, not only for financial security but also for personal achievement
in a business arena of high acceptance in the country's developing

society. His work presented the challenge he needed for his intellectual abilities, engineering knowledge, and skills. Young and vigorous, broad chested, large framed, and of medium height, he possessed physical strength and health that permitted him to pursue an active life for nearly sixty more years, a life that included untiring devotion to his work and frequent trips to inspect and appraise the woodlands he owned and managed in Maine and New Hampshire.

Coe spent hours estimating stumpage and overseeing all aspects of lumbering operations, including river drives, procurement of supplies, dam construction, and regulation of water levels, as well as visiting and lobbying the state legislature. He spent fully half his time in travel away from his home and office. Business occupied much of his attention; it was his pleasure. He worked with careful attention to detail, methodically recording the particulars of his business in his office memorandums and requiring frequent, descriptive reports from his employees. He carried on a voluminous correspondence, made copious notes about his business dealings, and maintained detailed accounting records. He kept everything. In short, he was in control.

Coe had other qualities that contributed to his influence in business and politics. Those who knew him spoke of his sound judgment, honesty and integrity, and self-confidence. Although he lacked in social contacts outside his business dealings, he was not without social skills: he was seen as courteous, pleasant, and possessing a sense of humor; he listened to the opinions of others; and he exhibited an ability to judge character and personality. Many attested to his charity and benevolence.[52]

Coe threw himself into his work for Pingree. Letters in the spring of 1844 showed that Pingree had obtained the services of a man astute in appraising the details of land opportunities and capable of giving sound advice. A letter Coe wrote to Pingree on May 13 noted that "the inhabitants of the town [Stetson] voted on Saturday at a public meeting to accept the new road . . . [and] I think we can reasonably expect a sale of quite a number of farming lots on that road this season as much of the land is very good and well situated." In a subsequent letter, he discussed Military Road and Aroostook Road as they affected Pingree's purchases, asking for instructions in lotting the land and cutting the timber and proposing to commence a survey. He discussed the threat of timber trespassing and tax implications of potential roads.[53]

On the advice of Coe, Pingree began purchasing townships around Chamberlain Lake. On July 16, 1844, the land agents of the commonwealth of Massachusetts and the state of Maine sold T7 R12 W.E.L.S. to Francis Blackman for $8,436.13. Less than a month later, on August 10, Blackman sold the township to Pingree for $8,000.00.[54] By 1846, Pingree owned five townships around Chamberlain Lake and two more on Eagle Lake. He had begun to issue cutting permits the year before, the value of which had been increased by Telos Canal.[55] Pingree had a letter drawn up on January 28, 1845, addressed "to the several persons lumbering under permits from D. Pingree," to enable Coe to adequately represent his interests:

> This will be handed you by Mr. Coe who visits your region as the representative of Mr. Pingree, and who is fully authorised to act in his behalf in all matters connected with his interest under permits to you.
>
> Please make Mr. Coe acquainted with your doings under such permits as also all matters connected with Mr. Pingrees interest which have or may come under your observation—please render him any aid or assistance he may need & you shall be duly paid for same.[56]

During the winter of 1845–1846, extensive cutting began on the

Pingree lands. Felling the trees, however, was one thing, and getting them out was quite another. Telos Canal made it physically possible by controlling the waters for log driving, but controlling the opportunistic desire for extra money by the canal owner, Rufus Dwinel, presented a serious obstacle. When the loggers attempted to drive their logs through the canal that spring, Dwinel forced them to pay what they considered an unfair toll. Pingree, who had built Chamberlain Dam as part of the system to supply driving water at Telos Canal, protested. But Dwinel would not budge, and to ensure that the logs would not go through until his toll was paid, he hired a menacing group of Bangor men armed with fearsome-looking knives. The loggers had no alternative but to pay, and their logs went through. The incident became known as the "bloodless Telos war." But it did not end there. Pingree and the other lumbermen took their grievance to the legislature, and evidence was presented at a hearing of the Committee on Interior Waters. The committee suggested a compromise toll, but Dwinel would not hear of it. The legislature finally resolved the issue by passing two acts: One gave Dwinel a deadline to accept a reasonable toll; if he did not, the other act would open the canal to public use. Dwinel accepted.[57]

In 1846 Coe and Pingree, like many other large landowners, faced the problem of transporting supplies to their lumbering operations. But they were self-assured men, confident in their ability to exert control over the land and overcome any obstacles to achieving their goals. Their solution was to build a large farm to provide hay, oats, and other produce, to summer oxen and other stock, and to serve as a centrally located depot for all kinds of needed equipment and other goods. Already, two such farms had been built: Trout Brook Farm, about twenty-five miles to the east, built in the late 1830s, and Grant Farm, thirty miles directly south, constructed in the 1840s.[58] But Chamberlain Farm, as they called it, was more remote and isolated. It could be reached in summer only by water and in winter by temporary roads over ice and packed snow, known as winter roads. With Coe in charge, clearing for the farm began at Apmoojenegamook Point, in a location that, according to one forest historian, "shows how far into the state the search for pine had been carried after the Telos gateway made greater areas accessible."[59]

Why, exactly, Coe chose this particular location on the shore of Chamberlain Lake is not documented, but certain facts, combined with an awareness of Coe's practical-mindedness, lead to a reasonable explanation. A fair expanse of land rises gently behind Apmoojenegamook Point. The soil is not swampy and wet; rather, it lies above the water table and beneath a low ridge to the north, from which erosion over thousands of years has built it to a suitable depth. Here, on a slope with a south-facing aspect and protection from the ridge, conditions tend to be drier and warmer and snow melts more quickly. Thus, the land is more conducive to the raising of crops. Behind the ridge is another body of water, Indian Pond, to which the farm would eventually extend and the frozen surface of which would provide access by a winter road. The point of land creates a small cove and protects it from the prevailing westerly winds that sweep down the lake and build huge waves; thus, it offers a sheltered place to land and anchor watercraft. Additionally, the farm is located between two dams—Chamberlain Dam, five miles away, and Telos Dam and Canal, thirteen miles by water to the southeast—and at the time it provided a base of operation for those repairing and tending them. Beyond these considerations and incidental to them, the site provides a beautiful view of the Katahdin mountain range.

The clearing would eventually grow to 600 acres of farmland with several large, shingled buildings constructed of eight-inch squared timbers.[60] The first buildings, according to one visitor in 1857, were made of logs and included a dwelling place, a storehouse, barns, and other structures.[61] That visitor was Henry David Thoreau, who at the very time of the farm's initial clearing could be

Chamberlain Farm, 1879

Thomas Sedgwick Steele, looking toward the southwest from the ridge
behind Chamberlain Farm, saw this view of the farm and Chamberlain Lake.
It is the earliest picture of the farm. Reprinted from Thomas Sedgwick
Steele, *Canoe and Camera: A Two Hundred Mile Tour through the
Maine Forests* (Boston, Mass.: Estes & Lauriat, 1880), 65.

found on Mt. Katahdin, attempting a climb. His influence would be
felt in this place to an extent unimaginable to those living then. But
for the remainder of the century, E. S. Coe would be the figure of
major influence.

The year 1846 held significance for Coe for other reasons. By this time, he owned several townships on Eagle and Churchill Lakes. To move the timber from them into Penobscot waters, he chartered and began planning two dams below Chamberlain Farm. The first was Heron Lake Dam (later called Churchill Dam), at the outlet of Churchill Lake at the head of the Allagash River. It would raise the level of the lakes and back up the water nearly to Chamberlain Dam, where a second dam would be built to serve as a lock in which logs could be raised to the level of Chamberlain Lake and floated into it. By this year, Coe also had begun to make a name for himself, as noted in the *Bangor Directory* of 1846: "Coe E. S. agent for timber lands, office over 6 broad, b'ds Mrs. Susan Patten."[62] And during this year, he married Mary Upham Barker.

Early the next year, 1847, Pingree sold Coe a "common and undivided" one-twentieth share of T7 R12. In this form of ownership, which still applies to a substantial area of Maine, no one individual owns a specific area of land; rather, each owner shares in the profits and losses from the property according to her or his proportion. It is difficult in this circumstance to develop or lease a piece of land unless all the owners agree. In this same year, Pingree sold an undivided share of T7 R12 to John Winn, and Pingree, Winn, and Coe separated out a 500-acre tract for Chamberlain Farm.[63] Also that summer, Pingree, who owned Katahdin Iron Works, located about sixty miles south of the farm, undertook construction of a road that would connect the iron works to a winter road leading to Chamberlain Lake and the lumbering region.[64] It appears that Pingree built it in part to aid the development of his timber interests as well as to serve the iron works.[65]

During the latter part of the 1840s, work was done on an east–west road thirty miles north of the farm, providing passage across the Allagash country and eventually connecting Ashland, Maine, to towns in Canada. Called the California Road for uncertain reasons, although some speculate the name related to the westward migration of the time, it served as a major supply route throughout most of the century.[66] In 1847, lumbermen penetrated this region near Umsaskis Lake. From that time on, throughout the century and into the next, loggers who drove the Allagash River resented Chamberlain Dam, which diverted water through Telos Canal. At times, the dam gates were forcibly opened and even dynamited.[67]

Outside the Allagash region during the mid-1800s, other developments promised changes in the vicinity of the farm. As white pines grew scarcer, lumbermen and mill owners began eyeing spruce trees for sawlogs.[68] Above Bangor there were perhaps as many as 250 sawmills, and steamboats had begun plying the waters of the Penobscot from Old Town to Winn. These years also saw the invention of wood-pulp paper, a development that would, before the end of the century, have a great impact on the forests around the farm.

In 1849, tragedy struck Coe. He lost his wife and their baby during childbirth. Sometime later, perhaps after his father died, in 1862, he went to live with his half brother, Dr. Thomas Upham Coe, and his wife in Bangor. He never remarried, and it appears that he became even more absorbed in his business interests. For the next fifty years, until his death, in December 1899, Coe accumulated an extensive record of activity at Chamberlain Farm in journals, inventories, supply lists, bookkeeping accounts, fire insurance papers, office memorandums, and correspondence. Through this record we learn how the attitudes and values of the time, specifically in the lumbering industry, influenced activities at the farm and contributed to the transformation of the wildland in the region. In the course of this change, Apmoojenegamook Point acquired another name: Hog Point, possibly from the presence of a nearby hog house. And throughout these years, E. S. Coe kept a tight rein over the farm.

From the beginning, Coe appears to have been a hands-on manager who wanted direct contact with his business enterprises. A clue to this attitude is found in a journal kept by a Mr. Brown, who worked for Coe. In March 1852, Coe and Brown made a business trip into the woods. Leaving Bangor in the morning of March 5, they traveled north by horse-drawn sleigh and eventually reached Fort Kent, at the top of the state, before returning to Bangor, a trip of more than 400 miles. Coe visited lumbering operations, stopped at Katahdin Iron Works, stayed at Grant Farm, ate moose meat, spent time at Chamberlain Farm, issued logging permits, and checked on the amount of timber being cut and other business details. The following are a few entries from Brown's journal:

> March 5th, Left Bangor for our journey into the woods. Travelling is very bad. Snow in the afternoon; 10th, Left Katahdin [Iron Works] for Grants in #2 R13. Got at Grants about 10 Ock in Eve. Had to walk the Horses all of the way from K.I.W. because the snow is deep & soft. Horses would Slump in up to their knees; 12th, Friday at Chamberlin farm rained in the afternoon. Mr. Coe arrived late in the afternoon; 15th, Monday Mr. Coe, Barker, Turner & Lampson went down to Telos. Hoisted the Gates. Took an inventory of the things there. . . . [A number of notes were inserted here, including the following.] 3/4 No 7 R 12 T E Crane & Co 6 ox & 6 horse teams hauling into Chamberlain Lake & Leadbetter Pond best logs cut on Chamberlin; 17th, Wednesday Left Chamber. Made a road of about 80 rods fr. 7 R 12 to 7 R 11. 3 men from Cranes shovel the path. Stayed all night at S. Boody Camp 8 R 10; 29th, Left Lincoln for Bangor.[69]

The farm's expansion can be traced throughout the last half of the century because of Coe's attention to detail and his penchant for orderly records. In April 1858, his personal ownership in the farm grew significantly, from one-twentieth to about one-quarter owner-ship, when David Pingree sold him nine-fortieths of the farm.[70] Two months later, Coe signed for himself and the other owners a policy with the Atlantic Mutual Fire Insurance Company, listing the following buildings for a total value of $3,650: "Cham. Farm House with L [ell, an extension at right angles to the building's length] and wood shed, all attached, warmed by three stoves; Store House; Barn No. 1, new; Barn No. 2; Barn No. 3, Stock Barn with open shed attached; Barn No. 4, Log Stable.[71] By 1869, the value had increased to $5,750, and a map showed additional buildings.[72]

Each year, Coe required a detailed accounting of all buildings, equipment, supplies, and livestock at the farm. These records also show the depot actively expanding its business. The 1859 inventory, for example, contained lengthy lists of items categorized by build-ings. Some idea of their diversity is found in the list of items in the storehouse for sale to lumbermen: 100 pounds of coffee, 53 wool and fur hats, 25 red flannel shirts, a lot of fishhooks, 12 five-gallon pails, 78 pounds of bar soap, 17 stovepipes, and 1 new bateau. That year, the barns stored nearly 100 tons of hay and 5 tons of oats. Some of the supplies received included seed for fifteen acres of burnt land, plough points, mule shoes, and food staples.[73] A year later, as the business grew, a desk showed up on the list of furniture for the farmhouse, along with a safe, possibly the very one now rust-ing away in the house's cellar hole.[74] By 1877, the inventory had grown to nearly sixty pages of items, quite an increase over the eleven-page inventory taken twenty-five years earlier.[75] Interest-ingly, the 1892 inventory reveals that Coe had a room at the farm-house.[76]

In keeping with the farm's growth, enlargement of its productive acreage continued. In 1875, workers cleared stumps from more than

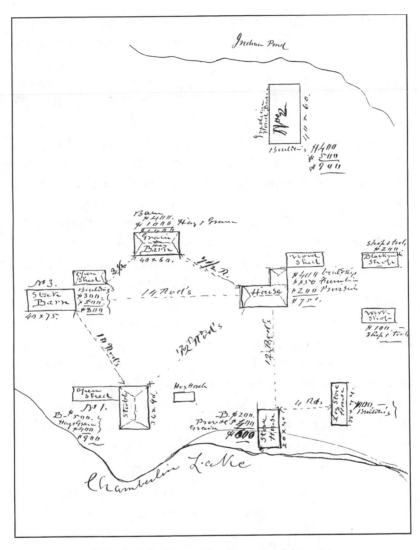

Chamberlain Farm Fire Insurance Map, 1869

From "Chamberlain Farm Fire Insurance Policy, Bangor Mutual Fire Insurance Company, 15 July 1869," E. S. Coe Chamberlain Farm Papers, Captain Myron H. Avery Collection, Maine State Library, Augusta.

seven acres, a process known as stumping. They also broke up four acres of new land, from which the heavy smell of newly spread manure soon scented the air. Farmhands also sowed about thirty-six acres in oats.[77] The 1876 record notes that the farm's workers ploughed forty-one acres; broke up fifteen rocky acres up the lake, above the stock barn, in the fall; broke up, stumped, ploughed, and harrowed three acres down the lake for the first time; and manured eight acres between the house and Indian Pond on the ridge and planted oats, which yielded well that year.[78] The farm log of 1881–1882 reads: "Stump & Ploughed about 16 acres down the Lake—Hard & Rocky—Some very good—6 more stumped." The log also notes that more than 100 sheep and lambs were raised.[79] And an 1882 list of freight contents and weights shows that 5,412 pounds of goods and supplies were shipped to the farm using a new railroad to Blanchard as part of its supply route.[80] History would show this to be only one effect of the railroad on Chamberlain Farm and the surrounding region.

Through the latter part of the century, Coe, in his seventies and eighties, continued to keep a crew actively running the farm. If someone in Bangor had picked up the *Bangor Daily Commercial* on the evening of Thursday, October 25, 1888, he or she might have read the following news item:

> A. R. Patten, who carries on the Chamberlain farm, the place so well known to the Bangor lumbermen, has been in the city today. He says that there will be very much lumbering in his section this winter. The farm is fast being brought up to its old standard. Seven men are employed there and among the products this year were 75 tons of hay and 700 bushels of oats. They raised other produce in proportion and are well satisfied with the yield.[81]

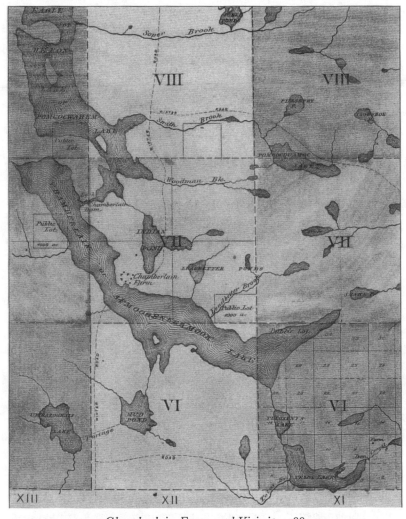

Chamberlain Farm and Vicinity, 1882
From George N. Colby & Company, "Timber Plan No. 3," *Atlas of Piscataquis County, Maine* (Philadelphia: F. Bourquin, 1882), 32.

No doubt Patten reported directly to Coe's office during this visit and received instructions to carry out on his return. Coe was on top of all facets of the operation. His office memorandums, for example, continue to show his control of water for the drives. In the spring of 1890, he noted: "April 9—W. R. Goodwin left today for Chamb. Lake to take care of Telos Webster Lake & Chamb Dams—for this spring gave him the same instructions as last year in regard to the management of the water."[82] And in an 1896 letter to Thomas McCard, foreman at the farm, he wrote:

> July 17th—Yours of the 4th At hand. . . . I hear to-day that Mr. Harvey came up the river past Chamberlain dam and said one of the gates was hoisted and that one of the farm men told him that they hoisted it to accommodate sportsmen. Now if any of your men did that or knew the gates was up and did not shut it, making it necessary for Mr. Grant to send a man up there to watch that dam, it is all wrong. I am surprised that your men should take such liberties to open the gates and allow the water to run that way, when the whole east branch drive were depending so much on the water from Telos. I should like to hear from you the facts in regard to it.[83]

This was only a hint of the impending conflict between landowners and recreationists.

For the period from 1895 to 1898, available bookkeeping records document the continuing value of the farm to lumbermen in the region. A news item dated March 11, 1898, reports the activities of a well-known logger: "Cornelius Murphy, of Old Town, is operating this season on the little Allegash stream, a tributary of Chamberlain lake, 12 miles west from Chamberlain farm. He has employed in the three camps 135 men, 38 working horses, with all the attendant tools and machinery necessary to carry on the lumbering business in northern Maine."[84] Farm records for that year's logging season show

Chamberlain Farm, 1890s

Tote teams gather on the snow-covered lakeshore in front of Chamberlain
Farm. Note that the farmhouse is a one-and-one-half-story building.
Another story would be built at the turn of the century.
Photograph courtesy of Patten Lumberman's Museum, Patten,
Maine, Carl Sprinchorn Collection, 508 N.

that Murphy purchased boots, potatoes, hay, meals, baked beans,
and other supplies totaling $371.99.[85]

Meanwhile, during the last half of the century, outside events
had occurred that related to Coe's interests in the logging industry.
In 1853, Maine acquired all remaining public lands by purchasing
those Massachusetts still owned. But the state was intent on selling
them, and in 1878 the Maine land agent reported that no public
land remained that the state could grant for homestead settlement.
In anticipation of this, both Coe and David Pingree Jr., who had
taken over the Pingree interests after his father's death, in 1863, had
filled out their holdings in the mid-1870s by buying parts of fifteen
separate townships, and Coe, independently, had bought land
rounding out eleven of his townships—an astounding proportion of
Maine's wildland area to be controlled by two individuals.[86]

Other developments promised even greater efficiency in the logging and lumber industry. In 1858, Joseph Peavey invented the
Peavey cant dog, an improved tool for handling logs, and in that

decade the double-bitted axe appeared. In Titusville, Pennsylvania, a new, practical source of power emerged with the drilling of the first oil well. Meanwhile, steam continued to power machines, and on the national scene after the Civil War, it would largely replace water power in factories and mill towns as a primary source of energy.[87]

During the war, the farm carried on its business with no apparent disruption. As usual, most supplies arrived over the winter roads from December through March, during the logging season. An 1863 publication noted, "The great supply road for Chesuncook Lake and that lumbering region leads from the [Katahdin Iron] Works among the mountains by the way of Grant's, and a very large business in teaming finds its way hither, and keeps the road in very excellent condition."[88] Over the years, supply routes to the farm continued to develop. In 1874, John M. Way Jr. published a map of the region that showed a winter road extending beyond the farm, intersecting with another road running east to Patten (later to be known as the Eagle Lake Tote Road), and connecting with Churchill Dam at the head of the Allagash River. Yet another winter road came to the shores of Telos Lake from the southern end of Chesuncook Lake.[89] A map made in 1881 by Thomas Sedgwick Steele also shows a road running from Patten to Trout Brook Farm and then on to Webster Lake and Telos Dam and Farm.[90] The traditional summer canoe access across Mud Pond Carry and down Mud Brook was improved in 1880 by Anse Smith Jr., who established the Mud Pond Toting Service, using horses for the first time. This service, later taken over by his brother, Frank, operated through most of the remaining century and contributed to the farm's business.[91] Little by little, the farm's inaccessibility changed, and so did the wildlands.

Other developments in transportation touched the farm and its surrounding forests during the latter half of the century. In 1869, the

Mud Pond Carry Toting Service

This team and buckboard hauled canoes over Mud Pond Carry
in the 1930s, continuing a horse-and-wagon carry business first
established by Anse Smith Jr. in 1880. Photograph courtesy of
Etta M. Hubbard, Bae Powers Collection.

European and North American Railroad completed a route from
Old Town to Mattawamkeag, only about seventy miles southeast of
the farm.[92] And in the last decade of the nineteenth century, the
Bangor and Aroostook Railroad was completed and began attract-
ing industry to the upper St. John region and creating greater logging activity in the woods.[93]

Meanwhile, the logging industry itself had been undergoing a
change. In the early 1860s, signs of a shift from pine to spruce for
sawlogs had become more evident as old-growth pine near accessible water transportation routes ran out. In 1861, trapper Manly
Hardy reported that the crew of a lumber camp near the foot of

Canoes in Mud Brook

This scene of canoeists wading through Mud Brook, shown here
in the 1930s, was common throughout the history of human travel
between the watersheds of the Penobscot and Allagash Rivers. The brook
was part of the popular route used to reach Chamberlain Lake and
Chamberlain Farm in spring, summer, and fall before roads were built
in the mid-1900s to provide access to the lake. Photograph
courtesy of Etta M. Hubbard, Bae Powers Collection.

Caucomgomoc Lake, fifteen miles east of the farm, was "hauling
spruce almost entirely."[94] Before the century ended, the cutting of
spruce trees would begin to increase even more dramatically as a
new use emerged: pulpwood for papermaking. In 1883, the sulfite
process came to Maine with the operation of the Penobscot Chemical Fibre Company in Old Town. Although at that time poplar
provided most of the wood pulp, spruce would generally replace it
early in the twentieth century.[95] This species is well suited for paper-

making because its long cellulose fibers, after being separated by grinding and chemical digestion of nonfibrous parts of the wood, can form a strong, tough paper.[96] Northern Maine had plenty of spruce trees, and the industry would draw heavily on the forests around Chamberlain Farm.

At the end of the century, an event occurred that must have cast a shadow over the future of the farm. It came with little warning. As usual, Coe's office memorandums for 1899 contained many entries about farm business. On August 31, for example, he expressed a long-standing concern about a severe threat of forest fires. Then, abruptly, in November the following notation appeared, written in another hand: "The Entry on opposite page, under date of 11th November, was the last Entry made in this book by E. S. Coe whose death occurred in December following."[97] "His last sickness was short and free of pain," reported the Reverend Henry L. Griffin, "and, in the ripeness of character, years and achievement, he fell asleep on the 9th day of December."[98] Thus ended a chapter in the history of Chamberlain Farm. It had lost the one person who had brought it into existence and taken a personal interest in its management and care, whose own career had been linked to it economically and, almost surely, emotionally. The next chapter in the life of the farm would be quite different. And so would that of the surrounding wildlands, for they would experience a different influence from what they had with Coe, a man who followed the surveyors into the woods, into their measured squares, all neatly quantifiable in economic value and bounded for legal private control, a man with the ability and vision to control the waters and get out the logs with extraordinary success.

At the time of Coe's death, the Coe-Pingree lands totaled more than a million acres, some of them owned jointly.[99] Coe, as manager of these lands, had controlled the permits for cutting rights and thus exerted a strong influence on the woods.[100] He died, however, at a time when even stronger forces were about to make greater changes in the industry and the forests.

As large as the Coe-Pingree lands were, their holdings would be no match for those being created at the turn of the century by the industrial giants, such as Great Northern Paper Company and International Paper Company. Their large investment in mills required a continuing supply of pulpwood and forced them to think and manage with a longer view of the forest's health and productivity. David Pingree Jr., for example, insisted on "sustained yield cutting practices in pulpwood with selective cutting in harvesting operations, rather than cut and abandon."[101] Five years into the twentieth century, Coe, too, was recognized for his prudent cutting practices: The *Bangor Daily Commercial* noted that he had "made it a rule to never cut a tree less than 16 inches in circumference at the butt. This is practical forestry. . . . Every wild land owner pays Eben S. Coe the tribute of sagacious appreciation of practical wisdom in caring for forests, and today his influence is potent in example."[102]

At the end of the century, the public showed signs of increasing recognition of the forest's public value. In 1891, for example, public support had contributed to the appointment of the first forest commissioner.[103] This occurred despite the fact that growing timber interests were exerting increasing pressure on Maine's government for control over the forests and timber harvesting. Years later, former secretary of the interior Stewart L. Udall would comment in his book *The Quiet Crisis* that Maine and such states as Wisconsin and Oregon were turned into "company states" during this time.[104]

Both public and private interest in the long-term health of the forest had a strong element of economics, which was consistent with the national interest in conservation that would emerge early in the next century. According to historian Richard Judd, this new view of the forest came at a time when the Allagash region had experienced only relatively light cutting in those areas beyond easy access to driving waters, and it was likely that some geographically isolated places still contained sizable stands of virgin spruce. The forest, he noted, "had changed surprisingly little since the 1830s."[105]

Changes, however, were to come. Already, developments in other places promised to drastically affect this remote bit of North America, as they would throughout the country. In 1892, Rudolf Diesel patented an internal combustion engine. The next year, Henry Ford built his first car, and two years later, in 1895, four automobiles were registered in the United States. In the spring of 1897, the Schenectady Locomotive Works in Schenectady, New York, built a ten-wheel railroad locomotive weighing 142,000 pounds and numbered it 109 for the Chicago, Hammond & Western Railroad—an engine that would one day break the stillness of Chamberlain Farm in a way it had never experienced before.[106]

The lumbering activities around T7 R12 and the other townships surrounding Chamberlain Farm reflected a national trend in the latter half of the nineteenth century. In the United States, production of lumber ranked second to production of cotton in the manufacturing industry.[107] For the forty years following the Civil War, it expanded dramatically as a result of several factors: an increasing demand for lumber; availability of wood in areas marginal for agriculture, such as those in the Allagash region; availability of means of transportation such as rivers and streams; and changing technology.[108] The culture of the time extolled the forest industry for its contributions to the advancement of society.

The changes seen in the vicinity of Chamberlain Farm from 1840 until the death of E. S. Coe, at the end of the century, rode the tide of these developments and reflected a perspective in which people saw themselves as apart from nature. Nature was in their service, to be controlled, and this was its main value. It had appeared inexhaustible, and few were concerned about its future sustainability.

This perspective, which was widely held and influential, shows itself even today. It is one that in many ways contributed to the development of the United States. But it was not without a cost, and the American public at the end of the century was neither unaware of nor unconcerned about the effects of this view. There was little question that the land and its forests and waters had suffered: the loss of virgin trees, the increased incidence of forest fires resulting from slash-and-burn forestry and human carelessness, the alteration of river and stream channels, and the effect of abandoned logs on streams all attested to that fact. These conditions were brought about by the way forests were harvested for wood. But this perspective was also evident in the people's view of the wildlife and other resources of the land.

Chapter 3

A Well-Stocked Country

ON THE AFTERNOON OF SEPTEMBER 7, 1858, a canoe came out of Mud Brook's inlet, crossed Chamberlain Lake, and continued on to Chamberlain Farm. One of the three young men to come ashore was a slight twenty-five-year-old by the name of Manly Hardy. As he and his companions, Hiram Leonard and William Staples, walked toward the farmhouse, one of the first things that struck them was the smell: They had exchanged the damp, fresh, balsam-and-cedar-scented forest for the familiar odor of dry fields, weathered wood, and manure. But this was soon forgotten, for coming down the path to greet them was Pial Antwine Tomah, a Huron Indian and the fourth member of their expedition. Hardy felt the excitement of anticipation now that they were all together. The four were gathering at the farm for a fall fur hunt on the Tobique River in Canada, some 200 miles away via the Allagash and St. John Rivers.

The arrival of the hunters and trappers did not appear unusual to A. B. Fogg, the young foreman in charge of the farm. He had grown accustomed to woodsmen and others stopping by to pick up supplies and spend a night or two. But he never would have guessed that the lean, woods-wise Hardy would in the future be one of Maine's most widely known naturalists, with a national reputation as a highly regarded collector of bird specimens; that he would be respected as a consultant and writer on natural history and the Maine woods; or that he would acquire a name as a furrier as well as an accomplished hunter and trapper.[1]

When Hardy and his friends arrived at Chamberlain Farm, game was very much on their minds, and the wildlife was there for the taking, even more so than the trees, for one did not have to own the land to remove its animal life. It was a time when few laws protected wildlife and little enforcement of them occurred. From the early part of the century, inland fish had been considered economically worthless; only the "money," or food, fish—the migrating salmon, shad, and alewives—were protected by the county's three fish wardens, whose jurisdiction was limited to the Penobscot River and its tributaries. Since the 1830s, bounties had been in effect, and Hardy could collect eight cents for each crow he shot, three dollars per bear, eight dollars per wolf, and one dollar for each bobcat and lynx. The only law protecting mammals had been passed twenty-eight years earlier, in 1830—a law allowing moose and deer hunting with no bag limit from September 1 through December 31.[2]

With few restrictions and a seemingly inexhaustible supply of game, the mood in the Allagash region during those years in the 1800s, like that all across America, was one of unrestricted exploitation. Only three years after this first visit by Hardy to Chamberlain Farm, a friend and another man hunting and trapping in the upper Allagash Stream country, mainly for hides and pelts, killed 40 moose and 1 caribou and trapped 100 sables, 20 lynx, 9 otters, 9 fishers, and quite a number of minks and beavers. That same year, Hardy learned from the headman at Chamberlain Farm that two brothers "had killed eighty-two moose north of Katahdin, between Telos and Sowadnehunk Mountains." Some claimed that 1861 was "the year of the greatest slaughter of Moose ever known." Years later, Hardy would take issue with this, arguing that the "hide hunters," as he called them, killed fewer than 400 moose that year, compared with a total of 461 killed by sportsmen in 1902 for heads and antlers.[3]

Manly Hardy, however, would live through a time when public attitudes toward wildlife changed from showing little concern about the decimation of species to supporting laws to protect some species and restore populations of others. He would see a growing public awareness of the ethics of hunting methods, and he would come to express publicly his own feelings and beliefs about the pursuit of game. His opinions would be respected because, from its very beginning, his life had been intertwined with the lives of wild animals.

The only child of Catherine Sears Atwood and Jonathan Titcomb Hardy, Manly was born into a family known for its achievements in business, literature, and the arts. His father was an astute and successful businessman who had interests in general trading, shipping, lumbering, timberlands, and the purchase and sale of furs. He passed on to his son his interest in the woods, hunting and trapping, and Indian lore. In 1836, four years after Manly's birth, the family moved to Brewer, where Manly lived the rest of his years. When he was twelve, a significant event occurred in his life when he met a Prussian nobleman, Count Karl Luther, who was traveling in America. The count taught him how to mount birds and cultivated in him an interest in ornithology, which extended through his lifetime. While in his teens, after attending public schools, Manly received tutoring at a private school conducted by the Reverend George W. Field, where he acquired an intimate knowledge of classical literature. One of his classmates was Thomas Upham Coe, half brother of E. S. Coe.[4] Despite his education in the classics, Hardy would turn out to have more in common with E. S. Coe than with Thomas Upham Coe: Both he and E. S. Coe would exploit the Allagash-Penobscot forests—Coe for their pine and spruce trees and Hardy for their game animals.

Hardy did not intend to pursue a career in the hunting and trapping business. During his youth, he had never been robust and had suffered from acute rheumatism and bouts of severe pain in his neck, shoulders, and eyes. Although studying was difficult and he admitted a dislike for it, he dedicated himself to studying for a religious career. At the age of nineteen, in his first journal, which he kept from June 11 to November 27, 1852, he began with the following: "Having as I hope given my heart to Christ . . . I will fit myself to be a Missionary." His entries reveal the emotions and conflicts of a youth seeking to clarify his future and his feelings toward his parents and God. He recorded regular attendance at religious lectures, sermons, and prayer meetings; serious study of Greek and Latin with the purpose of entering college; and attempts at writing poetry. To relieve the suffering that reading caused him, he made frequent trips into the country, visiting woods, fields, and waters to hunt, trap, and fish. In June, for example, he tried unsuccessfully to shoot two deer, wounded another, and killed crows, pigeons, a cuckoo, and a woodchuck. Some of his recorded hunting exploits that summer and early fall appear to have been undertaken just for sport and marksmanship practice: shooting a blue jay's head off, killing a nighthawk and a swallow on the wing. That October, he started trapping, and when his journal entries ended in late November, he had caught minks, a weasel, and two cats.[5]

Throughout his journal, Hardy wrestled with competing feelings, torn between a love for the outdoors and hunting and a desire to serve God. "I must not pursue it [his love for the woods and hunting] so closely as to lose sight of my great object to be a Missionary," he wrote. "I want to hold my heart and affections at God's dis-

posal and to feel willing to do whatever he requires of me at whatever sacrifice." Yet the pull of the outdoors was strong, as shown by
an entry he made that September:

> Another month of my life has passed and "old
> Autumn comes nodding o'er the plain." Soon our
> forrests will begin to don their many-colored attire
> and our uplands display a variety of tints which the
> Painters skill might try in vain to imitate. Soon
> game will be fit to kill and streched out at length by
> my camp fire neath the forrest shade I shall lay and
> gaze upon the fall-orbed Moon and the twinkling
> stars as they appear in the clear blue sky and think
> of him who made them and of the multitudes in
> past ages who have looked upon them and have
> passed away from the stage of existence.[6]

Years later Hardy's daughter, Fannie Hardy Eckstorm, wrote
that sometime after her father's last journal entry, on November 27,
1852, "his eyes gave him so much trouble that he had to give up
study entirely and for long periods could neither read nor write, so
that his education in the schools never was finished and he did not
go to college nor to the Seminary, nor become a Missionary. But he
went more and more in the woods, and among the men he was a
Missionary indeed by his example rather than by his precepts."[7]

It was not, then, an unusual event when Hardy took the stage
out of Bangor with his friend Hiram Leonard on September 2,
1858, to embark on a two-month hunting and trapping trip. After
"a tedious ride of 16 hours," they arrived at Greenville, where the
next day they took passage on the steamboat to the Kineo House at
Mt. Kineo, about seventeen miles up Moosehead Lake. On Saturday, September 4, they crossed Northeast Carry and started down
the West Branch of the Penobscot River. "I never saw so beautiful

reflections of trees in the water as I witnessed today," Hardy declared. "The colors were perfectly distinct even to the delicate tints of the changing leaves. Every knot or bunch of moss or the bunches of berries were distinctly visible." On Saturday and Sunday they camped on the river with hunters, one of whom, after an unsuccessful night of moose hunting, came back "swearing because he did not fire at some ducks for fear of scaring moose and vowing that the next time that he went out to hunt 'he would be like hell take all that came along ducks, muskrat and moose.'"[8]

On Monday, William Staples joined Hardy and Leonard at Chesuncook Lake, and the three paddled up Umbazooksus Stream and across the lake of the same name to Mud Pond Carry. Hardy called it "probably the worst carry for the distance in the state." They portaged by a clearing near the lake and a deserted house and barn, the latter surmounted by a pair of moose antlers. The party camped on the carry, halfway across, and early the next morning completed the portage to Chamberlain Lake. Hardy's journal describes their arrival at the farm:

> September 7. . . . We crossed over to the Chamberlain Farm 2-1/2. . . . Pial Antwine Tomah . . . is camping with a St. Francis Indian near the farm. We dined with them, had plenty of dried moosemeat and fat hanging over the fire. We bought another canoe here. The Chamberlain farm contains about 300 acres of clearing and 50 of felled timber; the smaller farms at Eagle Lake and Telos are included in this estimate. It is owned by Pingree and Coe and is at present conducted by a young man by the name of Fogg who is quite polite and showed us more attention than could have been expected. They have this year pressed 40 tons of

hay. They are however very deficient in proper tools such as a with-twister, a more modern haypress, etc. There is a store connected with the farm where provisions and camp tools, axes, clothing suitable for the woods, etc. may be had by paying twice what they are worth which is sometimes quite an accommodation. Flour is 8 cents per pound, potatoes $1 a bushel, molasses, common, $1, salt 3 cents a pound, tobacco forty cents a pound, needles and pipes two cents each.[9]

Hardy and his friends tented out at the farm, staying a total of four nights, interspersed with a two-day trip to Eagle Lake and Smith Brook. At the farm, they prepared their gear while waiting for Staples to recover from an unexpected illness. On September 13, they set off once again for the Tobique River. Hardy did not know then that he would return two more times, in both cases under very different circumstances. The party continued across the Allagash lakes to the head of the Allagash River. Hardy described one evening's paddle after dark:

> I never saw so wild and strange sight as I witnessed tonight. In the south was the new moon now about half grown and having a peculiarly red and bloody look; in the west was a comet, seen by us for the first time tonight with its tail leaving a long train of lurid light across the sky; in the north the aurora borealis shot its long trembling flickering spears of light; the stars shone brightly leaving their shimmery paths on the tremulous waters. Meteors frequently shot across the sky. Added to this we were just entering a large lake unknown to me. A bull

moose was calling on one side of the inlet and an
owl was hooting on the other. A heron and some
ducks which we disturbed went quacking off and
the fish and muskrats kept splashing continually in
the tall reeds. Altogether it was the strangest combination of sights and sounds I ever heard.[10]

The group continued down the Allagash River, killing a "fine old
bull" moose, from which they "took about 30 pounds of meat, the
marrow and hide"; trapping muskrats; shooting two sheldrakes, or
mergansers, as well as a partridge and two muskrats; and spearing
suckers and a turtle. After reaching the St. John River on September 17, they continued downstream to the mouth of the Tobique
and ascended the river to its headwaters, where they hunted and
trapped until the end of October.[11]

In early September of the next year, Hardy again took a stage to
Greenville, this time for a fall fur hunt with a trapping acquaintance,
Rufus Philbrook. The two made their way down the West Branch
of the Penobscot River to Chesuncook Lake, and rather than go east
across Mud Pond Carry into Chamberlain Lake, they proceeded
north into Caucomgomoc Lake country. There they trapped in an
area ten to fifteen miles directly west of Chamberlain Farm. They
built a log cabin and set out traplines several miles in length. Before
the last of November, they had taken four bears, four fishers, three
lynx, two otters, seven beavers, fifty sables, thirty-five minks, and
seventy-five muskrats. Hardy reported an absence of foxes, skunks,
and raccoons, a lack of caribou in Maine at the time, "although they
began to come in by 1861," and a scarcity of deer above Mt.
Katahdin, complaining that "this year we did not see one."[12]

The North Woods would continue to attract Hardy throughout
his life, and in his later years he would write about his experiences,
such as the killing of a moose not far from Chamberlain Farm in the

Stretched Skins of Trapped Beavers

In the mid-1800s, when Manly Hardy was a young man, there were few restrictions on hunting and trapping. Among the furbearing animals commonly trapped were beavers, the skins of which are seen here hung outside a trapper's camp. Photograph courtesy of Barry Lord.

spring of 1861. "Wishing a vacation, I thought I would take a trip up north and visit some of my hunting acquaintances," began Hardy in an article about the 1861 trip for *Forest and Stream*. He started for the head of Chesuncook Lake, hiring a driver with a horse and sleigh to travel the more than 100 miles from Bangor by way of Katahdin Iron Works. The road became so bad that he ended up walking the last 50 miles. At Chesuncook, he met a hunter, A. B. Farrar, who asked Hardy to guide him into Allagash Lake country. Farrar wanted to meet two hunters, Billings and Philbrook, who were spending the winter there, so he could engage one of them for a bear hunting trip the next spring. Hardy knew Philbrook, for he had trapped with him in the Caucomgomoc region in 1859.

Accompanied by Farrar's moose dogs, the two snowshoed more than 20 miles to the inlet of Allagash Lake, passing within 8 miles of Chamberlain Farm. On the way, they encountered the carcass of a large bull moose, which they later learned had been shot by Billings. At Ellis Brook Bog, Farrar's dogs jumped a moose, but the men did not stop because of the distance they had to go. When they arrived at the hunters' camp on Allagash Stream above the lake, Billings and Philbrook were away.[13]

The trip to the camp had ruined Hardy's footwear, but Farrar's, made of moose shanks (analogous to the area between the ankle and knee of humans), "had been perfectly dry." Hardy proposed that the next day they "go back to Ellis Brook Bog and kill that moose the dogs had been barking at in order to get some shanks." He described the event as follows:

> Getting to Ellis Brook Bog our dogs soon found the moose, which proved to be an immense bull. As an experiment, I shot him near the kidneys, when he rose straight up upon his hind legs and fell back perfectly dead. We skinned him out and then skinned off the shanks, which is a rather difficult undertaking for a novice. In order to skin a pair of moose shanks the hide is cut around about eighteen inches above the hock joint and below as much as the length of the foot requires. Then a knife has to be worked around the inside from both above and below until the whole skin has been freed from the flesh, after which the hoof has to be disjointed and the skin slipped off.
>
> We took the shanks, nose, tongue and perhaps twenty pounds of the steak. The hide we prepared for hauling in the usual manner, which is by folding

it lengthwise till it is about two feet wide, tying it in
several places to prevent its unfolding and then cutting a narrow strip from the upper edge of each of
the forelegs nearly to the ears and tying the two
ends together, so as to pass over the shoulders of the
one hauling it.[14]

The killing of a moose for its hide and the subsequent waste of
meat was common at the time, yet according to Philip Coolidge,
who chronicled the history of the Maine woods, game laws
changed often throughout this period in the nineteenth century, in
response to "the effects of decreasing game supply and of increasing hunting." Poor enforcement, however, encouraged violation of
the laws. This may have been the case when, on June 29, 1852,
Manly Hardy recorded in his journal that he had shot at three deer:
The lawful season for killing moose and deer, according to
Coolidge, did not open until two days later, on July 1. Open seasons continued to fluctuate until 1875, when moose hunting was
banned for five years. "Moose must have become scarce," Coolidge
noted. No bag limit existed for any animal during open seasons
until around 1883. At that time, hunters faced a limit of one moose,
one caribou, or two deer. In 1899 the caribou season closed, never
to be reopened. Around the end of the century, moose and deer seasons gradually shortened, with different laws in effect for different
counties.[15]

The year after his moose-killing incident, Hardy married a
cousin, Emeline F. Wheeler; the two would eventually have six children, but one died before the age of two. During the remainder of
the century, Hardy continued to take one to three trips each year
into the woods or along the coast. Through them, he acquired an
extensive knowledge of natural history, woodcraft, and Indian lore.
He became intimately acquainted with the northern counties, as

Manly Hardy and Daughters, 1876

Manly Hardy loved hunting and trapping and became well known as a
furrier and naturalist. Pictured here, from left to right, are Catherine Atwood
Hardy, age nine; Fannie Pearson Hardy, age twelve; Annie Eliza Hardy, age
five; and Manly Hardy, age forty-four. Fannie, Manly's oldest daughter,
shared many outdoor interests with her father, and together they made
canoe trips into the north country. In 1888 they stopped at Chamberlain
Farm, one of at least three visits Manly made to the farm. Photograph
by F. W. Hardy, courtesy of Bangor Public Library,
James B. Vickery Collection.

well as the coastal counties of Washington and Hancock and much
of Waldo County.[16]

At the death of his father in 1864, Hardy took over the family
business of buying and selling furs, becoming "remarkably expert in
the judgement of the quality of pelts." The business grew to become
the most extensive fur business in Maine, with exports to Europe.

Over the years, Hardy developed a reputation for being genial with a keen sense of humor, generous and charitable, and modest. He was known as energetic and purposeful in his pursuits. Throughout his life, he neither smoked nor drank alcohol. And one quality that pervaded his writing was his zealousness for truth and justice.[17]

It was Hardy's sensitivity to inaccuracies and biases in the written work of others that prompted one of his earliest published letters, which appeared in an 1884 edition of *Forest and Stream*. He took issue with a writer who had asserted that there were no more wolves in Maine, noting numerous sightings reported by reputable individuals whom he knew. Commenting on his opinion of an increased wolf population, Hardy declared that "Game Commissioners have done a good thing in increasing the bounty." Then, taking offense to the label of "poacher" for some Maine hunters, he bore in on a matter that chafed on him: "Why the man from another state, who pays no tax here, and comes in August and September and kills and wastes our game, is not as much a poacher, etc., as a man who kills deer and eats it after the law expires, is a very hard thing for common people to see."[18]

Hardy's interests, however, extended beyond hunting, trapping, and the fur business to include a fascination for natural history, especially that of birds—an interest Count Karl Luther had aroused in him when he was a boy. Sometime around 1874, he began buying "a few birds of plumage and had one small case of them to look at during evenings when he could not read." Three years later, at the age of forty-five, he tried his hand at taxidermy, attempting to mount a robin. His daughter Fannie, then a child, helped him. They—or the book they were consulting, as Fannie remembered it—forgot to include the neck, and the job turned out rather badly. Hardy resolved to do better, and over the years his collection increased to 3,300 birds from the United States, about 20 birds short of a complete collection. One of the earliest members of the

American Ornithologists' Union, Hardy became good friends with Major Charles Bendire of the National Museum in Washington, D.C.; William Brewster, curator of the Agassiz Museum at Harvard University; and many other collectors and authors.[19]

In 1878, Hardy wrote his first published article, "Nesting Habits of the Red-Bellied Nuthatch," which appeared in the *Nuttall Bulletin*. Most of his articles and letters, however, were published in *Forest and Stream* and *Shooting and Fishing*. Fannie listed more than fifty articles her father had written about animals, the Maine woods, and Indians, observing that he "never overstated and what he said or wrote was original." Although he did not enjoy writing, he felt compelled to write down what he alone knew and to correct the errors of others.[20]

In September 1897, Hardy was taken "critically ill" while on a camping trip. The illness was not identified, but his daughter Fannie noted that he got out of the woods "only by his indomitable will and the devotion of the man with him." She revealed that this incident influenced Hardy's motivation for future trips.[21] However, it did not dampen his interest in natural history, and there is no better illustration of this than a letter he wrote to a friend in the first decade of the 1900s in which he discussed an article about the drumming of grouse:

> I have always concluded that the drumming was produced by the wings striking the sides and Major Bendire in his "Life Histories of North American Birds," has my letter published in which I wrote of how I thought they did it. My friend William Brewster was sure that it was done by the concussion of the air and that the wings never touched the sides and as he is a very careful observer and surely states what he is not sure of, I did not wish to dis-

pute him in a case where there was no sure proof. . . . Did I ever tell you of shooting a drummer . . . by moonlight; I shot one at 9 p.m. I called it the best piece of still hunting I ever did and was a great deal better pleased than if I had shot a moose.[22]

Hardy's enthusiasm for nature and the study of animals continued to the end of his life. "Not more than an hour before he took to his bed the day before he died [December 9, 1910, at the age of seventy-eight]," Fannie wrote, "he finished an article for *Forest and Stream* upon the otter. He was in great pain; he knew that the end was probably near, but he felt that he must stick to this article and finish it."[23] Three months later, Fannie received a letter concerning the article from William Long in Stamford, Connecticut:

I have just read your father's last article on the otter. As usual his simple, direct narrative takes me away in spirit to the big woods. . . . But my chief feeling at this moment is one of profound personal regret that we shall no longer hear from him . . . his writing always gave me brief, flashing glimpses of a wider experience than he could express, and of a quiet, heroic spirit which he tried in vain to conceal.[24]

Manly Hardy's interest in writing about natural history, hunting, and trapping came later in his life and in part reflected a keen awareness of society's changing relationship with wildlife. Like Coe, who had seen a rising concern for conservation of the forests, Hardy witnessed the beginning of a similar change in public sentiment toward wild animals. This was reflected during the last half of the 1800s, when sportsmen organized fish and game clubs and became influ-

Manly Hardy, 1905
Over his lifetime, Manly Hardy witnessed a change in public attitude toward wild animals, from exploitation with little legal restraint to a greater concern for the ethics of hunting methods and passage of more protective legislation. Photograph of portrait painted by Annie E. Hardy courtesy of Fannie (Hardy) Eckstorm Collection, box 620, folio, Special Collections Department, Raymond H. Fogler Library, University of Maine, Orono.

ential in state management decisions.[25] For example, in 1896, the Maine Sportsmen's Fish and Game Association appealed to the state's citizenry and government to awaken to the possibility of making "there own state with its wonderful objects of nature . . . the most attractive of all this great natural park in this sublime country of the Northeast . . . by preserving our forests, our fish, and our game."[26] Influenced by nature writers, editors of major magazines, and examples set by prominent sportsmen such as Theodore Roosevelt, a new ethics appeared among elite hunters regarding the nighttime shooting of deer under jacklights and the use of dogs for hunting.[27]

Hardy saw conflicts about the adequacy of fishways between those who fished and those who owned mills and dams.[28] He was present when an interest in fish culture began in the mid-1860s, promoted by Ezekiel Holmes, an agricultural reformer and natural-

ist whom Hardy had accompanied to Chamberlain Farm.[29] Before
the end of Hardy's life, there were ten state-run hatcheries and feed-
ing stations.[30] In 1880, when he was forty-eight, Maine marked the
beginning of its Department of Inland Fisheries and Wildlife by
making the state's two fishery commissioners (appointments created
in 1867) responsible for enforcing game laws as well as fish laws.[31]
Hardy saw the development of a warden service and, by 1896, the
commissioning of forty-eight inland fish and game wardens. He was
on hand when laws were put into effect requiring license fees and
bag limits, banning exportation of game, calling for enforcement of
laws against night hunting, regulating the use of dogs, and establishing closed seasons (a closed season on furbearing animals was
instituted as early as 1866). Gone were the freedoms he had experienced during his early hunting and trapping days in the wildlands.[32]

Although Hardy supported protective game laws, he continued
to resent what he saw as the making of "class distinctions" among
hunters. In a rebuttal to an article in a sporting magazine that he
saw as favoring wealthy out-of-state sportsmen, he wrote, "What I
do object to is having any one calling the men who leave our trout
in piles to rot on the banks . . . and who kill our game in summer
and waste it, 'true sportsmen,' and calling other as good men 'thieves
and poachers,' if later they kill what they need to eat."[33] And he
defended bounties on bears and wildcats on the grounds of game
preservation: Both kill deer, and, he argued, bears were of no benefit to the state as a game animal.[34]

Manly Hardy's life reflected many of the values society attributed to nature during his time. He was drawn to the woods and
seashore and enjoyed hunting game, trapping furbearing animals,
and catching fish, activities he also saw as having utility for food,
clothing, and other uses. However, his taking of animal life had limits. Although he killed small birds, his daughter Fannie observed
that his collection was "scantiest in the commonest kinds [of little

insectivorous birds]. . . . Killing little birds and stealing their nests never seemed to him quite fit occupation for a man."[35] Birds were of special interest to him, and he found great pleasure in observing them, collecting them for study, and educating others about them.

Hardy's fascination with birds led him to return a second time to Chamberlain Farm when he was in his late twenties, three years after his 1858 visit. This time, he came to the farm under very different circumstances: He served as assistant naturalist and boatman for the Maine Scientific Survey, led by Ezekiel Holmes and Charles H. Hitchcock. Holmes, Hitchcock, and their associates were men of science, quite unlike the visitors the farm usually hosted, yet their visit to the region was motivated by a view of nature much like that of Coe and Pingree, who saw its economic value and potential for development—a view that had driven the growth of the country. For Hardy, however, the expedition would have an unexpected effect on his scientific interests, especially his study of birds.

It was on August 30, 1861, that the Maine Scientific Survey team arrived at Chamberlain Farm, three weeks after it had left Bangor. Hardy recorded the day's events in his journal:

> Fine and clear. Slept well last night buried in the hay [at Telos Farm]. Started at about three; shot a muskrat soon after starting. There was a slight breeze ahead and we passed first through Lake Telos then a thoroughfare to Round Pond at the head of which we dined and waited for Hitchcock. Farrar found an old French Hatchet here. We took Davis into our canoe and let the Doctor [Holmes] into the Crazy Jane [a name given to one of the

watercraft] till we got to Black Point on Chamberlain when the wind being high and a heavy sea we
took the Doctor in in place of Davis. The sea was
very high and we got very wet before we got to the
farm.[36]

Ezekiel Holmes was a medical doctor, naturalist, professor, editor, legislator, and progressive farmer. Although he held a view that
espoused control of nature for human ends, he had his own opinions
about the results of such control. At the end of the expedition, he
would conclude that Maine had made a terrible mistake in giving
over the Allagash region and other northern wildlands to men such
as Coe and Pingree, when the region could have been developed in
other ways. Ironically, his stay at Chamberlain Farm—a productive,
working agricultural enterprise supporting the logging of this wildland—may have helped him arrive at this conclusion.

Holmes had lived sixty years when he came ashore at Chamberlain Farm, wet and well shaken by the wild waves of Chamberlain

Ezekiel Holmes

Ezekiel Holmes, with Charles H.
Hitchcock, led the Maine Scientific Survey team that stayed at
Chamberlain Farm in 1861.
Holmes appreciated both the scientific and utilitarian values of
nature, seeing science as a means
of improving opportunities to uti-
lize natural resources. Photograph
courtesy of Special Collections
Department, Raymond H. Fogler
Library, University of Maine,
Orono.

Lake. His had been a life of accomplishment. Born in Kingston, Plymouth County, Massachusetts, on August 24, 1801, he grew up fond of books. He prepared for college at an early age and entered Brown University when he was sixteen. He became interested in botany, mineralogy, and chemistry; those who knew him remembered the enthusiasm for plants and animals he displayed on outdoor excursions. A fellow student recalled that he had been impressed by Holmes' "honest, outspoken, moral nature [and] his unconcealed and fierce hatred of all tyranny."[37]

The year of his graduation, at the age of twenty, he delivered a lecture, "The Utility of Philosophy to a Nation," at a meeting of the Philophysian Society, to which he belonged. He gave a reasoned and inspired argument for the role of science, a perspective that not only reflected his own thinking but also had begun to invade the Maine wildlands he would one day visit. His remarks included the following:

> Blest as we are with all that is beautiful, useful, and interesting, we should be indeed ungrateful in the highest degree, should we not improve those bounties which the Almighty has so generously bestowed upon us. It is a duty which we owe to Him. . . . Mr. President, and Gentlemen of the Philophysian Society. . . . your endeavors are to enhance the beauties of Nature by increasing the utility of her productions, and making them subservient to the wants of man.[38]

Following his graduation from Brown University in 1824, the events in Holmes' life that led him to Chamberlain Farm followed a circuitous route. After receiving a doctor of medicine degree, he married and settled in Gardiner, Maine, to practice medicine. Around the same time, he began teaching natural sciences at the

Gardiner Lyceum; later, from 1833 to 1837, he taught chemistry and natural history at Waterville College. Meanwhile, he had started the *Maine Farmer and Journal of the Arts*, which was later renamed the *Maine Farmer*. Holmes edited the journal for the rest of his life, gaining recognition for his ideas as the publication became widely known and influential.[39]

In 1837, while James Hodge explored the Allagash for Charles Jackson, the state of Maine employed Holmes to conduct a survey of the Aroostook Territory to "ascertain the practicability of a water communication between the two rivers [Penobscot and St. John]; to examine the geology and mineralogy of the country, and describe its topography as far as possible, with reference to its future settlement, as well as for its facilities for lumbering operations."[40] The trip foreshadowed the future expedition that would bring him to Chamberlain Farm.

Following the conclusion of his own survey and the completion of Jackson's survey in 1839, Holmes believed that much more work needed to be done to adequately survey the economic potential of Maine's wildlands. Therefore, when the first session of the newly formed Board of Agriculture was convened in 1853 with Holmes as secretary, it was not surprising that he had a hand in actions to encourage the Maine legislature to again support a survey of the state's natural resources.[41] But another eight years would pass before any action was taken. Then, on March 16, 1861, the legislature resolved "that the governor with the secretary of the Board of Agriculture is hereby authorized to contract with some suitable person or persons to conduct a scientific survey of the state."[42]

Later in the spring, Governor Israel Washburn Jr. received five letters of petition for the appointment of Ezekiel Holmes as superintendent of the survey. The petitions cited the "general satisfaction" Holmes would give the people, the good results that could be expected, the suitability of Holmes' character, and his "general abilities and scientific qualifications."[43] This was not unexpected, for the public-minded Holmes was well known in leadership circles. He had served several terms as representative and senator in the Maine legislature, run for the governorship twice, and held the position of secretary of the Maine State Agricultural Society. Through the years, readers of the *Maine Farmer* and audiences to whom he spoke had been impressed by his practical-mindedness and his ability to express himself simply and clearly. One individual who knew him well described him as "always ahead of the times in which he lived. He was affable, good-natured, and quiet; strong and eloquent when aroused, and very quick and keen in perception and repartee. He always had a fund of good humor and anecdote and was universally beloved."[44] On May 27, 1861, Ezekiel Holmes signed a contract to share leadership of the survey with one other, Charles H. Hitchcock.[45]

Charles Henry Hitchcock, only twenty-five years old when he signed on as geologist for the expedition, came as an experienced scientist. He had grown up in Massachusetts in an intellectual atmosphere. His mother, Orra White Hitchcock, educated in the classics and talented both scientifically and artistically, had given special attention to the education and moral and religious upbringing of her children, six of whom survived to maturity. His father, Edward Hitchcock, professor of chemistry and natural history at Amherst College and geologist for Massachusetts and Vermont, had taken young Charles into his work, sharing with the boy his interests, ideas, and discoveries. Charles exhibited his parents' abilities of observation and speculation, leading his mother to call him "the young philosopher." Set on an academic and religious path at an early age, Charles had, by the time he joined the Maine Scientific Survey, completed classical and college preparatory courses at Williston Seminary, graduated from Amherst College, studied chemistry and Hebrew for a year at Yale College, completed two years in theology at Andover Theological Seminary, and worked in Vermont as his father's assistant geologist.[46]

Holmes and Hitchcock began immediately to employ their assistants: George L. Goodale, botanist and chemist; J. C. Houghton, mineralogist; Alpheus S. Packard Jr., entomologist; and C. B. Fuller, marine zoologist. They divided the corps into teams to explore various sections of the state, following a general timetable. One of their instructions called for an investigation of the wildlands "up the east branch [of the Penobscot River] thereof to its head waters; thence across to the Alleguash river or other tributary of the St. John, and down said river to Fort Kent—thus visiting a section hitherto unknown to scientific exploration." The expedition's major purpose: to discover and assess the region's "resources and capabilities."[47] On August 7, 1861, Holmes, Hitchcock, Goodale, and Packard left Bangor for the East Branch.

On August 10, the party began ascending the river at Nicatow Village (now Medway). The four scientists were accompanied by seven assistants and boatmen, one of whom was Hardy. They entered a remote and unsettled country, there being but nine settlers between the mouth of the East Branch of the Penobscot and the mouth of the Allagash River. This fact did not go unnoticed by Holmes, who noted that "the cause of this may be attributed to the fact that every township in this route is owned by proprietors who have hitherto held it for lumbering purposes."[48]

Going up the East Branch can be difficult in places, and the party encountered stretches of strong current and numerous falls and pitches. It was strenuous work, poling a loaded bateau and three birch-bark canoes against the river's flow and carrying these and their equipment and supplies around obstacles. Although it was long after the spring log drives, the expedition quite likely encountered grounded and sunken logs in rocky areas, and, of course, dams upstream required carrying around. Hardy, though hired as an assistant naturalist, saw the need to help out with boatman duties, noting in his journal that after "some hard poling reached Grindstone [Falls, about nine miles upstream] at noon. Poled the boats by and carried the stuff."[49] Another eleven and a half miles brought them to Whetstone Falls, where Holmes reported that "it became necessary to unload and carry by, a distance of half a mile."[50] A few hours later, they arrived at Hunt Farm, where they stopped for a few days. Here, they met the Reverend Marcus Keep, who guided Hitchcock, Goodale, and Packard on a side trip up Mt. Katahdin. The others, meanwhile, repaired boats and explored the vicinity. Hardy hunted, fished, and "helped the Doctor [Holmes] skin and prepare a muskrat."[51]

Several days later, after the Katahdin team returned, the party continued upstream some thirteen miles and arrived at Grand Falls. This is a nine-mile stretch of falls and rapids; for the canoeist, it is an almost continuous din of tumbling, spraying water, alternating between the unrelenting hiss of rushing rapids and the roar of falls, of which the most spectacular is the twenty-foot fall known as Grand Pitch. "The whole form the most formidable obstruction in the river between Oldtown and Grand Lake," remarked Holmes.[52] It was here that Hardy had an accident: "At the Grand Pitch while warping a batteau I slipped from a ledge and fell in, hurting my back severely and bruising my arm. Lewis broke one of my suspenders pulling me out. I would not give up lugging although severely hurt."[53] Hardy helped carry the canoes and gear past another pitch after they had set up camp, and then he hunted up a small brook. The fall may have injured him more than he let on, given that he made no entry in his journal the next day.

Beyond the falls and rapids, the group came to a logging camp in T5 R8, which one of the assistants owned. There they stayed a few days for exploration, with members of the party going different ways. Hardy recounted that he accompanied Holmes and others on

Grand Pitch, East Branch of the Penobscot River
Grand Pitch, the largest of the falls on the East Branch of the Penobscot
River, presented a formidable obstacle for the Maine Scientific Survey team
on its 1861 trip up the river. Photograph by Dean B. Bennett.

a trip "in pursuit of a cave."[54] Two days later, the party proceeded
upriver two or three miles to Grand Lake Matagamon and, in the
words of Holmes,

> the commencement of a series of dams and other
> improvements, built at great expense by the propri-
> etors . . . extending from the foot of this (Grand)
> lake to the foot of Churchill Lake [more than sixty
> miles in the distance]. . . . The thorough structure
> of these fixtures, and the liberal expenditure over so
> large an area of country, reflect much honor on the
> enterprise and energy of the proprietors, and, we
> doubt not, are found to be profitable investments in

a money point of view. At any rate they are instrumental in giving the Penobscot lumberman successful triumph over the obstacles of nature, hardly
rivalled in any other country.[55]

Holmes, however, interjected a critical note, observing that
"thousands of acres of splendid interval land, on the banks of the
streams flowing into, and the connecting thoroughfares of, these
lakes, are submerged a great part of the year. . . . and to the eye of an
agriculturist seems to be rather a wanton destruction of so much
valuable soil." With some resignation, however, he admitted that "it
belongs to those who flow it, and they have a right to use it in such
way and manner as shall give them the most profit."[56]

After crossing Grand Lake Matagamon, they came to Trout
Brook, where "the Messrs. Pingree & Co., have made an excellent
farm (Trout Brook Farm)." There, they hired "two yokes of well
trained oxen" to take the bateau, equipment, and supplies on a sled
up to Webster Lake, ten to twelve miles distant over a tote road following Webster Brook. The assistants poled the empty canoes up
the brook. After crossing Webster Lake, they hired another team of
oxen from Telos Farm, near the dam at the head of Telos Canal.
Once on Telos Lake, Hitchcock discovered "very interesting fossils"
and decided to stay back a day to examine them while the rest of the
party "pushed forward with a view of reaching the farm on Chamberlain Lake before night. At that place it was agreed to make a
stand for a few days, from which we could make excursions to different parts of the adjacent region."[57]

Coasting up the southern shore of Chamberlain Lake in a brisk
wind and high waves, they came to a point of land, where, Holmes
reported, they "stopped to bail boat and 'take an observation.' . . .
From this point there is a fine view of the 'Chamberlain Farm' in the
distance on the opposite shore. The cluster of buildings situate on a

slope rising gently from the lake, looked like a little sea port in the wilderness." He attested that crossing the lake was difficult, with the wind and "spray from these frisky fresh water billows, dashing over the gunwales of our frail birchen cockle shells, . . . but we, however, succeeded in reaching our 'port' with no other damage than a little wetting of ourselves and cargo."[58]

The farm had been operating about fifteen years when Holmes gave the following description:

> We had letters to Mr. Locke, the foreman of the farm, and were soon domiciled in comfortable quarters. This farm has been established here by Messrs. Pingree & Co., and is conducted on a pretty large scale. Between 200 and 300 acres have been cleared and put into grass. A half a dozen men

Webster Brook Tote Road
Remnants of the Webster Brook Tote Road, over which the Maine Scientific Survey team portaged to Telos Lake in 1861, can still be found today. Photograph by Dean B. Bennett.

are constantly employed, and an immense amount of hay, grain and root crops is raised here, and used principally for supplies for men and teams in lumbering in the neighborhood. A large stock of cattle, horses and hogs is also kept at the farm. The crops of grain were then being harvested, teams were ploughing preparatory for another year's crop, and men were busy in felling trees to enlarge the area of cultivation, and get everything ready for a crop of grain "on a burn" the ensuing spring.[59]

Being a religious man, Hardy took the opportunity on a Sabbath day to explore some places at the farm that were familiar to him:

Sunday, September 1, 1861. Rose at 5-1/2; fine morning, clear and cool but windy. We have been strolling about, reading, etc. I went down today to see where we used to camp three years ago but it was all grown up, the grass and bushes where our campfire used to blaze. Thus things change and soon I too shall pass away. Shall I go above? I have just been reading in my journal of a Sabbath passed here September 12, 1858.[60]

After spending four days at the farm exploring the shores and waters of the lake, the survey team continued through the Allagash lakes and down the river to Long Lake, at that point splitting into three groups to explore the St. John River. Hardy and Holmes went down the Allagash to the St. John and up the St. Francis River before concluding their part of the survey.

The findings of the exploration were included in a 355-page report titled "Preliminary Report upon the Natural History and Geology of the State of Maine: 1861." Holmes' account of the East

Branch–Allagash expedition, titled "Notes and Sketches of the Wildlands Explored," has been called an excellent travel description that filled a blank spot in our knowledge of the early character of the northern country of Maine. The fact that the Maine legislature authorized continuance of the survey for another year also spoke to legislators' perceptions of its value to the state. Holmes himself believed that the survey made several distinct contributions, providing a better understanding of the region's potential for crop production and the raising of livestock; a catalog of birds and quadrupeds and their habitats; a compilation of notes and observations on the area's geography; and collections of specimens of plants, animals, rocks, minerals, and fossils for teaching and research. Some of the collections included discoveries of rare and unknown natural phenomena.[61]

Holmes, however, revealed one important regret: The state should not have sold the wildlands to the lumbermen. "Had the State retained these lands, and opened roads, and given facilities to settlers as it has in Aroostook," he opined,

> a very different condition of things would long ere this have existed there. Here is a healthy and naturally fertile territory, capable of supporting, at a very moderate computation, 150,000 inhabitants, completely shut up from settlement, and occupied at present by only about *forty persons.* . . . We . . . express our firm conviction that, if a different policy had been pursued in regard to our public domain in this, the very central portion of the State, many sections of these solitary wilds, where the "bear roams, and the wildcat prowls," would long since have yielded to the woodman's axe, and the silence that now broods over them given way to the hum of cheerful labor and productive industry.[62]

Fortunately for those who would one day work to preserve some of the region's wildness, the policy Holmes criticized helped delay the region's development and allowed its wilderness character to be more easily restored.

Although Holmes considered the survey a success, Hardy, according to his daughter Fannie, was disillusioned and disappointed by the experience. He had participated in the survey, she wrote, "because he hoped to learn something, particularly about the art of taxidermy." Instead, he discovered that although Ezekiel Holmes was a man of ability, "he knew nothing about ornithology and about taxidermy he knew considerable less. He could not skin a bird himself; nor tell anyone else how to do it, and had he not been thoughtful enough to provide the expedition with a little pamphlet published by the Smithsonian Museum, not a bird could have been preserved in the cruise." Fannie observed that her father's scientific aspirations were "nipped by a severe frost. It was many years before he made another attempt to study birds."[63] When he did, however, he went on to build one of the largest private bird collections of his day.

The next spring, Hitchcock returned to the region for additional study and stopped briefly at the farm for fresh supplies. Thus, the region of Chamberlain Lake at the end of 1862 had seen three scientific teams pass through its wildlands: one during Jackson's survey and two during Holmes and Hitchcock's survey. The Civil War prevented further scientific study of the state at this time, but as one biographer observed, "the very extensive investigations of 1861 and 1862 were of the keenest interest to the State government, to geologists, and of value in the work started in 1867 on the hydrographic survey."[64]

For Holmes, the survey brought him near the end of "a journey of studies in science begun over forty years before at Brown University."[65] After the survey, he returned to a previous interest in fish culture; in 1864, convinced that fish could be artificially bred to restore many of Maine's depleted lakes, he wrote a paper promoting the idea. He continued as editor of the *Maine Farmer* and took up the cause of establishing an independent college of agriculture for Maine, a movement that eventually succeeded with creation of the forerunner of the University of Maine. Holmes, however, never saw the outcome of his efforts: He died of pneumonia on February 9, 1865, at the age of sixty-three. In 1904, the Experimental Station at the University of Maine was rededicated as Holmes Hall.

After the survey, Charles Hitchcock served as curator and lecturer at Amherst College until 1865. He then studied at the Royal School of Mines in London before returning to take appointments as state geologist of New Hampshire and professor of geology and mineralogy at Dartmouth College. His professorship continued until 1908; during this time he conducted a geologic survey of New Hampshire, perhaps his most prominent work, and numerous studies on glaciation. He also published several maps; all told, he made more than 150 contributions to scientific literature. After retiring from Dartmouth, he moved to Hawaii and studied its volcanoes, living to the age of eighty-three.[66]

The scientific survey had been motivated by a public attitude toward nature that saw it as a resource to provide for human material needs. Science was seen as having practical value in the business of understanding and altering nature to make it more amenable to human use, even to the extent of reducing the scourge of insects and improving the climate. For example, Holmes, noting the difficulty farmers had in raising corn in these northern wildlands, predicted that "this anti-corn locality will be much reduced in extent by the clearing up of the land, and opening it to the sun and the warm southern breezes."[67]

Aside from their focus on the utilitarian aspects of their profession, Holmes and the other scientists delighted in making discoveries purely for their own scientific understanding of nature. Holmes revealed this when he related his feelings about Hitchcock's arrival at Chamberlain Farm after he had found fossils on the shore of Telos Lake that were not in the books: "There are no victories so really lasting and beneficial to the world . . . as the sinless and noiseless triumphs of mind over matter, as manifested in the scientific developments of the mysteries of nature."[68] This curiosity regarding the unknown is what drove those scientists to study the natural world—a world they viewed as set apart from themselves, to be investigated, described, and understood. However, during the period when Holmes and Hitchcock were leading the wildland surveys, the idea of separateness was just beginning to be challenged by Charles Darwin's theories of a human evolutionary connection with nature and its creatures—theories that would lead to the idea that to study

Brachiopod Fossils on the Shore of Telos Lake
The 400-million-year-old fossils seen here in an outcrop of Seboomook slate were quite likely some of the "very interesting fossils" discovered by geologist Charles H. Hitchcock during the Maine Scientific Survey of 1861. Photograph by Dean B. Bennett.

nature is to study ourselves. But for the time being, the natural world centered on humans, and its high purpose was to serve humanity.

This view of nature, seen in the loggers, hunters, and scientists who came to Hog Point and Chamberlain Farm, was about to be joined by a different perspective brought by other visitors to the region—an occurrence foreseen by none other than Holmes himself.

PART III

"Resting-Place for Weary Voyagers"

Harmony with Nature

ON AN AUGUST DAY IN 1861, Ezekiel Holmes, well tanned and camp-worn, came into Chamberlain Lake, seeing it for the first time. Impressed by its size and remoteness, he mused that "the time . . . is not far distant, when those who visit Moosehead in quest of health and pleasure, will be unwilling to return until they have also made a trip to Chamberlain and Telos."[1] And, indeed, he was right, for less than thirty years later, a popular travel guide would promote Chamberlain Lake and its farm as a destination for a growing number of people who hunted, fished, looked for adventure, or simply wanted to vacation: "The Chamberlain Farm, furnishing a resting-place for weary voyagers, is a large clearing on the northern side of the lake. . . . If you wish to stop here a few days you will find good accommodation."[2]

Today, thousands visit this lake each year. Like many of these visitors, I stay at such a resting place—a place called Nugent's Chamberlain Lake Camps. The camps, which remain the principal development on the lake, provide, as did the farm, a place to stay for those who come for hunting, fishing, and other outdoor activities. But we who continue to canoe Chamberlain Lake and wish to paddle to Nugent's are still faced with a difficult, sometimes impossible, crossing, just as Holmes and his party were when they made their way to the farm against a strong wind.

Possibly, Holmes was aware in his time of a different kind of energy only beginning to be felt in the country, an energy spawned by ideas that brought a more caring attitude and a longer view regarding productivity of the land and its waters, forests, and wildlife. Gradually, the force of the ideas grew stronger and swept across all social strata, from the common worker, worried about the future of resources needed to support a livelihood and outdoor pastimes, to the entrepreneur, needing dependable supplies of materials, and the public official, concerned about the financial future and welfare of the public at large. This new force carried words such as *conservation, management, scientific,* and *sustainability*—words spoken by powerful messengers who aroused the public's consciousness: George Perkins Marsh, President Theodore Roosevelt, John Muir, Gifford Pinchot. Because of these individuals and others like them, new ideas surfaced about forest conservation, wildlife protection, and the recreational benefits of nature.

These changing views were part of a perspective on the human relationship with nature different from that which had motivated control and alteration of waters, excessive killing of game animals, and short-term exploitation of forests. Such activities, for the most part initially unrestrained, took their toll on resources not only in the region surrounding Chamberlain Farm but all across the country. After the Civil War, the effects of this behavior toward nature were exacerbated as domestic energies launched into an industrial era bent on improving the American way of life and fueled by new technologies, improved manufacturing methods, more efficient transportation, and growing markets. The growth of cities, with their attendant problems of pollution, noise, and congestion, combined with new wealth to create a population that looked to the outdoors for its healthful benefits to mind and body.

There was, however, among this growing population an awareness of discord accompanied by ambiguity about the effect of the nation's "advancements" on a natural environment that was increasingly seen as offering more than just resources for new and expanding industries. The engines, roads, new modes of transportation, and diversity of products, all of which helped recreationists visit and enjoy wild and undeveloped places, at the same time invaded and diminished America's wildness. More roads, more vehicles, more airplanes, more motorized boats, more railroads, and more power-driven machines brought more people, more noise, more loss of privacy, more rules and regulations, and more pressure on the land and its wildlife. Those who sought the pleasure of the woods and waters for recreation and worried about conservation of natural resources began to see the need to balance competing values. Thus began a subtle shift in perspective toward the achievement of a more cooperative, harmonious relationship with nature. To be sure, nature was still seen primarily as in service to humans, but people began to see themselves more closely connected to nature, began to recognize the need to adapt to some of its elements, and began to understand the advantages of maintaining resources for the long term.

This perspective of cooperation with nature that began to exert itself in the latter part of the nineteenth century was, of course, not new. Over the centuries, many had viewed nature as more than just a source of food, fiber, and minerals to meet their physical and material needs. In the Western world, one who was recognized as influential in the early development of this view was parson and naturalist Gilbert White. He had roamed the countryside around his home in Selborne, England, in the 1700s, delighting in the natural world and trying to uncover its mysteries and demonstrate "the inherent beneficence of the universe."[3] While White enjoyed hunting and the material comforts of life provided by the nature he studied, he also found peace and tranquility. His goals, however, contrasted markedly with those of Park Holland, who had entered the woods to survey the wilds of Maine five years after publication of White's book *The Natural History of Selborne*. So committed was Western culture to the domination of nature that it would be well into the next century before White's views attracted a following.

As a writer with a scientific bent revealing the workings of nature, White inspired many nineteenth-century writers and naturalists, who in turn found receptive audiences in a growing America, motivating readers to seek out nature's delights and shaping their views and expectations. One of those writers was John Burroughs, who like White would make an original contribution to the writing of natural history and promote elements of a cooperative perspective toward nature. Burroughs' first book, *Wake-Robin*, was published in 1871. He aimed to interpret nature more artistically than had White with his scientific approach, seeking "to depict the immediate, total harmony between man and nature" even as "an element in nature." Burroughs, wrote one biographer, "invited his readers to the peace of the woods."[4]

Although it is not known to what extent Burroughs and other writer-naturalists, such as John Muir, influenced the public to seek out the wilds of America, people did so in great numbers during the latter half of the 1800s. Some of them came to Chamberlain Farm, bringing a different perspective from that of E. S. Coe, Manly Hardy, and Ezekiel Holmes. These new arrivals promoted the region for its health benefits and its opportunities for adventure, taught its lore and extolled its romance, shared their insights with those they guided and those who read their books, and cared for its woods and wildlife—and some even made it their home.

Chapter 4

Lore and Romance
of the North Woods

"*W*E CAN REST at Chamberlain Farm, with
its little red house so cosy and comfortable," suggested John Way Jr.
in his *Guide to Moosehead Lake and Northern Maine, with Map,* published in 1874.[1] Way must have been well acquainted with the farm's
attractiveness to the outdoor adventurers and other visitors who
were discovering this region after the Civil War. Writer Lew Dietz
recounted a story about Way that took place before publication of
his guide in which he would have more than welcomed the farm's
coziness. As a young man, Way had headed into the Allagash region
in the depth of winter on a hunting expedition. The party set up
camp near Eagle Lake, at Haymock Brook. Time passed, and they
ran low on food. Way, against the advice of the guide, decided to go
alone to Chamberlain Farm to replenish their supplies, a distance of
six to seven miles. Starting out on snowshoes, he got lost somewhere
around Leadbetter Pond. Luckily, when he failed to return, the
guide tracked him down and got him back to camp alive.[2]

Despite such mishaps, according to Dietz, Way's enthusiasm for the wilds of Maine overcame his background of wealth, education, and inexperience, and he became a "first-rate mapmaker and a seasoned Maine woodsman."[3] He also had the instincts of an entrepreneur, for his book and map came out at a time when tourists from middle and wealthy upper classes were seeking to escape unhealthful conditions of urban life or looking for respite from the fast pace and pressures of professional and managerial occupations. Whatever the reasons, the outdoors appealed to more and more people and drew them to the woods, lakes, and coast of Maine in ever increasing numbers. They constituted a vast market, national in scope, that rapidly spawned imaginative promotional efforts by railroad companies, steamship lines, resort hotels, and a host of other businesses, from outfitting to guiding services. And the promoters of this expanding tourism industry relied heavily on guidebooks and pamphlets for publicity.[4] Way's was the first for Maine's North Woods.

Way planned publication of his guidebook and map to coincide with the 1874 opening of the second Kineo House on Moosehead Lake. The hotel symbolized the changing view of the North Woods. One writer called it a "distinctive blend of opulence and rusticity that was the hallmark of Maine tourism."[5] Way himself noted that it could "furnish all the comforts and most of the luxuries of its city rivals" for as many as 150 guests, providing them with a spacious dining hall, private parlors, verandas, boats, guides, and other amenities and services.[6]

This kind of development in the North Woods was made possible, of course, by improvements in transportation. John Way's guidebook advertised the different ways people from Boston could reach Kineo House: They could travel by train or steamboat to Bangor and then by train to Guilford, by stage to Greenville, and finally by steamboat to the hotel. This would be only the beginning of transportation's effect on the woods.[7]

There was also a deeper change under way in 1874, one that extended across America. That was the year John Muir, guru of wilderness spirituality and preservation, wandered through the Sierra Nevada and John Burroughs settled at West Park, New York, on the Hudson River, a place he drew on for many of his writings about nature. It was also the year the magazine *Field and Stream* began publication and the National Sportsmen's Association was formed. Both advocated a new code of hunting and fishing ethics along with principles of conservation. Two years earlier, President Ulysses Grant had signed the Yellowstone Park bill. A shift in America's attitude toward the land and its wildlife was in the air, and John Way was catching its scent.

Within a few years, another writer and mapmaker, Lucius Lee Hubbard, took advantage of the growing tourist industry, coming out with a guidebook strikingly similar to Way's.[8] This work, published in 1879 and titled *Summer Vacations at Moosehead Lake and Vicinity: A Practical Guide-Book for Tourists*, was Hubbard's first. In it, he described a trip through Chamberlain Lake that "brings one to Chamberlain farm, where the most necessary articles of camp fare are usually to be had." Hubbard, echoing Ezekiel Holmes' aesthetic sensitivity of almost two decades earlier, alerted his audience to the unattractiveness of the lake's shores due to the litter of dead trees killed by the dam-raised water levels: "Some of the withered trunks still stand with bare arms, in marked contrast to their living neighbors, while others have fallen, and help make impenetrable any camping-ground which may be within."[9]

Lucius Hubbard had wide-ranging interests and talents. He was born on August 7, 1849, and grew up in Cincinnati, Ohio. After graduating from Harvard University in 1872, he went on to obtain a degree in law from the Boston School of Law in 1875 and practiced in that city for the next few years. During these years of education and lawyering, he spent his vacations in the woods of Maine.

Lucius L. Hubbard

Lucius Lee Hubbard, lawyer and geologist, also appreciated the aesthetic, healthful, and recreational values of nature. He explored the Allagash region in the latter half of the 1800s and capitalized on the post–Civil War interest in nature by publishing books and maps. Reprinted by permission of Bentley Historical Library, University of Michigan, Ann Arbor.

The experience in the outdoors and knowledge he gained, combined with a flair for entrepreneurship, led to his interest in producing books and maps.[10]

Hubbard published two more books and maps in the early 1880s. He dedicated *Hubbard's Guide to Moosehead Lake and Northern Maine*, published in 1882, "to the care-worn business man and overworked student, [for whom] no relaxation from the constant wear of their respective callings is so grateful as that which comes while camping in the woods."[11] Hubbard's third and last book on the Maine woods, *Woods and Lakes of Maine*, is his best known and, in fact, was reprinted in the early 1970s. It chronicles a 160-mile canoe trip he made in the autumn of 1881 with a friend and two Indian guides. The trip was an ambitious undertaking: Hubbard and his party began at the head of Moosehead Lake, crossed the Allagash lakes, portaged into the Musquacook waters, and went down the Allagash and St. John Rivers to Edmundston, New Brunswick, Canada.

During the trip, Hubbard kept a pocket-sized journal of the experience, from which he drew the details for *Woods and Lakes of*

Maine. It is interesting to compare his writings in the field with his published work. For example, at the end of the day of his arrival at Chamberlain Farm, September 24, he scrawled in his journal the following rather skimpy notes:

> Broke camp at 8 $\frac{1}{2}$ a.m. the skies having cleared, and the day promising fair. I poled one canoe down the brook, and Tom soon came with the other. We went to Chamb. Farm, delivd mail & other matter, ground the axes, drank a good deal of milk & lunched at the Locks. It is said to be 2 m. 40 rods from mouth of Mud Br. to the Farm, but it only took us 33 m. to paddle across—from which it appears to me to be the less.[12]

In contrast, Hubbard's book contains considerable more detail and color, illustrating how a few notes combined with a vivid memory can translate into an interesting account:

> Making our way with difficulty through the tangled mass of drift-wood which choked the mouth of Mud Pond brook, we entered Chamberlain Lake

Chamberlain Farm, 1881
Lucius L. Hubbard visited the farm in 1881, the year this drawing
was made. Reprinted from Thomas Sedgwick Steele, *Paddle and Portage,
from Moosehead Lake to the Aroostook River, Maine*
(Boston, Mass.: Estes & Lauriat, 1882), 49.

and struck across towards the farm. . . . The farm, which has grown to large proportions, is now owned by Hon. E. S. Coe of Bangor, and on it are raised yearly large numbers of cattle and sheep, and also potatoes, grain, and vegetables. So well do sheep thrive there, that a short time before our arrival one became so fat that, in the words of the superintendent, Mr. Nutter, they "had to kill him to save his life; couldn't lug himself around." Mr. Nutter also told us, that, when the season was not backward, he raised just as good corn as grew anywhere in the State of Maine. Good apples grow there, as we proved to our entire satisfaction.

There are on the farm, the year round, some six or eight men, a jolly and good-natured set. Woman's society is seldom or never vouchsafed them, and they are catered to by a man-cook,—at the time of our visit, a French Canadian. As this was the last human habitation we should see until we reached the lower parts of the Allagash, we improved the opportunity, and the cook brought forth from hidden storerooms a pan of rich, delicious milk, a plate of fresh cookies, and a basket of apples. The guides looked over their supply of tobacco, replenished it, refilled the potato-bag, and ground the axes.[13]

Hubbard wrote that he published his account of the excursion "to give the public a true and circumstantial delineation of the camper's life in the Maine forests . . . [and] to make known a number of Indian place-names." But he also wished to do more: He hoped to convey the pleasures of nature, "of learning to read her stones, her leaves and blossoms, and of forming a near kinship with the wild offspring that swim in her waters or roam through her groves."[14]

Hubbard was one of those gentleman sportsmen who came to the wilds of Maine to hunt and fish, and he espoused the sportsman's code of ethics advocated by many in the hunting community during this time. In his book, he related that soon after leaving Chamberlain Farm and entering Eagle Lake, the party heard the baying of a hound, followed by a gunshot. It was the work of "some reckless law-breaker," he wrote, knowing that hunting deer with dogs was illegal. Later, he saw a "quarter of moose-meat spoiling in the water." Before the trip was over, Hubbard himself shot a bull moose, and he made a point of saying that "the head and two hind quarters were at once sent to Moosehead Lake, and the greater part of the fore quarters was afterwards used at Chamberlain Farm, so that very little meat was wasted." Those who break the game laws, he wrote, "deserve . . . unqualified condemnation."[15]

Hubbard vacationed in the North Woods region for a period of thirteen years. His *Map of Northern Maine,* first published in 1879, proved popular (Warren K. Moorehead, for example, used it for his archaeological survey), and he continued to update and publish it for many years, producing the last edition in 1929. Science, however, claimed his career interests, and in 1886 he took degrees of A.M. (Artium Magister, or Master of Arts) and Ph.D. at the University of Bonn, Germany. Until his death, in 1933, he led an active life, serving as state geologist of Michigan, working in the mining industry, and writing numerous papers on geology.

In 1879, the year Hubbard published his first guidebook, Thomas Sedgwick Steele, a man of different talents, embarked on his fifth excursion to the North Woods, following his dream "to reach the solitudes of Maine, whose influences are so bewitching." On this canoe journey, the pleasant thirty-four-year-old jeweler,

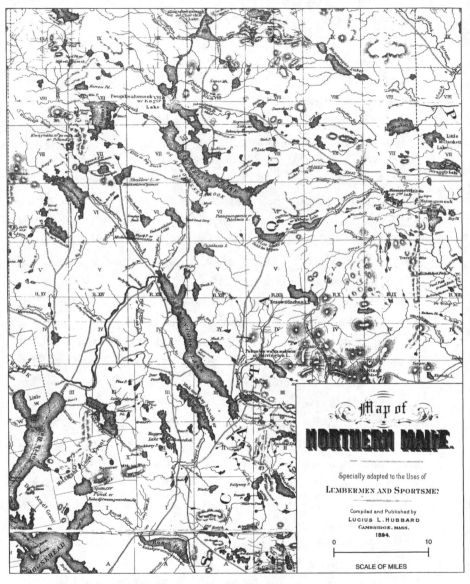

Map of Northern Maine, 1894

From Lucius L. Hubbard, *Map of Northern Maine*
(Cambridge, Mass.: Lucius L. Hubbard, 1894).

writer, and artist from Hartford, Connecticut, would stay for a while at Chamberlain Farm. Steele was something of a romantic when it came to the North Woods, and here he found escape and renewal: "There are reveries forced upon one, for which a city of brisk walls and dusty streets have no affinity. . . . In this fast world of ours, where the work of a week is crowded into a day, recreation is a necessity, and nowhere . . . has it greater recuperative power than in the depths of the forest." He declared that "there is something so free, so stimulating in the woods life . . . that after one season's enjoyment, a return to these wildernesses, and repeating its pleasures is the constant thought of the future." It teaches "self-reliance, and a philosophical endurance of many conditions of life, which will add to one's cheerfulness, while one is surprised how few of the necessities are essential to produce happiness." The trees and other plants, "coupled with the weird stillness of the forest, bring one nearer to God and His works."[16] These feelings he experienced in the wilds of Maine fulfilled longings he had felt from a very early age.

As a boy growing up and attending schools in Hartford, Steele developed an interest in drawing, painting, and the outdoors. He once wrote: "I can hardly remember when the sight of a gun or fish-

Thomas Sedgwick Steele

Thomas Sedgwick Steele, a Connecticut jeweler and artist, made many trips into the North Woods in the late 1800s. He wrote two books in which he described the Allagash wilderness in terms of its aesthetic, spiritual, healthful, and recreational values. Reprinted from *Illustrated Popular Biography of Connecticut* (Hartford, Conn.: J. A. Spalding, 1891), 281.

rod did not awaken within my boyish fancy a feverish desire to follow their lead, be the tramp ever so hard." And his journeys would
be difficult indeed, for it was the wild, remote North Woods that
captured his imagination and pulled at him. "How often in my early
years, while pursuing the study of geography at school," he related,
"did my pencil in drawing maps wander over this endless tract of
territory to the north and east of Moosehead Lake."[17]

In 1866, after high school, he joined his father as a partner in his
jewelry business in Hartford. Two years later he married, and in
1876, after the death of his first wife, he remarried. Steele continued his artwork at odd hours in and out of his place of business, and
his paintings garnered favorable notice by the public and by the
National Academy of Design in New York, presaging the day when
he would study art in Paris and become a professional artist.[18] He
also developed an interest in photography in the "old wet plate
days," becoming a serious amateur—so much so that according to
one writer, "his dedication to the craft in the face of all social conventions apparently left his friends no choice but to suffer his good-
humored photographic exploits."[19] In the 1870s, he began taking a
camera with him on his canoe trips into the North Woods of Maine,
encumbering himself also with a tripod, dozens of five-by-eight-
inch glass plates, a portable darkroom, and a kit of bottled chemi-
cals to coat and develop the glass plate negatives. Outdoor photog-
raphers today, with their compact equipment, can easily perceive the
difficulties he faced and understand why he sometimes had a photographic specialist along to help him.

So it was not surprising that an August day in 1879 found Steele
and an assistant photographer crossing Mud Pond Carry, trying to
protect fifty glass photographic plates from a sudden jar that might
"immediately subvert one of the principal objects of the exploration." For them the responsibility imposed, in some ways, a heav-
ier burden than carrying a canoe. The muddy path slowed Steele

and his group, which also included a friend and three guides, and by the time they reached Mud Pond all were aware of the low, setting sun and the need to hasten their progress. They crossed Mud Pond as quickly as possible and maneuvered their canoes down the brook. One can imagine their dismay when they were suddenly faced by "great weatherbeaten logs" clogging the entrance to Chamberlain Lake, which they had planned to cross before nightfall. The sound of axes rang out impatiently through the quiet cove as they tried to force a passage through the barrier. At last, they chopped out an opening large enough for a canoe, and with the sun "hardly half an hour above the horizon," they crossed the "beautiful lake two and a half miles to the opposite shore, and camped on its white pebbly beach at the foot of a farm."[20]

With good weather and a hospitable welcome, Steele decided to

Campsite in Front of Chamberlain Farm, 1879
Thomas Sedgwick Steele and his party camped on the shore in front of Chamberlain Farm during their visit in 1879. Reprinted from Thomas Sedgwick Steele, *Canoe and Camera: A Two Hundred Mile Tour through the Maine Forests* (Boston, Mass.: Estes & Lauriat, 1880), 68.

Interior of Farmhouse at Chamberlain Farm, 1879
Thomas Sedgwick Steele was shown into this room of the
farmhouse. Reprinted from Thomas Sedgwick Steele, *Canoe and
Camera: A Two Hundred Mile Tour through the Maine Forests*
(Boston, Mass.: Estes & Lauriat, 1880), 66.

stay for a few days to photograph the scenery. He also fished a little
and explored Indian Pond and the dams between Chamberlain and
Eagle Lakes. Steele's observant eye and ever present camera
recorded many details of the farm; he noted that it consisted of a log
house, eight to ten barns, and "about three hundred acres of cleared
land, if where in some portions you can jump from stump to stump
can be called 'cleared land.'" The commanding view of the lake and
country from the hillside behind the farm did not escape his eye, nor
did the two-story red farmhouse he visited, which provided him an
opportunity to describe its interior arrangement and decor.[21]

He noted that the house was whitewashed inside and had three
rooms on each floor. The room his party was ushered into "had low

ceilings of heavy logs, blackened by age and smoke from the big square iron stove which held undisputable possession of the center of the apartment." In one corner, he saw "a great box containing wood, which also served as a bed when other accommodations were not available. From the ceiling, hardly seven feet high, a clothes line was suspended on which hung a portion of the week's washing." The floor, he observed, "was made of logs with enough openings between them to admit plenty of fresh air." And, of course, he assessed the room's artistic sense and found that it "had not been wanting in the decoration of the log walls, and engravings cut from illustrated papers." In a prominent position, he noted, was a "portrait of a late unsuccessful candidate to presidential honors." Between two windows, rough shelves nailed to the sides of the walls "supported a roll of old papers, a Webster's dictionary, National fifth reader, Greenleaf's arithmetic, a Bible, and Testament, while at their side hung a mirror, and the family hair-brush and comb." But what struck Steele as "the most novel article in the room" was a fly trap. Although he thought "it displayed the inventive genius of the locality," he decided that it could "hardly have its model on the many shelves of the Patent office." It was "hung from the ceiling near the stove, and was manufactured from two shingles fastened together at the butts like an inverted V. On the inside was spread molasses, and as fast as the insects became interested in its sweets, it was the duty of the passerby to slap the boards together and destroy their contents."[22]

Following their pleasant and relaxing visit to the farm, the party broke camp on August 12, unaware of the difficulties that lay ahead. The trip to Telos Dam was uneventful, but they had no more than set up their tent when the "watery contents of the heavens began to descend." For the next three days, they were imprisoned by a heavy rainstorm. Then, to make matters worse, the weather turned freezing cold, leaving a heavy frost in the mornings and ice in their camp pails. Finally, they got a break and resumed their trip, but ahead of

Chamberlain Farm's Ingenious Fly Trap
On his visit to the farmhouse, Thomas Sedgwick Steele was most
impressed by this fly trap. Reprinted from Thomas Sedgwick Steele, *Canoe
and Camera: A Two Hundred Mile Tour through the Maine Forests*
(Boston, Mass.: Estes & Lauriat, 1880), 70.

them was Webster Brook, known for its furious rapids and haz-
ardous falls over "immense boulders and ledges . . . disputing one's
passage."[23]

For some time, the group had anticipated with excitement, and
perhaps a little anxiousness, Webster Brook's formidable stretches of
water. The guides had confidence in their birch-bark canoes but
questioned the durability of Steele's portable folding canvas canoe,
made specially for the trip. It was fifteen feet long, weighed forty-
five pounds, and could be collapsed into a bag measuring seventeen

by thirty-eight inches. One can imagine the scoffing and snickering that went on privately among the guides about this contraption. But it proved its worth, successfully competing with the birch-bark canoes in negotiating the rapids and actually going where they could not. The guides had to take back some of their ridicule. Said one of them: "You came over the 'rips' like a perfect duck."[24]

After crossing Grand Lake Matagamon, the party entered the difficult East Branch of the Penobscot River, with its many falls and rapids. But Webster Brook had been good training, and by the end of the month they had arrived intact at Medway and the confluence of the East and West Branches. It had been a memorable trip for Steele, filled with adventure, "grand old forests, noble waterfalls, picturesque lakes, and cascades." He came away convinced that the health benefits of such an excursion could not be overestimated. As an artist, he believed this was a region in which he could "linger many weeks with profit to both eye and brush."[25]

The next year, Steele published his account of the experience in a book titled *Canoe and Camera,* which included sixty illustrations and a map of the canoe tours of Maine. He wrote the book, he explained, because of a "desire to direct the attention of tourists, and more specifically artists, to a section of Maine *now but little known,* but which, if once explored, will yield to them a bright harvest of pleasure and studies."[26] His promotion both encouraged and served a developing interest in the region for its recreative, wholesome, and curative benefits.

In 1881, Steele was again in the same waters, having embarked on an exploration more ambitious than the one he undertook in 1879. At the same time, Lucius Hubbard was making his long Allagash–Musquacook trip. No record exists of the two encountering each other, although Steele inscribed a copy of *Paddle and Portage,* an account of his trip that year, to "Lucius L. Hubbard with the Author's compliments." This time, he carried a new camera for dry plate work, called the Tourograph camera, which, in the words of one writer, "upstate Mainers mistook for a newfangled patent coffee grinder."[27] On reaching Chamberlain Farm, Steele wrote: "We made a brief stay, and purchased an extra supply of hard tack, sugar, and molasses, as our stores were running short. Then turning our backs on the lovely peaks of Mt. Katahdin and the Soudahaunk range . . . we buffetted the waves of the lake for six miles, landing at the locks."[28] The remainder of the trip was long, with difficult portages from the Allagash waterway into the Aroostook River watershed, through which Steele and his party paddled to Caribou, Maine.

The publication of Steele's and Hubbard's books preceded a period of intense promotion of tourism in Maine and its North Woods region, which was accompanied by an expanding transportation system, including a large railroad network. In 1884, the Bangor and Piscataquis Railroad reached Greenville. That same year, the Maine Central Railroad published several pamphlets, devising the slogan *Maine, the Nation's Playground*. Five years later, the Canadian Pacific Railway pushed from Canada to Greenville and beyond to a junction with the Maine Central Railroad at Mattawamkeag. In 1895, the Bangor and Aroostook Railroad reached into Aroostook County, to Houlton. By the end of the century, it had built a spur to Millinocket, and in 1906 it proposed a branch through the Allagash region that would pass seven miles from Chamberlain Farm. That branch, however, was never built.[29] In 1895, the railroad began publishing annual regional guidebooks titled *In the Maine Woods*, and it continued to produce them into the middle of the next century. The books promoted fishing, big game hunting, and canoeing and included advertisements, laws, maps, and fares. Almost every issue, if not all, extolled the fishing, hunting, and other values of Chamberlain Lake, and occasionally an article mentioned the farm.

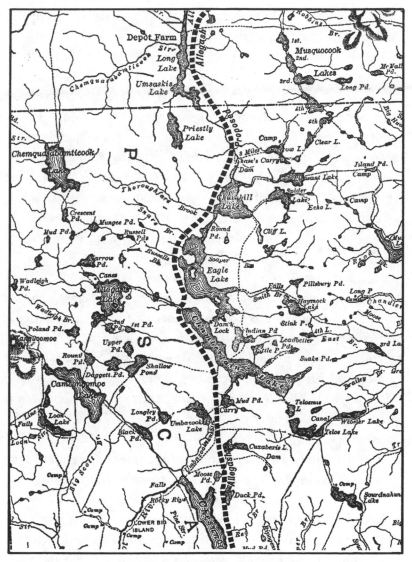

Proposed Allagash Railroad, 1906

From "Territory Reached by the Bangor and Aroostook R. R.,"
In the Maine Woods (Bangor, Maine: Bangor and Aroostook
Railroad Company, 1915), foldout map.

During the latter part of the century, enterprising individuals continued to capitalize on the demand for recreational information about the North Woods. For example, in 1889 Captain Charles A. J. Farrar produced *Farrar's Illustrated Guide Book to Moosehead Lake (and Vicinity)*, which covered a wide area surrounding Moosehead Lake and northward. Chamberlain Farm remained an outpost worthy of mention for those interested in hunting, fishing, and canoeing. It was Farrar who described the farm as "a resting-place for weary voyagers."[30] Maine's state government gradually took note of the economic opportunity of tourism, sponsoring displays and exhibits at the New Orleans Exhibition in 1884 and the Chicago World Fair in 1891 and taking measures to protect and restore its fisheries and game for sportfishing and sport hunting.[31] Historian Richard Judd saw Maine's concern about its wildlife in the 1890s as "part of a powerful new thrust in the American conservation movement . . . predicated on recreational rather than utilitarian concepts of land use, and on Romantic visions of the wilderness."[32] A later researcher concluded that in this same decade, "public attitudes toward wilderness were undergoing a radical transformation."[33] Before the end of the century, for example, an article in the *Atlantic Monthly* urged that northern Maine should be "permanently preserved to sport."[34]

Tourism continued its growth trend through the twentieth century, changing in response to social conditions and technological developments. Although it experienced declines during wars, depressions, and energy shortages, it always recovered. The affordability of automobiles, coupled with rising incomes and increased leisure time, changed the character of the industry. More and more people traveled to the North Woods for sport, adventure, recreation, and health. And with many of them, a new view of nature arrived at Chamberlain Farm.

As a group, these visitors to the farm and its surrounding wildlands came for reasons much different from those that had led to the cutting of timber and the building of dams for river driving. Instead, they found utility in the region's healthful qualities; in its beauty, peacefulness, quiet, freshness, remoteness, and mystery; and in the excitement of the experiences it offered. They indulged in the opportunity to meet and overcome its challenges and prove their ability and self-worth. They developed strong feelings for the natural environment they discovered, and they grew concerned when those qualities they had come to value were threatened or diminished in some way. Conservation and preservation found increasing numbers of advocates among them.

Thomas Sedgwick Steele and Lucius Lee Hubbard held emotional ties to this north country throughout their lives. Hubbard had the region in mind four years before his death when he wrote in a letter, "I wish I could find some one to collaborate with me in future improvements in the map."[35] He addressed the letter to a remarkable woman—a woman who came to Chamberlain Farm and the surrounding wildlands and left with a lifetime of insight that she would share with others throughout the country: a woman named Fannie Hardy Eckstorm.

Seven years after Steele and Hubbard crossed Mud Pond Carry, Fannie Pearson Hardy, then a young woman, came over the same trail. She was accompanied by her father, Manly Hardy, now in his mid-fifties and looking forward to seeing again the Allagash lakes he had first visited in 1858. With them was George Leonard, a guide Manly had hired to help on the carries and negotiate the rapids. Their trip across the carry had been delayed when one of the horses cast a shoe, but they still had most of the day ahead of them to reach their destination. On reaching Mud Pond, they set a leisurely pace for their paddle across and enjoyed the bright, sunny morning and the view of Mt. Katahdin, "lacking nothing of being a perfect mountain." Had they known what lay ahead, they might have not been so casual. When they arrived at the shore by the pond's outlet, Fannie and Manly took the carry path, and Leonard waded the canoe down the brook. It was then that Manly noticed the wind rising and began to fear the worst. At the meadows where Mud Brook wove its way to the lake, the two "stood on some stumps" and waited for Leonard. Launched once again in the canoe, they paddled through surging waves of marsh grass, blown by a now gusting wind. After passing newly built muskrat houses, they caught the smell of tainted meat—perhaps "some moose or caribou . . . left to spoil." Soon they came to Chamberlain Lake, and Manly's greatest concern was borne out. He knew they were going to be windbound.[36]

Fannie Hardy was twenty-three when she first saw Chamberlain Lake on that August day in 1888. In only a few months, she had gone from an education at Smith College to another in the wilds of the North Woods, and this time she was instructed not by professors but by her father. There had always been a special relationship between the two. They shared many interests, especially in natural history and writing. Near the end of her life, Fannie would say: "We were partners in everything. . . . I looked over and copied his stuff; he went over and criticised mine, suggesting but not interfering."[37] Through his influence, her father helped her to become a woman of notable accomplishment.

The 1888 trip that brought Fannie to Chamberlain Lake was the first of several she would take with her father in the North Woods between the time of her graduation from college and her marriage, in 1893. On all her trips, she kept detailed journals, recording what would become a foundation of experience and insight for her future writing about the North Woods and the people who lived and worked in them. Through her father, she learned about the changes the region had undergone, its geography, and its natural history. And it was this first trip that introduced her to Chamberlain Farm and impressed her with the extent of lumbering in the region and the resourcefulness of the men associated with it.

The journey had begun on August 20 at Bangor, where they boarded a train for Greenville, on Moosehead Lake, and traveled over a railroad line that had been extended to their destination only four years before. On the way, they picked up Leonard. They had dinner in Greenville, and afterward Fannie noted that she had "the honor of being the only woman at the tables." That afternoon, a steamer took them more than thirty miles up the lake to North East Carry. Their route over the next twenty-four days took them down the West Branch of the Penobscot River to Chesuncook Lake, up Caucomgomoc Stream, and over a carry where her father, referring perhaps to other travelers, "scolded a good deal at their leaving a carry in such shape as that for women to travel." They explored Caucomgomoc Lake and the surrounding ponds and streams in the area that Manly had first frequented thirty years before. Then they returned to Chesuncook and took the Mud Pond Carry route to Chamberlain Lake, where Fannie learned firsthand the lake's reputation for wind-driven ferocity.[38]

Fannie helped hold their canoe in the inlet of Mud Brook and "looked at the heavy sea which was running outside." The three of them "listened to the doleful creaking of the dead wood as the waves sawed one long tree against another, and subsiding showed ugly black snags sticking out, on which a canoe would be wrecked instantly." The farm on the opposite shore seemed so near, yet so far. Reluctantly, they drew back and "managed with some difficulty to get ashore on the right side of the stream, in a growth of sapling birch and poplar." Reconciled to waiting for the wind to subside, they prepared dinner, fortunately remembering to build their fire "where the smoke would not attract the attention of the men at the farm." They knew that "as in Thoreau's day, a smoke near the inlet is a signal for the farm to send a canoe across, some two miles and a half." Looking at the large, white-capped waves sweeping down the lake, they judged that it would be a difficult crossing even in the farm's "great sea canoes." Still, the knowledge that the farm was over there and its workers could be depended on for help if it were needed must have been a source of comfort. Fannie later recalled how Mr. Coe, the owner of the farm, had told her that "in winter they always leave a lamp burning all night, to guide any wandering lumberman belated on the lake."[39]

After dinner, the trio spent the remainder of the day bound to the shore by the wind. With time on her hands, Fannie had the opportunity to take in her surroundings. She saw "how beautiful across the angry lake the farm looked, seated on the sloping hillside among fields colored with the soft rich hues of growing grain, of grass land and of cultivated soil." From her experience, she concluded that not one of the other "supply" farms compared "with this in picturesqueness." She would write that "these great farms are a surprise to strangers. Here is Chamberlain, some 80 miles from the nearest railroad, and 60 from the nearest main road, one of the only two houses on a block of twenty-eight townships—a space larger than the State of Rhode Island."[40]

The next day, the three continued their trip across Chamberlain and the other Allagash lakes to the head of the Allagash River. Returning to Chamberlain Lake, they "went up to Chamberlain farm with a light wind almost in our faces. . . . On starting out again after getting our peck of potatoes we put across the lake." After leaving Chamberlain Lake, they crossed Telos Lake and went through the cut into Webster Lake. Fannie and her father walked the tote road to Second Lake while Leonard took the canoe down the difficult rapids of Webster Brook. They crossed Grand Lake Matagamon and proceeded down the East Branch of the Penobscot River, arriving at Medway on September 13, having traveled a total of 200 miles by canoe.[41]

The trip provided Fannie with many opportunities to further her education in the natural history of the North Woods. Her journal contains entries about specimens she and her father collected and prepared. For example: "After breakfast saw and shot a Canada Jay. He held to the tree and caused a lively scuffle in the rain to dislodge him. As he was spoiled as a specimen I made anatomical dissertations to Leonard. Timed his heart beating and after he was dead and began to stiffen it continued to beat over 55 minutes by the watch. His stomach contained two large beetles and some seeds." And another entry: "At one place we saw either a mink or a muskrat swimming but supposing it to be a muskrat father fired. The result was that he got both. The mink, a large one, had a kitten musquash in his mouth." They shot a young sheldrake (merganser duck) "still in the down," and later, "while the others pitched the tent," she wrote, "I sat on a log and tried to skin the sheldrake—but the sand flies and mosquitoes were so thick that it was all I could do to finish the job." While on Grand Lake Matagamon, they "landed on Louse Island and got a sprig of the Bank's Pine [jack pine]."[42]

Fannie filled her journal with other observations of plants, animals, geologic features, and the weather. For example, she encountered many spruce grouse, and after one such experience she wrote: "Father says that his father told him the spruce grouse sometimes drums flying, that is drummed as they fluttered down from the trees (like a quaker grasshopper). They make [as Fannie discovered] a great buzz as they fly and one of the two was so silly that she let us come within ten feet of her." Fannie heard loons, owls, log cocks (pileated woodpeckers), and the unusual sound of a tree falling during a quiet, windless time: "It was perfectly calm and there came first a sharp crack like the stroke of an axe, a rending and a crash." She saw two caribou and odd toads, "caught and played with a little orange bellied snake," and observed stones along the shore of a pond that were "peculiarly split, being almost exact rhomboids, or parallelograms." While going down the East Branch, she recorded its many waterfalls, deciding that the Hulling Machine was "the finest looking of the lot." She described and drew a new moon she saw when they got up by moonlight one early morning and set out on a calm lake to avoid getting wind-bound. She wrote about cooking trout and partridges, making cranberry sauce, and stewing duck and deer meat.[43]

She met many of her father's friends and acquaintances—guides, hunters, trappers, fishermen, woodsmen. She and her father visited with them around campfires and in their homes. She heard their stories and learned how they lived. She saw the log-driving rivers, stayed in deserted lumber camps, examined headworks and booms, studied how the dams and their gates operated, looked at logging operations, walked the woods roads, and stopped at working farms. She learned the Indian names of ponds, lakes, and other places. She met Indian guides and saw their campsites, and one even gave them some meat of a deer killed the night before.[44]

During the years 1889 and 1891, Fannie and her father explored the West Branch of the Penobscot, and she became further acquainted with the log-driving area she would write about one day. In 1890 and again in 1892, they paddled the Passadumkeag River, a tributary of the Penobscot. These trips gave the two many shared experiences and, without a doubt, increased the bond between them and strengthened the common views they held about the wildlands.

Born on June 18, 1865, in Brewer, Maine, Fannie was the first of Emeline and Manly Hardy's six children. Perhaps because she was the first child or perhaps because of their several mutual interests, Fannie developed a closeness to her father. In her later years, she said: "I was always with my father, following him into the woods round about, or listening to him and his friends talking at the dinner table. One day there would be seated such men as Deacon George A. Thatcher [a relative of Henry David Thoreau] and Professor Samuel Harris of Yale. . . . And the next day I might be listening to an Indian trapper. They were all treated with the same hospitality and they all contributed to my background."[45] In later years, her early acquaintances with Thatcher, the "gentlemanly hunter" Hiram Leonard, and the Penobscot Indian Joe Polis, all of whom figured in Thoreau's trips to the Maine woods, would influence some of her better feelings toward the Concord naturalist and philosopher, although, as we shall see, her feelings were mixed.

"It was my father's business [in furs] that brought such a diversity of wood life to our doors," she told an interviewer.[46] Another interviewer wrote: "Often as many as 30 or 40 Indians would come to their home for various reasons. Sometimes they came to trade or for social calls."[47] Nostalgically, Fannie related: "They told me stories, brought me baskets and little birch bark or carved canoes, and made a pet and plaything of me. I loved them all, without regard to comeliness. With all the white hunters I was the daughter of the

Fannie Pearson Hardy

As a girl and young woman, Fannie Hardy learned much from her father, Manly Hardy, about nature and the people who hunted, trapped, and made their living in the North Woods. Fannie later said, "There couldn't have been a childhood better designed to fit me for my future writing." Photograph courtesy of Bangor Public Library, James B. Vickery Collection.

regiment."[48] Clearly, she felt fortunate: "There couldn't have been a childhood better designed to fit me for my future writing."[49]

For years during her childhood, her family tented during summers on a point on Penobscot Bay, in Camden. She later wrote that there was hardly a road, beach, or back pasture she did not go over with her father. She picked blackberries, raspberries, and lilies by the armful from a pond, and she collected botanical specimens from everywhere. Her father guided and taught her, tramping the woods with her and teaching her to observe and learn the habits of animals and recognize their sign.[50] At his urging, she began at age eleven to take notes on her observations.[51] Because of her father, Fannie learned a little about the local Penobscot language and became familiar with the fur business, often accompanying him on his buying trips.[52] He also introduced her to ornithology. Together they learned taxidermy, and she helped him collect and mount a bird collection that would be the largest and most complete in Maine and one of the finest in New England. She said, "I have skinned everything from a golden eagle to a humming bird—from a bear to a mouse."[53]

Fannie grew up in Brewer, across the Penobscot River from Bangor, during a time when the area was reputed to be one of the greatest lumbering and shipping centers in the country, if not the world. One biographer wrote that "often she crossed to Bangor and walked through the Devil's Half Acre, Exchange Street and the water front districts where she saw woodsmen and river-drivers [and, according to Fannie], 'a motley crowd of gaunt, haggard, sunbaked, mosquito-bitten, bearded men,' whose clothes beggard description."[54] But periods of illness interrupted Fannie's active childhood and delayed her entrance into Smith College until she was twenty, even though she had readied herself for high school at age thirteen.[55] Relatively few women during this time had the opportunity to obtain a college education, but Fannie's extended schooling was consistent with the intellectual support her family had given her while she was growing up.

At Smith, her interest in natural history continued, and she and her father corresponded often, sharing observations and thoughts. In one of his letters, her father reported on birds he had seen, the quality of his furs, and a moose head he had sent to someone, remarking that the moose's "nose beats mine."[56] While at college, she made the acquaintance of naturalist and writer John Burroughs, who helped her and a friend organize the college chapter of the Audubon Society.[57] Twenty years later, when she herself had become a published writer, Fannie corresponded with Burroughs about their mutual interests in natural history. He asked permission to call on her and her father if he came to Maine and expressed hope that she might visit him if she ever came his way. Unfortunately, a meeting never occurred.[58]

In 1891, after graduation and her initial trips into the North Woods with her father, Fannie wrote a series of eleven articles for *Forest and Stream* titled "Six Years under Maine Game Laws." The series reflected her disgust at seeing wasted and illegally killed game in the woods. There is no doubt that her father strongly influenced the articles, for in them she examined an issue about which he had passionately written years before in a critical letter to *Forest and Stream* under the heading "The Wolf Cry in Maine." In her articles, Fannie protested the injustices of game-law enforcement in which wealthy sportsmen from out of state received favored treatment when laws were broken and the legislative influence they applied to promote laws that preserved game for their own sport. One biographer suggested that the articles provided a key to an attitude toward people that she held all her life: "her support of those born in Maine as opposed to 'outsiders,' and her feeling for the individual as opposed to the law."[59]

In the first article, she stated, "We are at a crisis in game matters," and "I am speaking for the farmers, lumbermen, explorers, guides, hunters, and all others . . . who may be classed as our rural population." She addressed in particular "the *gentlemen* who visit the Maine woods—a much smaller class, whom it may be hard to separate from the 'outsiders' and 'sports,' so called, for whom no great regard is professed." She declared that by conscious design, the laws shifted the game from rural to aristocratic hands. It is "a fact to be regretted by all, that game matters and game legislation are coming more and more to be regarded as a contest between rich and poor, non-resident and resident, sportsman and farmer." In support of this, she pointed out the lack of enforcement: "Did any one . . . ever see a warden in the woods anywhere over the whole Moosehead, East Branch, West Branch and Allegash country—the greatest hunting ground in the State—before the first of October [when the hunting season opened]?" She accused John Way, the Massachusetts man who produced the first guidebook and map of Moosehead Lake, of lobbying the Maine legislature to protect moose for sportsmen. "Mr. Way saw the need for this," she wrote. "The previous winter he had stayed six weeks at Haymock Lake . . . trying to kill a moose illegally."[60]

She drew on her trips with her father, pointing out that during the previous two years they had traveled in the woods during August and September, when it was illegal to kill any game animal, yet they had discovered fourteen violations of the game laws. "How a man," she stated, "can shoot at a moose when he knows he can use but 50 lbs. of the meat and that he must leave several hundred pounds equally good to spoil is beyond even our imagination; that is a positive sin, and if the man is a man he will not do it. We never forgive those who have done it." She evidently did not know, or chose to ignore the fact, that thirty years earlier her own father had killed a large bull moose for its shanks, nose, tongue, hide, and twenty pounds of steak. She spoke out against deer hounding, the illegal sale of game and fish, the number of poor wardens compared with the few good ones, and the deterioration in fishing and hunting. In her final article, she concluded that the existing laws were good, but stated that "we need a prompt reform in the equitable enforcement of those laws by competent and incorruptible officers," and such a reform must begin in the summer months.[61]

During the years of her summer trips, Fannie served as superintendent of the Brewer School System and then went with a Boston publisher as a reader of scientific manuscripts. In 1893 she traveled to Portland, Oregon, where she married Jacob A. Eckstorm, an Episcopal clergyman. Within the next few years, she gave birth to a daughter and a son. Her husband shared her interest in the outdoors and natural history, and together they spent what few outings they could get from his busy schedule in the woods and fields. During this time, with Jacob's encouragement, Fannie began writing two books about birds. Then, in 1899, tragedy struck: Her husband died. The loss was devastating, and she moved back to Brewer, where her father provided her with a house. Two years later, she lost her daughter. One can only imagine the anguish she felt; the deaths affected her health and her writing for some time. Fannie never remarried, and she remained a resident of the community for the rest of her life.[62]

Fannie had completed her bird books at the time of her daughter's death, and both were published that same year, in 1901. The first, *The Bird Book,* written for young people, provided a clue in the preface to her scientific view of nature: "Science is the green pasture of enthusiasms, and in the study of it there is no denying Shakespeare's dictum,—'There is no *good* Where is no pleasure ta'en.'"[63] Her other book, *The Woodpeckers,* she dedicated as follows: "To my Father, Mr. Manly Hardy—A Lifelong Naturalist." The book was intended to reward the reader with the pleasure of becoming acquainted with woodpeckers and finding answers to questions about them. "So much of man's pleasure in life," she wrote in the foreword, "depends on his ability to silence these persistent questioners [the birds, flowers, and bees who pose riddles], that this little book was written with the hope of making clearer the kind of questions Dame Nature asks."[64]

After the bird books were published and she recovered from her grief, Fannie turned to writing about the river drives and the singular, impressive actions of an unusual group of men, the river drivers. During her trips into the North Woods, she had become acquainted with the Penobscot River and the loggers and rivermen who depended on it. In 1904 she completed a book, *The Penobscot Man*, about the river and these men. Twenty years later, she republished it herself and added another chapter, in which she wrote:

> Hardly a greater story is there on record than this of a few common men, isolated in their location, many of them without neither capital nor education, taking hold of an engineer's problem of subduing a most unmanageable river and finally bitting and bridling it and training it to be *their* River, that brought their logs to market at their bidding. Few but the remnant who remain of those who did this, know how tremendous was the task of organizing and equipping the army that every year invaded the woods and brought the lumber down to the shrieking mills below.[65]

Throughout her life, Fannie Hardy Eckstorm continued writing, basing her work on meticulous research and a passion for truth. She became a recognized authority on the history of lumbering, folk songs, and the Indians of Maine. One of her first loves was the study of Indian languages. Most of her work was with the Penobscot language, although she did study the Passamaquoddy language

Fannie Hardy Eckstorm

Fannie Hardy Eckstorm became a respected Maine writer who shared with others her love and knowledge of natural history, Indian place-names, and the lore and romance of the Maine woods. Photograph courtesy of Fannie (Hardy) Eckstorm Collection, box 612, folder 91, Special Collections Department, Raymond H. Fogler Library, University of Maine, Orono.

to some extent. Early in life, noted Elizabeth Ring in a brief biography, "her father counseled her to win and deserve the confidence of the Indians, to learn their language and meaning of their nomenclature and to study their tribal customs."[66] She became friends with them and worked to accurately understand and communicate the meanings of their words. During her many years of study, she corresponded with Lucius L. Hubbard, Warren K. Moorehead, and others interested in the subject, and in 1941 she published the book *Indian Place Names of the Penobscot Valley and the Maine Coast.*

Over her lifetime, Fannie Hardy Eckstorm authored more than 200 separate writings, including books, chapters in books, book reviews, and articles. She wrote for the *Atlantic Monthly* and a number of other national publications. She received public recognition, including an honorary degree and honorary memberships in prestigious organizations. Five years before she died, she sent her friends a Christmas greeting on which were embossed words that reflected her philosophy: "There are but two kinds of people in the world, those who strive for what they can get out of it and those who strive to leave something in it."[67]

With her father as teacher, guide, and counselor, Fannie developed an intense attachment to the North Woods and the people who lived and worked there. Her writing, observed Lee Agger in the book *Women of Maine*, displayed "a love and respect for the land and wildlife."[68] She felt the poetry of the woods, as did Thoreau, whom she praised for it, and she identified with Thoreau's desire to simplify his life.[69] She was not above criticizing him, however, and one biographer noted that the writings of Thoreau's mentor, Ralph Waldo Emerson, had a greater influence on her.[70]

Through her special interest in the river drivers, she saw that people could capture the utility of nature while adding a dimension of fascination and awe, but when the drives began to disappear, she felt the effects of technological power over nature. "A log used to be a thing of romance," she wrote; "now it is only a tree cut down, and with a saw."[71] It grieved her to see the large paper companies transform the North Woods with their new machines and equipment, new methods of logging, and huge dams. One biographer even suggested that her book *The Penobscot Man*, while celebrating "the strong virtues of river drivers and woodsmen . . . [, attacked] by extension, the paper mills for taking over Maine's forests and rivers."[72]

But the changes in the North Woods and the wood industry witnessed by Fannie Hardy Eckstorm also brought to the region people who had a new perspective on the forest and lumbering—a view different from that which had ruled in the nineteenth century. The landowners needed a dependable supply of wood, and they looked to a new breed of forester to help manage the forests for that goal. One such man was George S. Kephart, and he would come to Chamberlain Farm. But it would be at a time when the farm, too, was changing.

Chapter 5

Minding the Wildlands

$\mathcal{G}$EORGE S. KEPHART came into this world a
Cornellian by family tradition, and expectations were high that he
would one day graduate from that institution of higher learning.
And in 1898, three years after his birth, a development occurred at
Cornell University that would influence his entire life's work: The
university became the first school in the United States to offer a full
four-year program leading to a bachelor's degree in forestry.[1] Here,
Kephart would prepare for a career in the country that had captured
the mind and heart of Fannie Hardy Eckstorm, and it would capture his mind and heart, too. Like Fannie, he would find himself
caught in a changing view of the human role in these wildlands. He
would write about and sing the praises of the river drivers, but he
would bring to Chamberlain Farm a view of the country different
from the one prevalent in their time. His ideas would embody the
meaning and spirit of a new forestry, a forestry that combined science and economics within the emerging idea of conservation.

The viewpoint Kephart represented did not gain a foothold easily, but it began earlier than one might suspect. As far back as 1844, George W. Coffin, land agent for Massachusetts, had warned: "He who visits the lands lying along the tributaries of the St. John, a hundred years hence, will probably see them despoiled of their wealth. That event will doubtless occur, sooner or later; legislation can hasten, or retard it. That Maine ought to endeavor to postpone it, we fully believe."[2]

The cutting continued without restriction all across New England until another voice gave further warning in the 1860s. A Vermonter, George Perkins Marsh, expanded on Coffin's apprehensions to include the ecological effects of overcutting and fire on flooding, erosion, and other detriments to natural communities. Marsh, a man with considerable intellectual ability and a broad worldview, experience in law and politics, and a love for nature, brought this message to the public in his book *Man and Nature,* which drew on the despoliation of the Vermont countryside he had seen and promoted a scientific and moral view of the human role in nature. He advocated cutting sparingly, reforesting, and, as far as possible, preserving land in its primitive condition so that it would regulate streams while also serving as a place for nature recreation. Looking back on Marsh a hundred years later, in the last half of the twentieth century, former secretary of the interior Stewart L. Udall saw him "most significant . . . as the framer of a new land ethic." David Lowenthal, in his 1958 biography of Marsh, observed that "until the twentieth century, no one except Marsh perceived the problem of conservation as one of interdependent social and environmental relationships."[3]

Coffin's and Marsh's early expressions of concern about the cutting of the forests began to penetrate the sphere of Maine's governmental consciousness in the late 1860s. The annual report of the Maine Board of Agriculture for 1869 appealed on moral and practical grounds for a bill to encourage the planting of trees in return for tax advantages.[4] Although Maine's government paid little attention to this and other early efforts, the concerns expressed by Marsh gained support among a broader constituency as logging increased during the last half of the century. In the view of historian Richard Judd, this growing support at the grassroots level reflected three "popular traditions—common stewardship, aggressive anthropocentrism, and reverence for nature."[5] In the 1880s, the Maine State Grange gave a collective voice to these beliefs and feelings of farmers and other rural inhabitants and, along with a number of influential people, took up the cause of protecting the forests. In 1891 the lobbying paid off, resulting in creation of the Maine Forest Commission and the position of forest commissioner.[6]

By the early part of the twentieth century, the practical advantages of conservation and scientific forestry had received recognition. The big landowners saw benefits that would further their economic self-interest. Others saw the forests as having public values, such as preservation of water control and supply, wildlife habitat, and scenery. However, attempts to pass laws making conservation and forest practices mandatory to protect these interests would be of limited success throughout the century, for the lumbering and wood products industries had too strong a voice in the state capitol.

The two factions did come together in the first decade of the 1900s to address one conservation problem: devastation of the forests by fire. A five-week drought in northern and eastern Maine in the spring of 1903 created conditions in the woods for a rash of destructive fires caused by human carelessness, lightning, and, in the minds of some, poor cutting practices. More than 200,000 acres burned, resulting in millions of dollars in lost property and timber, to say nothing of ecological damage and severe threat to human life. These conflagrations brought together public and private interests to combat the danger of future fires. But when the need for funding became apparent, the public looked to taxation of the landowners. The ensuing debate helped to define the legal responsibilities of the private property holders for the public interest—an interest that would continue to be clarified throughout the century and influence public policy for protection of a variety of forest values, from timber production to wilderness preservation.[7]

The immediate result of the public's efforts in forest protection was creation of the Maine Forestry District in 1909, which gave the forest commissioner full responsibility and authority to establish forest fire protection districts in parts of Maine, including the unorganized northern townships. By 1916, one could stand on Hog Point in front of Chamberlain Farm and see a fire lookout tower on the distant summit of Allagash Mountain. Another tower stood on the top of Soper Mountain, nine miles directly north of the farm.[8]

During this period, Fannie Hardy Eckstorm looked back and considered what had happened to Thoreau's Maine woods. "We hardly appreciate how great are the changes of the last fifty years," she wrote, "how the steamboat, the motor-boat, the locomotive, and even the automobile, have invaded regions which twenty years ago could be reached only by the lumberman's batteau and the hunter's canoe." As for the forest, she remarked with nostalgia and perhaps some sadness, the one Thoreau had come to see more than a half-century ago "has all but vanished, and in its place stands a new forest with new customs."[9]

Those customs were part of a dramatic change that took place around Chamberlain Farm following the end of E. S. Coe's era of influence, and it involved much more than the erection of fire towers on nearby mountains. The change could be laid to what one historian called a transition time—a time of advancements in technology and methods of logging, new industrial demands on the forest, the emergence of conservation concerns and less wasteful cutting practices, improved conditions for loggers, and the beginning of a subtle decline of the woods farms.[10] Especially significant was the change in industrial product: By 1906, pulp and paper had become the major manufacturing industry in Maine.[11]

Among these trends was one that had a major effect on Chamberlain Farm and its surroundings: the method of transporting logs. By 1890 in Maine, horses had gradually replaced oxen. The horse, however, would suffer a similar fate with the advent of the log hauler and tractor.[12] And behind these innovations lay a revolutionary development: the engine. Both steam-powered and internal combustion engines came into increasing use after the turn of the century and for a time brought a new vitality to the farm, but they would forever diminish a quality in the woods familiar to Coe and all before him: its silence.

At the dawn of the new century, two enterprising individuals, Fred W. Ayer and Herbert W. Marsh, obtained control of T8 R13, the town immediately northeast of T7 R12, which contained much of the Eagle Lake country. Faced with the problem of getting their logs out via the East Branch of the Penobscot River and with the dams and locks in disrepair, the two embarked on what has been called the "most ambitious transportation innovation" of the time.[13] Three miles northeast of Lock Dam, a narrow strip of land a little more than one-half mile wide separated Eagle and Chamberlain Lakes. Here, Ayer and Marsh proposed building a tramway, a kind of conveyor, to transport logs from Eagle Lake to Chamberlain Lake. It was a creative idea and must have challenged the imaginations of all who were aware of it.

Ayer and Marsh wasted no time in getting the project under way. In 1901, for about $150 per year, they leased Chamberlain Farm as their headquarters.[14] Early in the year, supplies were shipped by team from Palmer Brothers in Patten.[15] The farmhouse received an additional story.[16] New hands were hired, and the old depot suddenly had a new life and purpose.

That fall, they began hauling material from Northeast Carry to

Tramway, circa 1907
The development of the engine, combined with ingenuity, led to construction of the tramway—a creative method of moving logs from Eagle Lake to Chamberlain Lake, a distance over land of about one-half mile. Once in Chamberlain Lake, the logs were towed in booms by a steam-powered towboat to Telos Dam; from there, they were driven down Penobscot River waters to the mills. Photograph courtesy of Martha B. and Edward C. Werler.

the tramway site, including a 6,000-foot cable weighing fourteen tons, two large boilers, and a steam engine. The following spring, the tramway was under construction, and a year later, in 1903, it was ready to convey logs. One of the workers was twenty-year-old Ralph Miles, who was there the day the project started. Years later, he recalled in a letter that "at first it bothered as it was loaded top heavy but then they would put on a few logs as they tipped the hight of land those logs helped pull the others so in a short time it could be loaded full."[17]

It must have been a fascinating sight. The endless steel cable reached from the shore of one lake to the other and back. At intervals of ten feet, two-wheeled log-carrying trucks, clamped to the cable, ran on two railway tracks, one supported by a wooden trestle-like structure above the other. Trucks loaded with logs traveled on the upper tracks, and empty ones returned on the lower rails. At the Chamberlain Lake end, a nine-foot-diameter sprocket wheel pow-

Boom Towboat H. W. Marsh

The *H. W. Marsh*, a steam-powered side-wheeler, was built to tow booms of
logs to and from the tramway. It was retired on the shore of Chamberlain
Lake in front of the farm in 1913 along with a companion boat, the *George
A. Dugan*. Reprinted from *The Northern* 7, no. 8 (November 1927): 15.

ered by a steam engine moved the conveyor. Booms of logs were
towed to and from the tramway by two steam-powered boats that
had been built during construction of the tramway. One, the *H. W.
Marsh*, built at the Eagle Lake end of the tramway, was a side-
wheeler ninety feet in length and twenty-five feet at the beam. The
propeller-driven *George A. Dugan*, built at the Chamberlain Lake
end, was seventy-one feet long and had a twenty-foot beam. A. O.
Harkness, a man of mechanical ability who was sent to the farm to
supervise the *Dugan*'s construction, stayed on to run the tramway.
He estimated that the tramway moved 100 million feet of lumber
during its operation.

After five summers on Eagle Lake, the *H. W. Marsh* was moved to Chamberlain Lake, where it joined the *George A. Dugan* in tow-ing booms until about 1913, when the two boats were retired per-manently to the shore in front of Chamberlain Farm.[18] Their use-fulness, however, outlasted that of the tramway, whose fate was sealed the same year the project started: Alvin O. Lombard of Waterville, Maine, patented a steam-powered log hauler capable of moving 30,000 feet, or 125 tons, of spruce over iced winter roads. Production of the haulers began soon after, and by 1907 the massive tractors had become sufficiently competitive to replace the tramway operation.[19]

Meanwhile, the increasing network of roads, the appearance of the automobile and other motorized vehicles, and the ever growing popularity of railway travel were opening up the region to more and more people. Every year in the first decade of the century, the Ban-gor and Aroostook Railroad advertised Chamberlain Lake's attrac-tions to tourists and sportsmen and sportswomen. "Chamberlain Lake is one of the largest and best known bodies of water in north-ern Maine," an article declared in 1906, "and it is certainly one of the most picturesque." The farm, too, was mentioned occasionally, including its view of Mt. Katahdin.[20]

In 1914, another man who would enjoy that view came to the farm as manager for Lincoln Pulp Wood Company, the farm's renter.[21] A tall, lanky man with a bushy black moustache, his name was David Hanna. He lived to see the decline and end of the farm, for changes under way at the time of his arrival would outdate the usefulness of these lumbering supply depots. In 1915, for example, 1,098 trucks were registered in Maine,[22] and it would not be long before suitable roads for them would creep into the North Woods. "Highways 'In the Realms of Old King Spruce,'" announced one article in *The Northern,* a magazine published by Great Northern Paper Company. In 1916, the company began constructing a road to Frost Pond, twenty-five miles from Chamberlain Farm, and in

1919, the road was graveled and widened for trucks.[23] The big lumber companies were expanding their operations, transporting more of their supplies, improving their efficiency, conserving for the long-range use of the resource, and employing more professional foresters. One was George S. Kephart.

After his graduation from high school in 1912, in keeping with his parents' expectations, Kephart had begun making plans to attend Cornell University. However, family finances forced him to choose between the tuition-free colleges of veterinary medicine and agriculture. Ruling out the former, he tested the prospect of enrolling in the agricultural college and becoming a farmer by working the next year on his cousin's farm in Massachusetts. It was a wise move, for he later wrote: "During the year I did every assigned task in a left handed, semi-destructive manner that proved beyond a doubt that the farmer's life was not the life for me. At year's end I left the farm with an irreversible distaste for farming, a deep affection for the family horse, Daisy, and a friendship for my cousin, returned in kind by him, that had withstood the calamity of my inept efforts." Kephart returned to Ithaca in 1913 and entered the university, enrolling in the School of Forestry within the College of Agriculture. "It was a natural choice," he later said, "and should have been from the start, for here I felt completely at home."[24]

Kephart graduated from Cornell in 1917 with his forestry degree, one of fewer than 1,200 in the United States to have received the degree. He immediately entered military service in World War I and eventually served in France for eighteen months as a working forester in the Tenth Regiment of Army Engineers. While there, he met Harold Shepard, a forester with Lincoln Pulp Wood Company. After the war, with Shepard's help, Kephart joined that business concern.[25]

In the spring of 1919, the company, in keeping with the trend to bring conservation to its lands through corporate accounting and efficiency, assigned Kephart to a team of five woods cruisers to determine the quantity of timber on its holdings in the headwaters above Allagash Lake. Among those in the crew was Jim Clarkson, a man in his early forties and "of little schooling, but with profound knowledge of life in the woods." Born of Scottish and English parents, he had come to Maine from central New Brunswick and was destined to remain a figure in the history of the region around Chamberlain Farm for the next forty years. Clarkson exhibited resourcefulness in camping and woodcraft, respect for the training and values of the professional foresters in the group, pride in his own contributions, and interest in the work at hand. He had his moods, however, and after several months of unbroken, contented camp life, he would quite abruptly become brooding, "which meant," noted

George S. Kephart
George S. Kephart is shown here
in 1919 as a young forester in
Maine's North Woods. Photograph
courtesy of the Forest History
Society, Durham, N.C. Reprinted
by permission.

Kephart, "that he was due for a trip down river." Within a few days, Clarkson's bankroll would be gone. Then, after a call from him to the company, arrangements would be made for a cash advance and his return.[26]

The crew left Bangor and traveled by train, stage, tote sled, and snowshoes, and on the fourth day they arrived at Murphy's Camp on Telos Lake. A deep snowpack covered the northland. They stayed there until ice-out, running township lines and preparing to cruise company property in the vicinity. Soon after the lakes were free of ice, a motorboat was dispatched to take the men to Chamberlain Farm. Feeling a spirit of mild adventure, Kephart wrote, "It seemed to me that the boat was taking us ever farther from civilization, and ever deeper into the back country."[27]

When the crew came out of Chamberlain Thoroughfare and into Chamberlain Lake, they saw "an unbroken expanse of forest, receding from shore line to the horizon of low hills." For Kephart, it came as "a bit of a shock" when "Chamberlain Farm came into view, far ahead on the north shore." To him "it was, a symbol of civilization, carved into the forest. A bit of tilled land, some open fields, and a cluster of frame buildings," and he thought "its equal could be found throughout the more remote and less affluent areas of northern New England." But the farm had already begun to be affected by the changing means of supply for the logging businesses, and Kephart could tell that "Chamberlain Farm was already well past its hey-day of its existence." The party stayed at the farm two or three days, completing their outfitting and waiting out some bad weather. The interlude, Kephart wrote, "provided the minor thrills of eating meals prepared by a full time cook, reading some old magazines, and witnessing the stupendous feat of conversing over the telephone . . . [the] only winter time contact with the outside world."[28]

The party left Chamberlain Farm on the first fair-weather day and traveled up Allagash Stream into the country dividing the head-

Chamberlain Farm, Summer 1919

Chamberlain Farm, seen here as George S. Kephart saw it in 1919, was "a
symbol of civilization, carved into the forest." At far right is the boom towboat *George A. Dugan*, which was pulled up onto the shore and retired after
its years of service on Chamberlain Lake. Photograph courtesy of the Forest
History Society, Durham, N.C. Reprinted by permission.

waters of the Allagash and St. John Rivers. For the next eight
months they cruised the townships, working up detailed notes and
maps. "During this time," Kephart later wrote, "the thrills and nov-
elty of camping merged gradually into a more stereotyped acceptance of it as a way of life."[29]

Throughout their months in the woods, members of the team
traveled to Chamberlain Farm for supplies or used it as a stopover
on their trips downriver. Kephart recorded in a diary his trips out
and stops at Chamberlain Farm, noting that to get to Trout Brook
Farm he had to travel "about nine miles by canoe, the same afoot, &
twelve by motorboat." On one of his trips, he saw his first moose on
Webster Brook. Another time, the crew had to come out of the
woods and go to the farm to obtain flour to replace some on which
they had spilled kerosene.[30]

Sometime after 1920, Kephart noted, "[I] moved out of the

Chamberlain Farm, Early 1920s

Another view of Chamberlain Farm near the time of George Kephart's visit shows the *H. W. Marsh* in a much altered condition. The boat had deteriorated as a result of exposure to the elements, and its stern had been removed behind the paddle box when it was frozen in the lake one fall. To protect the engine, the forward part had been pulled up onto the shore. Photograph courtesy of Avis Harkness Black, whose father, A. O. Harkness, built the boat around 1903 at the tramway.

Allagash with a change of employers. And, as responsibilities changed over the following ten years, tenting out became less and less a part of my job." He observed that "winds of change were blowing through the Maine woods . . . but they were gentle breezes indeed." He was speaking of trucks, roads, powered logging machinery, and labor–management relations and their effects on the workers' attitudes.[31] The changes reflected what was happening in the country as a whole, and as Fannie Hardy Eckstorm had observed years earlier, the Allagash region, for all its remoteness, could not escape the transformation.

A year following Kephart's stint in the Allagash, the "Telos Cut," among Maine's "longest lasting and most profitable canals,"

Forestry Crew at Chamberlain Farm, 1919

A short stay at Chamberlain Farm provided an opportunity for the forestry crew that included George S. Kephart to outfit for work in the woods. Dave Hanna, farm manager, is third from left; Jim Clarkson, with hat, is fifth from left. Photograph courtesy of the Forest History Society, Durham, N.C. Reprinted by permission.

stopped operating.[32] In 1922, the East Branch Improvement Company repaired the old Lock Dam and built a roof over it, making it one of the most distinctive structures in the region. In that same period, Great Northern Paper Company completed a graveled road from Frost Pond to Duck Pond, only fourteen miles south of the farm.[33] The year 1922 also found Phinneus Sawyer completing a woods cruise of T7 R12, one of several that had been done by that year.[34] Information in the Maine state valuation of the township in 1924 indicated that Lincoln Pulp Wood Company owned it and placed its value at $184,629. The Chamberlain Farm lot in the township was still owned by D. Pingree and others, and its 500 acres were valued at $5,000.[35] But as Kephart had observed five years earlier, its buildings and fields were by then in decline.

At the farm during the 1920s, David Hanna most likely knew

Lock Dam, Outlet of Chamberlain Lake, circa 1930
Lock Dam took on a distinctive appearance when a roof was built
over it during a repair operation in 1922. Photograph courtesy of
Charles M. (Buck) Hamlin Jr.

about and even participated in some of the events in the region.
Having served as chief fire warden for a period of time, he undoubtedly knew of the wooden fire towers and perhaps helped replace
them with steel ones on Allagash and Soper Mountains in 1924.[36]
He probably received word of Dr. Fred Pritham's heroic effort on
January 4, 1925, to reach Ruth Vickery, who lived across the lake,
on Donnely Point. Pritham, who practiced in Greenville, received a
frantic telephone call from Ruth's husband, Earl Vickery, a forest
engineer for Great Northern Paper Company. His wife was having
a miscarriage. Pritham got into his snow machine, a Ford Model T
coupe connected to Caterpillar treads, and drove miles to a lumbering operation at Ellis Brook. Vickery met him there and guided him
six miles on snowshoes in the dark. The doctor carried out surgery

Chamberlain Farm, 1924
When this photograph was taken, Chamberlain Farm was in a slow decline
as expanding roads and use of trucks provided a more economical means of
supplying the logging operations. Photograph courtesy of Barry Lord.

under lantern light and probably saved Ruth's life. The Vickerys'
two young boys "watched the whole proceeding through the cracks"
in the floorboards of the room above.[37]

Hanna knew the family, because the next year one of the Vickery boys, Earl, then age five, received a new set of skis for Christmas
and skied across the lake to show them to Hanna at the farm. Earl
remembered Hanna as something of a hermit and the farmhouse as
a weather-beaten building in a snow-covered field that sloped up
from the shore of the lake.[38]

For Hanna, 1926 marked the beginning of a major development
in the region: On April 10, construction began on the Eagle
Lake–West Branch Railroad. The event suggested that even this
remote country was not completely isolated from the technological
revolution that, in the words of one historian, was being "witnessed

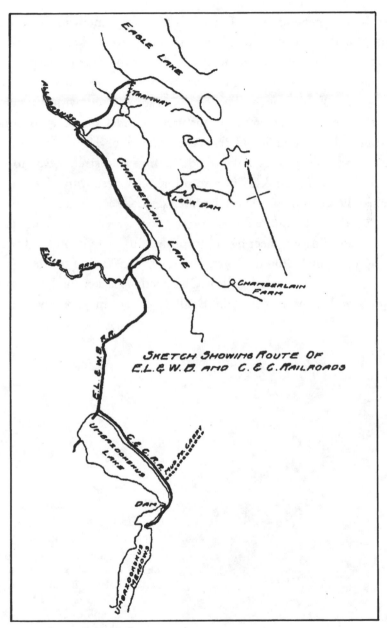

*Tramway and Eagle Lake–West Branch Railroad and
Chesuncook–Chamberlain Lake Railroad, 1927*

From *The Northern* 7, no. 8 (November 1927): 4.

by the first generation of Twentieth Century Americans."[39] Planning for the railroad had begun the year before when officials of
Great Northern Paper Company decided it would be less expensive
to take pulpwood down the West Branch of the Penobscot than
down the East Branch. The company contracted with Edouard
Lacroix, part owner of the Madawaska Land Company, to build
eleven miles of the railroad, from the tramway on Eagle Lake to the
head of Umbazooksus Lake. Another five-mile stretch was to be
built from Umbazooksus to a terminal on Chesuncook Lake and
called the Chesuncook and Chamberlain Lake Railroad.

By 1927, the railroad was in operation. Several interesting and
rather amazing engineering accomplishments were connected with
the project, including the construction of a 1,500-foot trestle across
Allagash Stream at the head of Chamberlain Lake; the hauling of
two large locomotives into the Eagle Lake terminus, one weighing

*Steam Engine on the
Chesuncook and Chamberlain
Lake Railroad, 1927*
This ninety-ton oil-burning
steam engine hauled pulpwood
on the Chesuncook and Chamberlain Lake Railroad, making a
round trip every three hours.
Photograph by M. Strauss,
reprinted from *The Northern* 7,
no. 8 (November 1927): 14.

seventy-one tons and the other ninety tons; and the transportation of an Erie steam shovel to the tramway site, along with some forty pulp cars and two gas-powered switching locomotives. An appreciation for the difficulty of the project comes from the realization that it was successfully completed without roads as we know them today or modern moving equipment such as cranes.[40]

Once the operational kinks had been overcome, the railroad moved an estimated 6,500 cords of pulpwood each week. At the Eagle Lake end, two 225-foot-long conveyors loaded a twelve-car train. At the Umbazooksus end, the cars were backed onto a trestle over the lake and the pulpwood emptied into the water.[41] The railroad operated until 1933, when the effects of the Great Depression on the market for paper products left Great Northern Paper with a

The "Casey-Jones," 1930

This heavy-duty railway motorcar and trailer, seen here at the Eagle Lake terminus of the Eagle Lake–West Branch Railroad, hauled men, mail, and supplies during the construction and operation of the railroad. Photograph courtesy of Charles M. (Buck) Hamlin Jr.

large inventory of pulpwood. The company terminated the operation and abandoned the engines and equipment in the woods, leaving them to be discovered by amazed visitors.

In 1927, following the startup of the railroad, Alfred Hempstead, head of the Social Service Department of Great Northern
Paper and editor of the company's monthly news magazine, *The
Northern,* visited Chamberlain Farm. As his boat approached the
shore, his first impression "was that of an old farm with a number of
unpainted buildings, some cultivated land and a large hillside hay
field that is growing up with trees. On the shore were two old
steamboats, both dilapidated and fallen to pieces to such an extent
that they can never be used again." He met Dave Hanna, who was
still in charge, and noted that Hanna had "a dog, Jack, a pair of
horses, a cow, six cats and a radio." In what sounds like a eulogy to
the old depot, Hempstead observed that the farm

> has been the only constant witness here of the
> changes of the last eighty years. Many are the tales
> told and enacted within its walls. The woodsman,
> the trapper and the sportsman have frequented it
> these many years. The birchbark canoes of earlier
> days are no longer hauled up on its shores; the bat-
> teau and the canvas covered canoe have taken their
> place; steam boats having served their time, have
> fallen into decay in its front yard. Now the whistle
> of a locomotive is heard across the lake more often
> than the cry of the loon. May this old landmark
> long remain.[42]

The operation of the railroad touched the farm in more ways
than by the sound of train whistles. Raymond Vigue, who worked
for Lacroix in 1928 as a teenager driving a Lombard log hauler,
recalled "many instances in which the Farm was a brief resting place

Wreck of the First Maine Forest District Airplane

This biplane, the first used by Maine for forest fire detection, was wrecked in Moosehead Lake on June 18, 1927, without loss of life. Its use signaled further changes in the Chamberlain Farm region brought about by technological advances. Reprinted from *The Northern* 7, no. 7 (October 1927): 7.

for woodsmen on the long treck from Greenville to the Allagash region, along with movement of tools, food and supplies supporting the Lacroix logging camps."[43] As early as June 1927, Edouard Lacroix wrote a letter to Auguste Lessard at the tramway, saying that "potatoes are very rare. Telephone Hanna at Chamberlain Farm; he offered us 40 barrels this spring."[44] On October 9, 1930, records from the Lacroix office, under the heading "Eastern Manufacturing Company," read: "10/9/30 2 live beef from Eastern's Chamberlain Farm." And an invoice signed by David Hanna from Lincoln Pulp Wood Company on that same date showed that two "beef creatures" were delivered, weighing a total of 1,410 pounds and costing $187.90.[45]

Other changes were taking place during the railroad's operation. The need for Lock Dam in river driving disappeared: Railroads had begun transporting logs and pulpwood that would have been driven down the St. John, and thus Churchill Dam could supply the smaller head of water needed for any necessary drives.[46] In 1927, the Maine Forestry District introduced the first aircraft for forest fire detection, and in 1929 and 1930 the agency chartered flights over the Penobscot watershed and other regions.[47] The drone of planes was added to the whistle of trains and putter of boats. Trucks and tractors, such as the familiar Caterpillar, would be in use before the end of the 1930s.[48] With them would come road improvements that after World War II would leave the company woods-farms unnecessary and unprofitable. In the midst of these events, George Kephart left the region to become a forester with the U.S. Department of the Interior's Bureau of Indian Affairs.

Visitors at Chamberlain Farm, 1930

Professor George H. Hamlin, third from left, stayed at the farm in 1930 while on an inspection tour of dams for the East Branch Improvement Company. Next to him, at far right, is David Hanna, manager; at far left is Jim Clarkson. The farmhouse burned the next year. Photograph courtesy of Charles M. (Buck) Hamlin Jr.

By the 1930s the big companies had, in the words of historian David Smith, "adopted scientific logging, forestry, [and] conservation, and were generally cultivating the woods as though they were a farm."[49] Just at this time, on October 3, 1932, one of Maine's large landowners died—David Pingree Jr., who had many years ago, at the turn of the century, seen the need to preserve an investment in Maine's forest heritage and advocated sustainable forestry. It would be only two decades until signs would begin to surface of a widespread public interest in this forested region for more than its production of timber.[50] But before that day came, Chamberlain Farm burned.

The fire occurred in April 1931. How the fire started is not known, but judging from old photographs, it appears to have been confined principally to the farmhouse, which it destroyed completely. In one of his columns about Lock Dam, outdoor writer Gene Letourneau expressed regret that "the most elaborate and complete records concerning the early days of the water diversion went up in smoke. . . . This farm [was the] center of all lumbering activities for nearly a hundred years."[51]

Its usefulness and condition already on the wane, the farm never recovered as a lumbering depot from this loss, and David Hanna moved to a cabin two miles down the shore. An article in the Bangor and Aroostook Railroad's 1937 edition of *In the Maine Woods* noted the "old Chamberlain Farm, now deserted and tumbling into ruin."[52] The Allagash lumbering industry had lost a part of its life, but it would not be the end of the farm. In a way, its demise marked a change in the region and the industry.

Three decades later, in 1963, George Kephart, then chief forester of the Bureau of Indian Affairs, saw the change clearly as he stood on the shore of Telos Lake. It had once taken him days to reach the lake, but this time he had found it less than a day's drive from Bangor. As he looked out over the lake, the memories came

"Old Chamberlain Farm, . . . tumbling into ruin."
A few years after the 1931 fire, with its farmhouse gone and its buildings
decaying and no longer maintained, Chamberlain Farm took on the appearance of a ghost town. Photograph courtesy of Gene L. Letourneau.

back, and for a moment he "saw the [Murphy] camp again as it was"
when he came to Telos on that April day in 1919. He could now see
how Murphy's crew had taken "its place in the continuing succes-
sion of loggers who had marched across the land from time to time,
beginning in the 1830's when the first loggers came to this area."[53]

Kephart himself valued the forest for its utility. He knew its
material worth, but like a growing number of people in his day, he
discovered other qualities that he appreciated. The fall coloring
filled him with a "sense of wonderment akin to awe." He became
disturbed at seeing the "desecration" of one of his old camping areas
by crowded tents, congested parking, and noise brought about by
too many people and easy access. He regretted having killed a bear
he had come upon one fall day when it was rooting for beechnuts.
He and the bear had seen each other at the same time, and after a

moment's debate with himself, he had shot it with his revolver for camp meat and its hide. Later, he reflected that he would have remembered his encounter with the bear with greater pleasure had he not killed it. Still, he wondered whether under the law of "survival of the fittest" all species could survive in the environment in which humans lived.[54]

At the same time, Kephart recognized how tied we are to nature's laws for our own survival and believed the human race itself to be threatened. He worried about the effects of our growing population, our crowded urban areas, and our lack of respect for others and the community as a whole. But he could bring himself only to partially condemn our "reckless exploitation" of natural resources, by which we had carved out from "this formerly wild and little-used land" a nation so rich, strong, and powerful that it survived two world wars and gave its citizens security, well-being, affluence, and leisure time. And he questioned what our lives would be like if his generation and others before had been more frugal in using natural resources and more gentle in dealing with their fellow man. At the same time, perhaps thinking of a need to make some amends, he argued that we should repay our debts, conserve our resources, heal an abused nature, and avoid thoughtless waste and pollution.[55]

George Kephart was privileged to have seen and experienced many changes in society and, in a lifetime that extended into his nineties, to have had the opportunity to develop a perspective on the role of humans in the world. Although he believed we should manage nature to the extent we can, he had respect for nature's laws and great faith in "Man's basic common sense." He believed that "the accepted life-style of the future will conform to the fundamental laws of nature and will also preserve the dignity of mankind."[56]

Chapter 6

Lure of Woods and Waters

*I*N HER LIVELY MANNER, Patty Nugent would have openly derided the idea that she and her husband, Al, would become legendary figures in Maine's sporting camp history. Al, in his quiet way, would have taken on an amused look had it been said to him. The story, however, would be told over and over: How they had chanced the difficulties of crossing Chamberlain Lake and set out on a July day in 1936, with Al in a boat towing a large raft that carried Patty, their belongings, and a brand-new Star Kineo cookstove. How they had landed on the shore near Leadbetter Brook, a little more than three miles east of the decaying remains of Chamberlain Farm, and commenced building a sporting camp. How their business had become known far and wide and they themselves had been sought after by writers and journalists. Less often told would be the story of how Patty and Al Nugent had encouraged a view of this region espoused by Thomas Sedgwick Steele, Lucius L. Hubbard, and others more than a half century earlier and in the process had changed the farm itself, from a place that had once supported cutting of the woods to a place where people came to take pleasure in them.[1]

Lila-Beatrice "Patty" Pelky was born on October 30, 1904, in Medway, Maine. She and her eight brothers and sisters grew up on the family farm learning the meaning of work. She also learned how to cook, taught by her father, who fed loggers in the woods camps. And he gave her something else: the dream of going to Chamberlain Lake. His work took him into that lake's vast, remote country, and Patty listened to his stories of the region with growing interest and wonder. But it would be years before Chamberlain Lake became more than an imaginative place to her.

After high school, Patty worked in the paper mill, and at the age of twenty-one, she married. The marriage, however, soon ended in divorce. While still in her twenties, she went to work for a nearby sporting camp on Rainbow Lake, where her brother Claude worked as a guide. "I loved that," she told an interviewer in her later years. "I did the cabin work, waitress work and I also helped with the cooking . . . and I always loved the woods." But the woods and the waters had another side. One day Claude disappeared, and his canoe turned up empty by the shore of a nearby lake. Among those who showed up to search for Claude was a tall, rugged man of twenty-nine by the name of Al Nugent. Al was there for almost a month before they found Claude's body. In the meantime, Patty had fallen in love. "I thought Nuge was the handsomest man I ever saw in my life. . . . Even my folks thought he was something," Patty would later say. From Al Nugent's perspective, the feeling was mutual.[2]

Allen O. Nugent was born at Caratunk, Maine, on January 1, 1903. As a boy, he had a knack for understanding mechanical things, and after leaving school he put his talents to work for the New England Telephone Company, building and maintaining telephone systems. But he had the north country in his blood, and by the time he met Patty, he had found employment with Great Northern Paper Company, working out of Grant Farm stringing telephone lines through the woods. After they met, Patty found work in nearby Kokadjo in order to be closer to him. During this time, Al's job took him into the country around Chamberlain Lake, which captivated him. Here was a strong taste of the frontier—unsettled, out-of-the-way, and wild. Here he could do what he really wanted to do—hunt, fish, trap, and guide.

At some point in the young couple's relationship, the idea of building a sporting camp crept into their minds, and as it grew, so did their excitement. There was little question about where the camp would be: The lure of the Chamberlain Lake region was too strong. The year was 1935 when they went into the country to look for a suitable location. It was Patty's first trip to Chamberlain Lake, and for her it must have been a thrilling experience, seeing the place she had imagined from her father's stories. After some exploration, they found the spot they wanted on a public lot—a parcel of land held in trust by the state for income to benefit education and other public needs. Following their return, they tried unsuccessfully to obtain a lease from the state. However, as the Nugents told it, they had lawyer friends who urged them to go ahead and settle on the land, and if they had trouble they would be defended.

That next winter, while Al worked for Great Northern Paper driving a tractor into the company's Sourdnahunk logging operation, about eight to ten miles south of Telos Lake, he started putting things for a camp into their storehouse. The next summer, after clearing out the old Murphy Road from Sourdnahunk Lake to Telos Lake, Al and Patty rented a team of horses and a wagon to haul their belongings and supplies over to Telos.

Getting their things safely across the lake was an enormous undertaking, fraught with potential difficulties. Their first task was to construct a large raft. When it was completed, they loaded it carefully with their belongings. Finally, with everything ready, they put off from shore on the evening of July 4 and traveled across the lakes at night, when the winds were less troublesome. Powered by a small motor and with two loaded canoes in tow, their raft slowly crossed Telos Lake and Round Pond, made its way through Chamberlain Thoroughfare, and came out into the daunting expanse of Chamberlain Lake. It was a difficult crossing, and some of their food got wet. But they made the far shore safely, and after tying up, Patty cooked their first meal on the cookstove while it sat on the raft.[3]

For their campsite, they selected the high ground beside Leadbetter Brook. Years later, Patty remembered saying, "Oh, this is a beautiful spot," when she saw the site. She recalled that "it was such a green knoll . . . all evergreens around, spruce and fir and a stream."[4] Al had other reasons for choosing the campsite: It was high ground, and the prevailing wind from the northwest came directly across the lake, making for breezy conditions; both of these factors would keep the flies away. Together, they climbed the knoll, Patty fondly recalled, "and I thought, 'This is an elegant view.' . . . Nuge put his arm on my shoulder and said, 'Just right, little girl. This is just right.'"[5]

Patty and Al Nugent were about to bring a long-held Maine tradition to Chamberlain Lake: a unique business called a sporting camp, which capitalized on the public's interest in fishing, hunting, and other outdoor recreational activities. Following the Civil War, promotion of the Maine woods by the railroads, hotels, and others had attracted wealthy clients from the big eastern cities. "Camps typically consisted of a main lodge for dining and socializing, with anywhere from eight to twenty cabins and outbuildings such as a woodshed, boathouse, guide's camp, ice house, barn and workshop," according to a brief history in *The Maine Sporting Camp Guide*. "The lodge and cabins were usually built of logs that had been cut on site. . . . The sporting camp . . . often had gardens, a cow and chickens." In addition to a staff to cook and to run the camp, "a mystical

Patty and Al Nugent, circa 1940
Patty and Al Nugent brought the
Maine sporting camp tradition to
Chamberlain Lake. With it came
people who visited the region to
hunt and fish and enjoy the area's
remoteness, beauty, and feeling of
wildness. Photograph courtesy of
Dabney Y. Hofammann.

Maine Guide . . . was the central figure in the guests' activities and
took the 'sports' to the secret spots for fishing, hunting or observing
wildlife."[6]

In the Allagash region as early as the 1890s, E. S. Coe had
recorded several inquiries from individuals interested in building
camps on his land. One came from Lucius Hubbard. Coe noted in
an office memorandum that Hubbard "would like lease of camp site
on 6 R15, 6 R14, 7 R14, & 15, 8 R14—one camp site—would like
to have general control against fire or slaughter game—with such as
are lawless but not against home people. To talk with owners about
the matter."[7] It is not clear whether Hubbard succeeded in securing
a lease, but others soon established camps in the region. As early as
1901, an advertisement for the Telos Lake Sporting Camps
appeared in the Bangor and Aroostook Railroad's guidebook *In the
Maine Woods*. The camps' 1902 advertisement contained a photograph with the following information:

Read What Telos Lake Offers and Come In!

Deer and moose from a deep wilderness. Big togue.
Richest Maine trout fishing only one and six miles
away by buckboard (at Coffee-los and Sourdnahunk [Nesowadnehunk Lake]). Cooper's Camps
serve fresh vegetables, milk, butter, etc. Special
rooms for ladies. Tents with floor, also cottages, to
let. Cooper's are the only camps in the Allagash
lake chain; are but 12 miles from usual Allagash
canoe route, and offer wide range of sport. Rates,
$2.00 a day. Guides, $3.00 a day. Two days ride in
by buckboard from Patten, or canoe from Northeast
Carry.[8]

At Mud Pond Carry in 1902, another set of sporting camps
appeared on Umbazooksus Lake. They were built by Howard Colby,
a wealthy sportsman from New Jersey. One source noted, "All of the
buildings were of logs, even to the ice house, the spring house, the
studio by the lake [for Mrs. Colby's photography], the storehouse
and other outbuildings." The Colbys entertained many guests; often
as many as twenty-two were accommodated at one time, along with
as many as ten guides. In 1916, the camps were taken over by the
Colbys' head guide, Ed Ronco, who operated them into the 1920s
and perhaps beyond.[9]

Although not a sporting camp in the traditional sense, Chamberlain Farm had served as a stopover for people coming to Chamberlain Lake to hunt and fish, but in the years before it burned, it
had served fewer and fewer visitors. When Patty and Al landed their
raft on that July day in 1936, only a few isolated cabins populated
the lakeshore. They were soon to learn of one cabin in the next cove,
on the outlet stream of Leadbetter Pond—the home of a trapper by
the name of Dave Hanna. After the fire at the farm, trapping had

become a major occupation for him. In this remote location, he had little competition for his trapping activity, so it was not long after Patty and Al arrived that Hanna showed up unhappy, certain that his new neighbors planned to trap in the area. But Al assured him that as long as Hanna trapped, he would not, and he never did.[10] The Nugents made a friend.

The first year was a hard one for Patty, Al, and Patty's brother Allie, who stayed with the couple. They first built a lean-to, which served as a home while they cleared the land and cut, hewed, and sledded logs for the cabins. Everything was built by hand; even the cabin sinks were made from wood. They had almost no money that first year and lived on the supplies they had brought in, the fish they

Cabin under Construction at
Nugent's Chamberlain Lake Camps, Early 1940s
An enormous amount of work went into building each of the several cabins
at the Nugents' sporting camps. Everything was built by hand, including
wooden kitchen sinks. Photograph courtesy of Charles M. (Buck) Hamlin Jr.

could catch, and a deer Al shot. Once, Patty ran out of white flour and had to make all her biscuits from buckwheat. When Dave Hanna found out about it, he brought over a sack of white flour. Patty later recalled that it was "one of the best gifts she ever received."[11]

Patty and Al depended on ingenuity, good health, and muscle power, as they would for the rest of their lives. It was not a place for sickness. Labor translated directly into survival and the success or failure of their venture. Both of them were physically strong, and according to Patty, at one time they both weighed the same—224 pounds. Al's strength was legendary. It was said that he single-handedly moved their cookstove up onto the knoll and into their kitchen, whereas it had taken five men to load it onto their raft. He could pick up a barrel of gasoline weighing nearly 500 pounds and put it into a canoe. Patty claimed she could shoulder a canoe and hundred-pound bags of beans and flour about as far as a man could.

That first fall, Patty and Al opened up the camps to deer hunters, but they had no money for furnishings, so the hunters had to sleep on the floor and use their jackets for pillows.[12] The people came anyway: Al had already established a reputation for guiding hunters. With their business started, word got out, and soon a seasonal routine became established, with the busiest times during spring fishing, right after ice-out, and fall hunting. But even in slow times, they were always busy—building, gardening, repairing, cutting and splitting firewood, cooking, cleaning, and transporting supplies, as well as doing their own hunting and fishing. It was a true partnership, for they divided their labor in ways that were most efficient. Al taught Patty to shoot, fly-fish, and tie flies. After Hanna's death, two years following their arrival, they added trapping to their source of income, and Patty had her own trapline. Al's line extended at least seventy-five miles. When he checked the traps, he would be gone for two weeks at a time, living in lean-tos and small cabins, which he had built every fifteen to twenty miles, and eating muskrat stew and boiled beaver.[13]

In those first years, there were few ways to travel to the camps. Visitors could come by canoe and cross Mud Pond Carry by horse and buckboard, or they could get to Telos Lake from Trout Brook Farm by tote road. The only other way was by plane. Flights into the region began in the 1930s and 1940s. As early as 1941, sportswriter Bill Geagan reported on a party of fishermen from Boston flying in and "stopping at the fine new sporting camp of [Allen] Nugent on Chamberlain Lake."[14]

Not long after the Nugents settled, a problem they had anticipated surfaced: The state tried to drive them out. Outdoor writer Gene Letourneau remembered one of the first incidents. He was visiting Albert Thibodeau, the district forest supervisor, at his headquarters at the tramway on Eagle Lake when Thibodeau got a telephone call. Letourneau wrote, "Albert caught my eye . . . [and] he casually asked me if I wanted to go see 'Nuge,' adding he had a message from the Augusta Forestry office to give him." The two were soon in Thibodeau's canoe, motoring down the lake to the Nugents' camps. When they arrived, Al was standing on his wharf. Letourneau related that after the canoe was tied up, the two men stood "facing each other on the narrow walk. They smiled, exchanged greetings. Then came a memorable piece of conversation. 'I've come to deliver a message to you from the Augusta office,' Thibodeau began. 'That so,' Nuge replied, 'what is it.' 'They want you to leave this place,' Albert replied. 'Did they say when?' 'No.' That was it." The three of them walked up to the cabins for tea and Patty's famous cookies.[15]

The state, however, would not give up easily. When the Maine Forest Service ran a telephone line past the camps, Al got a phone and hooked it into the line. Jim Clarkson, who in 1941 had become the dam tender at Lock Dam for the Bangor Hydro-Electric Company, was often instructed to "cut them off" from the phone line. But he and the Nugents had become good friends, so whenever Clarkson got word to cut the line, he would call Al up and they would meet at an agreed-on spot. Jim would cut the line, and Al would immediately splice it back together.[16] Eventually, in the mid-1940s, after years of failing to remove the Nugents, the state gave up and granted them a lease, and over the years the camps became a favorite retreat for state officials and the higher-ups in some of the woods-products companies. Even governors paid them visits.

World War II brought changes, and in 1941 Patty and Al closed the camps and went to work at Pratt and Whitney in Connecticut. They returned two or three years later, and by the end of the 1940s, their business was thriving, with full bookings. They did not place advertisements; outdoor writers did it for them, extolling their personalities, their pioneer spirit, and their ingenuity in living off the land. For example, Bob Elliot wrote in the *Boston Post* in 1946 that he "was thrilled by a visit to remote Chamberlain Lake and readily admitted that never had he seen such a genuine, down-to-earth set of buildings as those erected by the Nugents with axes, saws and perspiration."[17]

Gene Letourneau, writing for the *Waterville Morning Sentinel* and other Gannett Company newspapers in Maine, and Bud Leavitt of the *Bangor Daily News* wrote regularly about the Nugents and their camps. They spoke fondly of both Patty and Al. Their readers came to know Patty as lively, imaginative, gracious, hardworking, and forever busy—and they learned she could be feisty in protecting herself and the camps. Al, the reporters wrote, was powerful as a bull, a man who usually was exceptionally gentle but could be tough if provoked by actions he thought wrong or mean. He had a clear picture of right and wrong, but he looked at the good side of things and loved life. As a woodsman, he stood head and shoulders over most men. And his mechanical ability was well known and appreci-

Al Nugent Guiding Fishermen

By the end of the 1940s, the Nugents' business was thriving, and as the
years progressed, they attracted more and more guests, who heard about
them by word of mouth and by the many articles written about them.
This photograph was taken on the lake in front of the camps.
Photograph courtesy of Lidia and Miles Nugent.

ated by many who had a motor fail or experienced some problem
with a boat or snowmobile.

The reporters were fascinated by Al's stories and often quoted
them. For example, in response to a question about how much snow
they got around the camps, he had this story:

> Last year we had quite a lot of snow, six and a half
> feet. And I looked out in front here one day and I
> saw a hat. So I thought it was kind of odd and
> wondered if it blew off or something and went out
> and picked it up, and there was a man under it. And
> I said, "Can I help you?" And he said, "No thanks.
> I'm on horseback."[18]

As a couple, the Nugents possessed the self-sufficiency that made their kind of life possible. Despite limitations in suitable soil and garden space, they raised their own produce, including peas, corn, lettuce, beets, garlic, and potatoes. At the old Chamberlain Farm site, although the fields were beginning to grow up to forest, they were able to pick blueberries and obtain rhubarb from a large patch that still remained. Al noted that even when the farm was in operation, there "wasn't too much good land but they could raise hay in among the rocks very well. . . . Probably 100 or 150 acres of it is good land, soil about a foot and a half deep, good black soil." He told about seeing "piles of rocks . . . 20 feet across, five or six feet high," the result of clearing the land.[19] Over the years, the old farm itself provided many materials for the Nugents. They scavenged boards, hardware, scrap iron, and coal from the old blacksmith shop—several boatloads, to fuel Al's forge.[20]

Clarence Herrick, a former guide, remembered meeting the Nugents around 1949. A New Jersey sportsman, Walter Trow, had rented an old camp at Chamberlain Farm, now known as Nugent's Farm House, from George Rear, a Massachusetts businessman who had leased the farm in 1948 to start a sporting camp. Trow hired Herrick as his guide, and the two of them flew to the farm from Greenville for two weeks of spring fishing. Herrick recalled seeing the dilapidated paddle wheeler the *H. W. Marsh* on the shore, an old, weathered barn still standing, and—what was most unusual and would provoke a great deal of interest today—a mountain lion in the old field. While staying at the farm, the two men went up the lake almost every night for a delicious supper at the Nugents' camps. Herrick learned later, when he guided for the Nugents, that the small, rocky island they passed on their way, a gull nesting area, occasionally provided Patty with eggs for her cooking. Interviewed nearly a half century later, Herrick still had fond memories of the region. He had liked it because of its expansiveness and remoteness as well as its his-

Camp Converted from Old Chamberlain Farm Building, 1951
Since the late 1940s, this old building at Chamberlain Farm, perhaps
originally a boathouse, has been used as a cabin. Today, it is called the
"Farm House," operated by Nugent's Chamberlain Lake Camps.
Photograph courtesy of Harold Whiteneck.

tory. "I wouldn't like it now," he said. "Not compared to what it was
then." He acknowledged that the roads had changed his attitude.[21]

Through the 1950s, the Nugents depended on flying services,
such as Roger Holt's and Dick Folsom's out of Greenville, for much
of their business. A brochure the Nugents printed in the mid-1950s
advertised that the camps were "accessible by air only" and noted,
"Daily airplane deliveries keep us well stocked, with fresh eggs, butter, milk, cream, fruits and the choicest meats." Maine Flying Service pilots such as George Later also stopped by, ran errands, and
did duty in emergencies. When the planes were equipped with skis
for winter travel, Patty and Al saw their ice-fishing business expand
greatly, filling what had been a slow time of year for them. Guests
came from throughout New England and around the country.

Al and Patty also experienced some competition from one of their clients, Harold Whiteneck, a Boston coin dealer. Whiteneck had begun making yearly fishing trips to Nugent's Chamberlain Lake Camps in the 1940s, and he had become attracted to the area's remote, untamed, roadless character, its lack of people, and its abundance of wildlife. He decided that he would like to retire there when the day came. Even though he was only thirty-six at the time, he approached Al in 1950 about selling out to him. Instead, Al, in his amiable fashion, suggested that Whiteneck explore the possibility of leasing the farm and building his own camps there. By that time, George Rear had apparently abandoned his idea of establishing a sporting camp at the farm, and Whiteneck obtained a lease from the owners. In 1951, Whiteneck, with his brother Lloyd as a partner, selected a site on the shore at the eastern end of the farm lot. With Al's help, they began construction in 1952. Materials and equipment, including a jeep, a bulldozer, and a disassembled sawmill, were brought over tote roads to Telos Landing and then rafted or boated to the farm. A large stand of pine near Indian Pond provided logs for the buildings, and the sawmill, powered by the bulldozer's engine, produced dimension lumber from spruce, fir, cedar, and pine.[22]

By 1954, the Whitenecks' camps were operating from May through November as Heart O' Maine Sporting Camps. They included a large central dining hall with kitchen and lounge, three camps for sleeping, two light housekeeping cabins, a woodshed-garage, a machine shop, a gasoline storage shed, and a dug-out ice house. The brothers had their own plane for running errands and transporting guests. In the winter, Harold conducted his coin business in Boston and Lloyd made his home in Greenville, except for two winters when he stayed at the camps and took in ice fishermen. The work of running the camp from spring through fall depended on both of them, so when Lloyd hurt his back while putting their

Building at Heart O' Maine Sporting Camps, Chamberlain Farm, 1950s
Harold and Lloyd Whiteneck constructed this building and several others
in the early 1950s as part of Heart O' Maine Sporting Camps. The
camps were located on the Chamberlain Farm lot, on the lakeshore
east of the farm proper. Hog Point can be seen at far right.
Photograph courtesy of Harold Whiteneck.

plane in the water during the spring of 1960, they decided to sell out
to the Nugents.[23] Gene Letourneau included a small item in his
column: "Al and Patty Nugent have acquired the Chamberlain Farm
camps at the lake of that name. . . . They plan to turn these into
light housekeeping cabins.[24] From that time to the present,
Nugent's has included the Farm Camps.

In the 1960s, Patty and Al saw their business expand in another
way. After Harold Whiteneck sold out to the Nugents, he continued to visit the camps as a client in the winter, on a new machine
that was rapidly catching the fancy of outdoor enthusiasts—the
snowmobile. For Patty and Al, it soon became an indispensable
means of winter travel, and they were quick to capitalize on this new

opportunity to increase their winter business. Soon their brochure included the line "Where you can ride 'Ski-Doo' (the camps' unique new sled) across the ice or over snowy forest trails." Inevitably, they captured the hearts, and the business, of a new clientele. A letter to the editor of *Down East Magazine,* responding to an article about snowmobiling in the Allagash region, took the author to task for leaving out mention of "the congenial, hospitable, and lovable 'Al' and 'Patty' Nugent who own and operate the Chamberlain Lake Camps. To the numerous snowmobilers in the Millinocket area and many other areas the Nugents are what today may be called 'Super Hosts.'"[25] Interviewed in the mid-1970s, Al remarked that on some weekends they had 200 snow sleds at the camps.[26] The opening of more roads also allowed easier winter access for the snowmobilers, and in other seasons the roads made it easier for other outdoor enthusiasts to reach Chamberlain Lake and the camps. The Nugents saw their business grow while the flying services saw theirs diminish. And while this happened, the remote qualities around Chamberlain Lake and Farm began to disappear.

One event in the 1960s would influence the future of the region more than any other Patty and Al and their friends would experience: In 1966, after several years of pressure from the federal government to make the Allagash a national recreational area, and lobbying by citizen conservationists for a state-protected waterway, the state of Maine created the Allagash Wilderness Waterway. Citizens approved a bond issue to purchase a strip of land surrounding the watercourse, measuring 400 to 800 feet wide. More will be said about this later, but briefly, a key provision required that this narrow band of state-owned land, called the restricted zone, be managed for "maximum wilderness character" and buffered by a mile-wide area in which legal provisions and policies would control timber harvesting, roads, and development. Nugent's Chamberlain Lake Camps were located in the restricted zone. It was not unexpected, therefore, when in March 1971, Patty and Al received a letter from the director of the Maine State Park and Recreation Commission:

> As you recall, the Allagash Wilderness Waterway Act requires the State to purchase all land, all private camps and sporting camps within the restricted zone. . . . The purpose of this letter is to inform you that the appraisal . . . has been filed with the Commission . . . indicating that "value of the property (Mrs. Beatrice P. Nugent, T7, R12) consisting of buildings operated as sporting camps with the ordinary furniture and equipment used as part of the operation is $72,500." . . . The legislation of the Waterway Act provides that the Commission may lease back to the present owners or others "on terms and conditions determined by the Commission." I am sure it is the sentiment of the Commission that we hope you folks will stay on and operate the camps at Chamberlain for as long as you desire.[27]

Thus, Patty and Al were ensured the opportunity to live in their camps and continue to enjoy the spectacular sunsets over Allagash Mountain, the beauty of Mt. Katahdin, and their many guests and visitors for the duration of their lives. But the years were beginning to tell, and the physical labor required to keep the business running continued to make demands on them, despite the fact that they had hired help.

They were to have seven more good years together before the worst happened. "It was a Thursday," Patty recalled. "Nuge was hauling wood. . . . After a bit I realized I couldn't hear his tractor anymore. We found him sitting right there in the tractor. It was a massive heart attack. . . . They didn't want me to fly out with the body, . . . but I said, 'I *am* flying with Nuge.'" The newspaper announcement read: "Noble Allen O. Nugent, of Greenville, born at [Caratunk], Jan. 1, 1913, died Feb. 10 [1978] at Chamberlain Lake."[28]

"Al Nugent, dead? Impossible," wrote Bud Leavitt. "Those who knew Nuge over the years will recall him as the powerful gentleman of the outdoors, the man of scholarly curiosities, the man of shy dignity, the friendly man of gentle charm, the man of a thousand talents, the man of his beloved Patty's dreams."[29]

Two weeks after the funeral, Patty Nugent, in keeping with her indomitable spirit, returned home to the woods. She carried on with hired help, despite illness and difficulties in overseeing the operational details. "Aunt Patty is 80 and she received a Happy Birthday card from a fellow septuagenarian, Ranger Ronald [President Ronald Reagan]," noted Bud Leavitt in 1984.[30] In 1986, the *Moosehead Messenger* announced, "Patty Nugent Celebrates Fifty Years at Remote Chamberlain Lake":

> One of Northern Maine's most respected and admired sporting camp operators has celebrated her 50th year in the North Woods. About 300 people came by boat, canoe, airplane, and some even walked to reach Patty Nugent's camps on remote Chamberlain Lake, north of Greenville. People came from as far away as California, plus all parts of Maine and other New England States to pay their respects. In fact it was said the early July celebration was the largest gathering ever held in the virtually uninhabited Chamberlain Lake area.[31]

Ten days later, realizing the limitations age and health had put on her, Patty sent a letter to the director of parks and recreation for the Maine Department of Conservation. He responded: "Thank

Patty Nugent, 1986

In 1986, some three hundred people celebrated Patty Nugent's fiftieth
year at Nugent's Chamberlain Lake Camps. Photograph
courtesy of Gene L. Letourneau.

you very much for your letter of July 14, in which you indicate that
you desire to give up your lease to the camps at Chamberlain. Would
you please call me here, while you are in Millinocket, and we could
better discuss then a date when we can come to Chamberlain."[32]
With difficulty, Patty Nugent parted with the place of her dreams,
still remembering vividly the morning when from a raft she had first
seen her little green knoll.[33] On August 17, 1990, at the age of
eighty-five, the Little Old Girl of the Woods, as she was fondly
known, died at a nursing home in Brewer, Maine.

Patty and Al Nugent touched thousands who were drawn to the
country they loved. One such individual was Dabney Hofammann,
whose father worked with the Nugents during the summers of 1938
and 1939. In 1947, Dabney's parents honeymooned at the camps,
though belatedly because of World War II. In 1961, they introduced

Dabney, their young son, to the Nugents and their camps. So powerful was the impression on the boy that he returned as a young man in the mid-1970s to live with and work for Al and Patty. He came to know them well, learning their feelings for those woods and the changes they had experienced. He also knew them through his parents and thus had a two-generation perspective on their lives. Dabney left the Nugents to pursue a college education. Today, he is a practicing physician who remembers fondly, and with unusual insight, two exceptional people in his life. "The Nugents," he recalled,

> knew that the woods could be their friend, or could kill them. Neither ever lost respect for the environment in which they lived. Conversely, neither were they afraid of their setting. . . . They saw far better than those of us who passed through, that it was possible to live symbiotically with their surroundings. . . . They saw the need for paper, but fussed if the cutting was poorly done and silted a stream. The need for clean water was apparent, but do not tell them that they shouldn't use a motor boat on their lake. They had no tolerance for those who preached care of the woods, but who had not lived in it. If a man was hungry and needed food, an out of season deer was not a crime. Yet, taking game outside of the law simply for sport, was unpardonable. Trapping was making use of the wood's bounty, but leave stock for the future. It was an eminently reasonable creed.[34]

Hofammann continued: "Nuge understood the value of the waterway. He understood that had the state not come in then it well might have been the 'feds.' He realized that the state was a better landlord; the lesser of two evils. He did however express great reservations in the management of the waterway, and the way it implemented its mission. He always felt that this was the Maine Woods, and had not been a wilderness for over 100 years. The attempts of the state to make it a wilderness area were 'foolish.'"[35]

Overall, Hofammann's impression was that "they felt the concept of the Park was good, and that most people associated with it were solid. They were concerned that many rules seemed to come down to the Park from uninformed sources in 'the organized confusion,' as they considered the outside world. This tended to bother Patty more than Nuge. He tended to be more accepting of change than was she. Though Patty never would admit it," Hofammann remembered, "Nuge knew that the camps were transient. He once told me that he had carved the camps 'from the woods, and the woods will take them back.' That statement summed up his philosophy regarding the Allagash, the Park and their lives. I am sure today that he is 'Just Right!'"[36]

The woods, however, would not have a chance to take the camps back, for the year after Patty relinquished her rights to them, John Richardson and Regina Webster, another couple who saw Nugent's Chamberlain Lake Camps as "just right," were awarded a lease by the state. In one of those strange twists that life sometimes produces, these successors of the Nugents had gained their experience on Rainbow Lake, at the same camps where Patty had first worked and where she had met Al.

Both of them Vermonters and well acquainted with the rural nature of northern New England, John and Reggie, as Regina is known to her friends, left well-paying jobs and a home in the 1980s to pursue a dream of living in the woods. Mt. Katahdin and the surrounding region captured them, and when a job opened up at Rainbow Camps, they took it. Convinced that they wanted to run their own sporting camp but discouraged by the formidable obstacles of leasing land and building a camp or even of purchasing one already in operation, they jumped at the chance to bid on the Nugents' camps.[37]

Like their predecessors, these two new managers of the camps have a strong attraction to their spot on Chamberlain Lake and appreciate its openness and feeling of freedom. Reggie once told a reporter: "It's a great place to be. Even when it's harsh, it's exciting." And John says they love the "wicked views of Katahdin."[38] Both know their way in the woods and take great comfort in the remoteness; to this day, no roads provide access to the camps. It does not bother them to travel thirty miles to their mailbox.

True to the sporting camp tradition, they feel strongly about protecting the wildlife resources—obeying the laws, not wasting the kill, conserving for the future. The fact that hunting is an important component of their business does not preclude their developing strong attachments to some of the animals that appear in their camp yard. During their first spring, for example, a doe showed up at the camps nearly starved and with an injured hind foot. Under their care, she survived, and now, many years later, they continue to see her and her offspring around the camps.

In the years since the couple arrived, they have rebuilt the main camps and restored them to their former charm. Down at the Chamberlain Farm lot, they keep some of the old Whiteneck camps in serviceable condition as well as the one remaining building at the site of the farm. Today, visitors can still find a place to stay at the farm, but unlike the days of Manly Hardy and Lucius Hubbard, a different clientele joins those who hunt and fish in discovering the attractions of these lakes and woods. It was not surprising that one July morning sixty-five years after a raft with a cookstove pulled up to the shore of Chamberlain Lake, a group of men and women on a Maine Audubon Society trip boated up the lake from Nugent's Chamberlain Lake Camps to the farm. There, they walked the trail to Indian Pond, not to go fishing but to learn about the area's natural history and enjoy the sights and sounds of the North Woods.

Despite all the changes that have occurred during the history of Nugent's, one thing has not changed among those who come to the camps on this northern lake: their feelings for the place. One need only read the comments in the camp register:

> I finally found what I've been looking for.
>
> It doesn't get any better than this.
>
> A most beautiful piece of "God's Country."
>
> No better place on earth.
>
> This place restores my peace of mind.
>
> It's worth being here—a paradise!
>
> Back to the real values of life.
>
> Lovely wilderness! Will remember this forever!
>
> Thanks for the peacefulness and beauty.

One of the many enduring enticements of these woods and waters has always been the region's wildlife. Here, as elsewhere, there has been a trend in attitudes of those who hunt, fish, and trap and those who simply enjoy watching wild animals toward support for conservation and protective laws. And those such as the Nugents and their guides have always been aware that their livelihood depended on maintaining healthy populations of game species. As we have seen, the protection of fish and game also has been long viewed as a public responsibility; a long history of laws gives evidence of this. Those charged with enforcing the laws were the game wardens, a unique breed of outdoorsmen and women. One such individual, who was recognized for his years of dedicated service, who had a special love for this wild, remote country, and who knew the Nugents, was David Priest Sr.

❖ ❖ ❖

David Priest grew up in Maine's Penobscot County, in an area just west of the big lake country of eastern Maine. He lived most of his first ten years in the small rural town of Enfield, near his birthplace, in Burlington. In those formative years, he developed a consuming interest in the outdoors, and especially trapping. "From [the time I was] a small child I was crazy over hunting, fishing, trapping, and so forth," he recollected in his later years. Dave, as he came to be known, was influenced by both of his grandfathers, one a hunter and trapper who enthralled him with stories of the North Woods, and the other a farmer in nearby Lowell, where Dave visited and spent boyhood days exploring the woods and brooks.[39]

When Dave was ten, his parents moved to Brewer, where he finished grade school and then graduated from Brewer High School in 1930.[40] Interestingly, one of his jobs as a boy was mowing Fannie Hardy Eckstorm's lawn. And one time, as he prowled around the countryside of Brewer, he discovered an old, rusty trap with a tag showing that it belonged to Fannie's father, Manly Hardy. During these years, he started hunting, purchasing his first hunting license at the age of sixteen.[41] He also received a license to guide and, through the help of a cousin who guided for a living, obtained his first job, guiding a dentist on a fishing trip—for which he received a toothbrush as a tip.[42]

Dave continued to visit his grandparents' farm in Lowell, and he once shot a bear while hunting there. He also trapped on some of his visits and got two bobcats during one vacation. In an average year, he would make $200 on bounties and pelts.[43] All this occurred despite the fact that, as he put it in his later years, "My father, especially, was always against my hunting and trapping desires."[44] It was in the field of business that Dave's father saw his son's future.

After completing a program of study at the Maine School of Commerce in 1932, which he attended at his parents' insistence, he went back into the woods rather than into business. As he recalled: "I left home, temporarily at least, and moved into an old house my uncle owned in Burlington . . . and I stayed there alone in the fall and trapped until the hunting season." That winter, Priest spent time at remote Middle Pistol Lake, fourteen miles or so from Burlington and quite a hike across wooded country. His love for the woods was soon tested, however. Priest's father was still determined that his son get a job in business, so when his father received a telephone call from the Maine School of Commerce about a potential employer, he hired a man to walk nine miles at night to Middle Pistol Lake to get his son. Priest interviewed for the job. He was not pleased about it, however, and before his father got home from work, he headed back into the woods, much to his father's displeasure.[45]

From 1933 until the beginning of the 1940s, Priest worked nights for a pulp mill in Brewer. In the daytime, he hunted, fished, and trapped. He also guided out of a sporting camp on Nicatous Lake. Then, in 1941, he applied for a position as game warden, a secure job that would allow him to work outdoors. After taking the state examination and receiving the job, he was assigned to southern Maine. But it was not the kind of country he had envisioned; instead, he found it heavily populated with people and scrub oaks. After two weeks of disillusionment, he quit the job and went back to trapping. Economically, it made good sense to him. After all, a good fox or mink pelt brought an average of $35, whereas a warden's salary was only $21 per week. More than that, trapping was one of the things he liked most to do, and wardens were not allowed to trap, although they could hunt. Two years later, in 1943, Priest's outdoor life came to a temporary end when he entered the armed forces to fight in World War II. Late in the war, he was wounded while serving in Italy, and he spent the remainder of the conflict in a hospital.[46]

"I arrived back home late in November of 1945," Priest remembered,

> and immediately went back to trapping. . . . I
> guided springs and summers of 1946 and '47 out of
> the East Outlet Camps on Moosehead Lake. During the falls and winters I trapped. After the fishing
> season ended in September, I usually trapped bear
> for bounty until the season opened on foxes and
> raccoons and so forth late in October. . . . I had to
> take these bears to a warden to get them certified
> for bounty, and . . . it happened this day I took a
> bear out to get it certified, and the game warden
> asked me why I didn't go to Augusta the next day
> and take the warden's exam.[47]

Priest took the advice and passed the exam. On October 27, 1947, he received his commission as a game warden for District 77, a region of 800 square miles that included Chamberlain Lake. "The country then was just a wonderland for me," he recalled.[48] Here, he could carry out his warden duties in the kind of country he had wanted in his first job—a big, remote, well-wooded region with a taste of wildness. When not on the job, he could hunt bobcats with his dogs. He later said that he sometimes had the feeling he was doing more to protect deer by removing this predator than by catching poachers during the winter.[49]

When Priest entered the warden service, the number of game-law violations, especially night hunting of deer, was at an all-time high, as were violations of fishing without a license. The number of individuals hunting and fishing was steadily increasing. Fish and game had become more economically valuable to the state, and wildlife species that were hunted for sport were becoming increasingly managed. Ten years earlier, Maine had hired its first game

biologist. The number of fish hatcheries had increased, and preserves and sanctuaries had been set aside. The result of these
changes was more laws, more wardens with more enforcement
responsibilities, and more problems. To help the wardens, an annual
warden school had been initiated in 1937, and that same year a warden flying service had begun patrolling remote areas, stocking fish
aerially, and assisting in search and rescue operations. But funda-
mentally, the success of the state's protection of its fish and wildlife
depended on the wardens' "deep sense of devotion to duty and a sin-
cere interest in conservation."[50]

The job of a warden was not without hardship and risk. By the
time Priest assumed his duties, numerous assaults on wardens had
occurred during attempts to apprehend poachers. Some wardens
had even been murdered; others had lost their cabins in arson fires.
Many experienced accidental injuries while on duty in remote and
rugged terrain and in severe weather conditions. One observer suc-
cinctly summed up what it took to carry out that job: "The wardens
have to combine courage and common sense with tact and courtesy."[51]

Priest's work in game protection brought him into the Chamberlain Lake area from time to time. Many years later, when he was
well into his eighties, he remembered a visit to Chamberlain Farm
in the late 1940s: "I do recall some kind of an old boat being pulled
up on the shore of the Chamberlain Farm. But I can't visualize six
hundred acres of land being cleared there. . . . At the time I got up
there in the country, the fields had started to grow up quite a lot.
The opening was, oh, perhaps twenty-five or thirty acres, and there
were some fairly good-sized trees at that time."[52] There was one
inhabited building next to the shore, he said, in which George Rear
and his family lived.[53]

Priest recalled flying into the Nugents' camps one fall to follow
up on word from Patty and Al that they had heard some shooting

one night at Chamberlain Farm. Priest and another warden spent a couple of nights at the farm watching for night hunters. "Unfortunately," he reported, "the nights we were there, there was no activity." On another occasion, he bountied three lynxes for Al, who had trapped them during the winter. Another time, he had the opportunity to fish on Indian Pond with Al. They caught "three nice togue and a beautiful square-tailed trout." He recalled that it was good fishing in those days because no roads went to the pond.[54]

Flying was Priest's primary means of access into the region. Around 1951, the wardens in Priest's division built a log camp at Chamberlain Thoroughfare between Chamberlain and Telos Lakes, having chosen that location because of its easy access by plane under various wind conditions. There were no roads to Chamberlain Thoroughfare at the time, but shortly afterward lumbermen built a road to the site, a bridge, and a set of logging camps.[55] The event was significant, for the road was the first to come this close to Chamberlain Lake, and it would be only a matter of years before people traveled over it in search of the very remoteness it diminished.

During this time, Priest became acquainted with some of the others, besides the Nugents, who resided in the Allagash region and had known the country before the changes that came in the last half of the century. They, like the early guides, had enjoyed a more remote, freer life. One, of course, was Jim Clarkson, who was getting to be an old man when Priest met him. Priest had occasion to stay a few nights in Clarkson's cabin at Lock Dam, and he remembered the cabin as being immaculate.[56] Priest also recalled seeing another elderly man around Chamberlain Lake, Jake McEachern: "He was famous for his ability to use a broad axe in hewing logs and making camps."[57] The story is told that McEachern would lay ten matches on a chopping block and swing his razor-sharp axe to clip the heads, one at a time, just enough to light them. But he always missed one, explaining that he hoped to draw out a little wager from his audience. Another of Priest's acquaintances, a man he regarded as a friend, was Frank Cowan, who ran the portage from Umbazooksus Lake to Mud Pond. And at Allagash Lake there was Jean Dupree, whom he visited occasionally. Dupree was a trapper, and Priest remembered that he used to tell about going to the caves near the lake, where bats hibernated in winter, and collecting clusters of bats from the caves' roofs. He would fill half a burlap bag and use them to bait his bear traps.[58]

David C. Priest Sr. and Percival P. Baxter
Near Mt. Katahdin, circa 1960

As warden supervisor, David Priest Sr. accompanied Governor
Percival P. Baxter on his annual tours of Baxter State Park in the 1950s
and 1960s. During this time, Baxter finished assembling the 200,000-acre
park, which he gave to the people of Maine. Photograph courtesy of the
Maine Folklife Center, University of Maine, Orono.

In 1955, Priest was promoted to the position of warden supervisor and moved with his family to the town of Winn, on the Penobscot River above Lincoln. His jurisdiction covered large areas of four different counties, including Chamberlain Lake, and he supervised ten to fifteen wardens. A duty that Priest assumed in the spring of 1955 was accompanying former governor Percival Baxter on his tours of the park he had given to Maine, Baxter State Park. On his first such trip, he and the governor journeyed to Telos Landing and then boated to Telos Dam, where the dam tender, Clair Desmond, put on a big feed.[59] As we will learn, it was not Baxter's first trip into Allagash country.

Priest and the governor became good friends, and the two made several trips together each year to see the park and visit its campgrounds. Priest recalled that "the governor was very interested in anything outdoors, [and] he was quite a sentimental gentleman, an awfully nice old fellow." He insisted on placing a marker and artificial flowers at the grave site of a river driver who had met a watery death on Nesowadnehunk Stream in the park. "His big delight," Priest recalled, "was in going to the campgrounds and going around from one lean-to to another and talking with the campers and finding out what their interests were."[60] Priest was involved with Baxter State Park in other ways as well, such as assisting in Maine's first caribou reintroduction effort and conducting search and rescue missions.

Through his years of public service, Priest saw the duties of the warden service expand as increasing numbers of people were drawn to the woods for recreational activities, partly in response to growing affluence and leisure time, technological developments, increasing roads, new modes of travel, and the availability of better maps. Private flying services with light planes became more prevalent. Lakes and woods once difficult to gain access to gradually lost their remoteness and their feeling of wildness. Nationally, during the

1950s, a system of interstate and defense highways was established and the use of recreational vehicles grew, and both of these made the wildlands more accessible.[61] Publicity continued to attract increasing numbers of visitors to the North Woods and the Allagash region. Even the final issue of *In the Maine Woods*, published in 1957, made mention of Chamberlain Farm.[62]

Being a game warden became more complicated. Late in the 1950s, with more and more people able to afford boats, the state passed laws to regulate the registration and operation of motorboats, assigning enforcement to the wardens. And with the advent of snowmobiles in the 1960s, wardens were handed the responsibility of enforcing laws pertaining to their registration and operation. In the last quarter of the century, registration of all-terrain vehicles (ATVs) came under the jurisdiction of the Maine Department of Inland Fisheries and Wildlife, and the wardens found themselves dealing with safety, trespass, and other issues regarding their use. With increasing numbers of outdoor enthusiasts, the wardens were faced with a growing number of complaints, incidents involving nuisance wildlife and injured and dead wildlife, search and rescue operations, and drug and safety problems in addition to their traditional duties of enforcing hunting, fishing, and trapping laws. And during this time, they experienced the added pressure of a reduction in the number of field wardens and work hours.[63]

In the midst of these changes, on November 29, 1971, Dave Priest retired after twenty-four years of public service. Two days later, he was back in the Allagash, pursuing one of his great outdoor loves—trapping. Working out of the wardens' camp at Chamberlain Thoroughfare, he trapped beavers as part of a damage control effort to protect roads from inundation with water backed up by the beavers' dams. He also went back to guiding fishing enthusiasts, out of a camp on Munsungun Lake.[64] He hunted, trapped, and guided until the late 1970s, when he developed glaucoma.

Today, Priest still maintains an interest in the environment and conservation. He holds membership in several hunting, trapping, and warden organizations and continues to make his thoughts known to the public and to governmental officials. And even though his eyes have failed him, he can look back on a distinguished career that brought him recognition and honor. For example, his supervision of search and rescue efforts brought an acknowledgment of achievement from former governor Baxter. In the fall of 1963, a woman became lost while returning from a climb to the top of Mt. Katahdin, and a ranger who was attempting to find her also disappeared during a heavy ice and snow storm. Despite the rescuers' best efforts, the two were not found until the next spring, when another search was attempted. On November 19, 1964, Baxter wrote Priest a letter, saying: "You are to be congratulated on your tireless efforts to discover the bodies of Ranger Heath and the woman lost. Because of the courage and perseverance you displayed, I will long remember what you have done and when I see you in person later I shall certainly tell you that the people of the state owe you a debt of appreciation."[65] In 1992, the Maine Warden Service Association also honored Priest, with its Legendary Game Warden award.[66]

Priest is a principled man who is true to himself. Once, an author who was writing a book about Priest asked him how he would like to be known. His response: "I would like to be known as an honest man."[67] His life has been guided by what he believed was right. His strong attachment to the northern woods and lakes and the wild creatures that inhabit them occupied him from the days of his early childhood. Throughout his life, Priest was able to turn this love for the outdoors into a living—first as a trapper and guide and later as a game warden and warden supervisor—not only deriving an economic benefit but also gaining immense satisfaction from nature. He appreciated the beauty of a square-tailed trout, the presence of deer behind his home in Winn, and the wild character of the North

Woods. He once said: "My interest in that north country up there would be that there would be no more camps around the lakes; in other words, the lakes wouldn't be cluttered up with camps and big power boats, and like-a-that. . . . I would like to see it remain as much of a wilderness as it is at present."[68] Regarding the Allagash Wilderness Waterway, he said, "I think the idea of the waterway is a good thing."[69] But he continues to feel strongly that the wildlands in the North Woods should not be closed off to hunting and trapping.[70]

Priest saw it as his duty to protect the wildlife that he loved and was employed to safeguard. He realized that wild things need wild places, and today he worries about the effects of the increased human presence in the North Woods region, including pressure on fish and other wildlife. For instance, there were no ice-fishing shacks on Chamberlain Lake and the other Allagash lakes when he began his warden duties there, but today roads enable many people to fish during the winter.[71] He is disturbed by the introduction of exotic species of fish into the northern lakes, such as white perch and bass in Moosehead Lake. He argues forcefully for policies to protect the region's wildlife and believes it would be a "terrible mistake" to bring wolves back into the state. He considers the wolf a killer animal that would reduce the deer population and be detrimental to the moose herd, which has taken many years to be restored to a healthy population.[72]

Guiding was one of Priest's first jobs, and it was one of his last. In it, his avocation became his vocation. He enjoyed sharing his feelings about and knowledge of the outdoors with others and, by example, promoting the kind of use that would protect the natural environment he loved. As a group, those who obtain a livelihood from guiding today are among the citizens most sensitive to the loss of wilderness values. And many of them have become advocates for protection of these values in the Allagash.

Through the years, Chamberlain Farm saw many guided parties pass by, and occasionally a few would stop there. Individuals such as John Way Jr., Lucius Hubbard, and Thomas Sedgwick Steele all came with guides in search of wilderness adventure and hunting and fishing experiences in the old tradition. In the days before roads, vehicles, airplanes, camps, rangers, wardens, radios, cellular phones, and global positioning systems, people faced greater risk in going into the backcountry, so far from help in case of illness, accident, or becoming lost. Before guidebooks and accurate maps were published, adventurers encountered an unknown environment of vast and disorienting woods, dangerous rapids and falls, obscure trails and landmarks, and all manner of hazards and obstacles. For these reasons, they needed guides who knew the routes and were skilled in water travel, camp making, outdoor living, and hunting and fishing. From the late 1800s through the 1900s, the Allagash region saw extraordinary growth in the number of people seeking guide services. Historian Richard Judd reported that "as early as 1919 some 5,000 canoeists yearly made the portage across North East Carry . . . gateway to the Penobscot and Allagash headwaters."[73]

Many of the earliest guides were indigenous people of the Penobscot, Passamaquoddy, Maliseet, Micmac, and St. Francis tribes. Henry David Thoreau hired Joe Aitteon, a twenty-four-year-old Penobscot Indian, for his 1853 trip into the Maine woods and down the West Branch of the Penobscot River. Aitteon had previously guided moose hunters in the area. In 1857, Thoreau again hired a Penobscot Indian, Joe Polis, as a guide. Thoreau was especially interested in the indigenous people and wrote that in the case of Aitteon, he had "employed an Indian mainly to study his ways."[74] Fannie Hardy, on the trip with her father into the Allagash and down the East Branch, saw several Indian guides. Lucius Hubbard employed two native guides for his 1881 trip: One was a Maliseet Indian called Joe, whom Hubbard described as a very intelligent man of "great self-reliance" and "very well informed about the Northern Maine woods." The other was a member of the St. Francis tribe named Silas Wzokhilain, a hunter, trapper, and log driver who had distinguished himself in the Civil War.[75]

One of Maine's distinctive Indian guides was Chief Henry Red Eagle, born Henry Perley of Maliseet parents in Greenville on February 15, 1885. Laurence Lougee, a New York lawyer and a friend of Red Eagle, canoed Maine's North Woods with him for twelve years, beginning in the 1930s. He wrote that Red Eagle "was one of the best of a now almost vanished breed of outdoorsman. . . . His fellow guides would tell you few men could equal the Chief in handling a canoe with either paddle or pole."[76] But Red Eagle's work as a guide reflected only a small part of his talents: he was also a writer, storyteller, Wild West musician, lecturer, circus performer, vaudeville artist, actor, river driver, and counselor at boys' and girls' camps.[77]

In one of his many written works, "The Thunderous Wondrous Allagash," published in the 1952 edition of *In the Maine Woods*, Red Eagle drew on his guiding experience to describe the entire Allagash region, including Chamberlain Lake. Of the Maine guide, he wrote, "His canoemanship, his ability at woodcraft, and his experience, his knowledge of the country, the location of the best camp grounds, close to clean cool springs, of fishing pools and woods trails, etc., his companionship and advice may mean the difference between making the sojourn a pleasurable interlude or one which may be clothed with unhappy memory."[78]

The qualifications outlined by Red Eagle have been demonstrated by hundreds of talented guides over the past two centuries. Thomas Sedgwick Steele, who employed three guides for his 1879 trip, had good words to say about all three but singled out a fault in one of them, who he said "could scent a 'carry' three days ahead, and remember its hardships and burdens two days after."[79]

The Greenville area produced many guides. One was William D. Marsh, who guided during the 1920s and 1930s. Marsh loved the woods, recalled his daughter, Etta Hubbard. "The woods, hunting, fishing, berry picking were essential elements of a quality life for my father," she wrote. "The Allagash trip was a popular canoe trip . . . he guided trips there because that was the request of the sports." Chamberlain Farm was one of the places Marsh mentioned.[80]

Another guide, a contemporary of Marsh, was mountain man Walter Arnold, who was also a trapper, logger, hunter, fisherman, entrepreneur, and writer. "I was a guide to fishermen for 40 years," he related in an interview in 1972, when he was seventy-eight.[81] His diaries recorded most, if not all, of those forty years, including his guiding trips past Chamberlain Farm and down the Allagash River. In 1926, he made the following entry:

> Aug. 24. left Chesuncook at 7 oclock by steam boat. Went up to mouth of Amezusus [Umbazooksus] Stream. Put in canoe. . . . We paddled to Amezusus Lake. Got Team to Haul us to Mud pond. We had to make carry of about $^1/_2$ mile to Dead Water of Mud pond Brook—came down about 2 miles on Chamberlain lake. Made camp for night. Went fishing before dark caught 1 trout.[82]

Arnold was an ardent trapper and a prolific writer. He wrote and published six books on trapping and the preparation of scents as well as numerous articles on hunting, trapping, and other outdoor subjects. During the last twenty-one years of his life, from 1959 to 1980, he lived alone in a two-room log cabin thirteen miles into the woods on Indian Pond, about twenty miles west of Greenville (not

Walter L. Arnold

Walter Arnold, shown here in 1952 trapping beavers, was one of many Allagash guides who passed by Chamberlain Farm. He wrote prolifically about his hunting, trapping, fishing, and outdoor adventures. His diaries document several of his Allagash trips, and his articles describe his appreciation for the region's wildlife and the pleasures and thrills it offered. Photograph courtesy of Walter Lewellen Arnold Papers, Special Collections Department, Raymond H. Fogler Library, University of Maine, Orono.

the Indian Pond behind Chamberlain Farm). There, he wrote and trapped and fed his pet deer, Susie.

In 1971, he wrote an article titled "Allagash Waters" in which he summed up what an Allagash guide values about that region and life in the woods. He described the adventure of canoeing, the pleasures of camp life, and the attractions for those who came for the wildlife:

> Battling mountainous waves that go roaring across wind-swept lakes; Fighting foot by foot thru dangerous, swirling waters of rock infested rapids; Drifting quietly along beautiful avenues of deadwater, where nature is so enchanting in her peaceful moods; Partaking of tasty viands skillfully prepared by expert hands over glowing coals of the camp fire; Enjoying the many delights of camping in the open

spaces; The aroma of coffee and bacon arising from
pot and pan; The scent of the fragrant balsam
boughs in the bed; Stalking deer, bear, fox and other
wild life for shots with Kodak; Matching wits with
the wary trout that will furnish thrills aplenty with
his dashing and daring antics.

He concluded, "These and many more are the pleasures and thrills
experienced as one goes drifting along in contentment, over the
waters of that health restoring and picturesque Allagash."[83]

Another special kind of guide saw in the values described by
Arnold an opportunity to enrich the lives of young people. One was
Herbert Cochrane, who on a summer day in 1941 saw Chamberlain
Lake for the first time. From the mouth of Mud Brook, he gauged
the safety of its choppy surface as many had done before. Behind
him, the chatter of young voices filled the otherwise quiet cove.
With the carry behind them, the boys in his group knew they had
entered Allagash waters—a mark of accomplishment. In the distance on the far shore, Cochrane could see the opening of Chamberlain Farm, but he had no intention of crossing the lake at this
point, with the wind picking up. Someday, perhaps, when the wind
was right, he would take a party to visit the farm.

Cochrane was a man who felt he was a part of nature, who cared
about these wildlands he passed through, who loved the woods. He
was thirty-four the year of that Allagash trip, and a long way from
the city environment he had experienced during the first years of his
life. Fortunately for those whose lives he would touch, before
Cochrane was ten his family moved to the country, and that environment shaped his love for the outdoors. Later, as an undergradu-
ate at Springfield College in Massachusetts, he learned the rudi-
ments of canoeing. Following graduation, he pursued a career as a
physical education teacher, athletic director, and coach for private

Herbert Cochrane
Beginning in the early 1940s, Herbert Cochrane guided groups from summer boys' camps through the Allagash. He saw in this wild, remote area an opportunity to provide experiences that would instill in the boys a love for the outdoors and a sense of self-confidence and responsibility, helping them develop both physically and socially. Photograph courtesy of Warren Cochrane.

schools. His feelings for the outdoors and canoeing, combined with his devotion to teaching young people and helping them develop mentally and physically, led him to work during summers at boys' camps, first on Long Island Sound and later, in the 1940s, in Maine. In those years, he perfected his canoeing and outdoor skills.[84]

Writer Faye O'Leary Hafford, in her book *Waterway Wanderings: A Story of the People in the Allagash Wilderness Waterway*, described a three-week canoe trip Cochrane began running in 1950 for older boys attending Kewaydin Camp in Vermont. It would start in Jackman, in western Maine, and end at Portage Lake, in northern Maine—a trip of well more than 200 miles that passed through portions of several major watersheds and past Chamberlain Farm. "In 1953," she wrote, "when some boys asked to do an all-summer trip, Herb . . . began a six-week trip from Greenville, with side trips along the way."[85] By this time, Cochrane's son, Warren, had joined him in guiding trips.

When interviewed at the age of ninety-one, Herbert Cochrane still expressed in his eyes and voice his great love for the woods and lakes of northern Maine. The Allagash was in his blood. "I just wanted to share that place," he said. And this he did enthusiastically, for he was dedicated to instilling in youth a love for the outdoors, self-confidence, responsibility, and social skills. He saw his young campers grow physically, learn skills in paddling and outdoor living, and, especially, gain experiences they would never forget. His trips, for example, would take them through "tougher and tougher" rapids. After they had successfully negotiated a set, he would have them look back to see what they had paddled through and then point out their accomplishment, telling them, "You amaze me." He "marveled at how most of them learned." As a trip progressed and after he had decided the campers were ready, he would move them one by one into the lead canoe position. "I gave them every chance to have responsibility and to use their head," he said. He also taught them camp woodcraft and how to care for their campsites and properly dispose of waste. He saw his task as much like coaching.[86]

Through his business, Allagash Canoe Trips, Cochrane made the acquaintance of Frank Cowan at Mud Pond Carry, who assisted in carrying the canoes. At Lock Dam he met Jim Clarkson, who he remembered as a "mighty fine old timer who never talked much but always welcomed them [members of Cochrane's parties]." He invited Clarkson to every meal, and the dam tender once gave him a setting pole, a device used for poling canoes upstream, negotiating rapids, and carrying out other maneuvers. Clarkson, he recalled, had eight pet deer and had given each a name. On one of these Allagash trips, lake conditions allowed Cochrane and his son to take a group close to Chamberlain Farm to view the wreckage of the boom towboats.[87]

In the late 1950s, Jim Clarkson retired from his job at Lock

Dam and was replaced by a couple who became well known in the Allagash:

> Dorothy Boone Kidney, who spent 29 years (excluding winters) with her husband Milford, tending Lock Dam on Chamberlain Lake for the Bangor Hydro-Electric Company and registering canoeists for the Bureau of Parks and Recreation, was well acquainted with Herb Cochrane and his son Warren, who operated the Allagash Canoe Trips. It was one of the first of the many organized boys' trips to arrive in the spring.
>
> As she writes in her book *Away from It All,* Herb Cochrane *looked* the part of a director of a boys' canoe trip. He was sturdily built, deeply tanned from constant exposure to sun and rain.
>
> Planes, Dorothy reported, flew in crates of food before their arrival. After their arrival, Herb borrowed their sturdy, iron wheelbarrow to transport equipment and supplies from shore to campsite.
>
> A lot of Herb's campers were city boys who were afraid of animals in the wilderness. One boy, Dorothy reported, selected for his tent site a spot close to the foundation of their cabin making it impossible to use the front door! He slept directly under Milford's open window, just three feet away from Milford's bed!
>
> In her book, Dorothy writes about other observations of the boys in the Allagash Canoe Trip, for example, of a boy who borrowed her accordion for a few days and played sounds of wind, train whistles, and waterfalls. She wrote about their curiosity

bringing them into the cabin to ask questions about the fishing and hunting gear on the wall, the lack of electricity and about fishing.

At last, Dorothy says, one by one the canoes were pushed off from the bank of the stream to continue their one-hundred-fifty mile water trek to St. Francis.[88]

Faye Hafford wrote that "in 1961, Herb bought a camp on Sugar Island in Moosehead Lake [and] expanded his Allagash trips."[89] But changes were in progress in the waterway: Both federal and state officials were considering it for a recreational area, and roads were already encroaching. After establishment of the Allagash Wilderness Waterway and improvements in the roads, more people came to the area. Cochrane remembered this time sadly, calling the changes bad. "I could no longer advertise in the *New York Times* Allagash canoe trips in the wilds of Maine," he said. "It just ruined the place, and I ended up shortening the trips." As Warren observed, "limited access was key to that experience."[90]

Hafford wrote: "In the late 70's after making some custom trips, Herb retired . . . but he left a legacy to the Allagash Wilderness Waterway. His son Warren and grandsons Chip, Tris, and Bucky have stepped into Herb's shoes [Tris and Bucky no longer guide]. . . . Warren said of his father, 'Herb was an inspiring leader for young men.'"[91]

Herbert Cochrane was not the first guide to pass through Chamberlain Farm with youth groups. Wesley Herrick Sr. and his brother, Foster, started their boys' camp, Camp Wanderlust, in 1930. Wes and Foss, as they were called, led what were probably the largest groups. They would stay out for seven weeks, traveling north from Moosehead Lake to Fort Kent. Wes Herrick, in the words of his daughter, Priscilla, "had a keen sense of what teen boys needed.

He'd lost his own father when he was in his early teens. He knew a lot about cooking, first aid, and most particular the great outdoors. . . . He was a dreamer, a lover of nature, very artistic [he painted several Allagash scenes in oils], funny, charming, great story teller, musician who played many instruments but specialized with the banjo & trumpet. He was good at sports—particularly baseball. . . . One thing about my Dad," she continued, was that "he was very polite and kind. He loved animals. . . . Once a skunk got his head caught in a glass jar and allowed my father to help it get free without spraying."[92]

The Herricks' camp advertised: "Each boy is taught all phases of camping and woodcraft. By actual participation and daily practice he becomes skillful in making and breaking camp, handling his canoe and in general more self reliant and capable. He is encouraged to develop his own individuality and character . . . special attention is given to fishing and wild-game photography."[93]

Faye Hafford, who was at the time on the staff of the Allagash

Wesley Herrick Sr.
at Camp Wanderlust

Wesley (Wes) Herrick Sr., with his brother, Foster, founded Camp Wanderlust for boys in 1930. Like Herbert Cochrane, Wes saw the value of canoeing, camping, and woodcraft in young people's development. For most of his thirty or more years of canoe tripping, Herrick included Chamberlain Lake on his route through the North Woods. Photograph courtesy of Priscilla H. Bartlett.

Wilderness Waterway, wrote that the Camp Wanderlust groups were well organized. A ranger once observed Wes directing the boys to leave some campsite space for other travelers. "Wes often invited others to eat with his group," Hafford wrote. "He watched his boys, and kept them busy . . . and often entertained the boys by drawing and whittling."[94]

When the waterway was established, Herrick had a reaction similar to Herb Cochrane's. His daughter described it: "Before Dad retired he was very upset with the fact that this beautiful wilderness was taken over by the . . . government. It really angered him to see what the 'public' was doing to the 'Wanderlust trail' & all the camp sites that he & Foster had made."[95]

Without question, the waterway brought increasing regulations, created more public interest, and brought changes that affected the freedom of those using it. Hafford observed: "When the Allagash Wilderness Waterway became a reality, and more and more people started to come to the area, it seemed impractical to make summerlong trips. Interest in the long trips began to wane."[96] Guides such as the Cochranes, however, adjusted. Warren Cochrane, who took over his father's business, advertised in his brochure: "Although the Allagash Wilderness Waterway has more visitors now that it is a park, it is still the best summer canoeing area in the United States." In the 1970s, he and his sons began conducting shorter trips for teenage boys and girls and taking more parties of adults.[97] Today, Warren and his wife, Linda Koski, continue the Allagash Canoe Trips tradition.

In the late 1980s, another longtime Allagash guide, Gil Gilpatrick, put in a party at Chamberlain Lake for a trip. On the group's second day out, they stopped to visit "the remains of Chamberlain Farm." Later, an account of the trip was published by one member of the group, Mike Kimball. His lead: "Eight days paddling and camping on this legendary North Woods waterway is a wonderful way to put the rest of the world in perspective."[98] The guides, of course, had discovered this long ago, and today many of them express a view of nature and their relationship with it that reflects a deep and thoughtful understanding. They recognize that they are a part of nature, that it should be valued for its integrity and diversity, and that all of us must place limits on some of our actions for its future health.

Near the end of his book *Allagash: The Story of Maine's Legendary Wilderness Waterway,* Gilpatrick wrote:

> Man is part of the environment as much as any other animal and has been part of the Allagash environment for thousands of years. He has made mistakes, for sure, but his most ambitious projects are temporary and minute compared to what nature can do in one fell-swoop, and do for good![99]

Such a faith in the restorative powers of nature and perception of the place of humans in the natural world were a source of hope for those working to protect the Allagash region in the last half of the twentieth century.

PART IV

Restricted Zone

Oneness with Nature

IN MID-DECEMBER 1998, I made arrangements through Warren Cochrane and his wife, Linda Koski, to interview Warren's father, Herbert Cochrane. I remember cresting the hill overlooking Greenville, Maine, where they live, and seeing the spectacular vista of snow-covered Moosehead Lake, the historic starting point of so many North Woods adventures. Below me, the small town on the lake's shore was nestled against the hill. I met Warren at his home, and he took me across town to the nursing home where his father resided.

I looked forward to meeting the ninety-one-year-old former guide, who the previous fall had communicated with the Maine Bureau of Parks and Lands in response to a call for public comment on a management plan for the Allagash Wilderness Waterway. In his letter, he said that in his youth the woods, streams, and ponds of his northern Massachusetts home had been to him "God's Country," but now "it was spoiled by people cutting and developing the woods." He wrote that when he had first come to Maine for a canoe trip, he had felt "that this was really God's Country" and should not be misused. He concluded his letter as follows: "I'm confined to a nursing home now. I can't walk or move well. Although I would love to canoe the Allagash again, not being able to visit it because it is still isolated and takes effort to get to, is much better. If I could drive there and motor to any campsite, it wouldn't be worth visiting. I would like to know God's Country will be there for my great-grand-children much as it was for me, my son, and my grandsons who have all run trips on the Allagash."[1]

These words of Herbert Cochrane came to life for me when I met with him. He took me back to the Allagash region of the 1940s and carried me through the years with an enthusiasm that showed a deep, enduring love for that country and his guiding days. He recounted his experiences with wide-ranging emotion, laughing at humorous incidents he remembered, expressing the enjoyment and satisfaction he had received from watching the young people he guided grow and mature, conveying the disheartenment he now felt over the loss of the region's remoteness as roads pushed in, and revealing the sadness that swept over him when he saw his son leave on the canoe trips he was no longer able to take. But throughout my visit, one thing came through clearly: He still cared about the future of the Allagash. And like others who held similar values, he was concerned about what he perceived as increasing threats to its wilderness character.

Forty years before Cochrane made his plea to protect the sanctity of the land and waters he loved, others had raised their voices for its preservation. Because of their efforts, Maine acted to protect the waters of the Allagash from many of the intrusions and alterations America's lakes and rivers have increasingly experienced. At the core of the legislation passed by the people of Maine lies the restricted zone—a strip of land an average of 500 feet wide and 250 miles long surrounding the ponds, lakes, streams, and river that make up the nearly 100-mile-long Allagash Wilderness Waterway. Here, the law is explicit: The land and waters of the restricted zone must be managed for "maximum wilderness character." Beyond the zone, to a mile from the shores of these waters, this narrow band of land is further buffered by policies and management actions. As mentioned earlier, within the restricted zone sits Chamberlain Farm, once again influenced by humanity's changing views—but this time by a perspective that faintly echoes the view of the people indigenous to this land, who were there before the surveyors came: a view in which people saw themselves in unity with the other elements of the natural world.

After settlement of the north country, those who held aspects of this view began showing up sporadically in the Chamberlain Lake area. Through the years, their numbers grew and they came with increasing regularity, especially when the region became more widely known for its uniqueness as a wilderness waterway. One of the earliest to arrive at the farm—a man who anticipated this perspective of biocentric consciousness and expressed some of its themes in the nineteenth century—was Henry David Thoreau.[2]

Chapter 7

The Spell of the Wild

ON JULY 12, 1857, E. S. Coe had visitors in his office at 116 Hammond Street in Bangor, Maine. One was an acquaintance in the lumber trade, George A. Thatcher, who introduced Coe to his wife's cousin, Mr. Henry Thoreau of Concord, Massachusetts. The stranger was on the slender side, with brown hair and grayish-blue eyes, and was somewhat weathered looking, presenting an appearance that belied his capability of physically "enduring far more than the ordinary class of men."[1] To some, he could have appeared homely, but in "an honest and agreeable fashion."[2] Coe might have judged the man to be about his own age, and in fact Thoreau was nearly so, being three years younger. Interestingly, he had turned forty that very day.

The men talked about the country Thoreau was preparing to visit, a country Coe knew well—the Allagash region and the East and West Branches of the Penobscot River. Coe spoke about Chamberlain Farm, which he managed, calling it "our farm" in acknowledgment of his part ownership. The woods-wise proprietor

Henry David Thoreau, 1856
This daguerreotype was made by
Benjamin D. Maxham the year
before Henry David Thoreau came to
Allagash country. Thoreau brought a
much different perspective from that
held by the people he met at Chamberlain Farm. His visit to the farm anticipated a view of nature that has come to
be called ecocentric or biocentric.
Reprinted by permission, courtesy of
The Thoreau Society, Lincoln, Mass.

and land agent advised Thoreau's party to travel as lightly as possible and quickly scribbled a list of essentials: axe, canoe, blankets, frying pan, teakettle, dippers, tea, salt, hard bread and pork, pepper,
matches, ammunition, lines, hooks, and camphor.[3]

Coe and Thoreau were similar in several ways. Both were strong
outdoorsmen who loved the woods. They were capable of focusing
their energies on their interests, interpreting the many details they
saw, drawing conclusions, and keeping voluminous records of information about their activities and observations. And they shared one
common interest as a vocation: Both were surveyors and held the
title of civil engineer. This fact, however, belied some of their very
different outlooks toward the land.

For the successful, pleasant, and courteous businessman Thoreau
sat across from that day, surveying was a necessary step in the business of harvesting the forest, a skill that was fundamental to realizing his aspirations. To this end Coe had oriented his life: determin-
ing the locations and sizes of land parcels he wanted to purchase and

buying them at a price that would allow him to market the timber at a profit. For him, the forest was a commodity, and in its renewal there would be another crop of money.

Like Coe, Thoreau found that surveying took him into the outdoors and the woods he loved. But there was a sense of irony surrounding Thoreau's occupation as a surveyor. Although he practiced surveying as a means of making money, he also did so to provide himself time to pursue his other interests, especially his studies of nature, from which he drew inspiration and the grist for the intellectual explorations that fueled his writing and lecturing. Yet there were times when his employment in lotting the land was for the express purpose of selling it and cutting its trees, and this was something about which Thoreau, like Coe, had definite thoughts. Coe, facing a vast forested landscape, saw the challenge as getting the wood out, but Thoreau, who had tramped the heavily used landscape of Concord, saw a need to develop ideas about the sound management of woodlots.

It is likely that through the conversation, Coe learned about previous trips Thoreau and Thatcher had taken into the Maine woods and about Thoreau's desire to see a primitive uncut forest. But it is unlikely that he knew how strongly Thoreau felt about the values he placed on the North Woods he came to visit—the opportunities to observe and study nature in a landscape far more wild than Concord's and to appreciate its aesthetic and spiritual qualities. And though Thoreau did not reject civilization and viewed people as part of the natural world, he nevertheless could be disturbed by activities he saw as abusive to the land and as a threat to these values.[4]

Coe, therefore, would not have predicted that Thoreau, after seeing the damming and cutting of the Allagash region, would give his opinion in such terms: "The wilderness experiences a sudden rise of all her streams and lakes, she feels ten thousand vermin gnawing at the base of her noblest trees, many combining, drag them off, jarring over the roots of the survivors, and tumble them into the nearest stream, till the fairest having fallen, they scamper off to ransack some new wilderness, and all is still again."[5]

Nor would Coe have imagined the topic and tone of a piece Thoreau would write the following year about his 1853 trip to Chesuncook. In that article, published in the *Atlantic Monthly*, Thoreau commented that most people who come to the woods see the pine trees only as boards for the market: "The pine is no more lumber than man is, and to be made into boards and houses is no more its true and highest use than the truest use of a man is to be cut down and made into manure. There is a higher law," he proclaimed, "affecting our relation to pines as well as to men. . . . Every creature is better alive than dead, men and moose and pine-trees, and he who understands it aright will rather preserve its life than destroy it. . . . It is the living spirit of the tree . . . with which I sympathize. . . . It is as immortal as I am, and perchance will go to as high a heaven, there to tower over me still." This last sentence was dropped from the proof sent to Thoreau, and he responded with a blistering letter to James Russell Lowell, editor of the *Atlantic*, demonstrating how strongly he felt about his opinions and their faithful publication.[6]

Sitting in an office surrounded by the bustle of Maine's busiest city engaged in fulfilling its reputation as the lumber capital of the world, Coe probably was unaware that his friend's cousin had already taken messages to the lectern challenging his views of the North Woods as well as those of the game hunters and the scientific surveyors. Thoreau's statements spoke of a need for wildness, statements that he delivered as a lecture in 1851 and that would be published in 1862, shortly after his death, in an essay titled "Walking." In it, he would say: "Give me a wildness whose glance no civilization can endure." But perhaps even more radical to the ears of Coe would have been his statement "In Wildness is the preservation of the World."[7] One can safely say, however, that neither Coe nor Thoreau could have suspected that this last statement would become a rallying cry for wilderness advocates and would be heard across the world throughout the twentieth century and into the next millennium.

In contrast to Coe, Thoreau advocated for a simpler life, one in which material wealth and power would not consume his time and ambitions. He often spent a good portion of his day searching for a more intimate relationship with nature. Although he admitted that it was an extreme statement, he once spoke of "man as an inhabitant, or part and parcel of Nature, rather than a member of society."[8] And in a passage from *Walden:* "I was suddenly sensible of such sweet and beneficent society in Nature. . . . Every little pine needle expanded and swelled with sympathy and befriended me. I was so distinctly made aware of the presence of something kindred to me."[9]

The trip that brought Thoreau to Coe's office had begun to take shape earlier in the month with a letter to Thatcher: "Finding myself somewhat stronger than for 2 or 3 years past, I am bent on making a leisurely & economical excursion into your woods—say in a canoe, with two companions, through Moosehead to the Allagash Lakes, and possibly down the river to the French settlements, & so homeward by whatever course we may prefer." Thoreau invited Thatcher's son, Charles, to come along and indicated that he had two other men in mind, one of them possibly an Indian.[10]

Wilderness so fascinated the Concord writer that the Maine woods drew him back for this third time. His first excursion, in 1846 to Mt. Katahdin, had brought him face to face with a wild, desolate, mysterious world in which he confronted his essential being in relation to nature.[11] Five years later, he had stood behind a lectern to make his famous statements on the need for wildness. And in 1853, he had returned for a short trip down the West Branch to Chesuncook Lake with Thatcher and Joe Aitteon, their Penobscot Indian guide. Now, in 1857, he again embarked on a trip to the Maine woods, desiring to go not only deeper into the wildland but also deeper into himself. Here, immersed in a wilderness, he could experience the raw, powerful forces with which humans must contend physically and emotionally to survive. He could remove the civilizing buffers of Concord that worked against his obtaining a clearer view of a more direct human relationship with nature. He could find what is essential in life. That he found, for he came away renewed and all the more convinced of his views. When he got home, he wrote to his friend H. G. O. Blake:

> I flatter myself that the world appears in some respects a little larger, and not, as usual, smaller and shallower, for having extended my range. . . . It is a great satisfaction to find that your oldest convictions are permanent. . . . Ktaadn is there still, but much more surely my old conviction is there, resting more than mountain breadth and weight on the world. . . . As the mountains still stand on the plain, and far more unchangeable and permanent,—stand still grouped around, farther or nearer to my maturer eye, the ideas which I have entertained.[12]

Thoreau held a deep and lifelong interest in indigenous peoples and especially in their relationship to the land. Sometime during his Walden Pond experiment, around the time of his Katahdin trip, he began compiling notes on his readings of native peoples. Eventually, he accumulated twelve "Indian Books," as yet unpublished.[13] He had taken Joe Aitteon on his Chesuncook trip and decided to hire another Penobscot Indian guide for this trip to the Allagash. And so, on the morning of the day Thoreau visited with Coe, Thatcher took his cousin in his wagon to Indian Island, in nearby Old Town.

There they met forty-eight-year-old Joe Polis, whom Thatcher had known for many years. "He was stoutly built," Thoreau wrote, "perhaps a little above the middle height, with a broad face." Polis was known as "particularly steady and trustworthy," could read and write, owned land, and had once represented his tribe in the state capitol and in Washington.[14] Fannie Hardy Eckstorm and her father, Manly Hardy, knew him. "He was a very mysterious man, full of quiet drollery, [and he was] . . . fond of argument and enjoyed talking," Fannie observed. "Joe took a newspaper, had a bank account in Oldtown, and lived in the best and largest house on the island." He was a "keen business man," and because he "knew that the canoe in which he took Thoreau had been written about he kept it for years, hoping to sell it at a high price."[15]

Polis did not disappoint Thoreau. The two men exchanged banter throughout the trip, covering all manner of subjects—history, woodcraft, Indian customs, canoe making, hunting, fishing, telling of direction, and natural history. In a letter Thoreau wrote ten days after his return to Concord, he related: "I . . . think I have had a quite profitable journey, chiefly from associating with an intelligent Indian. . . . I have made a short excursion into the new world which the Indian dwells in, or is. He begins where we leave off. . . . The Indian, who can find his way so wonderfully in the woods, possesses so much intelligence which the white man does not,—and it increases my own capacity, as well as faith, to observe it.[16]

Thoreau's other companion was his friend Edward Hoar, a Concord lawyer who, like Thoreau, had been educated at Harvard University. Hoar was thirty-four at the time and had just returned from an eight-year stay in California. He was an enthusiastic botanist, and he and Thoreau botanized throughout the trip. Thoreau had planned to visit Katahdin at the end of the trip and study plants there, but Hoar was unable to do so because of an unfortunate incident. The two became lost on Mud Pond Carry and had to carry their heavy packs for five miles through rough, wet terrain and over and under blowdowns; according to one source, the ordeal left Hoar's feet in bad condition.[17]

The trip came during a period in Thoreau's life when his study of nature had taken an ecological turn and his observations increasingly included the patterns of interrelationship among plants and animals and their environment. "I have no time to go into details," he wrote in his manuscript *The Dispersion of Seeds*, "but will say, in a word, that while the wind is conveying the seeds of pines into hardwoods and open lands, the squirrels and other animals are conveying the seeds of oaks and walnuts into the pine woods, and thus a rotation of crops is kept up."[18] His unending curiosity, acute sensory awareness, and interpretive and poetic abilities would lead him to leave a broad, complex, and detailed record of his experiences on this excursion. He would record the sounds of birds, make lists of plants, describe a slick of melted pork on the water's surface, investigate glowing wood, observe the attraction of fish to the washing of dishes in a lake, comment on the range of devil's-needles, and examine Kineo "flint."

Early on the morning after Thoreau's visit with Coe and his busy day of preparation, he, Hoar, and Polis left on the stage for Greenville. One passenger who impressed him was Hiram Leonard, the hunter who would accompany Manly Hardy down the Allagash River to the Tobique River the following year. The next day, they launched Polis' birch-bark canoe and commenced an eleven-day trip that would take them across Moosehead Lake, down the West Branch of the Penobscot River to Chesuncook Lake, across Mud Pond Carry, into Allagash waters, down the East Branch of the Penobscot, and on the main river to Bangor.

After three days of paddling, they reached Mud Pond Carry. There, Thoreau and Hoar took a wrong turn and got lost, but the three reunited on the shore of Chamberlain Lake. Thoreau reported that they "could see the clearing called the 'Chamberlain Farm' with 2 or 3 log houses on the opposite shore—some 2 1/2 miles distant. The smoke of our fire on the shore brought over 2 men in a canoe from the Farm—that being the signal agreed on when one wishes to cross."[19]

The next day, the party proceeded north across Chamberlain Lake and into Eagle Lake as far as Pillsbury Island. There, Polis proposed going down the Allagash and through the more settled valley of the St. John River. The route Thoreau had planned to follow, however, was down the East Branch to Bangor. They took this latter route, as Thoreau later explained in a letter to Thomas Higginson, "not only because it was shorter, but because . . . it was wilder."[20]

After enduring a fierce thunderstorm on the island, they paddled back to Chamberlain and down the lake's northern shore, enduring rough water, and "landed on a point at the Chamberlain Farm." Thoreau related: "While my companions were pitching the camp I ran up to the house to get some sugar—our 6 pounds being gone. They were unwilling to spare more than 4 lbs.—since they only kept a little for such cases as this—& charged 20 cts. a pound for it—which I thought it was worth to get it up there. They unlocked a store house for it." He recorded that at the house,

> there were several men standing about the door there evidently ready to hear more news than I brought. When I got back it was dark—but we had a rousing fire to warm & dry us & for light—and while another shower was beginning I groped about cutting spruce & arbor vitae twigs for our bed. I Preferred the arbor vitae on ac. of its fragrance. The Indian went up to the house to inquire after a brother who had been absent a long time. The twigs

were very wet—but the heat of the fire reflected from the tent on to them dried them very quick. It rained soakingly in the night—but we slept soundly—& *these* were the best nights we had since the rain kept down the mosquitoes &c.—& lulled us asleep.[21]

When they awoke the next morning, "the fire was put out & the Indian's boots which stood under the eaves of the tent were half full of water."[22]

They left early the next morning to avoid being revisited by the wind and waves of the previous day. After crossing Chamberlain Lake, they continued for another six days before arriving in Bangor. The journey was not uneventful: Hoar became separated from the rest of the party on the Webster Brook Carry and spent the night alone, raising Thoreau's anxiety considerably. But when they arrived home, Thoreau viewed the trip as a success.

Entries in Thoreau's journal and his narrative account of the trip reveal ever more clearly his view of wilderness. Soon after the party had put into the waters of Moosehead Lake in the "still of the morning" and heard the dip of their paddles, Thoreau felt enlivened and free, "suddenly naturalized" in the sense of having become a part of the natural world he had entered. Later, after seeing the eerie glow of phosphorescent wood in the middle of the night by their dead campfire, he chose to forgo consideration of a scientific explanation, preferring instead to believe that the woods were "chokefull of honest spirits" and that for a few moments he had "enjoyed fellowship with them."[23] "Useful ignorance" is what Thoreau called this conscious openness to the existence of an unknown world, a state of mind that might lead to unimaginable discoveries.[24]

Throughout the trip, Thoreau exercised his curiosity, delighting in his observations and revealing those qualities of the wild that he valued. At night, he appreciated "the general stillness [that] is more impressive than any sound." And he derived pleasure from the "note of the white-throated sparrow, a very inspiriting but almost wiry sound." His reaction, therefore, was not surprising when he heard Polis firing his gun on a quiet evening while he and Hoar were fishing: "This sudden, loud, crashing noise in the still aisles of the forest, affected me like an insult to nature, or ill manners at any rate, as if you were to fire a gun in a hall or temple." He appreciated the "fantastic branches" of larch trees and the splendid, delicate flowers of the great purple-fringed orchids. But he "would have liked to come across a large community of pines, which had never been invaded by the lumbering army," and he disliked seeing the shores of the lakes in a "ragged and unsightly condition, encumbered with dead timber." He cautioned that the woods held values other than those seen by human society. "The Anglo-American," he wrote, "can indeed cut down, and grub up all this waving forest, and make a stump speech, and vote for Buchanan on its ruins, but he cannot converse with the spirit of the tree he fells, he cannot read the poetry and mythology which retire as he advances. . . . Before he has learned his a b c in the beautiful but mystic lore of the wilderness . . . he cuts it down."[25]

Those activities Thoreau did embrace were aimed at simplifying life and living with nature. On meeting a hunter who had been out in the wilds a month or more, Thoreau thought: "How much more respectable . . . is the life of the solitary pioneer or settler in these, or any woods,—having real difficulties, not of his own creation, drawing his subsistence directly from nature,—than that of the helpless multitudes in the towns who depend on gratifying the extremely artificial wants of society."[26]

Obviously, Thoreau, who laid out his views so sharply and in such opposition to society's dominative view of nature, would have his critics. One was Fannie Hardy Eckstorm. More than a half century after Thoreau's last trip, she wrote an article for the *Atlantic Monthly* in which she stated that his "abilities have been overrated." In her mind, he could not accurately estimate distance, area, and speed; he was not an ornithologist; he knew nothing of woodcraft; he never learned to feel at home in the Maine wilderness; and he was not a scientific observer. But Eckstorm did allow that he surpassed others as an interpreter: "He had the art to see the human values of natural objects. . . . It is . . . his attempt to reveal the Me through the Not Me, reversing the ordinary method, which makes his observations of such interest and value." And, she wrote, "the wonder is . . . that in three brief visits . . . he got at the heart of so many matters. . . . So, though he was neither woodsman nor scientist, Thoreau stood at the gateway of the woods and opened them to all future comers with the key of poetic insight. And after the woods shall have passed away, the vision of them as he saw them will remain."[27]

Another half century passed before a point-by-point rebuttal to Eckstorm's criticism of Thoreau appeared. Mary P. Sherwood, in "Fanny Eckstorm's Bias," published in the *Massachusetts Review*, acknowledged that "Mrs. Eckstorm was unusually qualified for making such a criticism, but her approach to discussing Thoreau as an outdoorsman was greatly warped," and furthermore "she resented anything coming in from outside [of Maine] . . . [and] she was at times prone to form an opinion first and test the accuracy of it afterwards." Sherwood defended Thoreau on his accuracy of measurement; the reasons why he may have missed the identification of seven of the thirty-seven birds he listed, including the fact that he never killed birds to identify them, as was the common practice at the time; his scientific observations and the wealth of scientific facts he accumulated, which had been mined by scientists over the years; and his woodcraft. She agreed with Eckstorm that Thoreau's vision of the woods will remain long after the woods are gone and concluded that "today Thoreau's *Maine Woods* appeals to the forester, the ecologist, the hunter, the adventurous canoeist and mountain climber."[28]

Thoreau's *Maine Woods* and other writings appeal to and inspire another group of individuals—those who seek to establish, protect, and restore a measure of wildness in the United States and elsewhere. In his essay "Walking," Thoreau observed that the preservation of "wild animals implies generally the creation of a forest for them to dwell in or resort to. So it is with man."[29] In his journal entry of November 8, 1858, he suggested that some old woods should be kept "to match the old deeds. Keep them for history's sake, as specimens of what the township was."[30] And in his manuscript *Wild Fruits*, he called for each town to "have a park, or rather a primitive forest, of five hundred or a thousand acres, either in one body or several, where a stick should never be cut for fuel, nor for the navy, nor to make wagons, but stand and decay for higher uses— a common possession forever, for instruction and recreation."[31]

One of his strongest pleas for preserving wildness came at the end of his account of his second trip to the Maine woods: "Why should not we . . . have our natural preserves, where no villages need be destroyed, in which the bear and panther, and some even of the hunter race, may still exist, and not be 'civilized off the face of the earth,'—our forests . . . for inspiration and our own true recreation?"[32]

Near the end of his life, Thoreau wrote that we should preserve our beautiful natural features that "have a high use which dollars and cents never represent. . . . So, if there is any central and commanding hilltop, it should be reserved for public use. Think of a mountain-top in the township, even to the Indians a sacred place, only accessible through private grounds. A temple, as it were, which you cannot enter without trespassing—nay, the temple itself private property." And in the same piece, he wrote: "I do not think him fit to be the founder of a state or even of a town who does not foresee the use of these things."[33]

A generation later, an individual would arrive on the scene in Maine who met Thoreau's standard of fitness and preserved such a mountaintop, that of Katahdin, and with it New England's largest wilderness area—an area in view of Chamberlain Farm. His name was Percival Proctor Baxter.

Dave Hanna at Chamberlain Farm might have seen them go by—a line of canoes moving northward almost imperceptibly along the far shore. Perhaps he had already heard that the flotilla was coming; news had a way of traveling through this remote area. Whenever someone arrived, almost everyone would ask about the news. When Thoreau landed at the farm and went up to the farmhouse, he found himself among a half dozen men ready for news. Even today, people who go into the Allagash region to see friends usually take along an extra newspaper to give them.

What Hanna may have known on that July day in 1923 was that the canoe party crossing Chamberlain Lake represented a singular event for the Allagash. It was the first time a governor of Maine had ventured into the region to canoe the river and its lakes. And although such a trip might have been unusual for a governor, it was not for this one; at forty-six years of age, Percival Baxter had spent much time in the woods of Maine.[34]

Baxter was born into a family of wealth and social prestige. His father, James Phinney Baxter, was a businessman and civic leader with an interest in history and a talent in art. As a youth, Percy accompanied his father on many fishing trips to the Rangeley Lake region of western Maine. The story is told that on one of their trips in 1884, when Percy was seven, his father attempted to liven up a "slow" fishing day by offering him ten dollars per pound for a trout weighing more than five pounds. Percy caught an eight-pound brook trout, and when he got home, he opened a savings account with the money. After his death, the fund, which had accumulated considerable interest, was used for wildlife education.[35]

Although fishing was a part of the outdoor experiences he had as a boy, hunting was not something his father engaged in, and consequently neither did young Percy. He grew up developing a strong affinity for animals and became especially fond of Irish setters. This attitude toward animal life would one day be reflected in his view of wilderness preservation.

Percival Baxter's interest in wildlife and the outdoors would be amply rewarded by the effort put into his Allagash trip, but he was also drawn to the region for another reason: a powerful attraction to Mt. Katahdin. He had been under its spell for many years prior to this canoe trip, and here, on the largest lake of the Allagash chain, Katahdin dominated the view. He had seen its beauty from Chesuncook Lake and then again on Mud Pond. But here on Chamberlain, it might have given him cause to reflect. Two years before his Allagash trip, he had shared his attraction to Katahdin in an address: "The grandeur of the mountain, its precipitous slopes, its massive cliffs, unusual formation and wonderful coloring cannot be surpassed or even equalled by any mountain east of the Mississippi River."[36] And only a few months earlier, he had proposed legislation to create a Mt. Katahdin state park, emphasizing recreation, excluding hunting, and allowing the cutting of live timber only so far as it would improve forest growth and not detract from scenic beauty. The proposal was defeated.[37] It was not his first attempt to protect the mountain, nor would it be his last.

Exactly when and how Baxter had become enraptured by the mountain and interested in its preservation is not known for certain. Baxter told Gene Letourneau, with whom he talked occasionally, that he had seen Katahdin for the first time in 1903, while on a fishing trip with his father at Kidney Pond, near the base of the mountain and southwest of its peak.[38] Irvin C. Caverly Jr., director of Baxter State Park, traced Baxter's idea to the same year and a time when he stood with two friends on a hill to the east of the mountain and said, "That mountain should belong to the people of Maine."[39]

Through the years from 1905 until he became governor, in 1921, Baxter served off and on in the state legislature. Beginning in his first term, when he supported a petition to preserve the natural beauty of the fields and forests of Maine, he became increasingly involved in efforts to protect Mt. Katahdin through legislation. As early as 1895, groups and individuals had advanced various proposals to set aside Katahdin and the surrounding region as a state park or reserve. Bills had even been introduced in the United States Congress for creation of a national forest reserve. Baxter's early attempts involved protection of land and water resources, to which end forests were especially valuable. In 1917, he introduced a bill for which he argued that it was not wise for Maine to have so much of its timber and water resources in "the hands of a few large landowners," that the people of the state should "buy back some of our squandered inheritance," and that for an example one had only to look at the holdings of the Coe estate of Bangor and Great Northern Paper Company, which together totaled 1.8 million of the 15 million acres of timberland in Maine.[40] The bill was defeated, but the significance of Baxter's public defense of such an attitude toward the timberlands graphically illustrated the change in viewpoint taking place.

In 1919, an undeterred Baxter introduced another bill to create state parks and forest reserves in the Katahdin region and elsewhere. Although it, too, was defeated, a weaker version was passed that permitted Maine to accept gifts of land, a provision Baxter would later use as a private citizen. In 1920, his commitment grew even more when he formed a five-day expedition to Katahdin with leading politicians, state officials, newspapermen, and others to "survey" the area for a "Centennial State Park." The next year, as governor, he supported "An Act Establishing the Mount Katahdin State Park" with much backing from legislators and the media. But the landowner lobby was again too strong, and the bill was defeated.[41]

Governor Percival P. Baxter's Allagash Trip, 1923

Governor Percival Baxter's 1923 trip to the Allagash region took him by Chamberlain Farm. He is shown here seated in the center of the group, dressed in a light-colored shirt and tie. By the time of this excursion, he had already come under the spell of Mt. Katahdin, as had Henry David Thoreau, and with the trip he made yet another connection with the Concord natural philosopher. Baxter would go on to create New England's largest wilderness area as a place to be forever left "in its Natural Wild State, free from the trappings and conventions of modern civilization. A wilderness which man may visit and enjoy but not desecrate." Photograph courtesy of the Maine State Library, Percival Proctor Baxter Collection.

By the time Governor Baxter saw the northern side of Katahdin and the surrounding mountains on his 1923 Allagash trip, he had suffered yet another defeat, only a few months earlier. He made the trip, the newspapers reported, to obtain firsthand information about the wilderness of northern Maine, especially its waterways, forests, and game reservations. The governor was interested in looking at the work of forest fire and game wardens and the potential of the lakes in the region to serve as reservoirs. This was also one of the few places in Maine Baxter had not visited.[42]

The governor's party consisted of his brother Rupert H. Baxter, who was a state senator and a member of his cabinet; Gilbert R. Chadbourne, his private secretary; Thomas A. James, curator of the Maine State Museum; Willis E. Parsons, commissioner of the Maine Department of Inland Fisheries and Game; five guides who were also game wardens; and a cook, who was said to have been "the most important personage in the outfit, next to His Excellency, the Governor."[43]

On Saturday, July 7, the party left Augusta, and on Sunday the group visited Ripogenus Dam and gorge and Nesowadnehunk Stream, where the members viewed Mt. Katahdin. The next day, "the real start for the Allagash," as Willis Parsons later wrote, was made when the group stepped "upon the deck of the Twilight, one of the steamers," and headed across Moosehead Lake to Northeast Carry. "Blessed with fair weather" that day, Moosehead Lake, "with its wooded isles, jutting points and broad expanse, never seemed more a sea of enchantment." They arrived early at the carry and spent the night there. The next morning, Tuesday, July 10, they launched their canoes on the West Branch of the Penobscot. They had "a fine run down the river" and were greeted by "an inspiring sight" when the party came out into the head of Chesuncook Lake and saw the remote Chesuncook Village "in gala attire," with flags flying. The people had come out in force to greet the governor, and the "mighty Katahdin range in the distance, reflecting the light of the westering sun, seemed to smile its approval and add to the beauty of the scene."[44]

The stopover at Chesuncook Village was an exciting event in the history of the small, isolated hamlet, which even today has no year-round road to it. The party was hosted by Ansel Smith, owner of the village hotel. At an evening gathering, Governor Baxter was presented to the group and, according to one account, spoke "in his own clear, easy way," telling the group "of his love of nature, his desire to be a good Governor, and his determination to know more of the great State of Maine."[45]

The next day, the party left for Umbazooksus Stream and Mud Pond Carry. Whether they stayed at Ronco's Camps on the carry is not known for certain, but it seems likely that they did because Parsons noted that they made their first camp two days later, "at beautiful Eagle Lake." Following Thoreau's route, they passed through Chamberlain Lake and by the farm before stopping for dinner at Pillsbury Island. That afternoon, the party proceeded up the lake to a warden's camp, where they spent the night. "The Governor's tent," wrote Parsons, "was pitched on the beach, or point extending out into the lake, that faces toward the outlet, a charming spot." The next morning, he reported, the point was christened "'Baxter's Point,' named in honor of Governor Percival P. Baxter, who Camped here July 12, A.D., 1923, being the first Governor to make the Allagash trip," and a notice was put up on a large pine tree.[46]

The party saw the "great waste of trees caused by flowage where the dams raised the water" and lumbermen who "were commencing to clean up the dead stumps on [the] sides of the lakes." The group experienced a "heavy electrical storm at Churchill Lake" with "rain so hard that it went through the tents." Overall, however, the "weather was pleasant most of the journey." They saw an abundance of game: "219 deer and hundreds of ruffed grouse and wild ducks."

In his report, Parsons, basking in the success of the trip, proclaimed in prose reminiscent of guidebook promotions that "this is the real canoe trip of the north, over clear water lakes of wonderful enchantment, down rapids and swift moving current, with ever-changing vista of contentment and beauty, that has been immortalized by Thoreau and many others who have written of the charm."[47]

When the party reached Fort Kent on July 17, they had covered 200 miles. The governor reported that "it was a fine trip with thousands of interesting things to see." Parsons wrote that for "one who admires nature, loves the artistic and yet sees not only beauty lavishly bestowed, but those wonderful resources, mighty forest and its wild life in abundance, there is not a dull moment."[48]

With his Allagash trip, Baxter had made another connection with that great publicist of his mountain, Henry David Thoreau. Although Willis Parsons had been moved to invoke the name of the Concord wilderness advocate, it is not known to what extent Baxter himself was influenced by him. As well read as he was and as passionate about the Katahdin region as he demonstrated himself to be, there is no doubt that he was inspired by Thoreau. After all, he was following the natural philosopher's example in his plea to establish preserves.[49]

The next year, 1924, was Baxter's last year in elective office. In his remaining days as governor, he worked for the introduction of another bill, in the next legislature, to create a Mt. Katahdin state park. In his farewell address to the people of the state, he again urged the creation of a park and offered the salary he had received as governor in 1923 and 1924 if the legislature would appropriate $20,000 and apply it toward that end for the next two years. When the legislature met, a bill was introduced as planned, but despite the support of Baxter's successor, Governor Ralph Owen Brewster, it failed, as did another attempt in Congress later that same year. Baxter, however, would not be deterred in his vision, though it would be five years before he took action.

Meanwhile, other voices could be heard among a small but growing number who advocated for preservation of the region's disappearing wild heritage. One was archaeologist Warren K. Moorehead, who had passed by Chamberlain Farm in 1912 using Baxter's route. Over the next few years, his work had taken him into wild and remote areas of New England, and there he had experienced and come to value an untouched nature. As the years passed, he had become alarmed at the encroachment of roads on the wildlands, the proliferation of automobiles, the lack of appreciation and understanding of nature on the part of many visitors, and wasteful cutting practices, widespread pollution, adverse effects of dams, and disregard of game laws.

In 1926, while serving as director of the Department of American Archaeology at Phillips Academy in Andover, Massachusetts, Moorehead wrote an article titled "The Rights of Nature: An Urgent Plea That Maine May Retain Her Woods in Their Present Wild and Untrammeled State." The piece was published in *Sun-Up, Maine's Own Magazine,* with a photograph of Mt. Katahdin on the cover. "Were Thoreau alive," he wrote,

> I am quite sure that he would speak in no uncertain tone concerning the contrast between the Great North Woods of today, and as he saw it years ago. . . . I am equally certain that he would have written *not* in his usual temperate and charming vein, but rather as a prophet seeking to call a wasteful nation to repentance. . . . I feel it a duty to warn the public that unless we change our policy with reference to conservation in the broad sense, the forest will soon be no more.[50]

He went on to predict that the industries involved with water power, timber, and pulp and paper would not agree with him.

Moorehead focused particularly on the need to preserve the wilderness of a large portion of northern Maine, including the St. John River, the Mt. Katahdin region, the Allagash River, and the head of the Aroostook River, all of which, he wrote, remained "as yet undisturbed." He argued that nature should have the right to carry on its natural processes free from human degradation. Giving voice to the opinion that those who controlled the large industrial and landholding companies had influence with legislators, he called for citizens to act in unison "in order that . . . a forest and mountain expanse unsurpassed in scenic beauty, in peace and quiet and impressiveness—be vouchsafed to mankind and his children; and here, since it cannot be done elsewhere, the Rights of Nature respected and maintained."[51] Although Moorehead and Baxter may not have been acquainted, the two men had similar thoughts and feelings, and in the years ahead, Baxter would use comparable language in defense of his mountain.

In August of the year after Moorehead's article was published, David Hanna of Chamberlain Farm had a visitor. His name was Myron Avery, and he was then twenty-seven years old. Like Baxter, he was born in Maine, graduated from Bowdoin College and Harvard Law School, was captivated by the region, and would promote it for its wilderness qualities. But he had far more experience than Baxter as a hiker, canoeist, and outdoorsman, and at the time of his visit to the farm he was gaining extensive and intimate knowledge of the Katahdin area, about which he would later write a large number of articles. Surprisingly, he would be one of Baxter's most vocal opponents.

Avery's visit to Chamberlain Farm came as he was exploring a new route to Mt. Katahdin. In fact, that would be the title of an article he would publish about the trip the next year, one of more than

100 articles and guidebooks he would write about hiking, canoeing, and camping in the Katahdin region and about the Appalachian Trail. The previous year, he had published an article titled "Northern Maine and Its Possibilities for Canoeing," in which he discussed the Allagash River, the West and East Branches of the Penobscot River, and the St. John River.[52]

Seven people made up the party that camped across the lake from the farm—two guides, three fishermen, and two mountaineers, Avery and Henry Buck, vice president of the Appalachian Mountain Club. It was their second day out; they had started from Bangor and journeyed to Chesuncook Village the previous day. That afternoon, following their arrival at the campsite, Avery and another member of the party paddled to the farm in the rain. They visited Hanna for about an hour and a half. Avery later noted in his journal that the farm was not in operation and the houses were "in dilapidated condition." Hanna told him he had been lumbering in the region since 1905, and he talked a good deal of the "early days." He showed them an original account book, which began in 1847, and said that Coe had the 1846 book. Avery, thinking ahead to the new route he was exploring, inquired about the Eagle Lake Tote Road, and Hanna said he had "hauled on there 13 years ago." This information was probably encouraging to Avery, and he and his companion may have discussed it as they paddled back across the lake in the rain to their camp.[53]

Avery's approach to Katahdin was unusual, to say the least. After leaving Chamberlain, the group paddled and portaged into Eagle Lake and up Smith Brook, around a set of falls, and into Haymock Lake, which was known for its fishing. Here the party split up, with Avery and Buck leaving the other five to fish and then return by canoe while they followed the Eagle Lake Tote Road southeast to Katahdin. For the next ten days, the two engaged in a physically demanding hike into the rugged, remote mountainous region north of Katahdin and eventually to the top of the mountain itself.[54]

Around 1931, Avery began a long tenure as chairman of the Appalachian Trail Conference, an organization that supervises the trail from Maine to Georgia. His life was extremely active—he hiked, wrote, promoted the Appalachian Trail and worked to complete and maintain it, practiced admiralty law, served as an officer in the United States Naval Reserve Force, and was a husband and a father of two children. With all this, he had a special interest in protecting the Katahdin area—an interest he had in common with Percival Baxter. How that protection was to be achieved, however, would be a source of bitter disagreement.

In 1931, Baxter's values regarding nature and wilderness came into sharp focus. That was the year he made his first gift of land to the state of Maine—5,700 acres, which included the summit of Mt. Katahdin. He stipulated that the land "shall forever be used for public park and recreational purposes, shall forever be left in the natural wild state, shall forever be kept as a sanctuary for wild beasts and birds, and that no roads or ways for motor vehicles shall hereafter ever be constructed thereon or therein."[55]

Over the next three decades, from 1930, when he was fifty-four, to 1962, when he reached the age of eighty-seven, Baxter purchased more than 200,000 acres and gave the land to Maine, thus creating Baxter State Park. The process involved negotiating at length; sorting out legal entanglements; buying and trading lands; dealing with water rights, cutting rights, and rights of way; obtaining legal opinions; compromising on timber harvesting, roads, and hunting; ceding the lands to the state in deeds of trust that would be difficult to break; and withstanding the uncertainties of World War II, the Korean War, and other conflicts. When it was done, he had patched together twenty-eight parcels. To this end he demonstrated vision, patience, perseverance, shrewdness, and—perhaps most important—the will to act on his values. He was aided by longevity, wealth, and what might be interpreted as a momentum of support as the park grew in size and the public became increasingly aware of it and Baxter's benevolence. As he added land to the park, he expanded his goals for its size, beginning with 50,000 acres in mind and progressing to 100,000 acres, then 150,000, and finally 200,000 acres. During his acquisition of the land, one situation probably pushed him more than any other to create a park of this size and define the project as his life's work: the threat of creation of a national park.

The idea to protect the Katahdin area as a national park and forest reserve had come up many years before Baxter started purchasing the land, but it had gone nowhere. The idea, however, returned with greater support in the 1930s as part of the New Deal. In 1933, despite Baxter's opposition, a congressional bill to create a national forest surfaced, with the support of Maine's governor and legislature. The bill was unsuccessful. In 1936, Myron Avery emerged on the scene as a major proponent and moving force behind the idea of a national park to surround the state park Baxter had created. He argued that increased access and lack of supervision had created pressures from visitors and brought about a deterioration of park conditions, especially around Chimney Pond, a beautiful tarn in a spectacular glacial cirque where abuse of the pond and destruction of the camping area environment had occurred. Maine, he charged, was not providing the necessary funding for park management. In response, Baxter requested a modest appropriation from the legislature to help care for the park. In early 1937, however, the legislature failed to fund the request, and Congressman Ralph Owen Brewster, with the help of Avery and the Appalachian Trail Conference in drafting a bill, introduced legislation to establish Katahdin National Park.[56]

The battle heated up. Baxter wrote letters and made public statements against the park and continued to buy land. Conservation groups were split. The Wilderness Society and the Appalachian

Mountain Club supported Baxter, but the Appalachian Trail Conference, with which Avery was strongly associated, supported the park. In 1938, Avery wrote two articles that argued strongly for the national park and criticized the roads, poor management, lack of funding, improper camping facilities, and lack of maintenance of the existing state park. He emphasized the need to preserve the area for its wilderness qualities, and he attacked Baxter's motives, suggesting that Baxter wanted it as a personal memorial.[57]

In the end, however, Baxter and the proponents of a state park prevailed. Brewster's bill died in the summer of 1938 when Congress adjourned without acting on it. The people of Maine favored a state park over a national one, and as John Hakola, who chronicled the story of the park, observed, the situation would be "reenacted three decades later in the Allagash Wilderness Waterway issue." However, the controversy and Avery's advocacy did prompt the state to begin improvements in the park despite inadequately financing them. Years later, Baxter took care of this problem by establishing a large endowment to pay the park's expenses. Time also softened Baxter's feelings toward Avery, and before Avery died, in 1952, Baxter indicated that he held no hostile feelings toward him.[58] Perhaps he realized that they both wanted the best for the mountain they loved.

In quite another way, Baxter's quest was again plagued by the federal government's interest in potential parkland in Maine. In 1962, while Baxter was attempting to purchase his last section of the park from Great Northern Paper Company—a piece of land critical to control of southern access to the park—and reach his goal of 200,000 acres, he ran into a problem. The National Park Service had its eye on a national recreation area surrounding the Allagash River and its headwaters. Great Northern Paper resisted selling to Baxter because the company feared the possibility of losing some of its forestland in the Allagash region to the federal government. Interestingly, Baxter was not above using this issue as a gentle prod by letting the company know that he had been contacted by the National Park Service for his views on the proposal and that his relations with the agency had been friendly.[59] When the company finally agreed to sell the piece of land, it did so with the stipulation that Baxter must agree to allow hunting and trapping, a condition the company made at the urging of employees who belonged to a local sporting club. To accomplish his dream, Baxter conceded, purchasing the land on November 8, 1962.[60]

Baxter lived to the age of ninety-two, and during that lifetime of nearly a century, he time and again projected values that revealed his view of the human relationship with nature and wilderness. In 1941, he said that "Katahdin always should and must remain the wild, storm-swept, untouched-by-man region it now is . . . where nature rules and where the creatures of the forest hold undisputed dominion."[61] The mountain was a place where "by day man stands spellbound in that solitude where man himself is an atom at the base of one of nature's noblest creations."[62] Baxter also held a particular reverence for the forests and wildlife: "Moose, deer, wildcats, bears, foxes and all the smaller animals and birds abound therein. All these creatures are safe from the hunters, and the sound of the axe and of falling trees never will echo through these forests."[63] And for people, the park would be a place where one could "get close to nature."[64]

Baxter wanted the park to be a place where everything is "left simple and natural, and [remains] as nearly as possible as it was when only the Indians and the animals roamed at will through these areas."[65] He believed that this would help correct what had been done to these lands "in which the rights of the people in a princely inheritance were given away or bartered for a song, for the folly of which future generations forever will pay." He saw the history of these lands as a story of violent speculation and fortunes won and lost, of great timber-owning families made wealthy, and of intrigue and corruption.[66] He longed for the day "when all of Maine will become a sanctuary for the beasts and birds of the forest and field, and when cruelty to the humbler orders of life no longer stalks the land."[67]

Over the years, Baxter, facing questions about allowed uses without clear decision-making information and confronting difficulties in acquiring land, compromised some of these principles. For example, in the 1950s, when resentment on the part of hunters over loss of their hunting areas surfaced in the legislature as opposition to his gift of land in the northern end of the park, he allowed hunting in some sections. But even as he approached the end of his acquisition efforts, he held that the park should be "maintained primarily as a wilderness, and recreational purposes are to be regarded as of secondary importance and shall not encroach upon the main objective of this area, which is to be 'forever wild.'"[68] In words that today bring to mind the language of the Wilderness Act, at that time still nine years away from passage, he responded on October 18, 1955, to a letter of praise for his benevolence by reiterating that the area is to be forever left "in its Natural Wild State, free from the trappings and conventions of modern civilization. A wilderness which man may visit and enjoy but not desecrate."[69]

By the time he completed his park, Baxter had received the admiration and appreciation of three outstanding men who would themselves be recognized for their work in conservation. One was Supreme Court Justice William O. Douglas, who wrote to Baxter on October 5, 1959, to say that he had just visited the park and was overjoyed: "All of us owe you a great debt for your generosity and your farsightedness. It is a wonderful creation and as a private citizen I thank you from my heart."[70] Three years later, Maine's senator Edmund S. Muskie, with whom Baxter had corresponded when Muskie was governor, accompanied Stewart Udall, secretary of the

U.S. Department of the Interior, to present the department's Conservation Service Award to Baxter.[71]

Over the years since Baxter's death, in 1969, the park has experienced a number of challenges involving its wild status and the interpretation of Baxter's wishes, including those related to snowmobiling, the cleanup of blowdown trees and those killed by a spruce budworm infestation, retention of cutting rights, the practice of scientific forestry, hunting, and roads. Such issues come before a three-member park authority consisting of the state attorney general, the commissioner of the Maine Department of Inland Fisheries and Wildlife, and the head of the Maine Forest Service. The authority, in turn, listens to the park director and an advisory committee as well as to user groups, conservation organizations, interested individuals, and members of the Baxter family. Policy decisions have resulted in, for example, the restriction of snowmobiles to a perimeter road and authorization of cleanup and restoration of areas damaged by "acts of nature," such as wind, fire, and insect infestation. Although the wilderness aspect of the park appears quite well protected, it has not been without what historian Neil Rolde observed near the end of his biography of Baxter: "the human pressures that . . . sometimes break like a stormy sea around the island of relative tranquility that he singlehandedly created."[72]

At the time of Baxter's last gift, just such a stormy sea was breaking in the shadow of Mt. Katahdin to the north—in the Allagash region. Out of the tumult would come a change in the wilderness surrounding Chamberlain Farm, a change that would be as significant for a unique wild river as the one Percival Baxter had created for an unusual mountain. And it would involve all three of the men who had praised Baxter for his great work—Douglas, Muskie, and Udall. But the idea had begun years earlier in the mind of one man in particular: Robert W. Patterson.

Chapter 8

The Struggle for Wildness

𝒰NBEKNOWNST TO AL AND PATTY NUGENT one October day in 1936, while they toiled at building their new camps on the shore of Chamberlain Lake as hunting season and winter bore down on them, a lone canoe slipped through the lake's cooling waters, past Chamberlain Farm, and toward a campsite across from Lock Dam. It was the first of many Allagash trips for Robert and Barbara Patterson and the beginning of Bob Patterson's involvement in events that would affect the lives of the Nugents in ways they could not then have imagined.

Originally from Massachusetts, the two Mt. Desert Island transplants were discovering that Maine offered the things they valued most, and one of those things, their "real bag," as Bob Patterson would say later, was the Maine woods. There, the two found renewal and closeness and a shared love for nature. Reflecting on his life years later, he would add that it was their marriage that made all things possible, for they saw eye to eye not only on how to live but also on why.[1]

275

For thirty-one-year-old Patterson, a Harvard University-educated architect and landscape architect, life would be filled with the realization of many possibilities. Like Percival Baxter, who was at the time beginning to put together his park, Patterson would become a considerable force in protecting another wilderness—the Allagash region. His Allagash trips would spawn a long love affair with the region, and that 1936 exploratory venture would set him on the path of advocacy and nurture a commitment strong enough to overcome difficulties not unlike those Baxter faced. But he and the others who would be embroiled in the effort would not have the wealth to purchase the land themselves, nor would they have the luxury of time, for they would face the real, imminent threats of roads, bridges, and flooding of the entire river by dams.

The second day after leaving their campsite on Chamberlain Lake, the couple reached the then roadless Haymock Lake, where they found all they "had hoped for: clear blue water, steep, wooded shores—remote, solitary, and silent." On their way out three days later, they crossed Mud Pond, and "on that afternoon," Patterson remembered, "it was a place of such beauty that we wanted to stay forever. The low sun turned the water to blue and gold. Ducks were everywhere, on and over the pond, and Katahdin, with its cloud cap, was a focal point seen across unbroken miles of autumn forest."[2] Whether he realized it or not, Robert Patterson had been caught in the spell of the Allagash.

Patterson had come to Mt. Desert Island in the mid-1930s to work as a landscape architect for Acadia National Park, bringing his wife and their daughter, Louisa. That year of his first Allagash trip, he established his own office. His work led him to specialize in using native plants, to design many homes, gardens, and other architectural works, and to consult on a variety of projects. He and Barbara preferred a simple, nonmaterialistic life. He saw humans as part of the web of nature, in which all life is interconnected. His love for the outdoors, his appreciation for the natural landscape and its features, his eye for aesthetics, and his sensitivity to emotional as well as practical considerations of environmental design heightened his awareness of the wild nature he discovered in the Allagash.

During the years of this professional life, he lived and worked on Mt. Desert Island, except from 1943 to 1945, when he served as assistant chief of land planning for the Federal Housing Administration. Throughout that time, he and his family, which by then included a son, Robert W. Patterson Jr., resided in Washington, D.C. They returned to Mt. Desert Island in 1945, and in 1947 a tragic fire swept the island, taking their home and everything in it. "A good way to clean out the attic," he once remarked with offbeat humor.

The Allagash trips continued. Patterson became a Maine guide and took his friends on trips. As his love for the area grew, so did his concern about the loss of its wildness and the changes he saw occurring in the Maine woods, especially as increased wood harvesting brought more roads closer to the waterway. As early as 1945, he spoke with Maine's senators about what he perceived as the "shaky future of the North Woods," and "got the brush-off," as he termed it.[3] He was not the only one who saw the Allagash as special and recognized the importance of its roadlessness to its wilderness character. Gene Letourneau, in one of his columns the next year, called it "Maine's last wilderness frontier."[4]

Access by vehicle to the region was about to change. It was on a family trip in 1953, recalled Patterson's son, Robert Jr., or Lee, as he prefers to be known, that they learned from Jim Clarkson at Lock Dam about a jeep coming to the shore of Telos Lake. Rumors that the road was going to be improved were confirmed by Harold and Lloyd Whiteneck, proprietors of Heart O' Maine Sporting Camps, when "they arrived from Chamberlain Farm, bringing magazines for Jim."[5] The wildness, recalled the senior Patterson in an article pub-

Robert W. Patterson Sr. and
Robert W. (Lee) Patterson Jr. at Lock Dam, 1955

Robert Patterson Sr. developed a love for the Allagash region through trips
with his wife and family that began in 1936. When he helped found the
Natural Resources Council of Maine in 1959, protection of the Allagash for
its wild and remote qualities was the organization's first major project. Photograph courtesy of Robert W. (Lee) Patterson Jr.

lished posthumously, "began to go. Lakes became noisy with out-
boards, families used the old campsites for long summer vacations,
and laundry appeared on the shores. Water-skiers appeared, . . .
alders choked the old carries, and the woods were changed forever."[6]
Before the 1950s ended, Patterson would act in a way that would
thrust him into the forefront of a bold move to reverse the trends he
saw.

In 1955, while Patterson's concerns were moving him toward
decisive action, another player in the events about to occur arrived
at the Nugents' dock on Chamberlain Lake. He was Maine's governor, Edmund S. Muskie. It was June, at the end of the legislative
session, and he was interested in taking a break where he could relax

Edmund S. Muskie at Nugent's Chamberlain Lake Camps, 1955
While serving as governor of Maine, Edmund S. Muskie, at far left, took a
break from his duties at the end of a legislative session to embark on a fishing trip into the Allagash region. In this north country, he would later write,
"we can find peace in the woods and on the lakes and streams, collect our
thoughts, and ready ourselves for whatever challenges the world brings."
Photograph courtesy of Donald E. Nicoll.

and fish in a wild, remote area. Fishing and camping was what he
had done with his father as a boy growing up in the hill country of
western Maine. The governor's party of six included assistants,
friends, and advisors, and the trip had been arranged through the
Maine Department of Inland Fisheries and Game. The group
stopped at Nugent's Chamberlain Lake Camps for lunch and then
flew west, past Chamberlain Farm, to the department's camp on
Allagash Lake.

The only member of that party living today is Donald E. Nicoll,
who at the time served as executive secretary of the Democratic
State Committee and "adjunct volunteer staff member" to the gov

ernor's office. Nicoll recalled that "Muskie had a long-standing general interest in the Allagash area, stemming from his reading, his general interest in the history of Maine and its development, his exposure to inland fisheries and game issues, and the general background interest in protecting the area against increased mechanization of timber harvesting."[7] He was also a friend of Gene Letourneau, who undoubtedly shared his own interest in the Allagash with the governor.

Muskie himself would later explain the feelings he developed for this area in his foreword to a 1971 reprint of Lucius Hubbard's book *Woods and Lakes of Maine*. Quoting Ralph Waldo Emerson's statement "In the woods we return to reason and faith," Muskie wrote that these words point out

> why we care so deeply for these untamed regions. . . .
> There is no more convincing proof of that wisdom
> than to stay a while in that wooded corner of Maine
> which Hubbard described, a corner where trees
> stretch to the shoreline, where the birds and the ani-
> mals live without fear, where the white water runs
> freely. . . . We can find peace in the woods and
> on the lakes and streams, collect our thoughts, and
> ready ourselves for whatever challenges the world
> brings.[8]

Three years after his Allagash fishing trip, Muskie was elected to the United States Senate, becoming the first popularly elected Democratic senator in Maine's history. He would have a long, successful career in Congress, receive his party's nomination for the office of vice president of the United States, and serve as secretary of state. He would be admired and respected for his accomplishments in the field of environmental protection. By 1970, he would be called "Mr. Clean" of the environmental crusade, "far and away the nation's best-known pollution fighter."⁹ But early in his career, the new senator would find himself immersed in a complex, politically sensitive, and contentious environmental issue—the future of the Allagash region.

Three months before Governor Muskie sought the restful qualities of the Allagash and during the time of Patterson's growing uneasiness about the loss of wildness in the region, a federal report emerged with recommendations for the "establishment of a river wilderness area featuring the Allagash River and its immediate surroundings," noting that "there are few sizeable rivers within the entire New England–New York region that now remain in a natural state. Of these the Allagash is one that is free of roads bordering the banks, free of man-made structures, and free of pollution." The Allagash, suggested the report, should be divided into two recreational areas with separate purposes: the area north of Lock Dam in the Allagash River watershed for wilderness recreation and the area of the Penobscot River watershed containing Allagash, Chamberlain, and Telos Lakes for outdoor recreation and generation of hydroelectric power. A small dam was proposed for Allagash Lake. Thus, as a consequence of the Telos Canal, made more than 100 years previously, Chamberlain Farm found itself on the shore of a proposed federal impoundment.¹⁰

The report was the result of a request made in 1950 by President Harry S. Truman to the secretaries of six federal agencies asking them to form a committee to survey the natural resources of the New England–New York region and make recommendations for their development, use, and conservation. Like all the other states in the region, Maine had a representative on the committee, so the federal interest was known to some in the state. As early as 1953, the committee had sent people into the Allagash to investigate the area.

Following the committee's report, the Secretary of the Interior's Advisory Board on National Parks, Historic Sites, Buildings, and

Monuments expressed concern for the future of the Allagash and declared it in the national interest for the region to be "retained unimpaired for the use and enjoyment of future generations."[11] In April 1956, a year after the report's release, a planning document prepared by the Maine State Park Commission in cooperation with the National Park Service recommended preservation of the natural conditions of the Allagash River and its immediate surroundings "because of the growing need for wilderness recreation areas."[12] In September of that year, Gene Letourneau reported that four representatives of the National Park Service were "looking over this vast wilderness area primarily to appraise its potential as a national park." Letourneau noted that many changes had come to the Allagash during the past thirty years with extensive lumbering and pulp operations, changes in equipment resulting in a large increase in mobile transportation, and the bulldozing and graveling of numerous private hauling roads. Seeking opinions on the possibility of a park, the journalist found "a rugged negative attitude" in one old-timer, but a "younger tenant countered . . . that as a park the Allagash wilderness might be perpetuated."[13]

In 1959, with the cooperation of the state of Maine, the National Park Service again sent a field party of park planners into the Allagash to make a careful survey of the area. Letourneau caught up with the four planners and their guides at a campsite on Pillsbury Island, on Eagle Lake. He found the survey team "more than impressed by the vast wilderness, the size of the lakes . . . and the unbroken stands of soft and hardwood timber." One member from the Washington, D.C., office observed that "there is nothing just quite like it left in this country."[14] But the team expressed concern for its future; they could not have missed seeing the hauling roads opening up the countryside.

Two months earlier, Letourneau had reported in a column that in 1958, Grafton Lumber Company of Ashland had opened logging roads to the public "that led to or close to practically every major fishing lake, pond and stream on the east side of the wilderness."[15]

A week after his Pillsbury Island interview, he noted in his column that "although a National Park Survey team found the Allagash Region the country's last frontier in unbroken wilderness, the network of roads continues to spread in the area." He went on to document a proposal to cut through the Allagash with a "high class road" that would link Maine's Route 11 and the Canadian boundary. And on a flight over the lower Allagash, he counted five new roads being built but noted that "there is no bridge across the [lower] Allagash as yet."[16]

In 1960, while the National Park Service was preparing its report, John F. Kennedy was elected president of the United States, and the Park Service came under the leadership of Secretary Stewart Lee Udall of the U.S. Department of the Interior. Udall had earned a reputation as a conservationist in the 1950s, when as a member of the U.S. House of Representatives from Arizona he had served on the Committee on Interior and Insular Affairs. As head of the Interior Department, Udall grew in stature as a champion of the environment. In 1963, two years after he took office, his book *The Quiet Crisis* was published, in which he told the story of the people and land of North America and expressed many of his thoughts and feelings about the American environment. He dedicated the book to the idea that we "must grasp completely the relationship between human stewardship and the fullness of the American earth." The *Saturday Review* noted that the book "reflects the vigor and ardor of its author—a man who likes to climb mountains, but who also is sensitive to the idealistic concepts expressed by philosophers and poets."[17]

Soon after his appointment, Udall was drawn into a growing controversy about the future of the Allagash. He was, in fact, caught between his Park Service's study about the feasibility of a national recreation area or park and a proposal for a tidal power project that called for hydroelectric dams on the St. John River, one of which would flood most of the Allagash River. Interestingly, both the park

Secretary of the Interior Stewart L. Udall,
President John F. Kennedy, and Maine Senator Edmund S. Muskie
in the Oval Office of the White House

In the early 1960s, Senator Muskie, right, arranged for a meeting
with Secretary Udall, left, and President Kennedy, center, to discuss
preserving the Allagash River and reviving the idea of building a tidal power
project at Passamaquoddy Bay on the coast of eastern Maine. Photograph
courtesy of Edmund S. Muskie Archives and Special Collections Library,
Photograph No. 5-20, Series 24, Edmund S. Muskie Collection,
Bates College, Lewiston, Maine.

and the power proposal originated from the same New England–New York Interagency Committee. The power project
included a major dam to be located eight and a half miles downstream from the mouth of the Allagash River, at a place called

Rankin Rapids. It would provide electric power to supplement that produced by harnessing the tides of Passamaquoddy and Cobscook Bays in the Canadian province of New Brunswick and the state of Maine. Studies showed that the Allagash watershed provided nearly one-third of the total flow of water at this point and, because of the nature of its watershed, a relatively stable seasonal supply of water. An alternative dam was proposed at Lincoln School, two miles downstream, which would limit flooding to the lower ten miles of the Allagash, up to Allagash Falls. This proposal also called for a larger dam to be built above the mouth of the Allagash, at Big Rapids on the St. John River, which would flood a large area of the upper part of this river.[18]

With the National Park Service report imminent and President Kennedy requesting that Udall evaluate the tidal power project for a recommendation, the fate of the Allagash appeared to depend on forces beyond state control. Surprisingly, for reasons involving Senator Muskie, Udall would exert the power of his office to force state preservation and control of the Allagash, but not without concern for the region's wildness. One thing was certain: the region around Chamberlain Farm would most certainly change.

Nearly a year before the Park Service issued its report, another advocate of keeping the Allagash wild passed by Chamberlain Farm—a man of high public office who expressed with uncommon eloquence his defense of the American wilderness and who would bring his considerable intellect and persuasive powers to the task of protecting the Allagash. He was Justice William O. Douglas of the United States Supreme Court.

Douglas was born on October 16, 1898, in Minnesota. He, like Muskie, came from a poor but loving family, but unlike the senator, he had experienced tragedy in early childhood: his father had died, and he had been stricken by polio. Initially, the disease paralyzed his legs, but he gradually regained their use. They were, however, thin and weak, and he grew self-conscious of them when he was taunted by children at school. As a result, he became a loner, compensating by excelling in his studies. He began exercising and hiking in the foothills of the Cascade Range near his home in Yakima, Washington, where his mother had moved the family after his father's death. In the mountains he found peace and tranquility, discovered the world of nature, and developed feelings that would lead to a lasting concern for the environment. He continued his hiking and outdoor activities throughout his life. He sought out remote, wild areas, and as he saw them encroached on, he became a highly visible and vocal crusader for their protection and preservation. A biographer wrote that Douglas' fight to preserve wilderness "may have been his finest battle."[19]

Douglas believed that the turning point in the nation's recognition of the need for wild places came when Henry David Thoreau articulated the view that wildness is needed to offset the progress of civilization by providing a retreat from urban life. The justice also embraced the writings of John Muir and Aldo Leopold, who advocated for wildness and the spiritual and community relationships with the natural world that people need to have. And he came to believe that all living things have a "being."[20] He would later write that "the very presence of a remote wilderness area that only a handful of people visit a year gives a new dimension to a nation. For it supplies an element of mystery and awe, a real sanctuary of a sort, a genuine frontier that man has not despoiled. In these things most citizens take pride."[21]

In 1960, Douglas was sixty-two and at work on his book *My Wilderness: East to Katahdin,* and the Allagash waterway was one of his destinations. As early as April, he wrote a letter to A. C. "Chub" Foster of Foster's Wilderness Camps on Grand Lake Matagamon asking whether he could see enough of the Allagash in a week during late September for him to have "an interesting chapter" in his wilderness book. Foster wrote back, saying that he had not taken the

Allagash trip since 1929 and warning Douglas that although it was at that time a "delightful trip through a continuous remote forest region, . . . the big lumber operators have opened up the entire country with truck roads and, as is usually the case, that grand wilderness region has lost some of its charm with the advance of progress." Foster had therefore investigated to see what the area was now like, and he did recommend a trip in September, "when the forest is in full color." In response, Douglas wrote that he would like to have Foster arrange for the trip and that his wife, Mercedes, known as Merci, and his friend Edmund Ware Smith would accompany him.[22]

Smith was a nationally known freelance writer and an editor of the *Ford Times*. He had written hundreds of articles and several books about Maine's woodsmen, hunters, hermits, and other outdoor people, some of whom were fictionalized. He was also a friend of Chub Foster. He and Foster were both about fifty-nine years of age. Smith and his wife, Mary, had come to know Chub and his wife, Fran, when they built a summer cabin on Grand Lake Matagamon.

A stream of letters flowed between Douglas, Smith, and Foster as preparations proceeded. Douglas was also corresponding with Commissioner Roland Cobb of the Maine Department of Inland Fisheries and Game for information and possible use of a state plane to fly him into the Allagash from Bangor. Cobb, however, wrote on August 1 that it would be difficult to arrange use of a state plane because two weeks of press persecution had just occurred after four members of the Governor's Council were picked up for a fishing violation after the department had flown them into a warden camp for a fishing trip.[23]

A few days after Cobb's communication, Douglas received a letter from John T. Maines, manager of woodlands for Great Northern Paper Company, inviting him to visit the company's woods operations on his trip. It seems Maines had seen a newspaper report about a speech Douglas had recently given in Oregon in which he said that "lumbermen have ground Maine to a pulp."[24] Although Douglas did not have an opportunity to see the operations on the ground, he did write to Maines after his Allagash trip to say he had seen some from the air and "noticed that they seemed to be almost exclusively bulldozer operations with a clean cut of everything." He wondered whether any of the operations about which Maines had written were "on a selective cutting basis."[25]

On September 20, the party began to assemble at a campsite on Telos Lake for a ten-day trip. Chub and Fran Foster arrived around four o'clock in the afternoon, followed by Ed and Mary Smith, who flew in an hour later. Four guides also arrived: Dave Jackson, Dana Shaw, and Willard Jalbert and his son Willard Jr. A change in the weather prevented the Douglases from flying in until the next morning.[26]

The leader of the trip, Willard Jalbert Sr., was known affectionately as "the Old Guide." His seventy-three years in the Allagash had built him a wide and enviable reputation. He was called a classic example of a Maine guide—good-looking, possessing a sense of humor, and highly skilled as an outdoorsman and canoeman. Douglas, who shared a canoe with him, said that despite his calendar age, Jalbert had the energy and vitality of a much younger man. The two talked and enjoyed a camaraderie for the whole trip. Mutual respect and admiration developed. Douglas was impressed with Jalbert's poling skills and knowledge, and Jalbert, interviewed in 1972 at the age of eighty-five, said that Douglas was a "great feller. I would say there's none better. . . . He's the most interesting person that we've ever met."[27]

The day after the Douglases arrived, the Old Guide raised the group at half past four in the morning with a rousing call: "Good morning sun! It's a nice day for singin' a song. A nice day for rollin' along." Smith said that although "the Old Guide's words had fire power and decibels," they contained "no smidgin of literal truth." In fact, the lakes were smothered by a dense, black fog. Before seven o'clock, they shoved off to the sound of the Old Guide's famous French-Canadian battle cry, which sounded like "Two la *prah!*" Douglas interpreted it to mean "All is ready," but according to Smith, one translation preferred by the Old Guide was "Let's get the hell out of here." The party headed for Eagle Lake in the fog, trying to follow the shoreline. Soon all were separated, each canoe invisible to the others. Smith wrote in his journal: "Strange mirages in fog. Justice Douglas proved to be a cedar post. What looked like the Statue of Liberty turned into my wife." Douglas saw a strange light possess the center of the lake as the sun almost penetrated the fog: "an eerie scene of black, boiling water that sent dark, vaporous clouds upward." The Old Guide said with a grin that "all it lacks is a witch." In this way, the party passed Chamberlain Farm without ever seeing it.[28]

On the second day, the group passed through the big lakes, past the remnants of Churchill Dam, into the white water of Chase Rapids, and on down the river. "As the rips and dead waters succeed each other, and the campsites likewise, there is a curious time compression," Smith observed. Their campfires were occasions of hearty, imaginative discussion, with Douglas, notebook in hand, probing endlessly about this place and its past. They fished, sang, engaged in playful banter, admired the "warmth and gaiety" of the fall colors, and registered excitement at the abundance of wildlife. But hanging over their trip, like the black fog that had swirled around them when they left Telos Lake, was the realization that bulldozed roads were increasing rapidly, penetrating the Allagash corridor every year and offering "an invitation to jeeps and other vehicles"—that the Allagash was "about to lose its remaining primeval qualities." This topic was in their "discussions at every camp from Telos to Fort Kent."[29]

William O. Douglas and Willard Jalbert, 1960
Justice William O. Douglas, at left, and Willard Jalbert, "the Old Guide,"
examine a setting pole at the ruins of Churchill Dam, below which the
Allagash River's first set of rapids begins. Douglas made the Allagash trip
while working on his book *My Wilderness: East to Katahdin.* He subsequently
became an eloquent proponent of the Allagash Wilderness Waterway.
Photograph by Mercedes (Douglas) Eicholtz, courtesy of Yakima Valley
Museum, Yakima, Washington.

As they sat around their last campfire on the St. John River,
downstream from its confluence with the Allagash, their talk turned
to an even more ominous threat, for they were at the site of the proposed Rankin Rapids dam, a project that could turn 97 percent of
the river they had just canoed into a large lake. The prospect was
unthinkable to Douglas, who expressed the thought that if the dam
were built, "civilization would condemn for all time a wilderness area
fashioned by time and nature, nourished by sweet water, and filled
with more wonders than man could ever catalog." After a long
silence, the Old Guide spoke: "Men think that nature was created
just for them, for their exploitation." Douglas agreed, acknowledg-

ing this as the key to explaining the human tendency to destroy
nature. He said he believed that only when we realize that nature is
for all living things, not for humans alone, will we have the humil-
ity to restrain ourselves and treat nature as sacred. The group talked
about these things around the campfire "until every star was out."[30]

The trip had a profound influence on Douglas. Although he had
traveled through wilderness areas all across the United States, in the
Allagash he had found "no hundred miles in America quite their
equal" and "certainly none [of] . . . their distinctive quality."[31] He
had witnessed the "great wonders on display" and been overcome
with a powerful sense of urgency for the Allagash to "become and
remain a roadless wilderness waterway. No more cutting of trees. No
invasions of any kind." And he believed there was still a chance to
"redeem in the Allagash some of the values we have lost" if people
had the "courage to act swiftly" and the "vision to see the enduring
values of wildness." If they did not, he foresaw, the Allagash would
join the "mass recreational areas where the quiet and peace of the
wilderness are gone forever."[32]

From the moment he stepped out of his canoe at Fort Kent,
Douglas launched himself into waters of a different kind—waters of
a growing controversy that had begun with little but a ripple, like his
entrance onto fogbound Chamberlain Lake. But now he was facing
turbulence not unlike that he had experienced in the difficult, rocky
stretch of Chase Rapids. "You would have one of the greatest recreation areas in the world," he announced, commenting on the idea of
setting aside part of the Allagash River area for public use. But he
also declared his opposition to its becoming a national park because
that would end hunting there and, he believed, probably lead to the
construction of roads: "I do think the federal government should
have a corridor along the river to maintain its natural state about a
half a mile or a mile on each side where there would be no cutting

of timber, but where camping, hunting, fishing and canoeing would be allowed. . . . Roads and resorts would ruin the area."[33]

On November 8, 1960, after returning to Washington, D.C., Douglas sent a private letter to Percival Baxter that began, "May I write to you confidentially for your advice and help?" He told Baxter how he had finished his Allagash trip "with a feeling of great concern that that fine wilderness river would soon be lost due to the encroachments of civilization." He wrote that "the roads are penetrating closer and closer." He proposed a solution: Put the Allagash under the Baxter State Park Authority. "I wonder," he went on, "if there are men in Maine of your proportions that have your vision and dimension of thought who would take steps to make that a reality?" At the end of his letter, he again emphasized that "this letter is for you and you alone."[34] On December 2, Baxter replied: "Your letter has come and I have read it with deep interest. . . . Your suggestion as to a corridor along the Allagash River is most interesting." But Baxter said he had little confidence that the legislature would take any action and thought that the important landowners "would oppose any project of such magnitude." He concluded, "I shall keep you informed."[35] Nothing of the idea came to pass.

Douglas, however, persisted in his vision of a protected Allagash waterway. In a letter to Conrad Wirth, director of the National Park Service, on December 4, 1961, he seemed to contradict his earlier opposition to creation of a national park. Indeed, he supported the idea, urging the Park Service to hold a public hearing on the matter and hinting that those in opposition could be his allies, depending on the policy adopted.[36] A year and a half later, he clarified his position in an article in *Field and Stream*, noting that a formula was being sought to allow some hunting, a popular activity in the Allagash. Hunting is normally prohibited in national parks, and Douglas believed this was the reason for strong local resistance to the park idea. He ended the article by stating, "The Allagash needs friends more than it ever needed them before."[37] One of those friends was Robert Patterson.

Two months before Douglas' fog-shrouded passage through Chamberlain Lake, Patterson and his wife had been on what had become almost an annual Allagash pilgrimage for them. A clearing sky greeted the two as they made their way along the northern shore of Chamberlain Lake. "We went on to a minute gravel beach," Patterson recorded in his journal, "and lunched; then on along the shore. Passed Nugent's, then Whiteneck's camps at Chamberlain Farm. We heard later that W. [Whiteneck] wants to sell out—about 500 acres and the buildings. There seemed to be no activity there. Near the old farm buildings, the wreck—very old—of what looked like an old side-wheeler." From the farm they went on to Lock Dam, where they met Milford and Dorothy Kidney. Then they motored on to the mouth of Allagash Stream, where they camped. The next day, July 15, they poled and dragged up to Little Allagash Falls, getting some unexpected help from a boys' group—a party of sixteen canoes. At the falls, they talked with the owner, Wes Herrick, who in his friendly way invited them to lunch.[38] The trip was a welcome rest and a source of renewal for Patterson, particularly after his efforts of the past year—efforts that would help save the Allagash.

During that year, 1959, Patterson's concern for the Allagash, along with the realization that Maine needed a voice for conservation-minded people, had motivated him to organize the Natural Resources Council of Maine, known as the NRCM. Largely through his efforts, the organization was founded on June 25, 1959. For the next six years, as its first president, he would work tirelessly to save the Allagash, one of the council's first major projects.[39] In January 1960 the NRCM published its first newsletter, devoted to educating the public about the value of the Allagash and the proposals affecting it. Besides the two federal interests, the

Rankin Rapids dam and a national park, these included a road from Ashland, Maine, to Daaquam, Quebec, Canada, that would bisect the waterway. Patterson and the council expected the park proposal to be released by the federal government shortly, but while they waited to see what form it would take, forces had already begun opposing it. In fact, even before the park survey team had started its work in 1959, Commissioner Cobb, the Maine Fish and Game Association, the American Legion, some legislators, and the timberland owners and loggers had spoken out against the park.[40]

The opposition was not unexpected. From E. S. Coe's day, when individuals and companies amassed large landholdings and created a forest products industry dominated by pulp and paper that became a cornerstone of the state economy, Maine's government had come under the industry's powerful lobbying influence. In American society, this is not unusual. Industry survives and grows on profits, and in order to reduce its risk of investment toward this end, it logically attempts to control those factors that influence its chances of success. The landowners were, of course, concerned about potential loss of land and their timber resource base. And at the time of the controversy, as historian Richard Judd noted, Maine's forestland owners enjoyed some of the country's lowest tax rates and controlled a labor market in the forest, and they feared that both situations would change with increased federal activity on the dam and park projects.[41] Additionally, many households were dependent on wood-related businesses for income and, ultimately, on use of the land to supply pulpwood, logs, and mill wood products. Maine citizens were also known for their independent-mindedness and strongly believed that state control was preferable to federal control in their lives. And as far as the land was concerned, it was too sparsely settled for many to see the need for zoning and other land-use controls, which further reinforced the feeling that landowners had the right to do what they wished with their property.

In this context, it was not surprising when in early 1960 Maine's forest commissioner, Austin Wilkins, told the members of a rotary club that a national park would strike a severe economic blow by removing 760,000 acres of timberland from production, with an accompanying loss of taxes and jobs. He said that companies were already following principles of conservation and welcoming hunters, trappers, and recreational visitors.[42] The following spring, a speaker at a public hearing on the Passamaquoddy Tidal Power Project "compared the preservation of the Allagash to the preservation of the back pasture on the farm, which could better be used as an industrial site."[43] A May 5 article in the *Portland Press Herald* reported that a petition bearing more than 7,000 names, representing a "goodly number of people of northern Maine," opposed the "unproposed proposal for a national park."[44] At the same time, the Allagash continued to be invaded by roads. Letourneau reported later in the month that the Telos Lake hauling road was improved to the extent that vehicles other than winch-equipped jeeps and tractors could gain access.[45]

In its June 1960 bulletin, the NRCM announced that the Allagash would be a topic of discussion at its upcoming first annual meeting and stated that it was unfortunate that the National Park Service had delayed its proposal. "There is evidence," it went on, "that the delay may be at least in part the result of pressures put on Maine's congressional delegation by certain business interests in the state." The article stressed that a proposal was needed as a rallying point, noting, "It is impossible to ask for widespread support without a definite plan." Nevertheless, the bulletin stated, there were thousands who wanted to save the Allagash. The publication also included a letter of congratulation from Justice Douglas on the fine work the council was doing to preserve the waterway.[46]

Conflicting views expressed at the NRCM's meeting that month led to publicity for the growing controversy. National Park Service officials said that an Allagash national recreation area would pose no economic threat, whereas representatives of Maine's Great Northern Paper Company alluded to jobs that could be lost. Patterson, reported the *Portland Sunday Telegram,* countered that the region would be of "tremendous value if kept as a wilderness, but he expressed fear that those characteristics may eventually be lost as more mechanization moves into the area."[47] Before the end of 1960, the owners of the land through which the Allagash flowed went on the offensive and announced a plan for timber harvesting, fish and wildlife management, and recreational use that would preserve the beauty of the waterside area, and John Maines of Great Northern Paper asserted, "Private ownership, free enterprise and the profit motive are still by far the best means of securing the greatest good for the greatest number of people in managing our Maine timberlands."[48] At the same time, Philip P. Clement, president of the Prentiss and Carlisle Company, which, he pointed out, represented "fairly substantial timberland interests," sent a letter to Senator Muskie in which he expressed concern about proposals in Washington, D.C., that he had heard could "seriously disrupt the orderly development and use of this timber resource." The letter included an "Allagash Land Management Policy" in which the major landowners in the Allagash agreed to, among other things, "grow and harvest forest products in the area in accordance with sound forest management policy" and "preserve the natural wilderness beauty of land bordering the lakes and water courses, and the canoeing tradition of the famous Allagash River."[49] As the year ended, the controversy was continuing to take shape and the arguments were becoming more focused, but still no national plan had materialized.

By late winter of 1961, events had begun to unfold. Udall had directed the National Park Service to release its report, and the

NRCM had engaged the Conservation Foundation in New York to conduct a thorough and impartial study of the Allagash. The foundation, a nonprofit corporation with a distinguished record of research, education, and publication in the field of natural resources, had begun to research the environmental, economic, and recreational value and potential of the Allagash and lay out and analyze alternatives for the waterway's future.[50] In June, a resolution passed in both houses of Maine's legislature, officially recognizing that "the Allagash River Valley is the last major waterway in the east still a wilderness area" and directing the Legislative Research Committee to "study what steps could be taken to secure these assets for the benefit of the people of the State of Maine." Patterson saw the resolution as an attempt to forestall creation of a national park but viewed it as encouraging regardless of the motives behind it.[51]

It was also in June that Udall and Muskie made a trip into the Allagash. Years later, Udall recalled:

> Ed Muskie asked me to accompany him on a Maine resource inspection trip. We flew on a float plane (just the two of us and a pilot) to Ross Lake [about twenty miles northwest of Chamberlain Farm] and stayed overnight. Next day we flew over the St. John river damsites and up the Allagash and over to eastern Maine where we inspected the area embraced by the Passamaquoddy Power Project. . . . I was impressed with Maine's wilderness—amazed actually that something so untrammeled existed in the East. I favored action to make the Allagash a National Riverway like the one that was emerging as a singular candidate project in the midwest, i.e., Missouri's Ozark National River. Ed, in his first term, was cautious and I could see he felt

a federal solution would cut against the grain of
Maine public opinion. It never became a candidate
for national protection, largely because I respected
Muskie and didn't want to push ahead if he was
opposed.[52]

"U.S. Park Service Releases Report on Allagash Area,"
announced a headline in the *Portland Evening Express* on July 7.
Finally, the long-awaited report was out. It proposed creation of a
national recreation area that would cover 246,500 acres of forestland
and contain sixty-three lakes and 360 miles of river and stream—a
total of 50,000 acres of water surface. Udall, the article noted, "has-
n't yet made up his mind about the proposal. . . . But the National
Park Service is solidly for the recreational area."[53] Muskie, in a carefully worded statement, commented that the proposal's recommendations deserved the "most careful and balanced review and
appraisal. . . . Udall has very wisely deferred making a judgment on
the report pending a thorough review."[54] An editorial in the *Portland Press Herald* observed that the proposal was sharpening the
debate on the Passamaquoddy Tidal Power Project in weighing it
against the benefits of wilderness.[55]

While these events were unfolding, an editorial in the *Portland
Evening Express* noted a determination among Americans to preserve the few wilderness areas that remained in the country, as evidenced by a congressional committee's recent approval of the
wilderness bill. "It is this awareness of public interest," the editorial
stated, that "encourages the belief the Allagash may be taken soon
as a national park."[56] Indeed, America was at this time beginning a
significant shift in attitude toward the environment, from utilitarianism to preservation and consideration of issues related to quality
of life and survival.[57]

In the fall, Patterson and the NRCM were seeing delays in the completion of the Conservation Foundation's study and feeling pressure to prepare for a decision to sponsor or support a plan for the Allagash.[58] The paper companies were continuing their public opposition. Representatives of International Paper Company stated that should any proposed park plan materialize, the company "would have to look immediately for a new source of raw wood to keep its two mills operating."[59] In Minnesota, a board member of the company was quoted as saying that the proposed Allagash national recreation area was "an example of the folly of single purpose land management."[60] And the Associated Industries of Maine came out in direct opposition, stating that the forest products industry would be injured by a park "locking up the Allagash for recreation."[61]

The year 1962 opened with a long statement in opposition to the park idea from an organization of landowners, companies, civic organizations, and citizens called the Association for Multiple Use of Maine Timberlands. The principal landowners were Great Northern Paper Company, International Paper Company, the Prentiss and Carlisle Company, and heirs to the Pingree holdings. To complicate matters, on January 31 President Kennedy's Outdoor Recreation Resources Review Commission sent a report to Congress in favor of setting up a kind of multiple-use recreation area in the Allagash while allowing logging to continue and apparently opposing the Rankin Rapids dam.[62] The pressure on Udall to make a decision went up another notch.

On February 12, the NRCM released the results of the Conservation Foundation's long-awaited fact-finding study, which was followed the next day by a public meeting led by the principal investigators and Patterson. "An increasing population and the demands for recreation caught up with Maine's Allagash country in 1957," stated the NRCM's bulletin in its introduction to the study.[63] The report itself presented an analysis of all the proposals for the Allagash, including one not advanced before—the establishment of a national forest in the region. It suggested that the idea had "considerable merit" and "ought to receive due consideration" as a compromise. Regulated timber harvesting, the report pointed out, could occur along with management of a wilderness recreation area that could be limited to a small area surrounding the river and major headwaters.[64]

Patterson and the NRCM began developing a set of broad objectives for the waterway's preservation. Patterson sought the advice of Sigurd Olson, an author and wilderness advocate who had been a leader in protecting the Quetico-Superior wilderness, along the boundary between Minnesota and Ontario, Canada. Olson replied that the Conservation Foundation's study and the NRCM's bulletin were exactly what Patterson needed to back up his argument. He mentioned that he had seen some of the Allagash country in 1954 but had never made a canoe trip down the river.[65] Patterson also met privately with Stephen Wheatland of the Pingree heirs, and in a letter to an NRCM board member, he said that Wheatland had indicated unofficially that the Pingrees could part with a 2,600-foot-wide strip next to the waters on land they owned.[66] Convinced that the NRCM should not yet be seen as taking sides, Patterson decided that the organization should publicize its "own ideas on minimum requirements that should apply regardless of who owns or controls the Allagash."[67]

Later that spring, the NRCM published its objectives, suggesting that a minimum area of 2,600 feet from all shores should be protected from cutting and that the characteristics of silence, solitude, a sense of remoteness from civilization, and a natural scene unaltered by human activity should be protected where wilderness conditions prevail. Further, no more than three or four access points to the shore should be allowed, and campgrounds accessible by cars, parking areas, and buildings should be no closer than 1,000 feet from the shore. Hunting and fishing should be allowed, and internal combustion engines should be used only on roads and at motor campgrounds.[68] If these aims could be attained, those who would one day visit the Chamberlain Farm site would do so in the old way, by canoe.

In mid-August, Patterson was at work writing the next NRCM bulletin, an edition devoted to the Allagash, and there was no better setting in which to do it than one of his and Barbara's waterway outings. Near the end of their trip, they found themselves on Chamberlain Lake with all campsites full. They were opposite Nugent's Chamberlain Lake Camps when it began to rain, so they stopped

Barn at Chamberlain Farm, 1962

This old barn was one of only two buildings remaining at Chamberlain Farm when Robert Patterson Sr. and his wife, Barbara, visited Nugent's Chamberlain Lake Camps in 1962. Photograph by Bill Cross, courtesy of Maine Department of Inland Fisheries and Wildlife.

there and took a cabin with meals. What started out as an overnight stay extended to three days. During that time Barbara banded birds, for which she now had a license, and Bob worked on the bulletin. Both took time to walk the trail toward Chamberlain Farm; to visit the old Hanna trapping cabin, which Nugent was remodeling; and to boat along the shore. The trip convinced Patterson of the urgent need to act soon because of incursions he had seen that were diminishing the region's wilderness character.[69]

The NRCM bulletin published on Patterson's return added a new note to the debate, giving serious consideration to state control. It proposed that all land in the Allagash watershed be given to the state by the owners and leased back to them for 999 years, except for a half-mile-wide wilderness strip along the shoreline. Timber harvesting would follow the best principles of forest management, and hunting and fishing would be allowed.[70]

Early in September, a Maine legislative research subcommittee, which had been directed to study the future use and development of the waterway, held a hearing in Augusta. Patterson took the opportunity to present the NRCM's views on the state and federal proposals but took no stand except that the wilderness character of the waterway should be preserved. One reporter observed that Patterson's presentation was "extremely dignified and effective and while other witnesses disagreed with some of his comments the main point he achieved was the serious belief that something needs to be done and done right away."[71] Three representatives of the U.S. Department of the Interior were present as observers. John Maines of Great Northern Paper Company, who was also president of the Association for Multiple Use of Maine Timberlands, testified at length against the proposals and argued that the area would retain its wilderness character for years under present management practices. But former state senator Ezra Briggs said the issue was simply "a conflict between some people who believe the Allagash is a unique wilderness canoe experience worth saving and a very large, powerful and influential group of landowners, mainly paper companies . . . who have launched one of the largest public relations campaigns against preservation of the Allagash ever seen in this state." The state commissioners of forestry and fish and game reflected Governor John H. Reed's support of the association. Commissioner Cobb said Udall had told him that unless the state agreed to ensure preservation of the Allagash's wilderness character, he would "recommend to President Kennedy that the Rankin Rapids dam be built, which would mean the end of the Allagash."[72] Udall denied having given any ultimatum and wrote a long public letter to Muskie refuting Cobb's statement. Muskie made a public statement supporting Udall.[73]

In early December, Lawrence Stuart, director of the Maine State Park and Recreation Commission, held a meeting with landowners and presented a five-page confidential statement and proposal, "sensing that if something concrete is not formulated very soon the Federal Government, thinking we can't solve it at the state level, will determine their own course of action independently." The plan had already been reviewed by members of the commission and by Commissioners Wilkins and Cobb. "It should be made clear," Stuart said, "that the Park Commission has no intention of promoting a State Park project in the Allagash. To do so would only add to an already confused situation. The Commission, however, would like to be of assistance in solving this problem if the landowners feel that the time has come when something needs to be done in the way of a compromise between suggested radical Federal proposals and the current 'status quo' condition." In discussing certain evaluations that formed the background for the proposal, Stuart noted: "The Allagash River is a great national wilderness area, and every effort should be made to preserve it. . . . The interests of the whole Nation, as well as of people outside the United States who are interested in this sort of an area, should be of paramount consideration." Notably, the proposal suggested that access to the waterway be provided only at three locations where access by car was already available—Telos Lake, Second Musquacook Lake (eleven miles west of Umsaskis Lake), and Michaud Farm (above Allagash Falls)—and called for the landowners to "agree not to open any more roads to the public than those currently in effect." Shorelands would be protected by purchase, lease, and zoning and by control of camp leases and inholdings. Parts of this plan, as will be seen, would surface in later, more official proposals.[74]

Just when the major elements in the Allagash issue seemed to have been identified, another appeared before the year ended. It came in the form of another major hydroelectric dam near Rankin Rapids. This time, it was a private initiative called the Cross Rock dam, and it would obliterate the Allagash waters all the way to Lock Dam, creating a 200,000-acre reservoir more than sixty miles long.[75] The matter had become more complicated than ever.

The year 1963 commenced with an effort by the state to sort things out. The Legislative Research Committee recommended a bill to the Maine legislature to create the Allagash River Authority and Advisory Committee. The authority would be charged with preparing and presenting to the legislature a specific agreement between the landowners and the state that would preserve the conservation areas of the Allagash region.[76] An editorial in the *Portland Press Herald* called it "an attempt by the state's pulp and paper industry to freeze the status quo and protect and preserve full exploitation by private interests of the Allagash's forest resources."[77] When Muskie was asked by state senator Edward P. Cyr to comment on the bill, he wrote back that "presumably, the establishment of such a wilderness area, if it is to be meaningful, should include the Allagash River and adjacent land areas as a contiguous and well defined entity irrevocably dedicated to its maintenance in a wilderness state. The bill does not clearly embrace such an objective." He saw the bill as an "effort to explore for two years the possibility of acquiring by negotiation with landowners a meaningful wilderness area on the Allagash River."[78]

At the March 21 hearing on the bill, Patterson, representing the NRCM, proposed amendments, including one that would direct the authority to "prepare a comprehensive plan for the permanent preservation and protection of the Allagash Watercourse."[79] The hearing garnered widespread support for the bill, but there was opposition from those supporting the power projects, for a bill was also being considered that would create an authority to build the Cross Rock dam. Almost immediately, a "Save the Allagash" committee was formed to oppose the dam—a committee that included Justice Douglas.[80] Muskie came out in favor of the federal approach to development of the upper St. John River's power potential rather than the proposed project at Cross Rock.[81] In May, Patterson, in a strongly worded letter to the editor of the *Portland Press Herald*, alerted the public to the "strong and well-heeled lobbies working in Augusta to destroy the Allagash" through the dam projects.[82]

In the meantime, Patterson had written a letter inviting Justice Douglas to speak at the annual meeting of the NRCM in June. Douglas accepted, whereupon Patterson wrote to Udall, asking him whether there was any possibility of telling Douglas anything about his decision on the Passamaquoddy–St. John–Allagash study. At the meeting, Douglas gave an address titled "Our Disappearing Wilderness," calling "the Allagash country a sleeping giant among the few remaining potential park and recreation areas in the northeast" and urging that it be saved. He made no mention of what Udall's pending decision would be.[83]

Two weeks later, on July 1, 1963, Udall made his recommendation to President Kennedy. He called for early authorization of the Passamaquoddy Tidal Power Project, with a dam above the mouth of the Allagash to "preserve in its entirety the free flowing nature of the Allagash River and its superb values." And in mid-August, Udall's Bureau of Outdoor Recreation released *A Report on the Proposed Allagash National Riverway,* recommending congressional action, proposing a smaller area than that originally proposed by the National Park Service, and recommending that a half-mile strip from the shore of the Allagash waters be acquired and preserved.[84] In a news report, Udall was quoted as saying "flatly that the U.S. Park Service would have control of the riverway."[85]

Not unmindful of the federal pressure, the state had already begun moving ahead on its own. Earlier in the summer, Governor Reed had signed into law the Allagash River Authority and the Allagash River Advisory Committee. The authority would be made up of five members: the commissioners of forestry, parks, and fish and game; the state attorney general; and the director of the School of Forestry at the University of Maine. The advisory committee would consist of seven appointed members. At the federal level, Muskie questioned the usefulness of the authority, but Udall was reported by Austin Wilkins to have said that "if the State did something on its own and would insure State ownership, he would refrain from pushing federal ownership."[86] The federal stick was still there.

In September, the act creating the Allagash River Authority went into effect, and soon afterward Patterson was nominated as a member of the advisory committee along with Clinton B. Townsend, an attorney and secretary of the NRCM. Both became members of the committee. That same month, the landowners began to step up the pressure. John Maines of Great Northern Paper, in a bold attempt to prove that the company's timber-harvesting policies were not harmful to the Allagash wilderness area, announced that the company would cut several million board feet of timber near the banks of the Allagash as a demonstration project.[87]

A different tack was taken that September by another major

paper company. Three representatives of the company met with Muskie to say that unless their questions regarding the proposed Allagash national riverway could be resolved, their plans to locate a new $50 million paper mill in Maine would probably have to be dropped. Muskie noted that what they needed most was reassurance of his and Udall's attitude of flexibility on three points: "(1) the amount of land taking for the riverway itself; (2) the number and location of access roads which would be permitted in the riverway area; and (3) the question of whether the area would be under the jurisdiction of the State or the Federal Government."[88] On September 23, Muskie and Udall met to decide on an appropriate strategy, and after their meeting Udall sent a letter to one of the company officials stating that he had an open mind regarding the details but was firmly committed to conserving the Allagash River. "I am sure," he wrote, "you can appreciate the fact that the results would involve a balancing of public interests, the steps required to protect the essential qualities of the Allagash, and the needs of the landowners. This, it seems to me, is fair and reasonable." Further, he believed "that public ownership and management is the only sure guarantee of the preservation of the Riverway in perpetuity. I have no inflexible position on the issue of State or Federal ownership." Muskie wrote to the same official to assure him of Udall's flexibility but took the opportunity to communicate his distress at Great Northern Paper Company's announcement of its intent to cut within 150 feet of Allagash Lake's shoreline. "This unilateral announcement," Muskie wrote, "in the midst of talk of possible agreements between the State and the landowners on protection of the area . . . is not likely to enhance the acceptance of professions of good faith on the part of the companies in the eyes of the public."[89]

And so the jockeying for power and the minds of the state's citizenry went on. Through the remainder of the year, the authority and the advisory committee held meetings with landowners, federal officials, and others. Pressure continued at the federal level: The U.S. Department of the Interior's Bureau of Outdoor Recreation conveyed to the authority that it was going ahead with its plans for a national riverway just in case an acceptable state plan was not forthcoming, and the agency also met with the landowners to discuss its plans.[90] The Interior Department published a flyer describing its concept of the riverway, stating that its purpose "would be to insure an area in the eastern United States of sufficient size and quality where present and future generations may experience a primitive northwoods canoeing adventure . . . [which] should take precedence over all other uses." Only if intensive use were excluded, the report stated, would the region maintain its remoteness, giving visitors the opportunity to know nature intimately and to lose themselves in time rather than distance—all of which would greatly enhance the value and usefulness of its water, forests, and wildlife.[91]

At the end of the year, Secretary Udall wrote a long letter to Governor Reed expressing concern about the landowners' attitude toward the riverway proposal and his grave doubts about their desire to conserve the riverway in its primitive state, especially after Great Northern Paper's announcement of its demonstration project. He asked for a three-way meeting of the authority, landowners, and the Bureau of Outdoor Recreation. The authority, however, recommended against it, and although Udall tried a second time, he was unsuccessful.[92] The federal government was being cut out.

During 1964, the authority and the advisory committee continued to work to draft a bill for the 102nd Legislature to consider in the winter of 1965. Muskie, in a letter to Wilkins of the authority, reiterated the test by which he and Udall would judge the state's plan, saying they both had believed from the beginning "that the key issue . . . is the preservation of the riverway as a free-flowing stream in a primitive and, insofar as possible, unspoiled forest area. To be meaningful, such preservation must be in perpetuity."[93] The authority held hearings that fall, and by the end of the year a draft proposal was under way for some form of legislative protection for the Allagash. Still, in a move that must have been frustrating to Patterson and the others who advocated the waterway's preservation, another bill was drafted for consideration by the legislature to create the Cross Rock hydroelectric dam.[94] Just when one dared to entertain a little optimism, another threat reared its head. Yet there was a ray of hope: The paper industry's magazine *Pulp and Paper* ran an article stating "on reliable authority" that both Muskie and Udall were of like mind that "the Allagash must be preserved from flooding" and "flanking forests on each side of the Allagash must be preserved in perpetuity, whether they are under state or federal control."[95]

In January 1965, the authority released its proposal for state control of the Allagash waterway. It proposed a zoned land area one mile from the high-water mark of the shoreline of the river and headwaters. Chamberlain Farm would not be included in the zoned area, for the plan excluded the area of Chamberlain Lake south of Lock Dam and Telos Lake. No woods operations would be allowed within 300 feet of the shore; beyond that, the first quarter mile would have selective cutting; and the remainder of the mile zone would be controlled by the Maine State Park and Recreation Commission. Consideration would be given to eventual acquisition of the 300-foot area. Roads and access would be approved by the commissioner of parks and recreation.[96] Soon after the proposal was made public, Patterson, obviously dissatisfied with the legislative plan and trying to move the process toward stronger preservation, wrote to Muskie expressing concern about the zoning provision and querying the senator about submitting a national riverway bill. Muskie wrote back, saying he thought that outright purchase of the shoreline strip of land would be essential and expressing his own concern about zoning and his reluctance to introduce a national riverway bill at that time.[97] Patterson also exchanged letters with

Udall in January and February expressing this concern, with which Udall agreed. Patterson also stated that he believed it would be a great mistake to leave out Telos Lake and most of Chamberlain Lake.[98]

The Cross Rock dam bill was printed on February 9, followed on February 24 by the bill to create the Allagash Wilderness Waterway. "War Clouds Gather over Allagash" was the headline of one article as hearings neared on the two bills. A unique alliance of conservationists, landowners, fish and game interests, and others formed to oppose the dams, especially Cross Rock.[99] A showdown was in progress. In mid-April, both Patterson and Townsend sent letters to the chair of the Allagash River Authority expressing their concerns about the Allagash bill, including the exclusion of Chamberlain and Telos Lakes. Patterson also suggested reservation of a 600-foot-wide strip of land along the shoreline, state purchase of the land, elimination of motorized watercraft except for those powered by small motors on Telos and Chamberlain Lakes, control of aircraft landings, and more clarity on road crossings.[100] Meanwhile, as the Allagash bill headed toward legislative consideration in early June, the landowners applied pressure by sending letters to the authority pledging to offer leases, sites for control stations, and access roads contingent on the legislature's acceptance of the Allagash waterway bill in the form recommended by the authority.[101] But the *Bangor Daily News* urged further study because of the conflict between the Cross Rock power proposal and still undefined federal proposals.[102]

Patterson had to make a stand. He sent a letter to Governor Reed, who supported the bill, saying regretfully that he, Townsend, and two other members of the advisory committee could not in good conscience go along with the bill as it stood because Telos and Chamberlain Lakes were not included, the 300-foot strip of land was too narrow to provide protection, and the land would not have permanent protection because the bill called for it to be acquired by short-term leases.[103] Opposition to the bill succeeded, and it was referred to the next legislature. The defeat was a blow to the landowners and to the authority. Years later, Patterson recalled that Justice Douglas had once remarked, referring to Maine, "that he had seen many company towns but never before a company state."[104] A small crack had just developed in the relationship. The Cross Rock dam bill also failed passage and was referred to a study committee. Hope still prevailed, and for Patterson, possibilities still existed. The view from Chamberlain Farm might still retain its wildness.

Unexpectedly, on May 30, just prior to the bill's failure, another avenue of hope for preservation of the Allagash had appeared as an editorial in the *Portland Sunday Telegram:* "Senator Muskie of Maine pulled a new surprise out of his hat last week when he introduced a measure that would permit states to administer wild river areas like the Allagash Waterway within the national Wild Rivers System. This, he indicated was an attempt to break the deadlock between state and federal interests over preservation of Maine's famous wilderness camping and fishing area."[105] Work on a wild rivers bill had been under way for some time, and in March Udall had sent it to Congress. Muskie saw it as an opportunity to resolve the Allagash problem.

On June 8, Muskie clarified his intent in a letter to Senator Henry M. Jackson, chairman of the Committee on Interior and Insular Affairs, in which he formally stated that on May 27 he had introduced an amendment to the act that would add state-designated and state-administered wild rivers. "Recently," he wrote, "I developed an approach which in my view will provide a vehicle for the compromise of Federal–State differences on the Allagash and other similar river situations throughout the country." He concluded by pointing to the need for the states and the federal government to work together as partners if the country was to preserve its unique wilderness and aesthetic values.[106] And on June 11, he commented in a letter to a constituent that the Allagash situation boiled down to "a comprehensive rather all inclusive federal plan on one hand and a rather weak State approach on the other. For some time I have been attempting to achieve a compromise between these two extremes. . . . In this approach 50 per cent federal funds would complement State monies for acquisition of property, easement, etc."[107] On June 14, Muskie's administrative assistant, Donald Nicoll, stated in a letter to Lawrence Stuart, "We have some evidence that the Wild Rivers bill supporters will accept the amendment."[108] Throughout the remainder of that month, Muskie continued to argue for his amendment, corresponding with members of the Committee on Interior and Insular Affairs, including Frank Church, Frank E. Moss, George McGovern, and Gaylord Nelson. In July, Muskie received support as well as suggestions from national conservation groups, including the National Wildlife Federation and the National Audubon Society.

Meanwhile, following the waterway bill's defeat, Richard Dubord, the authority's chair, wrote to all the landowners, saying that the authority's members were "deeply disappointed" and he hoped "that you feel, as I do, that the legislative setback was only a temporary one."[109] In early August, Commissioner Wilkins wrote a memorandum to the owners stating that a special legislative Allagash study committee had been set up on June 2 under Senator Elmer Violette, and he thought they would be interested to know that one of the early decisions was to "reactivate the Allagash Authority Study Team" for the purpose of providing information and entering into "discussion plans for an Allagash bill at the forthcoming special session of the 102nd Legislature."[110] Interestingly, in the legislative order establishing the new study committee, one of the reasons given for the committee was the fact that "there is now pending before Congress of the United States, a proposal to assist

states interested in the preservation of 'wild river areas' in cooperation with the Federal Government."[111]

On October 6, the committee held one of four statewide hearings in Portland. Patterson testified that the Allagash was the "last
thing of its kind in the East" and that Telos and Chamberlain Lakes
should be included in the state-controlled section. On November 9,
Edward Crafts, director of the Bureau of Outdoor Recreation,
appeared as a guest of the committee. He continued to keep federal
pressure on the state, saying that inasmuch as he could not say how
much longer the federal government would wait for state action, he
hoped the committee would present its recommendations during
the coming special session of the legislature.[112] By mid-November,
Chairman Violette stated that federal and state officials were "not
too far apart" on their plans for recreational use and control of the
Allagash. He hoped to have an acceptable proposal for preservation
ready at the next legislative session, early in 1966.[113]

On January 17, 1966, a new bill was printed for creation of the
Allagash Wilderness Waterway. It provided for inclusion of Chamberlain and Telos Lakes; state purchase of a restricted zone 400 to
800 feet wide to "preserve, protect and develop the maximum
wilderness character of the watercourse"; control over construction
in a quarter-mile zone; and some oversight on timber harvesting in
the remaining mile zone. Muskie, Udall, Governor Reed, and Patterson and the NRCM were given advance copies, and all gave the
proposed legislation favorable reviews.[114] This time, the effort was
successful, and in February the legislature enacted the bill, contingent upon voter approval of a $1.5 million bond issue "to develop
the maximum wilderness character of the Allagash Waterway," a
sum to be matched by the Bureau of Outdoor Recreation. The
wording was significant, for the framers of the act recognized that
the Allagash was no longer purely wild, but in order to meet the
intent of the act—that is, provide a wilderness-like setting and expe-

rience—the waterway's wilderness character needed to be restored or developed. With support from the state's political leaders and citizenry, 270,291 voters went to the polls on November 8, and 68 percent approved the bond issue, inaugurating, in the words of Udall, "a new concept, a new national era, of creative Federal–State conservation partnership."[115]

Chapter 9

A Need for Vigilance

*W*ITH PASSAGE OF THE ACT authorizing a bond issue for the purchase of land, the Allagash River escaped the fate of so many other rivers—development and obliteration by dams. The latter had happened, just as the Allagash battle was heating up, to the beautiful and wild Glen Canyon, through which the Colorado River flowed just above the famous Grand Canyon. Glen Canyon lost to public apathy and to strong state and federal support for a dam.[1] But the Allagash had been saved and could now join the Boundary Waters Canoe Area Wilderness as a protected wilderness canoe area of national significance. Like Sigurd Olson and the others who had saved Boundary Waters, Robert Patterson and a group of advocates, which included state and federal governmental officials, had succeeded in protecting a waterway of exceptional value. Both groups overcame opposition from powerful and politically dominating large private interests. Moreover, the battle for the Allagash, in the words of Richard Judd, "helped redefine an essentially western notion of untrammeled wilderness for the heavily used and sharply contested woods and rivers of the East."[2]

The accomplishment savored by the people of Maine in 1966 had not been easy—finding a way to protect the waterway had been like negotiating a twisting river of blind falls and rough rapids, sudden obstacles and sharp drops, and eddies and pools offering short respites. Multiple interests had converged on the Allagash and its headwaters, vying for control of its resources for logging, water power, hunting and fishing, wilderness canoeing, and other outdoor activities. The outcome had never been certain. The state had been pushed into the middle and pressured by the federal government, which wanted to create a recreational area or a power project or both; a group of landowners, who wanted to keep the status quo; private entrepreneurs, who wanted to reap profits from hydroelectric power; and conservationists, who wanted to preserve the waterway. Alliances had been formed, influence applied, and campaigns waged. At the root of the conflict was the range of values held by those drawn to Chamberlain Farm and its surroundings. In the end, the public chose to support the protection of wildness in the Allagash.

Not all were happy about the decision, and, of course, among those who had resisted were landowners. Even though the forest had been saved from flooding, the owners were now subject to more restrictions and some loss of land. Sometime after the vote, John Sinclair, an official with Seven Islands Land Company, which manages woodlands for the Pingree heirs, was asked by two of the Pingree landowners to take them into the Allagash to look at some of the lands they were to lose. Sinclair arranged for them to stay at Nugent's Chamberlain Lake Camps, and from there he took them by canoe to Pillsbury Island, in Eagle Lake. Around a little fire, as Sinclair recalled, the two gentlemen talked of the history of the lands that had been bought generations ago by E. S. Coe and David

Pingree and of the years the families had paid taxes and cared for their lands. At times, the two owners withdrew quietly into their own thoughts. Then they began to express their deep feelings about the taking of their land for the Allagash Wilderness Waterway, which to them and many others, Sinclair believed, was "crude and rude." Their stewardship and protection of the lands seemed to have been unappreciated, even ignored. The conversation continued long into the afternoon, and finally the two men stood and asked Sinclair to take them back. More than thirty years passed before Sinclair put this story in writing, because, as he explained, "it was such a sad event for them and myself."[3]

During the next several years, the state surveyed, appraised, and purchased land; appointed an advisory committee to help plan the area's management; and started work on a new dam at the head of the river to replace the old Churchill Dam and control water for canoeists. Patterson was appointed to the advisory committee, a position he would hold for more than a decade. In 1967, he shared some of the philosophy that had guided him during the Allagash controversy in an article titled "The Art of the Impossible," published in *Daedalus: Journal of the American Academy of Arts and Sciences*. "As we approach the end of our resources, insupportable overcrowding, and the loss of space and all wildness," he wrote, "more and more people realize that economic activity cannot provide certain necessities of life and can, in fact, destroy them." Then, in an obvious reference to the First Amendment to the United States Constitution: "As citizens, these have the same right as the potential destroyers to be heard. They deserve equal treatment, and at present they are not getting it. Their individual voices are lost in the wind, and they are heard only when they join together."[4]

On February 20, 1970, a news release from the Bureau of Outdoor Recreation announced the agency's final grant to Maine for the Allagash Wilderness Waterway. "The people of Maine, the Northeast, and the Nation can be proud of this magnificent accomplishment," the bureau's director, G. Douglas Hofe Jr., said. "Maine expects to complete the Allagash project by December 1971. The State then will have acquired more than 20,000 acres."[5]

In the spring of that year, Maine's governor, Kenneth M. Curtis, applied to Secretary of the Interior Walter J. Hickel for the entire Allagash Wilderness Waterway to be approved as the first state-designated wild river under the Wild and Scenic Rivers Act.[6] The act had been passed by Congress on October 2, 1968, and to Edmund Muskie's credit, his amendment had survived. Moreover, the Allagash Wilderness Waterway was specifically named in the act for inclusion in the system, pending application of the governor and

Abandoned Engine of the Eagle Lake–West Branch Railroad
Protection of the Allagash River as a wild river area included preservation of its rich logging history. One unusual reminder of that history is this steam engine, which was left in the woods when the railroad stopped running, in 1933. When this photograph was taken, in 1997, the engine had been jacked up on blocks and was awaiting a new bed and section of track for support.
Photograph by Dean B. Bennett.

meeting of the guidelines and criteria.[7] On July 17, a notice in the *Federal Register* announced approval of the state's application; the waterway met the criteria for classification as a wild river, the most stringent designation in the act.[8] With the approval, the state had an obligation under Section 10(a) of the act: "Each component of the national wild and scenic rivers system shall be administered in such a manner as to protect and enhance the values which caused it to be included in said system without, insofar as is consistent therewith, limiting other uses that do not substantially interfere with public use and enjoyment of these values. In such administration primary emphasis shall be given to protecting its esthetic, scenic, historic, archeologic, and scientific features."[9]

More specifically, the federal announcement that the entire Allagash Wilderness Waterway met the criteria and evaluation guidelines for its designation as a wild river area in the National Wild and Scenic Rivers System included the following:

1. Impoundments: "There are three small dams. . . . These . . . do not form impoundments which distract from or disrupt the wilderness character of the waterway and are of historic significance. . . . The operation of all three dams is governed by the policy . . . 'to preserve, protect, and develop the maximum wilderness character of the watercourse.'"

2. Accessibility: "Public access over private roads will be permitted to and along a portion of Telos Lake at the southern end of the waterway and to the northern boundary at West Twin Brook. Existing private roads within the waterway which have been developed for logging purposes will be closed to public use. . . . There are six established and designated areas for the landing and take-off . . . by aircraft. . . . During the winter, snowmobiles are permitted on designated roads, trails, and paths. The Allagash Lake and Stream are closed to all forms of motorized

travel including aircraft. Temporary bridges for short-term logging purposes may be authorized by the State. Any such crossing is designed to provide minimum impact on the wilderness
character of the waterway."

3. Essentially primitive: "The overall character of the Allagash
    Wilderness Waterway is an outstanding vestige of primitive
    America. . . . All existing structures have been removed except
    those essential to State service, maintaining water level control,
    and temporary structures necessary for watercourse crossing
    and access."

4. Unpolluted: "A concept of nondegradation will be followed
    whereby existing high water quality will be maintained to the
    maximum extent feasible." [10]

The dedication of the waterway on July 19, 1970, at the new
Churchill Dam officially celebrated the long, difficult effort to preserve the Allagash. The guest list included Patterson, Senator
Muskie, Governor Curtis, and representatives of the landowners,
Maine legislature, and the U.S. Department of the Interior. Those
who spoke at the event cited the meaning of the waterway in terms
of a conservation ethic, its national significance, and its management by generations of Pingrees, Coes, and others who had owned
and harvested the land. In the words of one speaker, the day was
"simply the beginning of a new chapter in the history of the Allagash."[11]

It would indeed be a new chapter for the Allagash, for Chamberlain Lake, and for Chamberlain Farm. The farm would no longer
face the threats of roads to its door, development as a resort, water-
skiers in its cove, and any number of civilization's other accou-
trements. The possibility of a private playground in the Allagash
open only to the elite had been removed; the area would be forever
open to all who wanted to enjoy a bit of the country's diminishing

wilderness. But its preservation would not have been possible without the values, vision, and perseverance of people such as Patterson, Muskie, Stewart Udall, William O. Douglas, and others who had the will to see the struggle through. Their leadership came at a time of change in the nation's view of its responsibility to the environment and the American wild; the first Earth Day had been celebrated only a few months before the waterway's dedication. The Allagash Wilderness Waterway was a symbol of this change and provided hope for wild rivers everywhere. Maintaining that symbol, however, would require no less an effort than had been exerted in its preservation.

At first, the steward for this wild river area, the Maine State Park and Recreation Commission, appeared to embrace the purpose and philosophy of the state's enabling legislation and the wild and scenic river designation, stating in 1970 that the river should "forever be maintained and operated in its wild condition to provide a wilderness canoe experience." In 1973, the Maine Bureau of Parks and Recreation (the agency's new name) stated in its *Concept Plan* for the waterway that it would be "protected, developed, and managed to the optimum extent possible, as a wilderness area.... Intensive day use is also not compatible with the wilderness experience and will not be allowed. The remoteness of the Waterway makes day-use an insignificant aspect."[12] How wrong this prediction would prove to be.

Guided by this view, the commission set out to develop the waterway's "maximum wilderness character." Patterson had given a sense of what this meant to him in a letter he had written earlier as a member of the advisory committee to the Allagash River Authority: "Wilderness character, I think, is a combination of *natural beauty,* a sense of *space and distance,* a sense of *remoteness* from civilization, the knowledge that some effort has been made to get into the area and to travel in it, and an absence of man-made *noise.*"[13]

The commission adopted policies to close all private roads as their usefulness ceased to the woods operator except to secure public access at the two ends of the waterway; to strictly control access from a road in the middle of the waterway should it continue to cross; and to manage the location and use of campsites and waste disposal.[14] In the restricted zone, as the legislation required, the commission demolished, torched, and otherwise eliminated structures all along the shoreline of the waterway, including a forestry headquarters, a shed housing the two engines of the Eagle Lake–West Branch Railroad, camps, docks, outbuildings, and other structures.

From the very beginning, the market for wood had set the tempo for the threat to wildness in the Allagash, and unfortunately, over the years following the waterway's creation, Maine found it lacked the ability to control timber harvesting and the resulting need for roads within the mile-wide buffer area outside the restricted zone. And so the cutting practices within that protective belt of forested land did not wholly conform to the reported rhetoric of the paper companies, which in the heat of the waterway battle had said it was in their best interest to carry out selective cutting and proper conservation management.[15] Instead, some large expanses of stump-stippled clear-cuts appeared up to the very edge of the narrow, fragile protected fringe of naturalness along the river's edge. Thus, a thin band of land conceived as a place for "wilderness character" acquired a new name: "beauty strip." And regardless of the silvicultural arguments, the public did not like what it saw. However, those who loved the wilderness waterway saw their efforts to ban clear-cutting and herbicide use cut down in legislative halls like the forests they fought to protect. In the end, only 18,000 acres of viewscape along the river north of Churchill Dam were left under state control—just 15 percent of the land that had originally required Maine's approval of cutting plans.[16] South of Churchill

Dam, harvesting could continue on private woodlands surrounding Chamberlain Farm and the headwater lakes with little consideration for the scars that might be seen on the ridges and hills. More ominous was the loss of approval of the location of principal haulroads for forest harvesting.[17]

Roads fractured the North Woods into a broken forest of wood-lots, each for the most part reflecting the economic dictates of the company operating there. The mosaic expanded into and through the mile-wide buffer area, making it indistinguishable from the rest of the working forest and discernible only on maps. The pattern developed all across the state. Between 1985 and 1999, secondary roads into Maine's woodlands increased by approximately 148 percent. The roads, combined with a 25 percent increase in the state's population, rising affluence and leisure time, and people's desire to escape from the artificiality and constraints of urban America, were major factors in the 28 percent increase in visitors to Maine's North Woods, from both within and outside the state, during the last quarter of the twentieth century.[18] They came propelled by almost every make and model of motorized vehicle. They made forays from second homes, camps, commercial campgrounds, and lodges—all within a day's striking distance. They were guided by flying services, outfitting services, and recreational services of all kinds. They used information gathered from the Internet, cellular phones, computerized maps, satellite images, and global positioning systems. In thirty years, summer visitors to the waterway tripled, and in twenty years, so did winter users.[19] More and more, they represented the kind of visitor the waterway's visionaries had failed to anticipate: the day user.

As a group, the day visitors favored easier, quicker access. Remoteness was not as much an issue for them as it was for the wilderness-seeking canoe campers, although it may be assumed that both groups appreciated a measure of solitude, privacy, quiet, and a

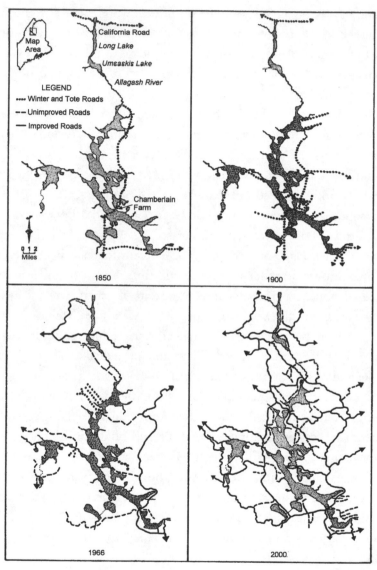

Allagash Wilderness Waterway Roads, 1850, 1900, 1966, and 2000

This depiction of roads in the Allagash waterway is based on a variety of sources. Improved roads are graveled, have culverts, and are generally passable by two-wheel-drive vehicles in all seasons, including winter if snowplows are in use. Unimproved roads vary in condition, depending on vehicle use and periodic upgrading. Winter and tote roads are passable by logging trucks and other logging machines during logging operations, usually in winter on frozen ground. Specific roads shown on the map may change from one category to another as use, maintenance, and road conditions change. Additionally, in some cases the categorization of roads may not be entirely accurate because of lack of information. *Map, 1850:* Information about the existence of the roads at this time is from Richard W. Judd, *Aroostook: A Century of Logging in Northern Maine* (Orono: University of Maine Press, 1989), 59–61; "Journey to the Woods, 1852," folder C15, E. S. Coe Chamberlain Farm Papers, Captain Myron H. Avery Collection, Maine State Library, Augusta; and inferences from historical documentation of the construction of dams and travel to Grant Farm and Trout Brook Farm. *Map, 1900:* See Harry A. Trink, *Map of Northern Maine* (Bangor, Maine: Bangor and Aroostook Railroad Company, 1897); Lucius L. Hubbard, *Map of Northern Maine* (Cambridge, Mass.: Lucius L. Hubbard, 1899); "TWP7 R12 W.E.L.S., 1908–1909," file F3-17, courtesy of James W. Sewall Company; and Joel W. Eastman, "A History of the Katahdin Iron Works" (master's thesis, University of Maine, 1965), 63–67. *Map, 1966:* See R. A. Vigue, "Pre-1966 Motor Vehicle Access to the Allagash" (Augusta, Maine: Maine Department of Conservation, Bureau of Parks and Lands, 1998), photocopy; "Proposed Allagash Wilderness Waterway," rev. 1966, map; A. Allen Murphy, "History of John's Bridge, Township 9, Range 13," 17 May 1998, photocopy, courtesy Seven Islands Land Company; 1966 aerial photographs, James W. Sewall Company; and Maine topographic maps, 15 Minute Quadrangle Series, including Chesuncook, 1958; Telos Lake, 1957; Allagash Lake, 1961; Spider Lake, 1954; Churchill Lake, 1962; and Umsaskis Lake, 1935 (Washington, D.C.: U.S. Geological Survey). *Map, 2000:* See "Allagash Wilderness Waterway," base maps (Augusta, Maine: Maine Department of Conservation, Bureau of Parks and Lands, 1990s); and *Maine Atlas and Gazetteer* (Yarmouth, Maine: DeLorme, 1999).

more intimate relationship with nature. The real issue, however, was the effect of increasing access on these qualities, and Robert Patterson was one who was sensitive to it. Patterson was one of them. In fact, he had been a member of the Maine State Park and Recreation Commission's first advisory committee in 1970 when policies were established limiting access and instituting other controls to maintain the waterway's wilderness character. Notably, at the end of the list of policies was the following statement: "It is the thinking of the Commission and its Advisory Committee that if users are not willing to take the Allagash trip on terms and conditions outlined above, then they should not undertake the Allagash trip." [20]

Despite these intentions, pressure for more access continued through the years to plague the waterway's managers. In 1977, while still a member of the advisory committee, Patterson, then in his early seventies, wrote to the director of the Maine Bureau of Parks and Recreation, expressing "a feeling that access to the Waterway is getting easier all the time."[21] Several years later, in the mid-1980s, the director voiced his own concern in an interview about the damaging effect of uncontrolled access and overuse of the waterway. "We are going to have to be very firm," he said.[22] But ease of access continued to prove a difficult problem. As Patterson observed, the public could still use most of the roads, and many who came to hunt and fish and even to take canoe trips found the convenience of the road system an acceptable exchange for the wildness it had destroyed.[23] Not surprisingly, with more and better roads leading to and into the mile-wide buffer of the waterway, lobbying for the approval of additional points of motorized access to the water's edge intensified over the years. As a result, the number of motor vehicle access points directly to the water or to campsites on the shore grew from two or three envisioned in 1970 to twelve allowed by rule making in 2000.[24]

With easier access and the resulting increase in visitors came the need for enforcement of rules. Unfortunately, management was unable to keep pace with the growing pressures. Over the years, the supervisors of the waterway gradually lost clout as the waterway lost its special position and individual budget in the agency's administrative hierarchy, going from a division in a department to one of six regions in a division and, finally, one park in a state of more than forty parks and historic sites. With each move, it suffered from competition for funds and staff. These changes occurred as the Maine Department of Conservation underwent reorganization and downsizing in cost-cutting and efficiency moves.

The changes also appeared to provide a strong incentive to treat the waterway in ways similar to other parks in the system and ignore the special management requirements imposed by the remoteness and wilderness protection mandates legislated by the state and spelled out in the Wild and Scenic Rivers Act and the federal designation. Some who favored more access and fewer restrictions used the opportunity to promote the view that the area was not a true wilderness in the sense of being untouched by humans as a way of justifying their demands. This attitude was completely opposite that which prevailed in 1970, when Lawrence Stuart wrote in *Parks and Recreation* that "although the Allagash is not a wilderness in the sense of its being untouched by man, it is a wilderness in the sense that those who visit it can enjoy primitive living under natural conditions. The Commissioners will lend every effort to ensure that the essential character of this beautiful area remains unchanged."[25] For consistency with this original objective, the argument that the Allagash was no longer a wilderness should have triggered an effort on the part of the state to examine the waterway's condition, especially its conformance with the 1966 mandate to develop its maximum wilderness character. Instead, the greater number of access points and developments, such as buildings in sight of the water, seemed to serve as an excuse to degrade the waterway's wild and remote qualities even further. In fact, many suspected that some would have liked to see the term *wilderness* removed from the waterway's name to advance this argument. And in keeping with this view, the state also appeared to favor a customer service management approach, along with a reluctance to train and otherwise equip and authorize rangers to strongly enforce the rules. In 1998, the Maine Center for Economic Policy would state in its report *Tourism and Maine's Future* that "from the Allagash Wilderness Waterway to Penobscot Bay's islands, wilderness values are being compromised as secluded places lose their remoteness and are 'loved to death.'"[26]

This slow erosion of the Allagash wilderness is not unlike that occurring in wild areas all across the United States. The difficulty of preserving roadless areas in national forests is but one example. The effect of off-road vehicles (ORVs) is another. Noisy and polluting, they are also capable of damaging land and disrupting wildlife. ORVs come in many types and include dirt bikes, all-terrain vehicles (ATVs), snowmobiles, jeeps, and four-wheel-drive vehicles, each having its supporters who want more and freer access. The pressure to use motorized canoes and high-horsepower boats and to build accessible launching facilities is also growing. Today, visitors to the Grand Canyon hear motorized rafts running the Colorado River. In the skies over many wildlands in the United States, airplanes and helicopters roar, and on the ground and in lakes, flying services seek more landing sites. The internal combustion engine is the bane of wilderness.[27]

Patterson, when in his eighties, was fully aware of such threats to the original vision of the Allagash Wilderness Waterway. Had he lived into the twenty-first century, he would have seen a continuing need for vigilance to protect the values he, Muskie, Udall, Douglas, Curtis, and so many others had worked to protect. In 1998, the state of Maine produced the first management plan for the waterway that contained detailed policies, objectives, and strategies. The new management plan, however, did not recognize how far the waterway had strayed from the conditions it was supposed to be held to in 1966 and 1970, nor did it take into account how strongly some members of the public felt about adhering to those conditions. The differences in public opinion came to a head in 2000 when the state, in accordance with its management plan, attempted to open an access at John's Bridge, a crossing between Eagle and Churchill Lakes.

A decision by the Maine Land Use Regulation Commission to allow the access is now being appealed in Maine Superior Court by several plaintiffs, including the Natural Resources Council of Maine. The organization's executive director stated: "The Council did not grasp the need for vigilance and ongoing advocacy to protect the wilderness character envisioned by our founders for the Allagash Wilderness Waterway. That lesson has been learned in poignant fashion, especially over the last several years."[28]

At issue today are the natural values Maine sought to protect when the waterway was originally created and later designated as a wild river area—values of natural beauty, integrity, and diversity that should characterize the wilderness character of the restricted zone. These values inherent in wilderness areas are at the crux of humanity's relationship with the rest of nature and provide both reason and motivation for saving wild areas. "The wilderness cannot be preserved against the pressures of population and 'progress' unless the guarantees are explicit and severely enforced, unless wilderness values become a crusade," wrote Justice Douglas in his book *A Wilderness Bill of Rights*.[29] Finding support for such a crusade is more possible today than it would have been in the mid-1800s, when Chamberlain Farm was built. At that time, beliefs in the separation of humans from nature and in human domination of nature prevailed in American society, supplanting the feeling of kinship with all things wild exhibited by those who had originally camped on a point of land in a lake they came to call Apmoojenagamook. But as

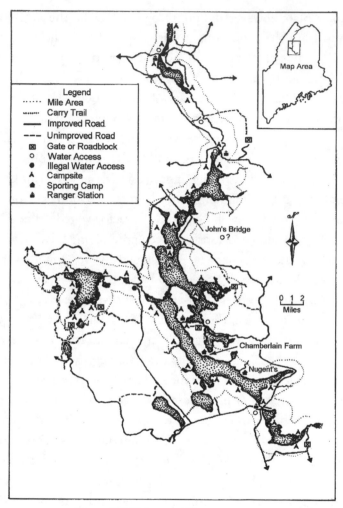

Allagash Wilderness Waterway, 2000

Modified from "Allagash Wilderness Waterway," base maps (Augusta, Maine: Maine Department of Conservation, Bureau of Parks and Lands, 1990s).

we have seen, other perspectives appeared at the farm through the years. People came with a view of being closer to nature, of living cooperatively with the land and being mindful of their effect on its future. Others saw themselves as part of the land and believed themselves obligated to preserve its integrity for the future of the earth and all living things. Although all these perspectives exist among those drawn to the Allagash today, a shift has occurred in their relative influence. The preservation of the waterway reflected this change, as does the ongoing reclamation of the farm by the forest from which it was carved.

This relative change in values mirrors a trend in the United States spanning a time from the 1800s, when widespread exploitation of forests, wildlife, waters, and other natural resources held sway, to the dawn of the twenty-first century, when increasing numbers of people were recognizing the value of conserving forests, protecting endangered species and their habitats, preventing air and water pollution, and expanding roadless wildlands (see appendix D). Today, more people favor nonmaterial values of nature, such as ecological protection and the expression of moral and ethical obligations to nature, over material commodity values and economic priorities. More now see the human connection with all living things in natural communities.[30]

For all the issues and problems that surround wilderness areas, people still see them as extraordinary natural places capable of evoking powerful feelings about our connection to nature and an appreciation for our history with the land. This is no more true anywhere than in the Allagash Wilderness Waterway, where a visitor can both capture a sense of the original wilderness and discover the human artifacts of changing cultural traditions. One need only explore the site of Chamberlain Farm to see this—to grasp the meaning of the name *Apmoojenegamook* when a storm sweeps across the lake's surface, to have the eye drawn to the red of a fire-cracked rock at the water's edge, to stumble across a stone wall or encounter a piece of rusting machinery, or to see a string of fishing traps in front of the old farm camp in winter or a line of canoes passing by in summer.

Places such as the Allagash Wilderness Waterway become all the more valuable as our world grows more crowded and developed, and once we have preserved them, we must be ever watchful. Robert Patterson learned this well, for he lived to see the wilderness character of the Allagash, which he had worked so long and hard to save, suffer from numerous encroachments. He especially decried the lack of control over the expanding network of roads and the increasing number of access points. In 1984, he wrote: "Whatever environmental lessons the Council [Natural Resources Council of Maine] may have learned in its first twenty-five years, the Allagash offers Lesson Number One: Never relax."[31]

Epilogue

SAFEKEEPING

John Richardson gently slides his boat against the dock in front of the Chamberlain Farm camp. Pieces of blue Styrofoam litter the beach: "Muskrats chewing the dock flotation," John explains in a tone that suggests he is thinking about the time it will take to pick up the scattered fragments. Piles of gravel hump up along the water's edge, where the winter's ice has pushed them. Farther down the shore, the high spring waters lap at the rusting remnants of the *H. W. Marsh*. There is little to suggest that it was once a boat. A scrim of budding poplars and birches, their silhouetted symmetry never more apparent, lines the narrow, jutting point, screening much of the view of the lake beyond.

I penetrate a barrier of alders beyond the end of the dock and emerge in an old field near some rusting machinery. The clear notes of a white-throated sparrow stop me for a moment, just long enough for blackflies to attack. Up ahead, I see the rotting wood of an old barn lying in a heap, an old mowing machine protruding through the jumble. My eye catches something else. Near the remnants of a harrow sits a fox, scratching its ear: I am not the blackflies' only victim. The fox watches me closely. I move, and it disappears. I follow, trying to step quietly on the soft, needled floor of a thick grove of pines, but I face a tangle of dry, dead branches and soon give up on the fox. Breaking out into a thicket of raspberries and red osier dogwoods, I walk along an animal trail containing piles of deer droppings. Soon, I reach the top of a low knoll surrounded by evergreens, where the farmhouse once stood.

*Remains of Boom Towboat
H. W. Marsh*

Chamberlain Lake and the distant mountains of the Katahdin
range can be seen beyond the
remnants of the steamboat *H.
W. Marsh,* now rusting away on
the shore in front of Chamberlain Farm. Photograph
by Dean B. Bennett.

The safe lies in the cellar hole as I remember it—rusting, flecked
with sunlight, and splotched with lichens. The door is still open, one
hinge broken. Stove parts lie scattered about. Through a flue hole in
one of them, a young birch tree grows. Part of a bed frame angles
across the leaf-covered earthen floor of the cellar. In one corner, near
the cellar's crumbling, moss- and lichen-covered stone walls, wood
ferns have found a niche. Birches and poplars rise up from the floor
to a height of thirty feet or more. Soon their canopies will leaf out,
and the cellar and its safe will be nearly concealed in the shadows.
And as the spring progresses, the surrounding vestiges of old hay
fields will fade beneath a cover of greening vegetation. Again, and
now more so than ever, I am struck by the symbolism of the safe, the
farm, and this waterway, for I now know more clearly how they sig-
nify humanity's changing relationship with nature and wildness.

From the moment early indigenous peoples first pulled up their canoes and camped on Apmoojenegamook Point, this piece of shoreline was nudged onto a course of change profoundly different from what it would have experienced without a human presence. For thousands of years the point remained under the influence of nature, with little effect from humans. Then, a little more than a century and a half ago, watercraft landing in the point's cove brought new visitors, who surveyed the land. Soon, others followed who saw wealth in the woods and a means to the markets in the lakes and streams. Dams soon raised the lake around the point, pushing back the shore and leaving a border of drowned and dying trees along the water's edge. In the forest, pines succumbed to the axe, and the land behind the point was cleared, stumped, and ploughed for farming. Buildings appeared, and bateaus and canoes lined the shore. Booms of logs passed slowly by, pulled by the muscle power of men. A different view had arrived at the point, and the land served a different purpose.

Years passed, and steamboats took over the job of pulling the booms of logs. Eventually they, too, were supplanted by new methods and technologies and were retired on the shore of the farm. Economies changed, and buildings fell into disrepair and disappeared. Only one remained, until new log cabins joined it some distance away, on the shore of the farm lot. They reflected different feelings about the region: an appreciation for its wildness and remoteness and its abundance of wildlife, as well as a concern for the sustainability of its resources. The old fields grew up, logging in the surrounding woodlands intensified, roads encroached, and trucks replaced the river drives. Float planes landed in the old farm's cove; gas-powered boats tied up at docks; canoes of canvas, fiberglass, and plastic replaced the birch-bark craft, and motors substituted for paddles; snowmobiles arrived. Many of these conveyances brought people who came to escape the cities and neighborhoods, to find peace and quiet, to indulge in the wildness and enjoy the solitude, and to engage in hunting and fishing opportunities provided by an abundance of wildlife. Most were aware of the invasion of roads and the changes they foretold.

A few came to the farm who viewed these encroachments on the region's wildness with alarm. They saw the threatened loss of an opportunity to experience a strong and close connection with the land; to obtain a sense of the beauty, integrity, and diversity inherent in a large expanse of relatively undeveloped wildland; and to gain a historical perspective on the character of the wilderness encountered by indigenous peoples and those who came after the first wave of European settlers. They expressed concern about the area's future protection and felt a need to act. They engaged in a long, successful political effort to preserve the waterway, and soon, after nearly a century and a quarter in private ownership, the farm again stood on public property. At first, the old farm's future hung uncertain, but in the end the camps remained and the farm's outdoor sports tradition continued.

Today, at the beginning of the twenty-first century, boats with high-horsepower engines can be seen tied to the dock in front of the farm or out on the lake beyond the cove. In winter, snowmobiles drive to its shore, transporting those who come to fish in holes drilled through the lake's frozen surface. Occasionally in the summer season, a through-trip canoeist stops by, but more and more of the visitors are on excursions of a day or two. Once in a while, someone staying at a road-accessible campsite on the far shore of Indian Pond behind the farm will boat across and walk a trail to the farm. The distant sounds of industrial logging are sometimes heard from the farm's camps, and at times dust clouds are seen rising over a sparsely wooded ridge across the lake. Occasionally, a plane will land on the lake and taxi to the shore at Nugent's Chamberlain Lake Camps. This is not a pure wilderness, and much must be done to recapture the conditions called for by the original state legislation and the "wild" designation under the Wild and Scenic Rivers Act, but here in the restricted zone, nature is slowly returning the farm to a semblance of the wilderness it once was.

When Senator Edmund Muskie spoke at the dedication of the Allagash Wilderness Waterway in 1970, he opened his remarks with a quote from E. B. White: "'Gradually the idea is taking form that the land must be held in safekeeping, that one generation is to some extent responsible for the next. . . .' Today," Muskie continued, "we bear witness to the practical application of that philosophy . . . the permanent preservation—in Maine, and for America—of some 200,000 acres of land and water, unspoiled by what we know as civilization."[1]

Chamberlain Farm at the End of the Twentieth Century
More than thirty years after it was placed in the restricted zone of the Allagash Wilderness Waterway, Chamberlain Farm was returning to its primitive character. Photograph by Dean B. Bennett.

The long struggle to save the waterway taught a valuable lesson in the preservation of wild places. But in the last thirty-year chapter of the Allagash story, the lesson was about the necessity of vigilance to keep safe that which has been preserved. The human attitudes and behavior and other pressures against the preservation of wilderness that Henry David Thoreau questioned, that Warren K. Moorehead railed against, that Percival P. Baxter worked to overcome, and that Robert Patterson and the other Allagash advocates opposed— all have continued to affect the farm and the entire Allagash

View from Chamberlain Farm, Still Much the Same as Thoreau Saw It

At the end of the twentieth century, the view from Chamberlain Farm retained many of the scenic elements Henry David Thoreau saw in 1857, thanks to Percival P. Baxter's preservation of the Mt. Katahdin region and Maine citizens who supported legislation to protect the Allagash. Today, at the beginning of the twenty-first century, threats, however, still remain, and many citizens and organizations are again mobilizing public support to restore and safeguard the wilderness qualities of the Allagash Wilderness Waterway. Photograph by Dean B. Bennett.

Wilderness Waterway. This is true of wilderness everywhere, and the problems and issues involved in maintaining wildness in the Allagash serve only to illustrate this.

Like those who brought that safe to Chamberlain Farm a century and a half ago to protect the wealth they gained from the land and its forests, today's seekers of wildness expect that what they value will be safeguarded. We cannot treat the Allagash Wilderness Waterway and other wild areas as that safe has been treated—left open, no longer protecting what was thought secure. Our society must not let down those dedicated people who entrusted this place and others like it to our safekeeping. Here in the Allagash, they left us a Chamberlain Lake shoreline as nearly undisturbed as when Thoreau saw it in the mid-1800s. Our responsibility is to keep it that way for future generations. The Allagash is not simply a vestige of primitive America: it stands in recognition of the values of wildness; it is a symbol of our hope for a wilder America. This is the view of the wilderness from Chamberlain Farm.

Before I leave the cellar hole, I look down at the open safe . . . and close it.

Postscript

The spirit that established the Allagash Wilderness Waterway is still alive. The generations that benefited from the efforts of its founders have recognized the need for vigilance. From all parts of Maine and across the nation, they have come to rally against the latest assaults on this wild river legacy. They are canoeists, fishermen, guides, youth group leaders, farmers, doctors, teachers, students, people with and without disabilities—men and women, young and old, all who cherish a wild, remote experience.

They have uncovered the waterway's history, examined the intent of those who set it aside, documented its record of management, explored its problems and issues, investigated its legal protections, monitored its care, raised public awareness, and enlisted the help of others. But above all else, their advocacy has been guided by the belief that the Allagash Wilderness Waterway is a symbol of hope for the future of all of America's wild and scenic rivers and deserves nothing less than the best stewardship efforts of Maine and the nation.

Appendix A

TIME LINE OF EVENTS
AROUND CHAMBERLAIN FARM

500–360 mya	Major geologic events form the region's bedrock (mya = millions of years ago).
2.6 mya	The last ice age begins.
25,000–11,000 B.P.	The Laurentide Ice Sheet forms, passes over the Allagash region, and recedes, creating the basin of Chamberlain Lake and a point of land sheltering a small cove on its northern shore.
CA. 11,000 B.P.	Indigenous peoples arrive in the Allagash region. For thousands of years, they follow an ancient canoe route through the lake, which they come to call Apmoojenegamook, camping occasionally on the point of land.
1606–1776	The Allagash region is under English and French possession at different times.
1783	A treaty following the Revolutionary War places Apmoojenegamook Lake within an area of disputed land between Canada and the United States.
1816	Moses Greenleaf proposes the construction of canals to Apmoojenegamook Lake.
1820	Maine becomes a state and separates from Mass-

achusetts. Land around Apmoojenegamook is owned jointly by Maine and Massachusetts.

1825–1833   The Monument Line is run south of Apmoojenegamook Lake and forms a baseline for laying out townships to the north.

1835   George W. Coffin's map indicates that Apmoojenegamook Point is in an unorganized township, although it is incorrectly drawn and labeled according to subsequent maps.

Harvesting of white pines in the Allagash watershed begins in the Telos Lake area.

1837   James Hodge passes by Apmoojenegamook Point on Maine's first scientific expedition, under the direction of Charles T. Jackson.

1839   George Featherstonhaugh passes by Apmoojenegamook Point while directing a survey for the British Boundary Commission and concludes that the lake belongs to Canada.

Shepard Boody investigates Apmoojenegamook (Chamberlain Lake) and Telos Lake as potential sites for dams to provide water for river drives.

1840   Zebulon Bradley and William Parrott survey the boundaries of T7 R12, surrounding Apmoojenegamook Point.

1841   Dams are constructed on Telos and Chamberlain Lakes, and waters of the two lakes are diverted into the East Branch of the Penobscot River.

1842   Telos Canal below Telos Dam is improved.

David Pingree, a wealthy merchant, hires E. S.

Coe, an engineer, as his land agent to investigate his landholdings in Maine.

1844   Land agents of Maine and Massachusetts sell T7 R12 to Francis Blackman, who sells it almost immediately to David Pingree.

1845–1846   David Pingree owns seven townships around Chamberlain and Eagle Lakes and begins extensive timber harvesting.

1846   E. S. Coe builds Chamberlain Farm behind Apmoojenegamook Point as a lumbering depot. Churchill Dam is built (known as Heron Lake Dam).

1847   David Pingree sells one-twentieth of the undivided land in T7 R12 to E. S. Coe.

Winter roads connect Chamberlain Farm to Grant Farm and Katahdin Iron Works to the south.

1857   Henry David Thoreau stays overnight at Chamberlain Farm on his trip through the Maine woods.

Eagle Lake Tote Road, a winter road from Patten, connects with Chamberlain Farm.

1858   David Pingree sells nine-fortieths of the undivided land in T7 R12 known as Chamberlain Farm to E. S. Coe.

Hunter and trapper Manly Hardy stays at Chamberlain Farm for a few nights while on a hunting and trapping trip.

1861   The second Maine Scientific Survey, under

Ezekiel Holmes and Charles Hitchcock, reaches Telos Dam on a tote road from Trout Brook Farm. The surveyors paddle across the lakes to Chamberlain Farm, where they spend several days.

1862   Members of the second Maine Scientific Survey make a brief stop at Chamberlain Farm to replenish their supplies.

1874   John Way Jr. publishes the first map and guidebook to the region for outdoor recreationists.

1879   Thomas Sedgwick Steele stays at Chamberlain Farm while on a trip through the region.

1881   Thomas Sedgwick Steele and Lucius Lee Hubbard stop at Chamberlain Farm on separate canoe trips.

1888   Fannie Hardy and her father, Manly Hardy, stop at Chamberlain Farm during a long canoe trip.

1899   E. S. Coe dies.

1901   Chamberlain Farm is leased as headquarters for construction of a tramway to convey logs between Eagle and Chamberlain Lakes.

1902   Sporting camps operate on Telos Lake and at Mud Pond Carry.

1903   The tramway begins operation, and the steam-powered boom towboats *George A. Dugan* and *H. W. Marsh* are constructed to operate on Eagle and Chamberlain Lakes.

1907   The tramway ceases operation because of competition from Lombard log haulers.

1912	Archaeologist Warren K. Moorehead passes by Chamberlain Farm on an expedition.
1916	The newly constructed Allagash Mountain fire lookout tower can be seen from Chamberlain Farm.
1919	George S. Kephart, a trained forester, stays at Chamberlain Farm off and on while doing wood-cruising work in the area.
1922	Lock Dam repaired and roofed.
1923	Governor Percival P. Baxter and his party pass by Chamberlain Farm on a trip.
1926	Construction of the Eagle Lake–West Branch Railroad begins. Maine guide Walter Arnold passes by Chamberlain Farm on a trip down the Allagash River.
1927	Myron Avery visits Chamberlain Farm on a canoeing and hiking trip. The Eagle Lake–West Branch Railroad begins operation.
1931	A fire destroys the farmhouse at Chamberlain Farm; many historical records are lost.
1930s	Airplane flights over the area begin.
1936	Al and Patty Nugent arrive at Chamberlain Lake and begin building a set of sporting camps on the lakeshore about three miles east of Chamberlain Farm. Robert Patterson Sr. and his wife, Barbara, canoe along the lakeshore across the lake from Chamberlain Farm.

late 1940s   Game warden David Priest Sr. visits Chamber-
                    lain Farm while George Rear and his family are
                    living in one of its old buildings near the shore.

early 1950s   A logging road is built to Chamberlain Thor-
                    oughfare.

1952   Harold and Lloyd Whiteneck begin building the
                    Heart O' Maine Sporting Camps on property
                    they have leased at Chamberlain Farm.

1955   Governor Edmund S. Muskie stops at Nugent's
                    Chamberlain Lake Camps on a fishing trip and
                    flies over Chamberlain Farm.

1959   A team from the National Park Service conducts
                    a reconnaissance study of the Allagash River
                    watershed for a proposed national recreation
                    area.

1960   Justice William O. Douglas and his party pass by
                    Chamberlain Farm in a thick, dark fog.
                        The Heart O' Maine Camps at Chamberlain
                    Farm are sold to Nugent's Chamberlain Lake
                    Camps.

1962   Robert and Barbara Patterson stay at Nugent's
                    Chamberlain Lake Camps.

1966   The state of Maine creates the Allagash Wilder-
                    ness Waterway and begins plans to purchase
                    land, including part of the Chamberlain Farm
                    lot, that will be managed for its "maximum
                    wilderness character."

1968   Great Northern Paper Company builds a road to
                    Indian Pond behind Chamberlain Farm.

1969   The Pingree heirs sell seventy-four lakeside acres of Chamberlain Farm to the state of Maine.

1970   The Allagash Wilderness Waterway is officially dedicated and designated as the first state-administered waterway in the National Wild and Scenic Rivers System.

1973   The *Allagash Wilderness Waterway Concept Plan*, which includes general guidelines for managing the waterway, is developed.

1999   The first management plan with detailed policies, objectives, and strategies is completed for the waterway.

2000   A proposed access point at John's Bridge becomes the center of a contentious legal dispute over the original intent of the Allagash Wilderness Waterway.

Appendix B

WILDERNESS CONTINUUM

One way to conceptualize the meaning of wildness or to assess the degree of wilderness in a place is to think of it in terms of a continuum. The one shown here is based on suggestions in *Wilderness and the American Mind* by Roderick Nash and *Battle for the Wilderness* by Michael Frome. Explanations of the categories follow.

A Wilderness Continuum

Purely Civilized (City)	Rural, Pastoral, Managed (Working Forest)	Purely Wild (Wilderness)

Perception of naturalness, remoteness, quietness, aloneness, ancientness

1	2	3	4	5

1. PURELY CIVILIZED

A landscape considered purely civilized is characterized by a dense human population in a highly designed environment. In a purely civilized landscape, engineered systems provide for transportation, communication, and other services, and artificial sights, sounds, smells, light, temperature, and other variables are strongly present.[1]

2. INTERVAL

Between a purely civilized landscape and one that is rural, pastoral, or managed is an interval landscape where some may perceive a degree of wilderness in an area "as small as one's backyard or a clump of wild plants or grass."[2]

3. RURAL, PASTORAL, OR MANAGED

A landscape categorized as rural, pastoral, or managed contains considerable patches of vegetation or naturally open areas reflecting various successional stages. Roads and other transportation developments divide the landscape, dams and other hydrologic developments are present, and dwellings and other structures are scattered about.

4. INTERVAL

Between a rural, pastoral, or managed landscape and one that is purely wild is another interval landscape, in which some wilderness may be present with "a feel for the original landscape."[3]

5. PURELY WILD

A landscape considered purely wild appears natural, wild, and unspoiled, with evidence of human presence substantially unnoticeable. Native plants and animals dominate, and ecological components and processes occur unaltered, without human control; an element of the unknown or unexplored mystery is present.[4]

Appendix C

TYPOLOGY OF PERSPECTIVES ON NATURE

An analysis is presented here of changing perspectives on nature seen in individuals associated with Chamberlain Farm. It is based on a typology developed from a review of research and thought in a number of fields, including philosophy, psychology, sociology, history, economics, education, and resource management. As summarized in the table, the typology identifies three major perspectives: *domination* (in control of nature), *cooperation* (in harmony with nature), and *integration* (one with nature). Analysis of the literature suggests that these viewpoints differ with respect to at least three parameters: the *place*, or position, in which people see themselves in relation to the rest of nature; the *values* people attribute to nature; and the *role* people see for themselves in nature. Each of these parameters is determined by beliefs, attitudes, and values that influence behavior associated with a particular perspective. The tendency toward behavior that preserves nature, especially wilderness, appears to become stronger as one moves toward the perspectives of cooperation and integration. See appendix D for some evidence of this.

Values, Perspectives, and Behavior

The typology is based on three assumptions: (1) people have needs that give rise to values concerning nature, which include beliefs and attitudes; (2) values can lead to behavior with either positive or neg-

Perspectives on Nature

PARAMETERS	DOMINATION	COOPERATION	INTEGRATION
Place of humans in nature	Separate from nature	Closely connected to nature	One with nature; integrated with nature
Values attributed to nature	Emphasize consumptive, utilitarian values to meet immediate material needs of humans	Emphasize both consumptive and nonconsumptive utilitarian values to meet long-term material and non-material needs of humans	Emphasize intrinsic, or inherent, values of nature to meet long-term needs of all life
Role of humans in nature	Dominate nature to maximize human welfare and remove negative aspects of nature	Adapt to some aspects of nature seen as negative and avoid others	Respect the integrity of the whole earth

ative effects on the natural environment; and (3) values can be categorized into major perspectives, or viewpoints, in reference to people and the rest of nature.

Regarding the first assumption, about needs and values, humanistic psychologist Abraham Maslow proposed in his theory of motivation that all of us have innate needs that must be met if we are to become fully developed and mentally healthy individuals. These needs may be grouped into two hierarchal categories. The first category contains basic physiological and safety (biological) needs, which, in relation to the natural environment, translate into direct consumptive values (such as clean water for drinking) and indirect consumptive values (e.g., unspoiled watersheds). The second category contains higher-order growth needs, including psychological needs (love, a sense of belonging, self-esteem) and philosophical, ethical, and aesthetic needs. These needs translate into nonuse values, characterized by no direct or indirect physical involvement, such as the satisfaction one receives when contemplating the existence of a beautiful lake, the satisfaction of knowing that preservation of a wild piece of nature will provide options for future generations, and the satisfaction of knowing that nature is protected for its own sake.[1]

Values can be thought of as deep-seated feelings about the worth of something that satisfies our needs and wants. Values consist of attitudes that include beliefs, feelings, and a tendency to act or respond to objects, events, and intangibles, such as ideas.[2] A deeper understanding of values is seen in the work of psychologist Shalom Schwartz, who proposed and tested a system of ten value types representing needs related to biological, social, and group survival and functioning. Two of Schwartz's competing value types that are important to this typology are universalism and power. He defines universalism in terms of the following goals: understanding, appreciation, tolerance, and protection for the welfare of all people and nature. This value type includes the following single values: broadmindedness, wisdom, social justice, unity with nature, and protection of the environment. Note that Schwartz's definition of universalism shows a strong relationship to Maslow's higher-order growth needs. Competing with the universalism value type is the power value type, defined in terms of the following goals: social status and prestige and control or dominance over people and resources. This value type is represented by the single values of social power, authority, and wealth.[3]

The second assumption on which the typology is based pertains to the relationship between values and behavior. Schwartz questions the assumption that priority given to a single value provokes and guides behavior. Instead, he suggests, "values may play little role in behavior except when there is a value conflict."[4] Using Schwartz's values theory, David Karp, as a Ph.D. candidate in sociology, studied the effect of values on predicting pro-environmental behavior. Notably, but not surprisingly, he found that a factor that included Schwartz's universalism value was a positive predictor of pro-environmental behavior. Schwartz's power value type, on the other hand, tended to be a negative predictor of pro-environmental behavior.[5]

The third assumption states that values and their inherent beliefs and attitudes form our cultural viewpoints, or perspectives, on nature. A large body of opinion points to the existence of two opposing viewpoints: the anthropocentric, or human-centered, perspective and the biocentric, or ecosystem-centered, perspective. Briefly, the human-centered viewpoint reflects human domination of nature to meet human needs, and the ecosystem-centered viewpoint reflects human integration in the rest of nature to protect values on which all living things, including humans, depend to meet their fundamental needs. It is useful to think of these two viewpoints as extremes of a continuum, as suggested by John Hendee, George Stankey, and Robert Lucas, authors of a valuable treatise on wilderness management. They noted that these perspectives "represent extreme polarized concepts about wilderness management, and it is unlikely either could be slavishly followed . . . it is difficult, if not impossible, to say that either idea is wrong or right."[6]

Between these two perspectives, I propose a third that contains transitional beliefs, attitudes, and values. To reflect this transition, I label these three viewpoints according to the kind of human position and interaction with elements of the natural world each characterizes: (1) domination, (2) cooperation, and (3) integration. This is, of course, only one of many ways to define the human relationship with nature. Psychologists, ethicists, and others continue to explore and define who we are and what we should be about in our natural world, as seen today in the continuing discussion of deep ecology, ecofeminism, and biophilia.

Perspective: Domination of Nature (Control of Nature)

The anthropocentric perspective in which humans dominate nature can be traced back to the rise of agriculture some 10,000 years ago, although it has always played a role in human survival.[7] Some see this perspective as having arisen from the philosophy of classical Greece, in which humans were seen as a dichotomy of mind and body. Because humans could reason, they were regarded as superior to the rest of nature, which could not reason. Freya Mathews' summary of the literature on this subject shows "that this assumption of humanity as the locus of all meaning and value was reinforced by Christianity, and finally clinched by the new science of the seventeenth century."[8] Donald Worster, who has explored the history of ecological thought, traced this viewpoint back to the time of Francis Bacon, a philosopher of science in the sixteenth and seventeenth centuries who believed that science and human management could create a utopia for humans. In such an ideal world, humans would acquire authority over all other creatures and find a place of dignity and honor. Worster observed that this perspective was given further legitimacy by the outstanding Swedish botanist Carl von Linné, or Linnaeus, in his essay "The Oeconomy of Nature," published in 1749. In the eighteenth century, the term *oeconomy* frequently referred to the divine government of the natural world. Worster noted that in the Linnaean model, humans "are like any other species living as subordinate parts of the divine order . . . [and] at the same time occupy a special place of dignity and honor," or, quoting Linnaeus: "All these treasures of nature . . . seem intended by the Creator for the sake of man. Every thing may be made subservient to his use." Worster suggested, however, that the Linnaean model, by promoting nature as perfection of God's work, might have served as a constraint for some people, as opposed to those who were influenced by Bacon.[9]

The following beliefs, attitudes, and values characterize the dominative perspective.

1. *PLACE* OF HUMANS RELATIVE TO THE REST OF NATURE AND ITS EXISTENCE

In the domination of nature perspective, humans are seen as separate from nature, which exists solely for their benefit. The belief that humans are set apart from the rest of the natural world is closely aligned with the idea that nature is there *for* humans. "Dominion over nature belongs to man by divine bequest," stated Francis Bacon.[10] In 1630, a few years after Bacon's death, John White, one of the first settlers in the New World, defended the idea thusly: "As for the colonies . . . replenishing wast and voyd . . . they have a cleare and sufficient warrant from the mouth of God."[11] This idea, placing humans in a position separate from nature, continues in the minds of many to this day. For example, the philosopher Max Oelschlaeger described the philosophy of resource conservation as based on, among other things, the belief that "human life takes place outside of nature, and the boundaries between wilderness and civilization are definite."[12] As a value, dominance also is well known. For example, it shows up not only in Schwartz's power value type but also in Yale University professor Stephen Kellert's studies of nine values of nature.[13]

2. *VALUE* OF NATURE

In the domination of nature perspective, humans value nature for its ultimate utilitarian purpose of satisfying human needs, especially material or physiological needs. According to Maslow's theory, basic needs must be met before we can move to higher needs. As mentioned earlier, such needs are illustrated by the utilitarian value of direct consumptive use, such as eating a duck, and indirect consumptive use, such as protecting the fish that ducks eat. However, nonconsumptive uses also have a utilitarian basis in meeting higher needs, such as enjoying duck-watching.[14] This idea of the utility of nature moving from physical needs to higher needs was observed by Ronald Inglehart, who studied attitudes, values, and behavior in relation to cultural shifts in advanced societies. He found that cultures begin as materialist, concerned with economic and physical security, and then shift toward the satisfaction of Maslow's higher-order needs—belonging and esteem, intellectual and aesthetic needs.[15] Kellert also identified the utilitarian value in his typology of values of nature. He found that it still remains strong today as an American value.[16] If humans see themselves as dominant in nature and believe they are the very reason nature exists, it is easy to see why they value that which meets their own needs over the rest of nature's.

3. *ROLE* OF HUMANS IN NATURE

In the domination of nature perspective, people regard nature as a machine to be engineered and run by them to maximize human welfare, and they believe that some aspects of nature are negative and should be removed. Such a perception of role follows logically from ideas about the human place in nature and the value of nature. By regarding nature as a machine and placing themselves outside it, people can easily imagine that they possess the power and ability to successfully run it.[17] Implicit in this view is the idea that human operation of the machine of nature will not be detrimental to the natural world. Some evidence of this comes from a study by Paul Stern and Thomas Dietz. They looked at the relationship between beliefs, attitudes, and values on the one hand and behavior toward nature on the other. Their findings suggested that "individuals who hold strong traditional and egoistic or materialistic values . . . tend to deny that human activities are harmful to nature."[18] Kellert, however, believes that people can be provoked to destroy or at least be unconcerned about the fate of creatures or natural areas toward which they have an aversion, such as wolves, snakes, and swamps.[19]

Perspective: Cooperation with Nature (Harmony with Nature)

People who are guided by the cooperation with nature perspective try to coexist peacefully with nature rather than work against it or exploit it without regard for its future health and sustainability. Donald Worster called this viewpoint the "Arcadian stance," after *Acadia,* a term that has come to mean any imaginary place that offers peace and simplicity. He traces it back to English parson and naturalist Gilbert White, who published *The Natural History of Selborne* in 1789.[20] The idea that this perspective is transitional between the views of domination and integration is evidenced by the beliefs, attitudes, and values with which it is associated.

1. *PLACE* OF HUMANS RELATIVE TO THE REST OF NATURE AND ITS EXISTENCE

In the cooperation with nature perspective, humans, though seen as separate from the rest of nature, are closer to it than in the domination perspective. People are aware that they have attachments to the land, both physically and psychologically, and that the natural world does not exist solely for their benefit. White, for example, believed that nature existed at least in part for humans, and through the efforts of God it had been made more amenable for human existence. To White, the relationship was characterized by a strong psychological connection, as evidenced in lines from his poem "The Invitation to Selborne": "The partial bard admires his native spot; / Smit with its beauties, loved, as yet a child."[21] Kellert also recognized this affinity for nature in the human relationship with wildlife, which, he noted, gives "people an avenue for expressing and developing the emotional capacities for attachment, bonding, intimacy, and companionship."[22]

2. VALUE OF NATURE

In the perspective of cooperation, people value nature for its utility in providing for human needs, with emphasis on higher needs after basic needs are met. From ancient times, a long record exists of human appreciation of nature beyond its material, utilitarian value. Although White, for example, saw that "forest and wastes are of considerable service to neighborhoods" and that worms "have much influence in the economy of Nature," being of great benefit to gardeners and farmers in the "chain of Nature," he also recognized other values, as expressed in these words of a poem: "These, NATURE'S works, the curious mind employ, / Inspire a soothing melancholy joy."[23] These higher values reflect the psychological and philosophical needs in Maslow's schema—peace of mind, a feeling of harmony with all life, aesthetic appreciation, and intellectual curiosity.[24] In economic terms, Lawrence Goulder and Donald Kennedy called these nonconsumptive, nonuse values, such as the pleasure of watching wildlife, and existence values, such as the satisfaction of contemplating the existence of some natural entity.[25] Kellert also noted in his study of values that "nature and living diversity . . . exert an extraordinary aesthetic impact on people" as we strive "after integrity, harmony, and balance in nature."[26] Finally, this expansion of human values to encompass more than the value of nature as an economic resource for material utilitarianism has become more closely aligned with the philosophical idea Max Oelschlaeger called preservationism, in which "human values go beyond those measured by the national income accounts to include the preservation of wild lands and life."[27] It was in this direction that Gilbert White turned his intellectual eye, seeing the relationships among seemingly independent creatures and objects. Earthworms, he noted, though appearing as "a small and despicable link in the chain of nature, yet, if lost, would make a lamentable chasm."[28]

3. *ROLE* OF HUMANS IN NATURE

In the perspective of cooperation with nature, humans, while obtaining a living from its resources, regard nature as not totally controllable and therefore seek to coexist with it, adapting to some of its aspects, conserving others for the future, and avoiding those that are repugnant, fearsome, or threatening. In the Arcadian tradition, White sought to live a peaceful life in his parish of Selborne. There, he lived, studied, and found enjoyment. The Royal Forest of Wolmer, he wrote, contained "many curious productions, both animal and vegetable; and has often afforded me much entertainment both as a sportsman and as a naturalist." And although he hunted, his utilitarian view was not devoid of ethical consideration regarding game animals. He criticized "unreasonable sportsmen [who] killed twenty and sometimes thirty brace" of partridges in one day in the royal forest when the birds were unusually plentiful. Although there was much in nature White felt unable to control, he had faith that knowledge, once acquired, would serve humanity well in this respect: "A full history of noxious insects hurtful in the field, garden, and house, suggesting all the known and likely means of destroying them, would be allowed by the public to be a most useful and important work." And in another passage: "Instead of examining the minute distinctions of every various species of each obscure genus, the botanist should endeavor to make himself acquainted with those that are useful."[29] These ideas of White regarding science were early indicators of Kellert's ecologistic-scientific value, which emphasizes and "probably . . . [instills] in the prudent person a cautious respect for maintaining natural systems and a reluctance to overexploit species and habitats."[30]

Perspective: Integration in Nature (Oneness with Nature)

Donald Worster detected themes of biocentrism in the writings of Gilbert White and later in Henry David Thoreau's works, but he credited Charles Darwin for helping to break down the idea of separateness between humans and other creatures.[31] The perspective of integration, here likened to the ecocentric-biocentric view, is characterized by the following beliefs, attitudes, and values.

1. *PLACE* OF HUMANS RELATIVE TO THE REST OF NATURE AND ITS EXISTENCE

In the integration in nature perspective, humans are viewed as an integral part of nature, united as one with the rest of nature. Humankind is an element in natural systems, not the reason for their existence.[32] Mathews, who observed a flood of eco-philosophies in the late twentieth century, noted that all were reaffirming the "intrinsic interconnectedness of the world, all portraying the world as a web or field of shared interpenetrating essences . . . insisting that everything participates in the identity of everything else." Moreover, she saw these philosophies as aiming to reestablish "our affinity, our kinship, with the natural world."[33] Paul Taylor, in his analysis of the biocentric outlook on nature, identified core beliefs that relate to the place of humans in nature, pointing out that we are interdependent members of a natural world in which no member is superior to another and all other living things are our kin. In this view, all forms of life coexist on the same terms, each unique and pursuing its "own good in its own way."[34] Inherent in this perspective is the idea that to truly become one with nature, we must transcend our ego and self-centeredness to discover our meaning and humanity. Maslow, in his hierarchy of human needs, noted that those individuals who satisfy their basic and self-actualizing needs may transcend their egos to develop a oneness with nature and humanity.[35] Notably, Schwartz called his universalism value a self-transcendence type, including in his definition the value of unity with nature.[36] On the basis of this kind of thinking, one might conclude that a sense of unity with the rest of nature is deeply embedded in the human mind, though its expression may be pushed back by other priorities.

2. *VALUE* OF NATURE

In the perspective of integration, nature is valued for those qualities that make it what it is. According to Oelschlaeger, "ecocentrists believe that natural systems are the basis of all organic existence, and therefore possess intrinsic value . . . [, which includes] diversity, stability, and beauty."[37] Mark Sagoff wrote that "as we come to depend on nature less and less for instrumental [utilitarian] reasons, we may recognize more and more the intrinsic reasons for preserving it." When we value something intrinsically, "we value the object itself rather than just the benefits it confers on us." Sagoff identified two forms of intrinsic value—aesthetic and moral—that relate to environmental policy.[38] Mathews similarly defined intrinsic value as value that "inheres in the things that possess it and is not relativized to the needs and desires, or interests, of external observers or agents."[39]

3. *ROLE* OF HUMANS IN NATURE

In the perspective of integration in nature, the role of humans in relation to the rest of nature has a strong ethical foundation. Judith Scoville concluded that "once the biotic community has been recognized as a center of value, ecology provides both an interpretation of the actions and interrelationships of that community and an increased understanding of what a fitting human response should be."[40] What such a response should be was suggested by Aldo Leopold: "A thing is right when it tends to preserve the integrity, stability, and beauty of the biotic community. It is wrong when it tends otherwise."[41] In this same vein, Holmes Rolston III wrote that humans "owe something to this beauty, integrity, and persistence in the biotic community. Ethics is not complete until extended to the land."[42] Oelschlaeger identified ecocentrists as those who believe that "ethical human actions (actions which provide the good life for humankind) necessarily promote all life on earth (preserve such intrinsic values as diversity, stability, and beauty)."[43] To summarize, the perspective of integration in nature reflects an acknowledgment that the global ecological system is a center of value in which humans are an important component and that humans have the ability to destroy those qualities of nature essential to all life. Furthermore, those with this perspective believe that humans have a moral capacity to be guided by an ethics that extends to all creatures; that recognizes the value of the integrity, or soundness, of the natural world; and that reflects a will to place limitations on their own actions for the good of the earth.

Appendix D

NATIONAL TRENDS
IN BELIEFS, ATTITUDES, AND VALUES
CONCERNING NATURE

Culture consists of a society's collectively shared attitudes, beliefs, and knowledge that are inherent in its values. The success of a culture depends in large part on its ability to resolve issues in an orderly manner with outcomes that respect these elements. Issues are defined as conflicts among society's values, and it is in resolving such conflicts that values can have a profound effect on human behavior. Behavior—the way members of a culture act in relation to themselves, others, and their environment—is the ultimate measure of a culture's ability to meet the needs of its members.

The act of preserving wilderness or wild nature—that is, setting aside natural ecosystems and limiting human use of them in order to protect their intrinsic worth—raises strong competing values and challenges fundamental cultural perspectives on our relationship to the natural world. Such an act especially challenges the perspective of domination and those values behind economic systems that are driven by and at the same time promote an insatiable thirst for the immediate use of nature's resources, too often with little regard for nature's health and future ability to sustain humans and other living things.

The studies cited here, though not exhaustive, are representative and show evidence that in the last half of the nineteenth century and throughout the twentieth century, a change occurred in Americans' views of their relationship with the rest of nature. Although a

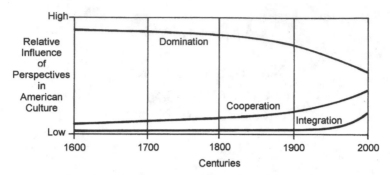

*Hypothetical Shift in Relative Influence of Perspectives
toward Nature and Wilderness Preservation*

The curves are conceptual constructs representing a hypothesis and
not strictly quantitative indicators of change. By the year 2000, the
perspective of domination, in relation to the perspectives of cooperation
and integration, remained strong and was a major influence in decisions on
environmental issues. This relationship among the perspectives received some
support in psychological and survey research, for example, in studies in
which respondents were asked to rate the importance of environmental
issues against other societal concerns and in collective public policy
decisions. Through the years, the transitional perspective of cooperation
showed steady gain; the perspective of integration grew relatively
stronger after the middle of the twentieth century.

human-centered perspective of domination of nature continued to
be strongly present, perspectives of cooperation and integration
became more important to more people. The figure, which shows a
hypothetical shift in perspectives, illustrates this trend for American
culture in general. This change was mirrored in the beliefs, attitudes,
and values of those who visited Chamberlain Farm and its surrounding wildlands.

Evidence of Change in American Beliefs, Attitudes, and Values

Evidence of changing American perspectives on nature and their
associated beliefs, attitudes, and values comes from a variety of
sources. Among them are documentations of historic events, opin-

ion polls and surveys, analyses of news media reports, studies of wilderness area use, and controlled research studies.

Early Events through the Nineteenth Century

Trends in changing perspectives are seen in anecdotal information of events over time.

Throughout the nineteenth century, wildlife was heavily exploited for hides, meat, and feathers. This was a time when the passenger pigeon was being exterminated. Popular literature emphasized the theme of man against nature in stories of Davy Crockett, Buffalo Bill, and other individuals who caught the American imagination. Toward the end of the century, however, public attitudes toward natural resources began to exhibit a major change. For example, in 1871 the first commissioner of fish and fisheries was appointed in the newly formed U.S. Fish Commission. In 1872, the United States Congress created Yellowstone National Park and had taken steps to protect Yosemite Valley in California. The year 1873 saw establishment of the position of forestry advisor to the secretary of the U.S. Department of Agriculture. In 1877, attention was called to the need to protect the headwaters of major rivers, and 1900 marked the passage of the Lacey Act, the first federal legislation to protect wildlife.[1]

Long-Term Studies in the Twentieth Century

A number of studies that document changing perspectives over one or more decades in the twentieth century reflect a systematic approach.

1900–1978

American attitudes toward animals, as revealed by an analysis of newspaper articles, showed a discernible decrease in the relative importance of the utilitarian value during the twentieth century, although it remained the most frequently occurring value. For example, in 1900 more than 50 percent of Americans expressed a strong utilitarian value, whereas in 1976 fewer than 40 percent expressed this value.[2]

1906–1965

A study of birth cohorts (groups) showed a change toward postmaterial values. Values of a given generation tended to reflect conditions prevailing during its preadult years. The intergenerational replacement showed diminishing emphasis on economic growth and increasing emphasis on protecting the environment and preserving the quality of life.[3]

1946–1990

USDA Forest Service wilderness areas expanded from 88 units in 1964 to 354 in 1990. Use of these areas grew by an average of 11.5 percent annually from 1946 to 1964 and by an average of 4.4 percent annually from 1965 to 1986.[4]

1950s–1994

Survey data before the mid-1960s hardly hint at an environmental consciousness. However, a review of surveys conducted in the early 1990s concluded that "Americans remained committed to the *goal* of protecting and improving the environment, but they no longer saw an urgent problem." Once society had agreed on the goal of protecting and improving the environment and spending money to do so, most Americans turned their attention to other things. Still, noted the authors of the review, "in the postindustrial era large majorities of American citizens across class and other social group lines are deeply committed to a safe, healthful, and attractive environment—and are prepared to support a variety of actions that seem reasonable in promoting those ends."[5]

1960s

The 1960s saw rapid growth in concern for the environment. Indicators included the following: (1) public opinion polls—the Harris Poll in 1965 showed that 43 percent of the population was concerned about water pollution; (2) publications—there was an increase in the number of books and newspaper articles about the environment and increased membership in conservation organizations (Sierra Club membership rose from 15,000 in 1960 to more than 85,000 in 1970); (3) wilderness visitation—numbers of visitors to wilderness areas doubled in the 1960s; (4) passage of legislation—many federal environmental laws were enacted during the 1960s.[6]

1973–1990

Public concern about the environment developed rapidly in the late 1960s, peaked around the first Earth Day, in 1970, and then declined throughout the rest of the 1970s. However, at the end of that decade, the public remained more concerned about environmental quality than was the case in the mid-1960s. There was a substantial increase in public support in the 1980s, and the spring of 1991 saw public concern at unprecedented proportions. Although environmental problems became more salient in the latter part of the 1980s, they still were seldom seen as the most important problems facing the country.[7]

1971–1989

Voting records in the U.S. House of Representatives showed increasing pro-environmental votes throughout the period 1971–1989.[8]

Short-Term Studies in the Twentieth Century

A number of studies pointed to perspectives on the environment near the end of the twentieth century. These looked at beliefs, attitudes, and values at a point in time.

1989–1993

A small, nonrandom anthropological study showed that only a small minority of Americans held a purely utilitarian view of nature, but respondents commonly expressed utilitarian arguments as one of many reasons for environmental protection. Seventy-two percent of the public agreed with the following statement: "Humans should recognize they are part of nature and shouldn't try to control or manage it." Eighty-three percent of the public agreed with the statement "Other species have as much right to be on this earth as we do. Just because we are smarter than other animals doesn't make us better." Eighty-three percent agreed that "all species have a right to evolve without human interference. If extinction is going to happen, it should happen naturally, not through human actions." The authors of the study concluded that "environmental values are now closely tied to many other deep value systems in American culture" and believed it unlikely that environmentalism was a passing fad.[9]

1994

A nationwide poll of 800 Americans conducted by telephone on May 21–24, 1994, showed that 65 percent believed that more land should be set aside for conservation (+/− 3.1% margin of error).[10]

1996

In a telephone survey of a sample of 1,003 Americans aged eighteen and older, a majority preferred a balance between environmental protection and economic development. Seventy-one percent favored protecting the environment by using resource management to conserve wildlife and natural places *over* preserving natural resources by preventing development and restricting use. Sixty-three percent said that environmental protection and economic development can go hand in hand, and 63 percent said that in an impasse between protecting the environment and developing the economy, they would opt to protect the environment.[11]

1997

In a nationwide survey of 1,002 Americans aged eighteen and older, two-thirds of the respondents favored protecting roadless, wild forest areas larger than 1,000 acres from development (+/− 3.1% margin of error).[12]

1995

A study of values, ethics, and attitudes held by 1,500 Vermont residents concerning management of Green Mountain National Forest in Vermont (50 percent response rate) showed the following: (1) nonmaterial values of the national forest clearly predominated; (2) individual values, such as recreation and aesthetics, were generally rated as most important; (3) societal values and more abstract values, such as ecological protection and the expression of moral and ethical obligations to nature, were rated as important; (4) the public subscribed to a diversity of environmental ethics, including anthropocentric utilitarian and stewardship ethics and bio-ecocentric ethics; (5) many values and ethics supported by respondents were highly dependent on the protection of ecological integrity; and (6) attitudes of respondents tended to favor nonmaterial benefits, including the protection of ecological integrity, over material benefits.[13]

1997

Studies of 1,000 New England households and 1,500 Massachusetts residents, both yielding about a 40 percent return, measured forest values, environmental ethics, and attitudes toward national forest management policy using White Mountain National Forest as a case study. The survey found the following: (1) aesthetic and ecological values received the highest importance ratings, and economic values received the lowest importance ratings; future-oriented values also received the highest importance ratings; (2) environmental ethics in the categories of utilitarian conservation, stewardship, and radical environmental ethics—that is, the views that animals should be free of needless human-caused pain and suffering, nature has a moral right to exist, and all things, including humans, are part of an interconnected community—tended to receive the strongest support; (3) attitudes toward national forest management policy issues tended to support policies that emphasized nonmaterial uses, such as those limiting current use for the sake of future generations and preserving remaining undisturbed forests, whereas policies that emphasized commodity values and economic priorities tended to meet with more disagreement than agreement; and (4) a relatively strong relationship existed among forest values, environmental ethics, and attitudes toward national forest management policy.[14]

1998

A telephone survey of a random sample of 1,900 people in the United States aged fifteen and older found that 55.7 percent believed there was not enough wilderness. About 75 percent of respondents rated each of the following wilderness values as very important or extremely important: protecting water quality, protecting wildlife habitat, protecting air quality, protecting wilderness for future generations, and protecting endangered species. More than 50 percent rated the following wilderness values as very important or extremely important: preserving ecosystems, scenic beauty, future option to visit, and just knowing it exists.[15]

Notes

Prologue: The Safe

1. Stephanie Kaza, "Ethical Tensions in the Northern Forest," in *The Future of the Northern Forest,* ed. Christopher McGrory Klyza and Stephen C. Trombulak (Hanover, N.H.: University Press of New England, 1994), 71.
2. This idea was eloquently expressed by Edwin Mickleburgh in *Beyond the Frozen Sea: Visions of Antarctica* (New York: St. Martin's Press, 1982), 195.
3. Wallace Stegner, *The Sound of Mountain Water* (Garden City, N.Y.: Doubleday & Company, 1969), 153.

Part I. Apmoojenegamook: Kinship with Nature

1. Joe Polis, Thoreau's Penobscot guide, said that *Apmoojenegamook* meant Lake That Is Crossed. See Henry David Thoreau, *The Maine Woods* (New York: Thomas Y. Crowell & Company, 1906), 356. Lucius L. Hubbard, in interviews with Penobscots beginning in 1881, found it to mean Cross Lake. See also Lucius L. Hubbard, *Woods and Lakes of Maine* (Boston, Mass.: Ticknor and Company, 1883), 195.

Chapter 1. The Dawnland

1. This description draws on R. B. Davis and G. L. Jacobson Jr., "Late Glacial and Early Holocene Landscapes in Northern New England and Adjacent Areas of Canada," *Quaternary Research* 23 (1985): 341–368; Woodrow B. Thompson and Harold W. Borns, eds., *Surficial Geologic Map of Maine* (Augusta: Maine Geological Survey, 1985); and David E. Putnam, Dariel McKee, and Tom Coon, *Archaeological*

Survey of the Churchill Dam Impoundment, Allagash Wilderness Waterway, Northern Maine (Augusta: Maine Historic Preservation Commission, 1997).

2. David E. Putnam, e-mail message to author, 19 November 1999.

3. For a brief discussion of the Paleo-Indian pursuit of game and procurement of stone, see Stephen G. Pollock, Nathan D. Hamilton, and Richard A. Doyle, "Geology and Archaeology of Chert in the Munsungun Lake Formation," in *NEIGC 94: Guidebook to Field Trips in North Central Maine,* ed. Lindley S. Hanson (Salem, Mass.: Salem State College, Department of Geology, 1994), 177.

4. The description of bedrock formation and associated events in the region is based on the following sources: Bradford A. Hall, *Stratigraphy of the Southern End of the Munsungun Anticlinorium, Maine,* Bulletin 22 (Augusta: Maine Geological Survey, 1970); D. W. Caldwell, *Roadside Geology of Maine* (Missoula, Mont.: Mountain Press Publishing Company, 1998); David L. Kendall, *Glaciers and Granite: A Guide to Maine's Landscape and Geology* (Camden, Maine: Down East Books, 1987); Chet Raymo and Maureen E. Raymo, *Written in Stone: A Geological and Natural History of the Northeastern United States* (Chester, Conn.: Globe Pequot Press, 1989); Pollock, Hamilton, and Doyle, "Chert in the Munsungun Lake Formation"; and a synthesis in Dean Bennett, *Allagash: Maine's Wild and Scenic River* (Camden, Maine: Down East Books, 1994).

5. See Bennett, *Allagash,* 13–14, 43.

6. An interesting account of this period of time following the retreat of the last glacier and, especially, its animal life is Arthur Spies, "Comings and Goings: Maine's Prehistoric Wildlife," *Habitat: Journal of the Maine Audubon Society* 5, no. 1 (January 1988): 30–33.

7. See Lucius L. Hubbard, *Woods and Lakes of Maine* (Boston, Mass.: Ticknor and Company, 1883), 194, 209, for the Penobscot name *Pockwockamus,* given to Mud Pond, and for a discussion of the name *Allagash.* See also William Willis, "The Language of the Abnaquies or Eastern Indians," in *Collections of the Maine Historical Society,* vol. 4 (Portland: Maine Historical Society, 1856), 104, for an explanation of the meaning of *Allagash* as Bark Camp.

8. Thoreau wrote that Pongokwahem Lake was also known as Heron Lake (now Eagle Lake); see Henry David Thoreau, *The Maine Woods*

(New York: Thomas Y. Crowell & Company, 1906), 252. See also Hubbard, *Woods and Lakes of Maine*, 209, in which the Penobscot meaning is given as Woodpecker Place. At least one scholar believes that this latter interpretation is not correct; Pauleena MacDougall, note to author, 13 March 2000.

9. For the quotations and a brief description of Moorehead's trip, see Warren K. Moorehead, *A Report on the Archaeology of Maine: Being a Narrative of Explorations of that State, 1912–1920, Together with Work at Lake Champlain, 1917* (Andover, Mass.: Andover Press, 1922), 15.

10. Douglas S. Byers, "Warren King Moorehead," *American Anthropologist* 41, no. 2 (1939): 288–289.

11. Bruce J. Bourque, "Prehistoric Indians in Maine," in *Maine: The Pine Tree State from Prehistory to the Present*, ed. Richard W. Judd, Edwin A. Churchill, and Joel W. Eastman (Orono: University of Maine Press, 1995), 21.

12. See Eva L. Butler and Wendell S. Hadlock, *A Preliminary Survey of the Munsungun-Allagash Waterway*, Bulletin 8 (Bar Harbor, Maine: Abbe Museum, 1962); and Milton Hall, "Results of a Search for Aboriginal Campsites along the Shores of the Headwater Lakes of the Allagash River, 1952–1953" (Bar Harbor, Maine: Abbe Museum, n.d.), photocopy.

13. David E. Putnam, "Exploring the 'Deep History' of the Waterway: Preserving the Archaeological Record for Future Waterway Users," 14 May 1997, photocopy.

14. Bourque, "Prehistoric Indians," 28.

15. This section and others describing vegetational change over the past 14,000 years in northwestern Maine draws on Davis and Jacobson, "Late Glacial and Early Holocene Landscapes"; George L. Jacobson Jr. and Ronald B. Davis, "Temporary and Transitional: The Real Forest Primeval—the Evolution of Maine's Forests over 14,000 Years," *Habitat: Journal of the Maine Audubon Society* 5, no. 1 (January 1998): 27–29; and George L. Jacobson Jr. and Ann Dieffenbacher-Krall, "White Pine and Climate Change: Insights from the Past," *Journal of Forestry* 93, no. 7 (July 1995): 40–41.

16. Putnam, McKee, and Coon, *Archaeological Survey*.

17. Davis and Jacobson, "Late Glacial and Early Holocene Landscapes";

Jacobson and Davis, "Temporary and Transitional"; Jacobson and Dieffenbacher-Krall, "White Pine and Climate Change," 41.

18. Bourque, "Prehistoric Indians," 28.

19. Putnam, McKee, and Coon, *Archaeological Survey.*

20. See Pollock, Hamilton, and Doyle, "Chert in the Munsungun Lake Formation," 167–172; and David Sanger, "The Ceramic Period in Maine," in *Discovering Maine's Archaeological Heritage,* ed. David Sanger (Augusta: Maine Historic Preservation Commission, 1979), 110.

21. Putnam, "Exploring the 'Deep History' of the Waterway."

22. Butler and Hadlock, *A Preliminary Survey,* 27.

23. David Sanger, "The Original Native Mainers: A Synopsis of the Lives and Times of Maine's Pre-European Inhabitants," *Journal of the Maine Audubon Society* 5, no. 1 (January 1988): 37.

24. Putnam, "Exploring the 'Deep History' of the Waterway."

25. Kenneth M. Morrison, "Mapping Otherness: Myth and the Study of Cultural Encounter," in *Beginnings: Cartography in the Land of Norumbega,* ed. Emerson W. Baker et al. (Lincoln: University of Nebraska Press, 1994), 120.

26. J. Baird Callicott, *In Defense of the Land Ethic: Essays in Environmental Philosophy* (Albany: State University of New York Press, 1989), 179.

27. For additional sources and discussion of these Wabanaki beliefs, see Harald E. L. Prins, "Children of Gluskap: Wabanaki Indians on the Eve of the European Invasion," in *Beginnings: Cartography in the Land of Norumbega,* ed. Emerson W. Baker et al. (Lincoln: University of Nebraska Press, 1994), 95–96, 111. See also Joseph Nicolar, *The Life and Traditions of the Red Man* (1893; reprint, Fredericton, New Brunswick, Canada: Saint Annes Point Press, 1979), 5.

28. Prins, "Children of Gluskap," 109.

29. Morrison, "Mapping Otherness," 123.

30. Callicott, *In Defense,* 189–190.

31. Calvin Martin, *Keepers of the Game: Indian–American Relationships and the Fur Trade* (Berkeley: University of California Press, 1978), 186.

32. Annie L. Booth and Harvey L. Jacobs, "Ties That Bind: Native American Beliefs as a Foundation for Environmental Consciousness," *Environmental Ethics* 12, no. 1 (spring 1990): 34–35.

33. Hilda Robtoy et al., "The Abenaki and the Northern Forest," in *The Future of the Northern Forest*, ed. Christopher McGrory Klyza and Stephen C. Trombulak (Hanover, N.H.: University Press of New England, 1994), 29.
34. Hubbard, *Woods and Lakes of Maine*, 191–214.
35. Ibid., 213.
36. Pollock, Hamilton, and Doyle, "Chert in the Munsungun Lake Formation," 159, 177.
37. Martin, *Keepers*, 187.
38. Morrison, "Mapping Otherness," 121–122; Frank G. Speck, "Penobscot Tales and Religious Beliefs," *Journal of American Folklore* 48, no. 187 (January–March 1935): 5–6; Nicolar, *Life and Traditions*, 83–84.
39. Speck, "Penobscot Tales," 10, 39.
40. Callicott, *In Defense*, 216–218.
41. Prins, "Children of Gluskap," 100.
42. David E. Putnam, personal communication, 7 July 1999.
43. See Martin, *Keepers*, 187.
44. For more discussion of the native role in exercising an environmental ethics, see Callicott, *In Defense*, 192–195.
45. Booth and Jacobs, "Ties That Bind," 31.

Part II. T7 R12 and the Farm: Control of Nature

1. Charles T. Jackson, *Third Annual Report on the Geology of the State of Maine* (Augusta, Maine: Smith & Robinson, 1839), 39–40.

Chapter 2. Wealth in a Bounded Land

1. Francis Higginson, *New England's Plantation* (1630; reprint, New York: New England Society in the City of New York, 1930), B.
2. William Bradford, *Of Plymouth Plantation: 1620–1647*, ed. Samuel Eliot Morrison (New York: Alfred A. Knopf, 1959), 62.
3. John Josselyn, *New-Englands Rarities Discovered* (1672; reprint, Bedford, Mass.: Applewood Books, distributed by Globe Pequot Press, Chester, Conn., 1992), 4.

4. See footnote 3 in Myron H. Avery, "The Telos Cut," *Appalachia* 21, no. 3 (1937): 381.

5. Edgar E. Ring, *Seventh Report of the Forest Commissioner of the State of Maine, 1908* (Waterville, Maine: Sentinel Publishing Company, 1908), 36.

6. An excellent set of maps that trace the early grants and charters for Maine, including the Allagash region, is in Gerald E. Morris, ed., *The Maine Bicentennial Atlas: An Historical Survey* (Portland: Maine Historical Society, 1976), plates 7–10.

7. This text is from Louis C. Hatch, *Maine: A History* (1919; reprint, Somersworth, N.H.: New Hampshire Publishing Company, 1973), 247.

8. Ring, *Seventh Report of the Forest Commissioner,* 45–46.

9. B. J. Holland, "Park Holland, Life and Diaries," part 3, "Survey Lands of Bingham Purchase, 1841," copied by Mary H. Curran, University of Maine at Presque Isle, photocopy, 49.

10. Joseph W. Porter, "Park Holland and His Family, 1915," University of Maine at Presque Isle, photocopy, 78–81.

11. See Holland, "Holland, Life and Diaries," 49.

12. Ibid, 50.

13. See Austin H. Wilkins, *Ten Million Acres of Timber: The Remarkable Story of Forest Protection in the Maine Forestry District (1909–1972)* (Woolwich, Maine: TBW Books, 1978), 7, for a description of early surveying practices and difficulties.

14. See Holland, "Holland, Life and Diaries," 50.

15. Ibid, 50–51.

16. Ibid, 54–55.

17. Ibid, 57, 61.

18. Ibid, 65.

19. Moses Greenleaf, *Statistical View of the District of Maine; More Specifically with Reference to the Value and Importance of its Interior. Addressed to the Consideration of the Legislators of Massachusetts* (Boston, Mass.: Cummings and Hilliard, 1816), 29–30, 120–121, 130–139.

20. Ibid., 132–136.

21. Richard G. Wood, *A History of Lumbering in Maine: 1820–1861* (Orono: University of Maine Press, 1935), 48–49.

22. Ring, *Seventh Report of the Forest Commissioner,* 77.

23. John E. McLeod, *The Northern: The Way I Remember* ([East Millinocket, Maine]: Great Northern Paper, [1981]), 15.

24. See Gordon G. Whitney, *From Coastal Wilderness to Fruited Plain: A History of Environmental Change in Temperate North America from 1500 to the Present* (Cambridge, England: Cambridge University Press, 1994), 175–176.

25. Joseph W. Porter, ed., *The Bangor Historical Magazine*, vol. 5 (Bangor, Maine: Joseph W. Porter, 1889–1890), 77.

26. Shirlee Connors-Carlson, *The Proudwood People: 1886–1986, 100 Years as a Way of Life* (Allagash, Maine: Town Crier, 1986).

27. Maine Department of Transportation, "A History of Maine Roads: 1600–1970" (Augusta: Maine Department of Transportation, 1970), photocopy, 3.

28. See *A Plan of the Part of the State of Maine Which Was Explored from Mars Hill to the Sebois in 1828 by Geo W. Coffin and Dan'l Rose and from the Sebois to the Head of the N.W. Branch of the Penobscot River by Dan'l Rose in 1829* (Augusta: Maine State Library); and Geo. W. Coffin, *A Plan of the Public Lands in the State of Maine, 1835*, cage box 2, Oscar Fellows Papers, Special Collections Department, Raymond H. Folger Library, University of Maine, Orono.

29. These developments in transportation are documented in John W. White, "Early Transportation in Northernmost New England, 1820–1870," *New England Social Studies Bulletin* 1, no. 3 (1955): 18–24; Maine Department of Transportation, "Maine Roads: 1600–1970," 5; and Connors-Carlson, *Proudwood.*

30. Charles T. Jackson, *First Report on the Geology of the Public Lands in the State of Maine* (Boston, Mass.: Dutton and Wentworth, Printers to the State, 1837), 12–13.

31. Charles T. Jackson, *Second Annual Report on the Geology of the Public Lands, Belonging to the Two States of Massachusetts and Maine* (Boston, Mass.: Dutton and Wentworth, State Printers, 1838), 57.

32. Ibid., 57–58.

33. Jackson, *First Report,* 12.

34. Jackson, *Second Report,* vii.

35. See Alec McEwen, ed., *In Search of the Highlands: Mapping the Canada-Maine Boundary, 1839* (Fredericton, New Brunswick, Canada: Acadiensis Press, 1988), 9–81.

36. See William P. Parrott and Zebulon Bradley, "Map of Part of the Undivided Lands: Being Townships Five, Six, Seven, and Eight in the Eleventh, Twelvth, and Thirteenth Ranges West from the East Line of the State, Surveyed *1840*," roll 1, vol. 3A; and "General Description of Township 7 in the 12th Range," roll 15, book 63, in *Land Office Plan Book* (Augusta: Maine State Archives), microfilm.

37. Ibid.

38. See Roderick Nash, *Wilderness and the American Mind*, 3rd ed. (New Haven, Conn.: Yale University Press, 1982), 6; and Michael Frome, *Battle for the Wilderness*, rev. ed. (Salt Lake City: University of Utah Press, 1997), 12.

39. For an interesting and informative overview of the boundary commission's work and use of the camera lucida, see William David Barry and Geraldine Tidd Scott, "Charting a Wilderness," *Down East: The Magazine of Maine* 41, no. 11 (June 1995): 58–63, 83–84.

40. "Reports of Principal Assistant Engineers Employed in the Exploration and Survey of the North Eastern Boundary of the United States in the Years 1840, 1841, and 1842, under the Direction of A. Talcott, Commissioner," E 107, envelope 2, folder 2, National Archives and Records Administration, College Park, Md.

41. Jackson, *Second Report*, viii, xii.

42. Richard Judd, "Route to a New Frontier: The Allagash River and the Creation of a Wilderness Concept," *Habitat: Journal of the Maine Audubon Society* 3, no. 6 (June–July 1986): 18.

43. Philip T. Coolidge, *History of the Maine Woods* (Bangor, Maine: Furbush-Roberts Printing Company, 1963), 42, 50–51.

44. Oscar S. Smith, "The Lumber Industry on Penobscot Waters," *The Northern* 4, no. 5 (August 1924): 4.

45. Coolidge, *History of the Maine Woods*, 44, 46–47, 67.

46. Jackson, *Second Report*, 57; *St. John Courier*, 23 March 1833.

47. See Richard W. Judd, *Aroostook: A Century of Logging in Northern Maine* (Orono: University of Maine Press, 1989), 62–63, for a discussion of river improvements.

48. Coolidge, *History of the Maine Woods*, 46.

49. "The Evidence before the Committee on Interior Waters, on Petition of Wm H. Smith, Daniel M. Howard, Warren Brown, and Theodore H. Dillingham, for Leave to Build a Sluiceway from Lake Telos to

Webster Pond," reported by Israel Washburn Jr., 134493 Telos Canal [1846], 1, Maine State Law and Legislative Reference Library, Augusta.

50. Ibid, 2–3.

51. William M. Pingry, *A Genealogical Record of the Descendents of Moses Pengry, of Ipswich, Mass.* (Ludlow, Vt.: Warner & Hyde, Book and Job Printers, 1881), 68–70.

52. Information on the life and manner of E. S. Coe is from Henry L. Griffin, "Commemorative Address," in *Services in Memory of Eben S. Coe, The Congregational Church, Northwood Center, N.H., June Twenty-Ninth, Nineteen Hundred,* ed. G. W. Bingham (Derry, N.H.: Charles Barttlett, Printer, 1901); Elliott C. Cogswell, *History of Nottingham, Deerfield, and Northwood, Comprised within the Original Limits of Nottingham, Rockingham County, N.H., with Records of the Centennial Proceedings at Northwood and Genealogical Sketches* (Manchester, N.H.: John B. Clarke, 1878), iv, 559, 657–659; and Joseph Gardner Bartlett, *Robert Coe, Puritan, His Descendants* (n.p. [privately printed], 1911).

53. E. S. Coe to David Pingree, 13 May 1844 and 5 June 1844, E. S. Coe Chamberlain Farm Papers, Captain Myron H. Avery Collection, Maine State Library, Augusta.

54. Land Agents of Maine and Massachusetts to Francis Blackman, 16 July 1844, book 12, p. 117; Francis Blackman to David Pingree, "Twp. 7 R. 12," 10 August 1844, book 9, p. 349, Piscataquis County Registry of Deeds, Dover-Foxcroft, Maine.

55. "Evidence before the Committee," 5–6, 29.

56. Samuel Smith to the Several Persons Lumbering under Permits from D. Pingree, 28 January 1845, Coe Papers, Special Collections Department, Raymond H. Fogler Library, University of Maine, Orono.

57. The so-called Telos war has been widely documented. See "Evidence before the Committee"; and Myron H. Avery, "The Telos Cut," 380–395.

58. See David C. Smith, *A History of Lumbering in Maine, 1861–1960* (Orono: University of Maine Press, 1972), 21–23; and Everett L. Parker, *Beyond Moosehead: A History of the Great North Woods of Maine* (Greenville, Maine: Moosehead Communications, 1996), 36–59.

59. Coolidge, *History of the Maine Woods,* 57.

60. A. G. Hempstead, "A Visit to Chamberlain Farm," *The Northern* 7, no. 8 (November 1927): 7, 14–15.

61. Henry David Thoreau, *The Maine Woods* (New York: Thomas Y. Crowell & Company, 1906), 243, 262.

62. *The Bangor Directory* (Bangor, Maine: Samuel S. Smith, 1846), 16.

63. D. Pingree to John Winn, "Undivided 4/20 Twp. 7 R. 12," 9 January 1847, book 15, p. 304; D. Pingree to E. S. Coe, "Undivided 1/20 Twp. 7 R. 12," 2 January 1847, book 15, p. 309; D. Pingree, John Winn, and E. S. Coe to Jefferson Lake, "Undivided One-Half of 500 Acres in Twp. 7 R. 12 (Known as Chamberlain Farm)," 1 January 1847, book 19, p. 102, Piscataquis County Registry of Deeds, Dover-Foxcroft, Maine.

64. See William R. Sawtell, *Katahdin Iron Works: Boom or Bust* (Milo, Maine: Milo Printing Company, 1982), 19.

65. Joel W. Eastman, "A History of the Katahdin Iron Works" (master's thesis, University of Maine, 1965), 65–67.

66. For a discussion of the California Road and its history, see Judd, *Aroostook,* 59–61; and Lew Dietz, *The Allagash* (New York: Holt, Rinehart & Winston, 1968), 253–254.

67. "Telos Canal and Chamberlain Dam," box 2, Oscar Fellows Papers, Special Collections Department, Raymond H. Fogler Library, University of Maine, Orono.

68. Coolidge, *History of the Maine Woods,* 65.

69. "Journey to the Woods, 1852," folder C15, E. S. Coe Chamberlain Farm Papers, Captain Myron H. Avery Collection, Maine State Library, Augusta.

70. D. Pingree to E. S. Coe, "Undivided Nine-Fortieths of Chamberlain Farm, Twp. 7 R. 12," 4 April 1858, book 35, pp. 466–467, Piscataquis County Registry of Deeds, Dover-Foxcroft, Maine.

71. "Chamberlain Farm Fire Insurance Policy," June 1858, E. S. Coe Chamberlain Farm Papers, Captain Myron H. Avery Collection, Maine State Library, Augusta.

72. "Chamberlain Farm Fire Insurance Policy," July 1869, E. S. Coe Chamberlain Farm Papers, Captain Myron H. Avery Collection, Maine State Library, Augusta.

73. "Inventory of Chamberlain Farm," 1859, and "Merchandise and Supplies," E. S. Coe Chamberlain Farm Papers, Captain Myron H. Avery Collection, Maine State Library, Augusta.

74. "Inventory of Chamberlain Farm," June 1860, E. S. Coe Chamberlain

Farm Papers, Captain Myron H. Avery Collection, Maine State Library, Augusta.

75. "Chamberlain Farm Inventory," 1 July 1877, E. S. Coe Chamberlain Farm Papers, Captain Myron H. Avery Collection, Maine State Library, Augusta.

76. "Inventory from A. K. P. Patten to Thos. McCard," 5 and 6 April 5 1892, E. S. Coe Chamberlain Farm Papers, Captain Myron H. Avery Collection, Maine State Library, Augusta.

77. "Chamberlain Farm House Account," 1875, E. S. Coe Chamberlain Farm Papers, Captain Myron H. Avery Collection, Maine State Library, Augusta.

78. "Chamberlain Farm House Account," 1876, E. S. Coe Chamberlain Farm Papers, Captain Myron H. Avery Collection, Maine State Library, Augusta.

79. "Chamberlain Farm Log," 1881–1882, E. S. Coe Chamberlain Farm Papers, Captain Myron H. Avery Collection, Maine State Library, Augusta.

80. "Chamberlain Farm, List of Weights and Contents," 25 December 1882, E. S. Coe Chamberlain Farm Papers, Captain Myron H. Avery Collection, Maine State Library, Augusta.

81. *Bangor Daily Commercial,* 25 October 1888.

82. "E. S. Coe Office Memorandum," 1889–1898, Coe Papers, Special Collections Department, Raymond H. Fogler Library, University of Maine, Orono.

83. E. S. Coe to Thos. McCard, 17 July 1896, E. S. Coe Chamberlain Farm Papers, Captain Myron H. Avery Collection, Maine State Library, Augusta.

84. "Murphy's Camp at Allegash," *The Northern* 3, no. 10 (January 1924): 10.

85. "E. S. Coe Chamberlain Farm Account Records," 1 February 1897–1 February 1898, Coe Papers, Special Collections Department, Raymond H. Fogler Library, University of Maine, Orono.

86. See Wilkins, *Ten Million Acres,* 2; and Smith, *History of Lumbering, 1861–1960,* 190–191.

87. James B. Trefethen, *The American Landscape, 1776–1976: Two Centuries of Change* (Washington, D.C.: Wildlife Management Institute, 1976), 8–10.

88. Charles T. Jackson, *Katahdin Iron Works, Katahdin, Maine, 1863* (Boston, Mass.: T. R. Holland, 1863), 7.

89. John M. Way Jr., "Map of Moosehead Lake and the Headwaters of the Penobscot and St. John Rivers," *Guide to Moosehead Lake and Northern Maine, with Map* (Boston, Mass.: Bradford & Anthony, 1874).

90. Thomas Sedgwick Steele, *Map of the Headwaters of the Aroostook, Penobscot, and St. John Rivers, Maine* (Boston, Mass.: Estes & Lauriat, 1881).

91. "Ronco's Camp and Mud Pond Carry," *The Northern* 6, no. 8 (November 1926): 6.

92. John W. White, "Early Transportation in Northeasternmost New England, 1820–1870," *New England Social Studies Bulletin* 12, no. 3 (1955): 19.

93. See Jerry Angier and Herb Cleaves, *Bangor and Aroostook: The Maine Railroad* (Littleton, Mass.: Flying Yankee Enterprises, 1986).

94. Manly Hardy, "A Maine Woods Walk in Sixty-One, Part III," *Forest and Stream* (4 April 1903): 263.

95. Smith, *History of Lumbering, 1861–1960*, 235.

96. Whitney, *From Coastal Wilderness*, 183.

97. "E. S. Coe Office Memorandum," 1899, Coe Papers, Special Collections Department, Raymond H. Fogler Library, University of Maine, Orono.

98. Griffin, "Commemorative Address," 19.

99. Coolidge, *History of the Maine Woods*, 615.

100. "The Wildlands: Who Owns Them?" *Bangor Daily Commercial*, 7 February 1905.

101. Stephen Wheatland, "History of Pingree Heir Timberland Ownership," *Biennial Report of the Forest Commissioner* (Augusta, Maine: Forest Commissioner, 1969–1970), 120.

102. "The Wildlands: Who Owns Them?"

103. Wilkins, *Ten Million Acres*, 25, 53.

104. Stewart L. Udall, *The Quiet Crisis* (New York: Avon Books, 1963), 110.

105. See Judd, "Route to a New Frontier," 19–20.

106. *Proposed Plan of Preservation and Interpretation: Tramway Historic District, Allagash Wilderness Waterway* (n.p., 1994), 12, 15.

107. Thomas R. Cox et al., *This Well-Wooded Land: Americans and Their Forests from Colonial Times to the Present* (Lincoln: University of Nebraska Press, 1985), 111.
108. Whitney, *From Coastal Wilderness*, 173–176.

Chapter 3. A Well-Stocked Country

1. "Sudden Death of Manly Hardy," *Bangor Daily News*, 10 December 1910; and "Manly Hardy," *Journal of the Maine Ornithological Society* 13, no. 1 (March 1911): 1–9.
2. See Harvey Elliot, "Fish and Game Management in Maine: The Early Years," *Maine Fish and Game* (spring 1961): 13; and Philip T. Coolidge, *History of the Maine Woods* (Bangor, Maine: Furbush-Roberts Printing Company, 1963), 689.
3. Manly Hardy, "A Maine Woods Walk in Sixty-One, Part III," *Forest and Stream* (4 April 1903): 263.
4. "Sudden Death"; "Manly Hardy."
5. Manly Hardy, "First Journal," 1852, Fannie (Hardy) Eckstorm Collection, box 614, folder 73, pp. 41–59, Special Collections Department, Raymond H. Fogler Library, University of Maine, Orono.
6. Hardy, "First Journal," p. 52.
7. See editorial note by Fannie Hardy Eckstorm. Ibid., 59.
8. Manly Hardy, "Notes of a Trip to Tobique—1858," Fannie (Hardy) Eckstorm Collection, box 614, folder 73, p. 7, Special Collections Department, Raymond H. Fogler Library, University of Maine, Orono.
9. Ibid., 8–9.
10. Ibid., 10.
11. Ibid., 13–19.
12. Manly Hardy, "A Fall Fur Hunt in Maine," *Forest and Stream* 74, no. 21 (21 May 1910): 810. The full article was published as a series in vol. 74, nos. 19, 20, 22, 23, and 24.
13. Manly Hardy, "A Maine Woods Walk in Sixty-One, Part I," *Forest and Stream* (21 March 1903): 223–224.
14. Ibid., 224.
15. Coolidge, *History of the Maine Woods*, 686–688.

16. "Manly Hardy," 2, 6; and William B. Krohn, letter to author, 10 August 2000.
17. "Manly Hardy," 2–9; "Sudden Death."
18. Manly Hardy, "The Wolf Cry in Maine," *Forest and Stream* 23, no. 6 (20 March 1884): 1.
19. "Manly Hardy," 3–8.
20. Ibid., 6–8.
21. Ibid., 6.
22. Manly Hardy to C. Ames, 11 November 1905, Fannie (Hardy) Eckstorm Collection, Special Collections Department, Raymond H. Fogler Library, University of Maine, Orono.
23. "Manly Hardy," 7.
24. William J. Long to Fannie Hardy Eckstorm, 15 March 1911, Fannie (Hardy) Eckstorm Collection, box 617, folder 38, Special Collections Department, Raymond H. Fogler Library, University of Maine, Orono.
25. Richard W. Judd, *Common Lands, Common People: The Origin of Conservation in Northern New England* (Cambridge, Mass.: Harvard University Press, 1997), 207.
26. J. F. Sprague, "Our Association's Mission," *Industrial Journal* (24 January 1896): 2.
27. Judd, *Common Lands*, 214.
28. Ibid., 133–141, 165–166.
29. Ibid., 156.
30. Maine Department of Inland Fisheries and Wildlife, ["History of Maine Department of Inland Fisheries and Wildlife"] (Augusta: Maine Department of Inland Fisheries and Wildlife, n.d.), photocopy.
31. Elliot, "The Early Years," 14.
32. Maine Department of Inland Fisheries and Wildlife, ["History"].
33. Manly Hardy, "Reply to Special," 1891, "Father's Articles about Game," Fannie (Hardy) Eckstorm Collection, box 618, folder 3, p. 169, Special Collections Department, Raymond H. Fogler Library, University of Maine, Orono.
34. Manly Hardy, "On Bear Bounty," *Bangor Daily Commercial,* February 1901.
35. "Manly Hardy," 6.

36. Manly Hardy, "Notes Taken on Trip Maine Scientific Survey—1861," Fannie (Hardy) Eckstorm Collection, box 614, folder 73, p. 34, Special Collections Department, Raymond H. Fogler Library, University of Maine, Orono.

37. N. T. True, "Biographical Sketch of Ezekiel Holmes, M.D.," *Tenth Annual Report of the Secretary of the Maine Board of Agriculture: 1865* (Augusta, Maine: Stevens & Sayward, Printers to the State, 1865), 209.

38. "Ezekiel Holmes: Memorials, Journals, and Correspondence, Early Years," *The Home Farm* 4, no. 32 (19 June 1884): 1.

39. See True, "Biographical Sketch," 207–222.

40. Ibid., 215.

41. Lawrence M. Sturtevant, "Ezekiel Holmes and His Influence: 1801–1865" (master's thesis, University of Maine, 1948), 372.

42. Chaps. 84 and 85, *Acts and Resolves Passed by the Fortieth Legislature of the State of Maine 1861* (Augusta: Stevens & Sayward, Printers to the State, 1861), 41.

43. "Ezekiel Holmes Petition," 1861, S-530, misc. box 20/17, Research Library Collection, Maine Historical Society, Portland.

44. True, "Biographical Sketch," 213–220.

45. "Contract for Scientific Survey of Maine," 1861, Maine State Archives, Augusta.

46. Background on Charles H. Hitchcock is from Warren Upham, "Memorial of Charles Henry Hitchcock," *Bulletin of the Geological Society of America* 31 (1920): 64–80; and "Sketch of Charles Henry Hitchcock," *Popular Science Monthly* (December 1898): 260–268.

47. Ezekiel Holmes and Charles H. Hitchcock, "Preliminary Report upon the Natural History and Geology of the State of Maine: 1861," *Sixth Annual Report of the Secretary of the Maine Board of Agriculture: 1861* (Augusta, Maine: Stevens & Sayward, Printers to the State, 1861), 93–94.

48. Ibid., 333.

49. Hardy, "Notes on Maine Scientific Survey," 29.

50. Holmes and Hitchcock, "Preliminary Report," 333.

51. Hardy, "Notes on Maine Scientific Survey," 30.

52. Holmes and Hitchcock, "Preliminary Report," 335.

53. Hardy, "Notes on Maine Scientific Survey," 31.

54. Ibid., 32.
55. Holmes and Hitchcock, "Preliminary Report," 340–341.
56. Ibid., 341.
57. Ibid., 341–344.
58. Ibid., 345.
59. Ibid., 345–346.
60. Hardy, "Notes on Maine Scientific Survey," 34.
61. Sturtevant, "Ezekiel Holmes," 374–376; Holmes and Hitchcock, "Preliminary Report," 359–360.
62. Holmes and Hitchcock, "Preliminary Report," 353–354.
63. "Manly Hardy," 2–3.
64. Sturtevant, "Ezekiel Holmes," 377–378.
65. Ibid., 378.
66. See Upham, "Memorial," 64–80; and Upham, "Sketch," 260–268.
67. Holmes and Hitchcock, "Preliminary Report," 357.
68. Ibid., 346.

Part III. "Resting-Place for Weary Voyagers": Harmony with Nature

1. Ezekiel Holmes and Charles H. Hitchcock, "Preliminary Report upon the Natural History and Geology of the State of Maine: 1861," *Sixth Annual Report of the Secretary of the Maine Board of Agriculture: 1861* (Augusta, Maine: Stevens & Sayward, Printers to the State, 1861), 345.
2. Charles A. J. Farrar, *Farrar's Illustrated Guide Book to Moosehead Lake* (Boston, Mass.: Lee and Shepard, 1889), 245–246.
3. Gilbert White, *The Natural History of Selborne*, ed. Paul Foster (1789; reprint, New York: Oxford University Press, 1993), xiii.
4. See Edward J. Renehan Jr., *John Burroughs: An American Naturalist* (Post Mills, Vt.: Chelsea Green, 1992), 95–98 (quotes, 96).

Chapter 4. Lore and Romance of the North Woods

1. John M. Way Jr., *Guide to Moosehead Lake and Northern Maine, with*

Map (Boston, Mass.: Bradford & Anthony, 1874), 40. Note: map covers Moosehead Lake and the Penobscot and St. John Rivers.

2. Lew Dietz, *The Allagash* (New York: Holt, Rinehart & Winston, 1968), 149.

3. Ibid., 148.

4. See Richard R. Wescott, "Tourism in Maine," in *Maine: The Pine Tree State from Prehistory to the Present*, ed. Richard W. Judd, Edwin A. Churchill, and Joel W. Eastman (Orono: University of Maine Press, 1995), 432–438.

5. Ibid., 434.

6. Way, *Guide to Moosehead Lake*, 22.

7. See Way, *Guide to Moosehead Lake*.

8. Published materials with the exhibit *Maine Wilderness Transformed: Timber, Sporting, and Exploitation of the Moosehead Lake Region* (Portland: University of Southern Maine, Osher Map Library and Smith Center for Cartographic Education, 22 May 1997–7 January 1998).

9. Lucius L. Hubbard, *Summer Vacations at Moosehead Lake and Vicinity: A Practical Guide-Book for Tourists* (Boston, Mass.: A. Williams and Company, 1879), 102–103.

10. "Dr. L. L. Hubbard," *Michigan Miner* 3, no. 1 (1 December 1900): 1.

11. Lucius L. Hubbard, *Hubbard's Guide to Moosehead Lake and Northern Maine* (Cambridge, Mass.: Lucius L. Hubbard, 1882), v.

12. Lucius L. Hubbard, "Journal of the Musquacook Trip Sept. and Oct. 1881," Lucius L. Hubbard Papers, box 5, Bentley Historical Library, University of Michigan, Ann Arbor.

13. Lucius L. Hubbard, *Woods and Lakes of Maine* (Boston, Mass.: Ticknor and Company, 1883), 75–77.

14. Ibid., 7–10.

15. Ibid., 79–83, 151–154.

16. Thomas Sedgwick Steele, *Canoe and Camera: A Two Hundred Mile Tour through the Maine Forests* (Boston, Mass.: Estes & Lauriat, 1880), 11–12, 15, 20, 22.

17. Ibid., 12, 75.

18. Information on Thomas Sedgwick Steele's life is from *The Steele Family: American Genealogical Research* (Washington, D.C.: Heritage Press, 1975), 81–82; and *Illustrated Popular Biography of Connecticut* (Hartford, Conn.: J. A. Spalding, 1891), 281; and, courtesy of The

Connecticut Historical Society, Hartford, Connecticut, the following: "T. Sedgwick Steele," *Hartford Courant,* 11 September 1903; and H. W. French, *Art and Artists in Connecticut* (New York: Kennedy Graphics, Da Capo Press, 1970), 156–157.

19. William F. Robinson, *A Certain Slant of Light: The First Hundred Years of New England Photography* (Boston, Mass.: New York Graphic Society, 1980).

20. Steele, *Canoe and Camera,* 35, 61–63.

21. Ibid., 64–65.

22. Ibid., 66–70.

23. Ibid., 78–81, 97.

24. Ibid., 75–106.

25. Ibid., 139.

26. Ibid., 16.

27. Robinson, *Slant of Light.*

28. Thomas Sedgwick Steele, *Paddle and Portage, from Moosehead Lake to the Aroostook River, Maine* (Boston, Mass.: Estes & Lauriat, 1882), 49–50.

29. Carlton J. Corliss, "Railway Developments in Maine" (address at Ricker Classical Institute and Ricker College Alumni Association Banquet, Maine State Library, Augusta, 8 June 1953), photocopy, 13–16; Jerry Angier and Herb Cleaves, *Bangor and Aroostook: The Maine Railroad* (Littleton, Mass.: Flying Yankee Enterprises, 1986), 37.

30. Charles A. J. Farrar, *Farrar's Illustrated Guide Book to Moosehead Lake* (Boston, Mass.: Lee and Shepard, 1889), 245–246.

31. Wescott, "Tourism," 434–437.

32. Richard W. Judd, *Common Lands, Common People: The Origin of Conservation in Northern New England* (Cambridge, Mass.: Harvard University Press, 1997), 197.

33. Charles G. Roundy, "Changing Attitudes toward the Maine Wilderness" (master's thesis, University of Maine, 1970), 68.

34. Alvin F. Sanborn, "The Future of Rural New England," *Atlantic Monthly* 80 (July 1897): 82–83.

35. Lucius L. Hubbard to Fannie Hardy Eckstorm, 21 September 1929, Fannie (Hardy) Eckstorm Collection, Special Collections Department, Raymond H. Fogler Library, University of Maine, Orono.

36. This account is excerpted from Fannie Pearson Hardy, "Windbound on Chamberlain," *Forest and Stream* (7 November 1889): 303; and Fannie P. Hardy, "Trip Down the East Branch via North East Carry," 1888, "Journals of Fannie P. Hardy (Mrs. Eckstorm)," pp. 71–72, Fannie (Hardy) Eckstorm Collection, Special Collections Department, Raymond H. Fogler Library, University of Maine, Orono.

37. Fannie Hardy Eckstorm to Ralph S. Palmer, 2 February 1946, quoted in Elizabeth Ring, "Fannie Hardy Eckstorm: Maine Woods Historian," *New England Quarterly* 26, no. 1 (March 1953): 52.

38. Hardy, "Trip Down the East Branch," 60–72.

39. Hardy, "Windbound," 303.

40. Ibid.

41. Hardy, "Trip Down the East Branch," 72–82.

42. Ibid., 64, 66, 69, 79.

43. Ibid., 61, 68–69, 74, 78–81.

44. Ibid., 60–82.

45. Mildred Wasson, "Fannie Hardy Eckstorm: Celebrity and Next Door Neighbor," *Bangor Daily Commercial,* 29 November 1924.

46. "Bird-Lover in Oregon: Sketch of the New Writer, Fanny Hardy Eckstrom [sic], Her Life in the Maine Woods," *Portland Sunday Oregonian,* 28 April 1901.

47. Wasson, "Fannie Hardy Eckstorm."

48. "Bird-Lover in Oregon."

49. Wasson, "Fannie Hardy Eckstorm."

50. Ring, "Fannie," 51.

51. Wasson, "Fannie Hardy Eckstorm."

52. John A. Garraty and Edward T. James, eds., *Dictionary of American Biography: Supplement Four, 1946–1950* (New York: Charles Scribner's Sons, 1974), 248.

53. Wasson, "Fannie Hardy Eckstorm."

54. Ring, "Fannie," 47; for quote, see Fannie Hardy Eckstorm, *The Penobscot Man,* 2nd ed. (Bangor, Maine: Jordan-Frost Printing Company, 1924), 342–343.

55. Wasson, "Fannie Hardy Eckstorm."

56. Manly Hardy to Fannie Hardy, 11 March 1886, Fannie (Hardy) Eckstorm Collection, Special Collections Department, Raymond H. Fogler Library, University of Maine, Orono.

57. "Bird-Lover in Oregon."

58. John Burroughs to Fannie Hardy Eckstorm, 4 July 1907, 18 July [190?], 9 August [190?], Fannie (Hardy) Eckstorm Collection, box 610, folders 90–97, Special Collections Department, Raymond H. Fogler Library, University of Maine, Orono.

59. See Ring, "Fannie," 54–56, for a brief, well-written summary of Fannie Eckstorm's position.

60. Fannie Pearson Hardy, "Six Years under Maine Game Laws," *Forest and Stream* 36, 37 (March–August 1891): 189, 227–228.

61. Ibid., "Six Years," 249–250, 516, 45–46.

62. "Bird-Lover in Oregon"; Ring, "Fannie," 45.

63. Fannie Hardy Eckstorm, *The Bird Book* (Boston, Mass.: D. C. Heath & Company, 1901), iii.

64. Fannie Hardy Eckstorm, *The Woodpeckers* (Boston, Mass.: Houghton Mifflin Company, 1901), 1–2.

65. Eckstorm, *Penobscot Man,* 350.

66. Ring, "Fannie," 51–52.

67. Ibid., 45.

68. Lee Agger, *Women of Maine* (Portland, Maine: Guy Gannett Publishing Company, 1982), 95.

69. Fannie Hardy Eckstorm, "Thoreau's Maine Woods," *Atlantic Monthly* 102 (August 1908): 242–250.

70. Fannie Pearson Hardy, *Tales of the Maine Woods: Two Forest and Stream Essays (1891),* ed. Pauleena MacDougall (Orono: University of Maine, Maine Folklife Center, 1999), 2.

71. See footnote 6 in Ring, "Fannie," Fannie Hardy Eckstorm to Alfred G. Hempstead, 6 December 1927, 47.

72. Garraty and James, *Dictionary,* 248; and Ring, "Fannie," 46–47.

Chapter 5. Minding the Wildlands

1. George S. Kephart, "Return to Telos" (Durham, N.C.: Forest History Society, 1970), photocopy, 1. This is the original, unedited manuscript of *Campfires Rekindled* (Marion, Mass.: Channing Books, 1977). Manuscript provided courtesy of the Forest History Society.

2. George W. Coffin, *The Forest Lands of Maine: Report of the Land Agent*

of the Commonwealth of Massachusetts, Laid before the Legislature, January 10th, 1844.

3. See Stewart L. Udall, *The Quiet Crisis* (New York: Avon Books, 1963), 81–94; Roderick Nash, *Wilderness and the American Mind,* 3rd ed. (New Haven, Conn.: Yale University Press, 1982), 104–105; and David Lowenthal, *George Perkins Marsh: Versatile Vermonter* (New York: Columbia University Press, 1958), 246.

4. *Fourteenth Annual Report of the Secretary of the Maine Board of Agriculture, 1869* (Augusta, Maine: Stevens & Sayward, Printers to the State, 1870), 82–83, 85.

5. Richard W. Judd, *Common Lands, Common People: The Origin of Conservation in Northern New England* (Cambridge, Mass.: Harvard University Press, 1997), 11.

6. See Austin H. Wilkins, *Ten Million Acres: The Remarkable Story of Forest Protection in the Maine Forestry District (1909–1972)* (Woolwich, Maine: TBW Books, 1978), 30–31.

7. Ibid., 29, 39–44. See also Richard W. Judd, *Aroostook: A Century of Logging in Northern Maine* (Orono: University of Maine Press, 1989), 211–215.

8. See Wilkins, *Ten Million Acres,* 43–47, 95–97, 109–111; and David N. Hilton, *From York to the Allagash: Forest Fire Lookouts of Maine* (Greenville, Maine: Moosehead Communications, 1997), 82, 158.

9. Fanny [sic] Hardy Eckstorm, "Thoreau's Maine Woods," *Atlantic Monthly* 102, no. 2 (August 1908): 242.

10. See David C. Smith, *A History of Lumbering in Maine, 1861–1960* (Orono: University of Maine Press, 1972), 385–392.

11. Charles G. Roundy, "Changing Attitudes toward the Maine Wilderness" (master's thesis, University of Maine, 1970), 62–63.

12. Smith, *History of Lumbering, 1861–1960,* 392.

13. Ibid., 395.

14. Fred J. McLeary, "Neighborhood Data," in *Real Estate Appraisal of Chamberlain Farm Property, Township 7, Range 12, WELS, Maine,* 26 September 1968, p. 8. McLeary notes that Chamberlain Farm was leased in 1906 for $150 per year.

15. "Palmer Bros. Account Book," 1900–1902, No. 616, donated by Frank McElroy, Patten Lumberman's Museum, Patten, Maine.

16. A. G. Hempstead, "A Visit to Chamberlain Farm," *The Northern* 7, no. 8 (November 1927): 7.

17. Ralph I. Miles to David Withee, 17 April 1961.

18. See Hempstead, "Visit to Chamberlain Farm," 7; O. A. Harkness, "The Eagle Lake Tramway," *The Northern* 7, no. 8 (November 1927): 5–6, 14; *Proposed Plan of Preservation and Interpretation: Tramway Historic District, Allagash Wilderness Waterway* (n.p., 1994), 8–11; and Smith, *History of Lumbering, 1861–1960*, 395–396, 405.

19. Smith, *History of Lumbering, 1861–1960*, 392–393.

20. See *In the Maine Woods* (Bangor, Maine: Bangor and Aroostook Railroad Company, 1901–1910); for the quote, see the 1906 edition, p. 43.

21. See Hempstead, "Visit to Chamberlain Farm." Hanna's name is spelled by some as *Hannah*, but invoices that he signed show the correct spelling to be *Hanna*.

22. Maine Department of Transportation, "A History of Maine Roads: 1600–1970" (Augusta: Maine Department of Transportation, 1970), photocopy, 8.

23. "Highways 'In the Realms of Old King Spruce,'" *The Northern* 5, no. 6 (September 1925): 5–6.

24. Kephart, "Return to Telos," 2.

25. Ibid., 1–4.

26. Ibid., 7–10.

27. Ibid., 25.

28. Ibid., 25–28.

29. Ibid., 34.

30. Ibid., 52, 77–78.

31. Ibid., 34, 80–81, 91.

32. Joel W. Eastman, "Transportation Systems in Maine, 1820–1880," in *Maine: The Pine Tree State from Prehistory to the Present*, ed. Richard W. Judd, Edwin A. Churchill, and Joel W. Eastman (Orono: University of Maine Press, 1995), 314.

33. "Highways 'In the Realms of Old King Spruce,'" 6.

34. Phinneus Sawyer, "1923 Woods Cruise of T7 R12," no. R-2081, Great Northern Paper Company Archives, Millinocket, Maine.

35. *Maine State Valuation, Piscataquis County Wildlands*, 1924, p. 165.

36. See Maine Forestry District Map, Chamberlain District, Penobscot Watershed, ca. 1925.

37. Dorothy Clarke Wilson, *The Big-Little World of Doc Pritham* (New York: McGraw-Hill Book Company, 1971), 213–215.

38. Earl (Bud) Vickery, letters to author, 9 October 1996, 23 October 1996, 9 November 1996.

39. See James B. Trefethen, *The American Landscape, 1776–1976: Two Centuries of Change* (Washington, D.C.: Wildlife Management Institute, 1976), 10–14, for an overview of the technological revolution in the first part of the twentieth century.

40. "Another Advance Step in Woods Transportation," *The Northern* 6, no. 8 (November 1926): 3–5, 15; Emerson F. Blodgett, "The Pulp Wood Express," *The Northern* 7, no. 8 (November 1927): 3–5.

41. Blodgett, "Pulp Wood Express," 3–5.

42. Hempstead, "Visit to Chamberlain Farm," 7, 14–15.

43. Raymond F. Vigue, letter to author, 26 November 1997.

44. Edouard Lacroix to Auguste Lessard, 28 June 1927, courtesy Raymond F. Vigue.

45. Documents from the Lacroix office, courtesy Raymond F. Vigue.

46. For a discussion of changes related to the need for Lock Dam, see Judd, *Aroostook,* 170.

47. Wilkins, *Ten Million Acres,* 156–162.

48. John E. McLeod, *The Northern: The Way I Remember* ([East Millinocket, Maine]: Great Northern Paper, [1981]), 147–149.

49. Smith, *History of Lumbering, 1861–1960,* 374.

50. Roundy, "Changing Attitudes," 128.

51. Gene L. Letourneau, "Famous Lock Dam at Chamberlain Is Again under Fire," *Portland Sunday Telegram,* 15 January 1939.

52. *In the Maine Woods* (Bangor, Maine: Bangor and Aroostook Railroad Company, 1937), 16.

53. Kephart, *Campfires Rekindled,* 18–19.

54. Ibid., 133–144.

55. Ibid.

56. Ibid., 142.

Chapter 6. Lure of Woods and Waters

1. The story of the Nugents is from visits and talks the author had with them, from information given to the author by others who knew

them, and from articles based on interviews by writers spanning nearly fifty years. Some dates and stories reflected minor inconsistencies, which the author cross-checked as much as possible. Some inaccuracies, however, may still exist.

2. Lynn Franklin, "A Woman in the Wilderness," *Maine Sunday Telegram*, 26 June 1977, section D.

3. Lynn Franklin, "Oh for Good Old Days of Beaver and Muskrat Stew!" *Maine Sunday Telegram*, 22 August 1976.

4. Franklin, "Woman in the Wilderness."

5. Mel Allen, "An Allagash Love Story," *Yankee Magazine* (July 1986): 68.

6. Maine Sporting Camp Association, *The Maine Sporting Camp Guide* (Jay: Maine Sporting Camp Association, n.d.).

7. "E. S. Coe Office Memorandum," 1889–1898, Coe Papers, Special Collections Department, Raymond H. Fogler Library, University of Maine, Orono.

8. "Read What Telos Lake Offers," *In the Maine Woods* (Bangor, Maine: Bangor and Aroostook Railroad Company, 1902), 151.

9. "Ronco's Camp and Mud Pond Carry," *The Northern* 6, no. 8 (November 1926): 6–7.

10. Gene Letourneau, "Sportsmen Say," *Waterville Morning Sentinel*, 29 June 1986.

11. Ibid.

12. Franklin, "Woman in the Wilderness."

13. Bud Leavitt, "Outdoors," *Bangor Daily News*, 15–16 March 1986; Henry Fiola and John Ehlert, "The Nugents of the Allagash," *Snowsports* (ca. mid-1970s): 49; Franklin, "Oh for Good Old Days."

14. Bill Geagan, "Down the Trail with Bill Geagan," *Bangor Daily News*, 31 May 1941, p. 17.

15. Letourneau, "Sportsmen Say," 29 June 1986.

16. Dabney D. Hofammann, letter to author, 11 September 1997.

17. Bob Elliot, "Chamberlain Lake Couple Live in Real Pioneer Log Cabin," *Boston Post*, 13 October 1946.

18. Taped interview with Allen Nugent, ca. 1975, collection of Paul J. Fournier.

19. Franklin, "Oh for Good Old Days."

20. Hofammann, letter, 11 September 1997.

21. Clarence Herrick, interview with author, Guilford, Maine, 23 September 1997.

22. Harold Whiteneck, interview with author, 14 January 1997; letter to author, February 1997; Heart O' Maine Sporting Camps brochure.

23. Whiteneck, interview, 14 January 1997.

24. Gene Letourneau, "Sportsmen Say," *Waterville Morning Sentinel,* 6 August 1960.

25. Charles A. Pratt, letter to editor of *Down East Magazine,* 25 January 1972.

26. Taped interview, collection of Paul J. Fournier.

27. Lawrence Stuart, director, State Park and Recreation Commission, letter to Al and Patty Nugent, 3 March 1971.

28. Allen, "Allagash Love Story," 107; "Noble Allen O. Nugent," n.p., n.d., in possession of the author.

29. Bud Leavitt, "Outdoors," *Bangor Daily News,* n.d.

30. Bud Leavitt, "Outdoors," *Bangor Daily News,* 3 December 1984.

31. "Patty Nugent Celebrates Fifty Years at Remote Chamberlain Lake," *Moosehead Messenger,* 16 July 1986, p. 8.

32. Herbert Hartman, director of parks and recreation, Maine Department of Conservation, letter to Patty Nugent, 17 July 1986.

33. Allen, "Allagash Love Story," 108.

34. Hofammann, letter, 11 September 1997.

35. Ibid.

36. Ibid.

37. John Richardson and Regina Webster, interview with author, 28 March 1999.

38. Roberta Scruggs, "Winter of Their Content," *Maine Sunday Telegram,* 25 February 1996; Richardson and Webster, interview, 28 March 1999.

39. David C. Priest Sr., audiotapes to author, 19 June 1997 and 3, 7 August 1997; William S. Warner, *An Honest Woodsman: The Life and Opinions of Dave Priest—Maine Trapper, Guide, and Game Warden* (Orono, Maine: Northeast Folklore Society, 1983), 19–23.

40. Priest, audiotapes, 3, 7 August 1997.

41. Warner, *Honest Woodsman,* 27.

42. Priest, audiotapes, 3, 7 August 1997.

43. Warner, *Honest Woodsman,* 26–28.

44. Priest, audiotapes, 3, 7 August 1997.

45. Ibid.

46. Priest, audiotape, 19 June 1997; Priest, audiotapes, 3, 7 August 1997.

47. Priest, audiotapes, 3, 7 August 1997.

48. Priest, audiotape, 19 June 1997.

49. Priest, audiotapes, 3, 7 August 1997.

50. Quote from Charles S. Allen, "Maine's Warden Service: A Proud Past ... and a Challenging Future," *Maine Fish and Game* (fall 1994): 23. See also Harvey Elliot, "Law Enforcement through the Years," *Maine Fish and Game* (fall 1960): 8; Harvey Elliot, "Fish and Game Management: The Recent Years," *Maine Fish and Game* (fall 1961): 22; and Maine Department of Inland Fisheries and Wildlife, ["History of Maine Department of Inland Fisheries and Wildlife"] (Augusta: Maine Department of Inland Fisheries and Wildlife, n.d.), photocopy.

51. Quote from Philip T. Coolidge, *History of the Maine Woods* (Bangor, Maine: Furbush-Roberts Printing Company, 1963), 705. See also Maine Department of Inland Fisheries and Wildlife, ["History"].

52. David C. Priest Sr., audiotape to author, 5 January 1999.

53. David C. Priest Sr., telephone conversation with author, 19 May 1997.

54. Priest, audiotape, 19 June 1997.

55. Ibid.

56. Priest, audiotapes, 3, 7 August 1997.

57. Priest, audiotape, 19 June 1997.

58. Ibid.

59. Ibid.

60. David C. Priest Sr., audiotape to author, July 1997.

61. James B. Trefethen, *The American Landscape, 1776–1976: Two Centuries of Change* (Washington, D.C.: Wildlife Management Institute, 1976), 20–21.

62. *In the Maine Woods* (Bangor, Maine: Bangor and Aroostook Railroad Company, 1957).

63. Allen, "Maine's Warden Service," 27; Timothy E. Peabody and Thomas A. Santaguida, *The Maine Warden Service and the State of Maine: A Contemporary and Historical Overview* (Augusta: Maine Department of Inland Fisheries and Wildlife, [1999]).

64. Priest, audiotape, 19 June 1997.

65. Kevin J. MacLean, "Ex-Warden Claims Gov. Baxter Allowed Hunting in Park," *Katahdin Times,* 6 January 1998, p. 5.

66. Priest, audiotapes, 3, 7 August 1997.

67. Ibid.

68. Priest, audiotape, July 1997.

69. Priest, audiotapes, 3, 7 August 1997.

70. See MacLean, "Ex-Warden Claims."

71. Priest, audiotapes, 3, 7 August 1997.

72. Priest, audiotape, 19 June 1997; Priest, audiotape, July 1997.

73. Richard Judd, "Route to a New Frontier: The Allagash River and the Creation of a Wilderness Concept," *Habitat: Journal of the Maine Audubon Society* 3, no. 6 (June–July 1986): 20.

74. Henry D. Thoreau, *The Maine Woods* (New York: Thomas Y. Crowell & Company, 1906), 103.

75. Lucius L. Hubbard, *Woods and Lakes of Maine* (Boston, Mass.: Ticknor and Company, 1883), 31–33.

76. Chief Henry Red Eagle, *Aboriginally Yours,* ed. Eleanor R. Williamson, Juana D. Perley, and Madalene F. Burnham (Greenville, Maine: Moosehead Communications, 1997), v.

77. Ibid., xvii.

78. Chief Henry Red Eagle, "The Thunderous Wondrous Allagash," *In the Maine Woods* (Bangor, Maine: Bangor and Aroostook Railroad Company, [1952]), 28–29.

79. Thomas Sedgwick Steele, *Canoe and Camera: A Two Hundred Mile Tour through the Maine Forests* (Boston, Mass.: Estes & Lauriat, 1880), 36–37.

80. Etta Hubbard, letter to author, 4 November 1999.

81. Frank Donovan, "Life in the Maine Woods," *Boston Globe,* 7 March 1972.

82. Walter L. Arnold, "Diary—1926," Walter Lewellen Arnold Papers, Special Collections Department, Raymond H. Fogler Library, University of Maine, Orono.

83. Walter L. Arnold, "Allagash Waters—Part One," original manuscript for *Hunter-Trader-Trapper,* 22 June 1971, Walter Lewellen Arnold Papers, Special Collections Department, Raymond H. Fogler Library, University of Maine, Orono.

84. Herbert and Warren Cochrane, interview with author, 18 December 1998.

85. Faye O'Leary Hafford, *Waterway Wanderings: A Story of the People in the Allagash Wilderness Waterway* (Allagash, Maine: Faye O'Leary Hafford, n.d.), 51.

86. Cochrane, interview, 18 December 1998.

87. Ibid.

88. Dorothy Boone Kidney, letter to author, 14 December 1999.

89. Hafford, *Waterway Wanderings*, 51.

90. Cochrane, interview, 18 December 1998.

91. Hafford, *Waterway Wanderings*, 51.

92. Priscilla Bartlett, letter to author, 20 May 1999.

93. Wesley Herrick Sr. and Foster Herrick, *Camp Wanderlust: Canoe Trips along the Allagash* (Henniker, N.H.: Camp Wanderlust, n.d.).

94. Hafford, *Waterway Wanderings*, 51.

95. Bartlett, letter to author, 20 May 1999.

96. Hafford, *Waterway Wanderings*, 54.

97. Ibid.

98. Mike Kimball, "Canoeing the Allagash," *Yankee Magazine's Travel Guide to New England: Summer–Fall 1989* (Dublin, N.H.: Yankee Publishing, 1989), 197.

99. Gil Gilpatrick, *Allagash: The Story of Maine's Legendary Wilderness Waterway* (Skowhegan, Maine: Gil Gilpatrick, 1995), 227.

Part IV. Restricted Zone: Oneness with Nature

1. Herbert Cochrane to Tom Cieslinski, Maine Bureau of Parks and Lands, 3 June 1998.

2. Both Worster and Oelschlaeger saw Thoreau as among the first to have anticipated and expressed elements of the biocentric viewpoint. Max Oelschlaeger, *The Idea of Wilderness: From Prehistory to the Age of Ecology* (New Haven, Conn.: Yale University Press, 1991), 169–170, 294; Donald Worster, *Nature's Economy: A History of Ecological Ideas* (Cambridge, England: Cambridge University Press, 1985), 179–180.

Chapter 7. The Spell of the Wild

1. Daniel Ricketson, on meeting Thoreau in 1854. Quoted in Milton Meltzer and Walter Harding, *A Thoreau Profile* (New York: Thomas Y. Crowell & Company, 1962), 239.

2. Nathaniel Hawthorne, after meeting Thoreau in 1842. Quoted in Meltzer and Harding, *Profile*, 91.

3. Henry David Thoreau, *The Journal of Henry D. Thoreau*, vol. 9, ed. Bradford Torrey and Francis H. Allen (1906; reprint, New York: Dover Publications, 1962), 487.

4. For a provocative interpretation of Thoreau's views of civilization and nature, see Daniel B. Botkin, *No Man's Garden: Thoreau and a New Vision for Civilization and Nature* (Washington, D.C.: Island Press, 2001). For Thoreau's accounts and views of his New England countryside, see also David R. Foster, *Thoreau's Country: Journey through a Transformed Landscape* (Cambridge, Mass.: Harvard University Press, 1999).

5. Henry David Thoreau, *The Maine Woods*, (New York: Thomas Y. Crowell & Company, 1906), 250.

6. Ibid., 132–133, 250. See also letter to James Russell Lowell and editorial comments in Henry David Thoreau, *The Correspondence of Henry David Thoreau*, ed. Walter Harding and Carl Bode (Westport, Conn.: Greenwood Press, 1958), 501, 515–516.

7. Henry David Thoreau, "Walking," in *Henry David Thoreau: The Natural History Essays*, ed. Robert Sattlemeyer (Salt Lake City: Peregrine Smith, 1980), 112–113.

8. Ibid., 93.

9. Henry D. Thoreau, *The Illustrated Walden*, ed. J. Lyndon Shanley (Princeton, N.J.: Princeton University Press, 1973), 132.

10. Thoreau, *Correspondence*, 485–486.

11. Although a popular interpretation of Thoreau's Mt. Katahdin experience suggests it was traumatic for him and challenged his romantic view of nature, others make a strong argument that it was a revelation for him, helping him find himself and his true relationship with nature. See Henry David Thoreau, *Wild Fruits*, ed. Bradley P. Dean (New York: W. W. Norton & Company, 2000), xiv–xv.

12. Thoreau, *Correspondence*, 491–492.

13. Bradley P. Dean, letter to author, 24 May 2000.

14. Thoreau, *The Maine Woods*, 173, 215, 317–318.

15. Fannie Hardy Eckstorm, "Joseph Polis," Fannie (Hardy) Eckstorm Papers, box 618, folder 10, Special Collections Department, Raymond H. Fogler Library, University of Maine, Orono.

16. Thoreau, *Correspondence*, 491.

17. See Ray Angelo, "Edward S. Hoar Revealed," *Concord Saunterer* 17, no. 1 (March 1984): 9–15; see also Thoreau, *Correspondence*, 491.

18. For a discussion of Thoreau's interest and work in the scientific observation of nature, see Henry D. Thoreau, *Faith in a Seed: The Dispersion of Seeds and Other Late Natural History Writings*, ed. Bradley P. Dean (Washington, D.C.: Island Press, 1993), xi–17; quote, 106.

19. Henry David Thoreau, "Thoreau's Journal," no. 23, 27 July 1857, transcribed by Joseph J. Moldenhauer, MA 1302:29, The Pierpont-Morgan Library, New York.

20. Thoreau, *Correspondence*, 507.

21. Thoreau, "Journal," 27 July 1857.

22. Ibid.

23. Thoreau, *The Maine Woods*, 180, 196–199.

24. Thoreau, "Walking," 127–128.

25. Thoreau, *The Maine Woods*, 211, 229–230, 251, 301.

26. Ibid., 267.

27. See Fanny [sic] Hardy Eckstorm, "Thoreau's 'Maine Woods,'" *Atlantic Monthly* 102, no. 2 (August 1908): 242–250.

28. See Mary P. Sherwood, "Fanny [sic] Eckstorm's Bias," *Massachusetts Review* (autumn 1962): 139–147.

29. Thoreau, "Walking," 117.

30. Thoreau, *Thoreau: An American Landscape*, ed. Robert L. Rothwell (New York: Marlowe & Company, 1991), 182.

31. Thoreau, *Wild Fruits*, 238.

32. Thoreau, *The Maine Woods*, 171.

33. Thoreau, *Wild Fruits*, 236–237.

34. "Governor Percival Baxter's Allagash Trip," *Portland Sunday Telegram*, 8 July 1923; *Bangor Commercial*, 20 July 1923; *Kennebec Journal*, 23 July 1923; Willis E. Parsons, "Governor Baxter Makes the Allagash Trip," 2 August 1923; Scrapbook, vols. 2, 11, 20, Percival Proctor Baxter Collection, Maine State Library, Augusta.

35. Gene L. Letourneau, *Sportsmen Say* (Augusta, Maine: Guy Gannett Publishing Company, 1975), 213–215.
36. Percival P. Baxter, "Mount Katahdin State Park" (address to Maine Sportsmen's Fish and Game Association, Augusta, Maine, 27 January 1921).
37. John W. Hakola, *Legacy of a Lifetime: The Story of Baxter State Park* (Woolwich, Maine: TBW Books, 1981), 102.
38. Letourneau, *Sportsmen Say*, 217.
39. Quoted in Neil Rolde, *The Baxters of Maine: Downeast Visionaries* (Gardiner, Maine: Tilbury House, 1997), 148.
40. Hakola, *Legacy*, 50.
41. Ibid., 51–61.
42. "Baxter's Allagash Trip," *Portland Sunday Telegram*, 8 July 1923.
43. Parsons, "Baxter Makes Allagash Trip."
44. Ibid.
45. "Governor Baxter at Chesuncook," *The Northern* 3, no. 6 (September 1923): 7.
46. Parsons, "Baxter Makes Allagash Trip."
47. Ibid.
48. Ibid.
49. See Rolde, *Baxters of Maine*, 230, for a discussion of Baxter and Thoreau.
50. Warren K. Moorehead, "The Rights of Nature: An Urgent Plea That Maine May Retain Her Woods in Their Present Wild and Untrammeled State," *Sun-Up, Maine's Own Magazine* (December 1926): 26–29.
51. Ibid., 27–29.
52. See Myron H. Avery, "Northern Maine and Its Possibilities for Canoeing," *Water Sports: The Club News* 16, no. 189 (September 1926): 164–167.
53. Myron Avery, "Journal," August 1927, Captain Myron H. Avery Collection, Maine State Library, Augusta.
54. See Myron H. Avery, "A New Route to Mt. Katahdin: The Pogy Trail and One Party's Adventure in Making the Climb," *In the Maine Woods* (Bangor, Maine: Bangor and Aroostook Railroad Company, 1928), 13–26.
55. See Hakola, *Legacy*, 101–123, for an insightful discussion of Percival Baxter's wilderness concept.

56. See Hakola, *Legacy,* 141–159; and Rolde, *Baxters of Maine,* 250–256, for accounts of the national park controversy.

57. See Hakola, *Legacy,* 141–159.

58. Ibid., 141–159, 299; quote, 158.

59. Ibid., 97–98.

60. Irvin C. Caverly Jr., letter to author, 25 April 2000.

61. *Portland Sunday Telegram,* 30 November 1941, quoted in Constance Baxter, Judith A. Hakola, and John W. Hakola, *Greatest Mountain: Katahdin's Wilderness* (San Francisco: Scrimshaw Press, 1972).

62. Baxter, "Mount Katahdin State Park."

63. *Portland Sunday Telegram,* 30 November 1941.

64. Percival P. Baxter, "Communication to Governor H. A. Hildreth and the Ninety-Second Legislature, Portland, Maine, 2 January 1945," quoted in Baxter, Hakola, and Hakola, *Greatest Mountain.*

65. Baxter, "Communication, 2 January 1945."

66. Baxter, "Mount Katahdin State Park."

67. Baxter, "Communication, 2 January 1945."

68. *Portland Evening Express,* 20 June 1957, quoted in Baxter, Hakola, and Hakola, *Greatest Mountain.*

69. Percival Baxter to Payson Smith, 18 October 1955, folder 58, "Baxter State Park, Correspondence (General)," Percival Proctor Baxter Collection, Maine State Library, Augusta.

70. William O. Douglas to Percival Baxter, 5 October 1959, folder 58, "Baxter State Park, Correspondence (General)," Percival Proctor Baxter Collection, Maine State Library, Augusta. Published by permission of the William O. Douglas Estate.

71. See Rolde, *Baxters of Maine,* 312–314.

72. Ibid., 323–324, 329.

Chapter 8. The Struggle for Wildness

1. Background on Robert W. Patterson is from *Harvard Class of 1927: Fiftieth Anniversary Report* (Cambridge, Mass.: President and Fellows of Harvard University, 1977), 546–547; "Bob Patterson, Conservation Leader, Dies at Age Eighty-Three," *Bar Harbor Times,* 25 February 1988; and Robert W. Patterson Jr., interview with author, Ellsworth, Maine, 23 September 1999.

2. Robert W. Patterson, "Wilderness No More," *Down East* 37, no. 11 (June 1991): 48.

3. *Harvard Class of 1927*, 547.

4. Gene L. Letourneau, "Allagash Remains Our Last Frontier," *Portland Sunday Telegram*, 1 September 1946.

5. Patterson Jr., interview, 23 September 1999; Robert W. Patterson, journal entry, 31 August 1953, journal in possession of Robert W. Patterson Jr.

6. Patterson, "Wilderness No More," 48.

7. Donald E. Nicoll, letter to author, 10 March 1999.

8. Hubbard, *Woods and Lakes of Maine* (1888; reprint, Somersworth, N.H.: New Hampshire Publishing Company, 1971), 1–2.

9. Theo Lippman Jr., and Donald C. Hansen, *Muskie* (New York: W. W. Norton & Company, 1971), 142; "Mr. Clean" quote by columnist Richard Wilson.

10. New England–New York Inter-Agency Committee, *The Resources of the New England–New York Region*, 2 pts., 15 March 1955. See especially pt. I, "The General Report on the Comprehensive Survey," I-1; pt. II, chap. 3, "Saint John River Basin, Maine," X-7, X-12; and pt. II, chap. 5, "Penobscot River Basin, Maine," VII-11, X-1–9.

11. U.S. Department of the Interior, National Park Service, *Proposed Allagash National Recreation Area*, (Washington, D.C.: U.S. Department of the Interior), June 1961.

12. Maine State Park Commission and National Park Service, United States Department of the Interior, *A Recreation Plan for Maine*, (Augusta, Maine: Maine State Park Commission, 1956), 1–3, 21–23.

13. Gene Letourneau, "Allagash Area under Survey," *Portland Press Herald*, 26 September 1956.

14. Gene Letourneau, "Allagash Region Real Wilderness," *Portland Sunday Telegram*, 5 July 1959.

15. Gene Letourneau, "Allagash Hinges on Conservation," *Portland Press Herald*, 29 April 1959.

16. Gene Letourneau, "Roads Knife Allagash, Last Frontier," *Portland Press Herald*, 13 July 1959.

17. Stewart L. Udall, *The Quiet Crisis* (New York: Avon Books, 1963), viii; *Saturday Review* quote from frontispiece.

18. Conservation Foundation, *Report on the Allagash to the Natural*

Resources Council of Maine (New York: Conservation Foundation, 1961), 10–18.

19. For background on William O. Douglas, see Melvin I. Urofsky, ed., *"The Douglas Letters": Selection from the Private Papers of Justice William O. Douglas* (Bethesda, Md.: Adler & Adler, 1987), ix–xxi, 231–232 (quote, 232). See also William O. Douglas, *Go East, Young Man: The Early Years* (New York: Random House, 1974).

20. Douglas, *Go East*, 206.

21. William O. Douglas, *A Wilderness Bill of Rights* (Boston, Mass.: Little, Brown & Company, 1965), 85.

22. William O. Douglas to A. C. Foster, 18 April 1960; A. C. Foster to William O. Douglas, 6 June 1960; William O. Douglas to A. C. Foster, 10 June 1960, William O. Douglas Papers, container 650, Allagash and Maine folders, Manuscript Division, Library of Congress, Washington, D.C. Published with permission of the William O. Douglas Estate.

23. Roland H. Cobb to Nan Burgess, secretary to William O. Douglas, 1 August 1960, William O. Douglas Papers. Published with permission of the William O. Douglas Estate.

24. John T. Maines to William O. Douglas, 11 August 1960, William O. Douglas Papers. Published with permission of the William O. Douglas Estate.

25. William O. Douglas to John T. Maines, 1 October 1960, William O. Douglas Papers. Published with permission of the William O. Douglas Estate.

26. The description of Douglas' Allagash trip is from William O. Douglas, *My Wilderness: East to Katahdin* (Garden City, N.Y.: Doubleday & Company, 1961), 239–265; and Edmund Ware Smith, *Upriver and Down: Stories from the Maine Woods* (New York: Holt, Rinehart & Winston, 1965), 220–240.

27. Frederick Pratson, interview with Willard Jalbert, September 1972, no. 713, p. 11, Northeast Archives of Folklore and Oral History, Maine Folklife Center, University of Maine, Orono.

28. Douglas, *My Wilderness*, 239, 246–247; Smith, *Upriver and Down*, 227–231; Edmund Ware Smith, "Allagash Trip Journal, 1960," p. 5, Edmund Ware Smith Collection, Special Collections, Miller Library, Colby College, Waterville, Maine.

29. Smith, *Upriver and Down*, 238; Douglas, *My Wilderness*, 260.

30. Douglas, *My Wilderness*, 260–261.

31. Ibid., 244.

32. Ibid., 262–263.

33. See "Against Allagash Park: Supreme Court Justice Ends Eight-Day Canoe Trip," *Bangor Daily News*, 29 September 1960; and "Justice Douglas Calls for Preservation of Allagash," *St. John Valley Times*, 29 September 1960.

34. William O. Douglas to Percival Proctor Baxter, 8 November 1960, folder 84, Percival Proctor Baxter Collection, Maine State Library, Augusta. Published with permission of the William O. Douglas Estate.

35. Percival Proctor Baxter to William O. Douglas, 2 December 1960, folder 84, Percival Proctor Baxter Collection, Maine State Library, Augusta.

36. William O. Douglas to Conrad L. Wirth, 4 December 1961, Urofsky, *Douglas Letters*, 245–246.

37. William O. Douglas, "Why We Must Save the Allagash," *Field and Stream* (July 1963): 29, 57.

38. Robert W. Patterson, journal entries, 14–15 July 1960, journal in possession of Robert W. Patterson Jr.

39. "Bob Patterson," *Bar Harbor Times*.

40. See Letourneau, "Allagash Region," 5 July 1959; Gene L. Letourneau, "Legion Voices Opposition to Allagash Park," *Portland Press Herald*, 7 September 1959; and Gene L. Letourneau, "McIntire Opposes Allagash Park," *Portland Evening Express*, 8 October 1959.

41. Richard Judd, "A Last Chance for Wilderness: Defining the Allagash Wilderness Waterway, 1959–1966," *Maine History*, 40, no. 1 (Spring 2001).

42. "Maine Seen Hurt by Using Allagash as National Park," *Portland Press Herald*, 16 January 1960.

43. *Natural Resources Council Bulletin* 1, no. 4 (June 1960): 2.

44. May Craig, "Seven Thousand Opposed to Allagash Park," *Portland Press Herald*, 5 May 1960.

45. Gene L. Letourneau, "Allagash Region Remains State's Vast Wilderness," *Portland Sunday Telegram*, 26 May 1960.

46. *Natural Resources Council Bulletin* 1, no. 4 (June 1960): 1–3.

47. "Allagash Recreation Area Could Be Source of More Revenue, Group Told," *Portland Sunday Telegram*, 26 June 1960.

48. "Great Northern Frames Allagash Management Plan," *Portland Press Herald*, 10 November 1960.

49. Philip P. Clement to Edmund S. Muskie, 17 November 1960, U.S. Senate: Senate Office (180-8), Edmund S. Muskie Collection, Edmund S. Muskie Archives, Bates College, Lewiston, Maine.

50. Robert W. Patterson to Ezra James Briggs, 21 March 1961, in possession of Robert W. Patterson Jr.; *Natural Resources Council Bulletin* 2, no. 2 (June 1961): 1–3.

51. Robert W. Patterson to Charles A. Pierce, 20 June 1961, in possession of Robert W. Patterson Jr.; *Second Supplemental Journal of the Senate*, Additional Papers from the House, A-1, Joint Order, 7 June 1961.

52. Stewart L. Udall to author, 1 September 1997.

53. "U.S. Park Service Releases Report on Allagash Area," *Portland Evening Express*, 7 July 1961.

54. "National Recreation Area along Allagash Proposed," *Portland Press Herald*, 27 June 1961.

55. "Park Service Idea on the Allagash Will Sharpen Debate on Quoddy," *Portland Press Herald*, 29 June 1961.

56. "Allagash Next?" *Portland Evening Express*, 24 July 1961.

57. See Charles G. Roundy, "Changing Attitudes toward the Maine Wilderness" (master's thesis, University of Maine, 1970).

58. Robert W. Patterson to Natural Resources Council of Maine officers, executive committee, and advisors, 10 October 1961.

59. Gene Letourneau, "If Park Plans Materialize, Company Faces Problems," *Portland Press Herald*, 2 September 1961.

60. "Hinman Opposes Making Allagash Recreation Area," *Portland Press Herald*, 17 October 1961.

61. "AIM Opposes U.S. Takeover of Allagash," *Portland Press Herald*, 2 December 1961.

62. May Craig, "Recreation Area in Allagash with Logging Permitted," *Portland Evening Express*, 31 January 1962.

63. *Natural Resources Council Bulletin* 3, no. 1 (February 1962): 1.

64. Conservation Foundation, *Report on the Allagash*, 176–177.

65. Sigurd F. Olson to Robert W. Patterson, 3 March 1962, Sigurd Olson Papers, box 21, Minnesota Historical Society, Saint Paul.

66. Robert W. Patterson to Ezra James Briggs, 6 March 1962, in possession of Robert W. Patterson Jr.

67. Robert W. Patterson to Charles Pierce, 10 March 1962, in possession of Robert W. Patterson Jr.

68. *Natural Resources Council Bulletin* 3, no. 2 (April 1962).

69. Robert W. Patterson, journal, pp. 74–77, 15–17 August 1962, in possession of Robert W. Patterson Jr.

70. *Natural Resources Council Bulletin* 4, no. 1 (August 1962).

71. "Allagash Hearing, Complete Report on Testimony," *Enterprise*, 13 September 1962.

72. Donald C. Hansen, "Sec. Udall May Urge Flooding of Allagash," Guy Gannett Portland Papers, 6 September 1962.

73. May Craig, "No Udall Ultimatum on Allagash: Muskie," and "Udall Reiterates Denial of Allagash Ultimatum," *Portland Press Herald*, 12 September 1962.

74. Lawrence Stuart, "Confidential . . . Meeting, December 6, 1962, with Landowners," U.S. Senate: Senate Office (688-5), Edmund S. Muskie Collection, Edmund S. Muskie Archives, Bates College, Lewiston, Maine.

75. "Proposal Surprises U.S., State Officials," *Portland Evening Express*, 21 December 1962; "Reed, Power Interests Discuss Allagash Project," *Portland Press Herald*, 21 December 1962.

76. One Hundred First Legislature, Legislative Document no. 115, *An Act Creating an Allagash Authority for State of Maine*, 10 January 1963; Donald C. Hansen, "State Multiple-Use Control of Allagash Proposal," *Portland Press Herald*, 13 February 1963.

77. "Hearing on Allagash 'Authority' May Illuminate a Tangled Problem," *Portland Press Herald*, 12 January 1963.

78. Edmund S. Muskie to Edward P. Cyr, 11 April 1963, U.S. Senate: Senate Office (180-5), Edmund S. Muskie Collection, Edmund S. Muskie Archives, Bates College, Lewiston, Maine.

79. *L. D. 115 Amendments Proposed by the Natural Resources Council*, March 1963, in possession of Robert W. Patterson Jr.

80. "Panel Organized to Fight Allagash Power Proposal," *Portland Evening Express*, 25 March 1963.

81. "Muskie Stand on St. John Power Project Questioned," *Portland Press Herald*, 16 May 1963.

82. Robert W. Patterson, "Augusta Lobbyists Aim at Allagash's Destruction," *Portland Press Herald,* 13 May 1963.

83. Robert W. Patterson to Justice William O. Douglas, 15 April 1963; Robert W. Patterson to Justice William O. Douglas, 8 June 1963; Robert W. Patterson to Stewart L. Udall, 8 June 1963; William O. Douglas, "Our Disappearing Wilderness" (address at annual meeting of the Natural Resources Council of Maine, 14 June 1963), in possession of Robert W. Patterson Jr. Published with permission of the William O. Douglas Estate.

84. U.S. Department of the Interior, Bureau of Outdoor Recreation, *A Report on the Proposed Allagash National Riverway* (Washington, D.C.: U.S. Department of the Interior, July 1963).

85. "Allagash Riverway Proposal May Become First in U.S." *Portland Evening Express,* 16 July 1963.

86. M. H. O'Brien, "Allagash Report Study is Urged," *Portland Sunday Telegram,* 30 June 1963; Austin H. Wilkins to Frank Hancock, Ronald Speers, Lawrence Stuart, and A. D. Nutting, 15 August 1963.

87. Donald C. Hansen, "Firm Will Cut Timber Near Allagash Banks," *Portland Sunday Telegram,* 22 September 1963.

88. Edmund S. Muskie to Files, "Allagash Project," 12 September 1963, U.S. Senate: Senate Office (180-5), Edmund S. Muskie Collection, Edmund S. Muskie Archives, Bates College, Lewiston, Maine.

89. Stewart L. Udall to Lawrence Kugelman, 23 September 1963, U.S. Senate: Senate Office (180-5), Edmund S. Muskie Collection, Edmund S. Muskie Archives, Bates College, Lewiston, Maine; Edmund S. Muskie to Lawrence J. Kugelman, 24 September 1963, U.S. Senate: Senate Office (180-5), Edmund S. Muskie Collection, Edmund S. Muskie Archives, Bates College, Lewiston, Maine.

90. "Allagash National Riverway Possible within Three Years," *Portland Press Herald,* 25 October 1963.

91. *Something about Conservation: The Allagash National Riverway* (Washington, D.C.: U.S. Department of the Interior, 1963).

92. Stewart L. Udall to John H. Reed, 31 December 1963; John H. Reed to Frank E. Hancock, 6 January 1964; Frank E. Hancock to John H.

Reed, 15 January 1964; Stewart L. Udall to John H. Reed, 7 March 1964; Frank E. Hancock to John H. Reed, 7 April 1964.

93. Edmund S. Muskie to Austin H. Wilkins, 18 November 1964, U.S. Senate: Senate Office (227-4), Edmund S. Muskie Collection, Edmund S. Muskie Archives, Bates College, Lewiston, Maine.

94. Natural Resources Council of Maine, *Conservation Bulletin* (December 1964).

95. Albert W. Wilson, "Udall Withdraws Allagash Charge—Administration's Riverway Demands Revealed," *Pulp and Paper* (14 December 1965): 9.

96. Allagash River Authority, *Allagash Wilderness Waterway—a Proposal for State Control*, January 1965.

97. Robert W. Patterson to Edmund S. Muskie, 5 January 1965; Edmund S. Muskie to Robert W. Patterson, 14 January 1965; Robert W. Patterson to Edmund S. Muskie, 29 January 1965; Edmund S. Muskie to Robert W. Patterson, 9 February 1965.

98. Robert W. Patterson to Stewart L. Udall, 5 January 1965; Stewart L. Udall to Robert W. Patterson, 4 February 1965; Robert W. Patterson to Stewart L. Udall, 22 February 1965.

99. "War Clouds Gather over Allagash," *Portland Sunday Telegram*, 28 February 1965.

100. Robert W. Patterson to Richard J. Dubord, 14 April 1965; Clinton Townsend to Richard J. Dubord, 16 April 1965.

101. Great Northern Paper Company to Richard J. Dubord, 7 May 1965; International Paper Company to Richard J. Dubord, 7 May 1965; Pingree Heirs to Richard J. Dubord, 7 May 1965; Irving Pulp and Paper Limited to Richard J. Dubord, 11 May 1965; Bangor Hydro-Electric Company to Richard J. Dubord, 7 May 1965.

102. "Too Vital for Hasty Action," *Bangor Daily News*, 28 May 1965.

103. Robert W. Patterson to John H. Reed, 31 May 1965; Robert W. Patterson, Clinton B. Townsend, George Emerson Jr., and Weston S. Evens to Carlton D. Reed Jr., president of the Maine Senate, and Dana W. Childs, speaker of the Maine House, 1 June 1965.

104. Patterson, "Wilderness No More," 73.

105. "The Real Problem," *Portland Sunday Telegram*, 30 May 1965.

106. Edmund S. Muskie to Henry M. Jackson, 8 June 1965, U.S. Senate:

Senate Office (228-1), Edmund S. Muskie Collection, Edmund S. Muskie Archives, Bates College, Lewiston, Maine.

107. Edmund S. Muskie to Malcolm Stoddard, 11 June 1965, U.S. Senate: Senate Office (228-1), Edmund S. Muskie Collection, Edmund S. Muskie Archives, Bates College, Lewiston, Maine.

108. Donald E. Nicoll to Lawrence Stuart, 14 June 1965, U.S. Senate: Senate Office (494-10), Edmund S. Muskie Collection, Edmund S. Muskie Archives, Bates College, Lewiston, Maine.

109. Richard J. Dubord to John T. Maines, Maurice R. Wing, John G. Sinclair, Robert N. Haskell, and Stephen Wheatland, 10 June 1965.

110. Austin H. Wilkins to John Maines, John Sinclair, Morris Wing, Robert Haskell, and George Carlisle, 4 August 1965.

111. "Legislative Order for a Special Allagash Study Committee, 2 June 1965, Allagash Study Committee 1965–1966," Legislative Materials, Maine State Archives, Augusta.

112. Allagash Study Committee, 1965–1966, "Committee Minutes and Public Hearing Notes," 17 August 1965–December 1965, Maine State Archives, Augusta.

113. "State and Federal Officials Near Accord on Allagash," *Portland Press Herald,* 10 November 1965.

114. "Udall Gets Advance Peek at Allagash Plan," *Portland Press Herald,* 13 January 1966; "Governor Reed, Natural Resources Council Praise Plan for Control of Allagash," *Portland Press Herald,* 15 January 1966.

115. Press release, State Park and Recreation Commission, Augusta, Maine, 30 November 1966.

Chapter 9. A Need for Vigilance

1. For accounts of the beauty and the loss of Glen Canyon, see Roderick Nash, *Wilderness and the American Mind,* 3rd ed. (New Haven, Conn.: Yale University Press, 1982), 228–229; and Edward Abbey, *Desert Solitaire: A Season in the Wilderness* (New York: Ballantine Books, 1968), 173–220.

2. Richard Judd, "A Last Chance for Wilderness: Defining the Allagash Wilderness Waterway, 1959–1966," *Maine History,* 40, no. 1 (Spring 2001).

3. John G. Sinclair, "Waterway Notes," 4 June 1998, photocopy, 17–18.

4. Robert W. Patterson, "The Art of the Impossible," *Daedalus: Journal of the American Academy of Arts and Sciences* 96, no. 4 (fall 1967): 1029.

5. "Final Grant Made to Assist Maine in Establishing Allagash Wilderness Waterway," press release, U.S. Department of the Interior, Bureau of Outdoor Recreation, 20 February 1970.

6. Kenneth M. Curtis to Walter J. Hickel, 10 April 1970 and 4 May 1970.

7. See Public Law 90-542, 90th Congress, S.199, 2 October 1968, *An Act to Provide for a National Wild and Scenic Rivers System, and for Other Purposes*, 1.

8. "Allagash Wilderness Waterway, Maine, Notice of Approval for Inclusion in National Wild and Scenic Rivers System as State Administered Wild River Area," *Federal Register* 35, no. 138 (17 July 1970): 11525.

9. Public Law 90-542, 10.

10. "Allagash Wilderness Waterway, Maine, Notice of Approval," 11526.

11. Bradford S. Wellman, president, Seven Islands Land Company, representing landowners of the northern Maine Allagash Watershed, address delivered at Churchill Dam at dedication of the Allagash Wilderness Waterway, 19 July 1970, 3.

12. Maine State Park and Recreation Commission, *The Allagash Wilderness Waterway: April 1970*, report to support the governor of Maine's application for inclusion of the waterway in the National Wild and Scenic Rivers System (Augusta: Maine State Park and Recreation Commission, 1970), 13–14. See also Maine Bureau of Parks and Recreation, *Allagash Wilderness Waterway Concept Plan* (Augusta: Maine Bureau of Parks and Recreation, November 1973), 13, 23.

13. Robert W. Patterson to Frank S. Hancock, 7 December 1963.

14. Maine State Park and Recreation Commission, *Allagash Wilderness Waterway: April 1970*, 13–14.

15. John Allan Long, "Shooting the Allagash," *Christian Science Monitor*, 24 August 1964; also statements by the Association for Multiple Use of Maine Timberlands, January 1962 and September 1962, stressing selective cutting of mature trees (which keeps the land in its original

character and allows young trees to continue growing), in possession of the author.

16. David D. Platt, "Designer Wilderness: The Allagash Isn't as Wild as It Looks," *Maine Times* (18 August 1989): 9; John W. Forssen, "More Protection for the Allagash," *Maine Fish and Wildlife* (fall 1985): 25.

17. Maine Department of Conservation, Bureau of Parks and Lands, *Allagash Wilderness Waterway Management Plan* (Augusta: Maine Department of Conservation, Bureau of Parks and Lands, January 1999), appendix exhibit I, p. 3; Mitch Lansky, *Beyond the Beauty Strip: Saving What's Left of Our Forests* (Gardiner, Maine: Tilbury House, 1992), 179–180; Maine House of Representatives, 116th Maine Legislature, *An Act to Protect the Allagash Wilderness Waterway*, Legislative Document no. 954, 18 March 1993.

18. Timothy E. Peabody and Thomas A. Santaguida, *The Maine Warden Service and the State of Maine: A Contemporary and Historical Overview* (Augusta: Maine Department of Inland Fisheries and Wildlife, [1999]).

19. See Maine Department of Conservation, *Allagash Wilderness Waterway Management Plan*, appendix exhibits D, F.

20. Maine State Park and Recreation Commission, *Allagash Wilderness Waterway: April 1970*, 13–14.

21. Robert W. Patterson to Herbert Hartman, 27 December 1977, in possession of Robert W. Patterson Jr.

22. Forssen, "More Protection," 25.

23. Robert W. Patterson, "Wilderness No More," *Down East* 37, no. 11 (June 1991): 76.

24. Thomas Morrison, e-mail message to author, 30 April 2001.

25. Lawrence Stuart, "The Allagash . . . Three Years Later," *Parks and Recreation* (April 1970): 62.

26. David Vail et al., *Tourism and Maine's Future: Toward Environmental, Economic, and Community Sustainability* (Augusta: Maine Center for Economic Policy, 1998), 24.

27. See, for example, The Wilderness Society's quarterly newsletter, vol. 2, nos. 1, 2 (winter 1999–2000, spring 2000).

28. Everett B. Carson to author, 19 October 2000.

29. William O. Douglas, *A Wilderness Bill of Rights* (Boston, Mass.: Little, Brown & Company, 1965), 87.

30. See Robert Manning, William Valliere, and Ben Minteer, "Values, Ethics, and Attitudes toward National Forest Management: An Empirical Study," *Society and National Resources* 12 (1999): 421–436; and Robert Manning et al., *Forest Values, Environmental Ethics, and Attitudes toward National Forest Management* (Burlington: University of Vermont, School of Natural Resources, 1998).

31. Robert Patterson, "A Council Seemed to Be the Answer...," *Twenty-Five Years of Environmental Leadership in Maine, NRCM Bulletin* (June–July 1984): 6.

Epilogue: Safekeeping

1. Remarks made by Edmund Muskie at the dedication of the Allagash Wilderness Waterway, 19 July 1970.

Appendix B. Wilderness Continuum

1. Roderick Nash, *Wilderness and the American Mind,* 3rd ed. (New Haven, Conn.: Yale University Press, 1982), 6.

2. Michael Frome, *Battle for the Wilderness,* rev. ed. (Salt Lake City: University of Utah Press, 1997), 12.

3. Ibid.

4. Nash, *Wilderness and the American Mind,* 6; Frome, *Battle for the Wilderness,* 12.

Appendix C. Typology of Perspectives on Nature

1. See Rod Farmer, "Self-Actualization and Culture," *Social Development Issues* 7, no. 2 (summer 1983): 63–72, for an overview of Maslow's theory and its cultural implications. See also Lawrence H. Goulder and Donald Kennedy, "Valuing Ecosystem Services: Philosophical Bases and Empirical Methods," in *Nature's Services: Societal Dependence on Natural Ecosystems,* ed. Gretchen C. Daily (Washington, D.C.: Island Press, 1997), 24–28.

2. See Michael J. Caduto, *A Guide on Environmental Values Education* (Paris: UNESCO, 1985), 16.

3. Shalom Schwartz, "Value Priorities and Behavior: Applying a Theory of Integrated Value Systems," in *The Psychology of Values: The Ontario Symposium*, vol. 8, ed. Clive Seligman, James M. Olson, and Mark P. Zanna (Mahwah, N.J.: Lawrence Erlbaum Associates, 1996), 2–6.

4. Ibid., 1–2.

5. David Gutierrez Karp, "Values and Their Effect on Pro-environmental Behavior," *Environment and Behavior* 28, no. 1 (January 1996): 111–133.

6. John C. Hendee, George H. Stankey, and Robert C. Lucas, *Wilderness Management*, 2nd ed. (Golden, Colo.: North American Press, 1990), 18.

7. Max Oelschlaeger, *The Idea of Wilderness: From Prehistory to the Age of Ecology* (New Haven, Conn.: Yale University Press, 1991), 293.

8. Freya Mathews, "*Terra Incognita:* Carnal Legacies," in *Restoring the Land: Environmental Values, Knowledge, and Action*, ed. Laurie Cosgrove, David Evans, and David Yencken (Carlton, Victoria, Australia: Melbourne University Press, 1994), 38–39.

9. See Donald Worster, *Nature's Economy: A History of Ecological Ideas* (Cambridge, England: Cambridge University Press, 1985), 30, 36.

10. Fulton Henry Anderson, *The Philosophy of Francis Bacon* (New York: Octagon Books, 1971), 185.

11. John White, *The Planter's Plea; or the Grounds of Plantations Examined and Usual Objections Answered* (1630; reprint, New York: Da Capo Press, 1968), 9–10.

12. Oelschlaeger, *Idea of Wilderness*, 287.

13. See Stephen R. Kellert, *The Value of Life: Biological Diversity and Human Society* (Washington, D.C.: Island Press, 1996), 20–21.

14. Goulder and Kennedy, "Valuing Ecosystem Services," 24–28.

15. Ronald Inglehart, *Culture Shift in Advanced Industrial Society* (Princeton, N.J.: Princeton University Press, 1990), 133–135, 152.

16. Kellert, *Value of Life*, 10–11, 42–43.

17. See Oelschlaeger, *Idea of Wilderness*, 287, which notes *Homo sapiens'* external relationship to the ecomachine as one of the defining characteristics of the resourcism philosophy.

18. Paul C. Stern and Thomas Dietz, "The Value Basis of Environmental Concern," *Journal of Social Issues* 50, no. 3 (1964): 76.
19. See Kellert, *Value of Life*, 24–25, for a discussion of his negativistic value.
20. Worster, *Nature's Economy*, 3–25.
21. Gilbert White, *The Natural History of Selborne*, ed. Paul Foster (1789; reprint, New York: Oxford University Press, 1993), 1, 47.
22. Kellert, *Value of Life*, 21.
23. White, *Selborne*, 23, 62, 182–183.
24. Farmer, "Self-Actualization," 65–67.
25. Goulder and Kennedy, "Valuing Ecosystem Services," 25.
26. Kellert, *Value of Life*, 14–15, 17.
27. Oelschlaeger, *Idea of Wilderness*, 289.
28. White, *Selborne*, 182.
29. Ibid., 20–21, 79, 195.
30. Kellert, *Value of Life*, 13–14.
31. Worster, *Nature's Economy*, 179–180.
32. See Oelschlaeger, *Idea of Wilderness*, 194–195.
33. Mathews, "*Terra Incognita*," 39.
34. See Paul Taylor, *Respect for Nature: A Theory of Environmental Ethics* (Princeton, N.J.: Princeton University Press, 1986), 99–119.
35. Farmer, "Self-Actualization," 65.
36. Schwartz, "Value Priorities," 3–5.
37. Oelschlaeger, *Idea of Wilderness*, 294.
38. See Mark Sagoff, "Zuckerman's Dilemma: A Plea for Environmental Ethics," *Hastings Center Report* 21, no. 5 (September–October 1991): 32–40.
39. Freya Mathews, *The Ecological Self* (London: Routledge, 1991), 119.
40. Judith N. Scoville, "Value Theory and Ecology in Environmental Ethics: A Comparison of Rolston and Niebuhr," *Environmental Ethics* 17 (summer 1995): 129.
41. Aldo Leopold, *A Sand County Almanac* (New York: Oxford University Press, 1949), 224–225.
42. Holmes Rolston III, *Environmental Ethics: Duties to and Values in the Natural World* (Philadelphia: Temple University Press, 1988), 188.
43. Oelschlaeger, *Idea of Wilderness*, 294.

Appendix D. National Trends in Beliefs, Attitudes, and Values concerning Nature

1. Stephen R. Kellert and Miriam O. Westervelt, *Trends in Animal Use and Perception in Twentieth-Century America* (Washington, D.C.: U.S. Department of the Interior, U.S. Fish & Wildlife Service, 1981), 2–3, 5; James B. Trefethen, *The American Landscape, 1776–1976: Two Centuries of Change* (Washington, D.C.: Wildlife Management Institute, 1976), 10.

2. Kellert and Westervelt, *Trends in Animal Use and Perception,* 39–42.

3. Ronald Inglehart, *Culture Shift in Advanced Industrial Society* (Princeton, N.J.: Princeton University Press, 1990), 56, 436.

4. John C. Hendee, George H. Stankey, and Robert C. Lucas, *Wilderness Management* (Golden, Colo.: North American Press, 1990), 380.

5. Everett Carll Ladd and Karlyn H. Bowman, *Attitudes toward the Environment: Twenty-Five Years after Earth Day* (Washington, D.C.: AEI Press, 1995), 2, 5, 50–51.

6. Kellert and Westervelt, *Trends in Animal Use and Perception,* 21–22.

7. Riley E. Dunlap and Rik Scarce, "The Polls—Poll Trends: Environmental Problems and Protection," *Public Opinion Quarterly* 55, no. 4 (1991): 651–672.

8. Samuel P. Hays, "Environmental Political Culture and Environmental Political Development: An Analysis of Legislative Voting, 1971–1989," *Environmental History Review* 16, no. 2 (1992): 15.

9. Willet Kempton, James S. Boster, and Jennifer A. Hartley, *Environmental Values in American Culture* (Cambridge, Mass.: MIT Press, 1995), 99, 102–103, 107, 111, 114–115.

10. The Nature Conservancy, nationwide telephone survey conducted by KRC Communications Research, Newton, Mass., 21–24 May 1994.

11. Roper Starch Worldwide, *Report Card: Environmental Attitudes and Knowledge in America: The Fifth Annual Survey of Adult Americans* (n.p.: National Environmental Education and Training Foundation, 1996).

12. Lake Sosin Snell Perry & Associates, Inc., memorandum to The Wilderness Society, 28 October 1997.

13. Robert Manning, William Valliere, and Ben Minter, "Values, Ethics,

and Attitudes toward National Forest Management: An Empirical Study," *Society and Natural Resources* 12 (1999): 434–435.

14. Robert Manning et al., *Forest Values, Environmental Ethics, and Attitudes toward National Forest Management* (Burlington: University of Vermont, School of Natural Resources, 1998), 12, 16, 21–24, 51.

15. H. Ken Cordell et al., "How the Public Views Wilderness," *International Journal of Wilderness* 4, no. 3 (1998): 28–31.

About the Author

DEAN B. BENNETT is professor emeritus at the University of Maine at Farmington. Born and raised in Maine, he received a Ph.D. degree in resource planning and conservation from the University of Michigan and a master's degree in science education from the University of Southern Maine. He has devoted much of his professional life to teaching and writing in the fields of science and environmental education, natural history, and human relationships with nature. This is his fourth book in the field of nature and the environment; like the others, it involved extensive observation and study outdoors in natural areas and drew on his background in art and photography. His books include *Maine's Natural Heritage: Rare Species and Unique Natural Features; Allagash: Maine's Wild and Scenic River;* and *The Forgotten Nature of New England: A Search for Traces of the Original Wilderness.* He and his wife, biologist Sheila K. Bennett, enjoy hiking, canoeing, and skiing in the North Woods of Maine.

Index

Note: Italicized page numbers refer to illustrations.